SOCIALIST
REGISTER
2 0 0 2

THE SOCIALIST REGISTER
Founded in 1964

EDITORS:
LEO PANITCH
COLIN LEYS

FOUNDING EDITORS
RALPH MILIBAND (1924-1994)
JOHN SAVILLE

CONTRIBUTING EDITORS:

GREGORY ALBO
HUW BEYNON
VARDA BURSTYN
PAUL CAMMACK
DAVID COATES
GEORGE COMNINEL
DIANE ELSON
BARBARA EPSTEIN
NORMAN GERAS
SAM GINDIN
JUDITH ADLER HELLMAN
URSULA HUWS
STEVE JEFFERYS
SHEILA ROWBOTHAM
JOHN S. SAUL
HILARY WAINWRIGHT
ELLEN MEIKSINS WOOD
ALAN ZUEGE

CORRESPONDING EDITORS:

AIJAZ AHMAD, NEW DELHI
ELMAR ALTVATER, BERLIN
PATRICK BOND, JOHANNESBURG
GERARD GREENFIELD, HONG KONG
MICHAEL SPOURDALAKIS, ATHENS

Visit our website at:

http://www.yorku.ca/org/socreg/
for a detailed list of all our issues, order forms and an online selection of
past prefaces and essays,

...and join our listserv by contacting
socreg@yorku.ca
for a discussion of the essays from this volume and issues relevant to socialists.

SOCIALIST REGISTER 2002

A WORLD OF CONTRADICTIONS

Edited by LEO PANITCH and COLIN LEYS

MERLIN PRESS
FERNWOOD PUBLISHING
MONTHLY REVIEW PRESS

First published in 2001
by The Merlin Press Ltd.
PO Box 30705
London
WC2E 8QD

British Library Cataloguing in Publication Data
1. The Socialist Register. —2002
I. Panitch, Leo 1945-   II Leys, Colin 1931-
355'. 005

Canadian Cataloguing in Publication Data
National Library of Canada Cataloguing in Publication Data
Main entry under title:
  A world of contradictions : Socialist register 2002
Includes bibliographical references.
ISBN 1-55266-058-3
  1. International economic relations. 2. Globalization. 3. Socialism.
I. Panitch, Leo, 1945- II. Leys, Colin, 1931-
HX44.5.W67 2001   337   C2001-902701-X

ISSN: 0081-0606

Published in Europe by The Merlin Press
0 85036 501 5 Paperback
0 85036 502 3 Hardback

Published in the USA by Monthly Review Press
1 58367 049 1 Paperback
1 58367 048 3 Hardback

Published in Canada by Fernwood Publishing
1 55266 058 3 Paperback

Typeset by Jon Carpenter
Printed in Great Britain
by CPI Bookcraft

CONTENTS

PREFACE

In the last two or three years people everywhere have become more aware of, anxious about, and hostile to the scale and complexity of, contemporary capitalism — its scope, its reach into daily life, and the nature and speed of the changes that are now driven by global market forces. The costs involved for the vast majority in the global 'south', and for growing numbers in the 'north', who are victims of the drastic aggravation of injustice and inequality that globalization is producing, have become more and more clear. Also becoming clearer are the problems the neoliberal order itself faces: yet another decade beginning with the threat of an economic recession, a classic crisis of overproduction in the 'leading-edge' global telecommunications sector, increasing evidence of financial instability in 'key emerging markets', and growing nervousness from Wall Street to Tokyo as the stock market heads downwards. Capitalism is also now beset by highly visible problems in both services and accumulation resulting from the privatization of the public sphere in such areas as electricity supply (California), rail transportation (UK), water supply (Canada, Bolivia, South Africa), etc.

The increasingly powerful 'anti-corporate' movements, spearheaded by young people, are both an expression of and a reaction to these developments. The counterpart to the widespread disillusion with electoral politics, as all political parties both embrace and surrender to global market forces (witness the astonishing collapse of voter participation in the British general election in June 2001), is a huge range of extra-party activism. This occurs around dozens of major issues, from the environment to racism, which are increasingly understood to be insoluble without — at a minimum — a collective challenge to, and assertion of democratic control over, capital: so that more and more activists now define themselves as, precisely, *'anti-capitalist'*.

The Socialist Register has consistently focused on the processes driving globalization, as well as its costs — from our much-cited 1994 volume, *Between Globalism and Nationalism,* to our 1999 volume, *Global Capitalism versus Democracy.* In the present volume we have sought to take this a step further. The task of resubordinating the market forces that now control the world depends not only on understanding them, but on understanding them in their contradictoriness: seeing how they depend on structural relationships that produce problems and vulnerabilities, incoherence and conflict. The energy and commitment that brought so many tens of thousands of people to Seattle and Québec City — not to mention the thousands of movements evolving in every city and many rural areas of the world, from Soweto to Chiapas — need to be backed by careful analysis of the way that capitalism's contradictions are now manifested on a global terrain.

This task is the primary focus of the 38th annual volume of the *Register* now in your hands. Our concept of contradiction has not been mechanical or theo-logical. We were not looking for 'primary contradictions', let alone *the* primary contradiction. Still less do we mean to suggest that there are contradictions that will bring down capitalism of their own accord. On the other hand, we have been concerned with systemic contradictions as opposed to just tensions, conflicts, mere paradoxes, 'ironies' and the like; i.e., our focus is on structural relations inherent in capitalism which at the same time constitute or give rise to obstacles to its smooth or even continued expansion, and which offer opportu-nities for effective socialist practice.

The continued importance of Marx's fundamental concept for understanding the world today was ironically illustrated for us, as we were writing this Preface, by the Chinese Communist Party's efforts to grapple with the consequences of its turn to capitalism. This came in the shape of a front-page article in the *New York Times* of June 3, 2001 about a Central Committee Report entitled 'Studies of Contradictions Among the People Under New Conditions'. It is not clear whether the Central Committee's understanding of the concept of contradiction has progressed significantly from the time when the Party still offered advice to the people, based on the maxims of Mao, on such subjects as 'Solving the Principal Contradictions of Onions'. In contrast with all misuse and abuse of Marx's fundamental concept, Ellen Wood's concluding essay to this volume (from which we have purloined the above gem) lucidly sums up the theoretical strength and explanatory power of the concept when it is employed as Marx meant it. The essays that precede hers use contradiction in this way to anatomize the central dynamics of neoliberalism; analyze the way contradictions manifest themselves in such diverse fields as culture, communications and crime; dissect the strategies and structures used by the managers of global 'governance' to try to contain conflict and cope with contradiction; reveal how those who suffer, materially and psychologically, under contemporary capitalism, themselves try to cope with and negotiate their deprivation, alienation and marginalization; and, not least, probe the possibilities — and the limits — of the new movements of protest and resistance.

Among the contributors, Naomi Klein is the author of *No Logo* and a colum-nist for *The Globe and Mail* and *The Guardian*; and André Drainville teaches political science at Laval University in Québec City. Gérard Duménil and Dominque Lévy are researchers in Paris at MODEM-CNRS and CEPREMAP-

CNRS. Elmar Altvater is Professor of Political Science at the Free University of Berlin; David Harvey has recently taken up a professorship in anthropology at the Graduate School of the City University of New York; Graham Murdock and Peter Golding both teach media studies at Loughborough University in England. Reg Whitaker and Guglielmo Carchedi have recently retired from teaching political science and economics, respectively, at York University, Toronto and the University of Amsterdam. Susanne Soederberg teaches political science at the University of Alberta in Edmonton; and Paul Cammack, a contributing editor to the Register, teaches in the Department of Government at the University of Manchester in England. Marta Russell, a Los Angeles-based journalist, is the author of *Beyond Ramps*, and Ravi Malhotra, an Ottawa-based disability rights activist, is currently pursuing graduate studies at the Harvard Law School. Michael Kidron is an independent writer working in London; and David Miller, a member of the Media Research Institute at Stirling University in Scotland, wrote his essay while a visiting scholar at the Institute for the Study of Social Change at the University of California, Berkeley. Pablo González Casanova is head of the Instituto de Investigaciones Social at UNAM in Mexico City, and Ellen Wood, York University professor emeritus of political science, currently lives and writes in London.

We want to thank all our contributors, while reminding the reader that neither they nor the editors necessarily agree with everything in the volume. We are also grateful to Martijn Konings for his highly efficient work since taking over as editorial assistant from Marsha Niemeijer, who continues to give invaluable assistance in looking after our website (www.yorku.ca/socreg). We continue to be indebted to Tony Zurbrugg and Adrian Howe at the Merlin Press for their creative and committed work in producing the Register.

In conclusion, we are happy to report the return of John Saul as a contributing editor of the Register; but we are very sad to have to note the passing of a long-term comrade and contributor to the Register, Daniel Singer. No one showed greater dedication to keeping the spirit of revolution alive through the dark decade of the 1990s.

L.P.
C.L.

June 2001

FAREWELL TO 'THE END OF HISTORY': ORGANIZATION AND VISION IN ANTI-CORPORATE MOVEMENTS

NAOMI KLEIN

'We are here to show the world that another world is possible!' the man on stage said, and a crowd of more than 10,000 roared its approval.[1] What was strange was that we weren't cheering for a specific other world, just the possibility of one. We were cheering for the idea that another world could, in theory, exist.

For the past thirty years, a select group of CEOs and world leaders have met during the last week in January on a mountaintop in Switzerland to do what they presumed they were the only ones entitled to do, or capable of doing: determine how the global economy should be governed. We were cheering because it was, in fact, the last week of January, and this wasn't the World Economic Forum in Davos, Switzerland. It was the first annual World Social Forum in Porto Alegre, Brazil. And even though we weren't CEOs or world leaders, we were still going to spend the week talking about how the global economy should be governed.

Many people said that they felt history being made in that room. What I felt was something more intangible: the end of The End of History. Fittingly, 'Another World Is Possible' was the event's official slogan. After a year and a half of global protests against the World Trade Organization, the World Bank, the International Monetary Fund, the Word Economic Forum, both major US political parties, and Britain's Labour Party — to name just a few — the World Social Forum was billed as an opportunity for an emerging movement to stop screaming about what it is against and start articulating what it is for.

The particular site was chosen because Brazil's Workers Party (Partido dos Trabalhadores, the PT) is in power in the city of Porto Alegre, as well as in the state of Rio Grande do Sul and has become known world-wide for its innovations in participatory democracy. The conference was organized by a network of Brazilian unions and NGOs, as well as ATTAC France. The PT made sure that no expense was spared: state-of-the-art conference facilities, a star-studded roster of speakers and international musicians, delegates greeted by officials from the local tourism department, as well as by friendly police officers — quite a culture shock for a group of people growing accustomed to being met by authorities with clouds of pepper spray, border strip searches and 'no-protest' zones. If Seattle was, for many people, the coming-out party of a resistance movement, then, according to Soren Ambrose, policy analyst with 50 Years Is Enough, 'Porto Alegre is the coming-out party for the existence of serious thinking about alternatives'.

The charge that this movement lacks alternatives — or at least a coherent focus — has become something of a mantra since the Battle in Seattle in November 1999, a criticism summed up by an article on 'The New Radicals' in Newsweek: 'One thing that seems to be lacking today is a mission statement, a credo, that gives the movement, such as it is, some focus'.[2]

There is no doubt that in the absence of such media-friendly packaging, critics have had free reign to portray young activists as everything from tree-wearing, drum-beating bubble brains, to violent thugs bent only on destruction.

Addressing this perceived vision deficit was the *raison d'être* of the World Social Forum: the organizers clearly saw the conference as an opportunity to whip the chaos on the streets into some kind of structured shape. And in 60 lectures and 450 workshops, there were indeed plenty of ideas flying around — about new systems of taxation, like the Tobin Tax, co-operative, organic farming, participatory budgets and free software, to name just a few. But I found myself asking a question that often pops up at similar, smaller-scale events. Even if we did manage to come up with a ten-point plan — brilliant in its clarity, elegant in its coherence, unified in its outlook — to whom, exactly, would we hand down these commandments? Put another way: who are the leaders of this movement — or are there any?

Last April, after a portion of the protests against the Free Trade Area of the Americas turned violent, the press and the police engaged in a game that might be described as 'Find the Leader'. Mark Steyn, a columnist with Conrad Black's *National Post*, pointed at Maude Barlow, chair of the Council of Canadians (one of the world's largest and most committed anti-free trade NGOs), insistently referring to a group of 50,000 people as 'Maude's Mob' and even going so far as to threaten retaliation against Barlow herself. 'The next time a member of Maude's Mob throws a rock at me, I intend to take it home, and chuck it through her window', he wrote.[3]

The police, for their part, claimed that Jaggi Singh, one of the organizers of the Anti-Capitalist Convergence, ordered his minions to attack the fence that surrounded much of Quebec City. The main weapon the police cited was a theatrical catapult that lobbed teddy bears and other stuffed animals over the fence. Singh had nothing to do with the catapult, nor did he do anything at the protest but give speeches about state violence. Yet the justification for his arrest, and for later being denied bail, was that he was a kind of protest puppet master, allegedly pulling the strings behind the actions of others. The story has been similar at other protests. During the demonstrations against the Republican National Convention in Philadelphia in August 2000, John Sellers, one of the founders of the Ruckus Society, had his bail posted at $1 million. Two months earlier, David Solnit, one of the founders of the puppet-making political theatre group Art and Revolution, also faced a pre-emptive arrest, this time in Windsor, Ontario during a meeting of the Organization of American States.

The systematic police targeting of protest 'leaders' goes a long way towards explaining the deep suspicion of traditional hierarchies that exists in this new movement. Indeed, the figure that comes closest to a bona fide 'leader' is Subcomandante Marcos, a man in the mountains of Chiapas who hides his real identity and covers his face with a mask. Marcos, the quintessential anti-leader, insists that his black mask is a mirror, so that 'Marcos is gay in San Francisco, black in South Africa, an Asian in Europe, a Chicano in San Ysidro, an anarchist in Spain, a Palestinian in Israel, a Mayan Indian in the streets of San Cristobal, a Jew in Germany, a Gypsy in Poland, a Mohawk in Quebec, a pacifist in Bosnia, a single woman on the Metro at 10 p.m., a peasant without land, a gang member in the slums, an unemployed worker, an unhappy student and, of course, a Zapatista in the mountains'.[4] In other words, he is simply us: we are the leader we've been looking for.

This critique of hierarchies goes far beyond charismatic leadership. Many of the participants in the anti-corporate protest movements are equally suspicious of one-size-fits-all ideologies, political parties, indeed of any group that would centralize power and organize the parts of this movement into subordinate cells and locals. So while the intellectuals and organizers up on stage at the World Social Forum may help shape the ideas of the people on the streets, they most emphatically do not have the power or even the mechanisms to lead this street movement. In this amorphous context, the ideas and plans being hatched at the World Social Forum weren't irrelevant exactly, they just weren't important in the way they clearly hoped to be. They were destined to be swept up and tossed around in the tidal wave of information — web diaries, NGO manifestos, academic papers, home-made videos, *cris de coeur* — that the global anti-corporate network produces and consumes each and every day.

To those searching for replicas of more traditional anti-capitalist politics, this absence of clear structure makes the anti-corporate movement appear infuriatingly impassive: Evidently, these people are so disorganized they can't even get it together to respond positively to those who offer to organize them. Sure they've got guts when it comes to protesting, but these are MTV-weaned activists, you can practically hear the old guard saying: scattered, non-linear, no focus.

Only maybe it's not quite so simple. Maybe the protests, from Seattle to

Quebec City, look unfocused because they are not demonstrations of one movement at all but rather convergences of many smaller ones, each with its sights
trained on a specific multinational corporation (like Nike), a particular industry
(like agribusiness) or a new trade initiative (like the Free Trade Area of the
Americas), or in defence of indigenous self-determination (like the Zapatistas).

Look a little closer and it's clear that these smaller, targeted movements are
indeed battling the same forces, forces perhaps best outlined by the Zapatista
National Liberation Army when it began its uprising on January 1, 1994 (the day
the North American Free Trade Agreement came into law). The strategic victory
of the Zapatistas was to insist that what was going on in Chiapas could not be
written off as a narrow 'ethnic' or 'local' struggle — that it was universal. They
did this by identifying their enemy not only as the Mexican state but as 'neoliberalism'. The Zapatistas insisted that the poverty and desperation in Chiapas was
simply a more advanced version of something happening all around the world,
and which began with the first acts of colonialism. Their 500 year head start
graces the indigenous people of Chiapas' place at the political vanguard now. In
his communiqués, Marcos pointed to the huge numbers of people being left
behind by prosperity, whose land, and work, made that prosperity possible. 'The
new distribution of the world excludes "minorities." The indigenous, youth,
women, homosexuals, lesbians, people of colour, immigrants, workers, peasants;
the majority who make up the world basements are presented, for power, as
disposable. The distribution of the world excludes the majorities.'[5]

If neoliberalism is the common target there is also an emerging consensus that
participatory democracy at the local level — whether through unions, neighbourhoods, farms, villages, anarchist collectives or aboriginal self-government —
is where to start building alternatives to it. The common theme is an overarching
commitment to self-determination and diversity: cultural diversity, biodiversity,
and, yes, political diversity. The Zapatistas call this a movement of 'one "no" and
many "yeses"', a description that defies the characterization that this is one movement at all, and challenges the assumption that it should be.[6]

Rather than a single movement, what is emerging is thousands of movements
intricately linked to one another, much as 'hotlinks' connect their websites on the
Internet. This analogy is more than coincidental and is in fact key to understanding the changing nature of political organizing. Although many have
observed that the recent mass protests would have been impossible without the
Internet, what has been overlooked is how the communication technology that
facilitates these campaigns is shaping the movement in its own image. Thanks to
the Net, mobilizations are able to unfold with sparse bureaucracy and minimal
hierarchy; forced consensus and laboured manifestos are fading into the background, replaced instead by a culture of constant, loosely structured and
sometimes compulsive information-swapping.

Despite media descriptions that portrayed the events in Quebec City as two
protests — one a 'peaceful' labour march, the other a 'violent' anarchist riot, there
were, in fact, hundreds of protests over the course of the weekend. One was

organized by a mother and daughter from Montreal. Another by a vanload of grad students from Edmonton. Another by three friends from Toronto who aren't members of anything but their health clubs. Yet another by a couple of waiters from a local café on their lunch break. Sure there were well-organized groups in Quebec City: the unions had buses, matching placards and a parade route; the 'black bloc' of anarchists had gas masks and radio links. But for days the streets were also filled with people who simply said to a friend, 'Let's go to Quebec', and with Quebec City residents who said, 'Let's go outside'.

In the four years before Seattle, similar convergences had taken place outside WTO, G-7 and Asia Pacific Economic Cooperation summits in Auckland, Vancouver, Manila, Birmingham, London, Geneva, Kuala Lumpur and Cologne. What is emerging is an activist model that mirrors the organic, decentralized, interlinked pathways of the Internet — the Internet come to life. Interestingly, the Washington-based research centre TeleGeography has taken it upon itself to map out the architecture of the Internet as if it were the solar system. Last year, TeleGeography pronounced that the Internet is not one giant web but a network of 'hubs and spokes'.[7] The hubs are the centres of activity, the spokes the links to other centres which are autonomous but interconnected.

It seems like a perfect description of the so-called anti-globalization protests. These mass convergences are activist hubs, made up of hundreds, possibly thousands, of autonomous spokes. During the demonstrations the spokes take the form of 'affinity groups' of between two and twenty protesters, each of which elects a spokesperson to represent them at regular 'spokes council' meetings. At some rallies, activists carry actual cloth webs. When it's time for a meeting, they lay the web on the ground, call out 'all spokes on the web' and the structure becomes a street-level boardroom.

The affinity groups agree to loosely coordinate their actions, and, at some events, to abide by a set of non-violence principles (at the very least, they agree not to endanger one another by engaging in violence during a portion of a protest that is planned as non-violent). Apart from that, however, the affinity groups function as discrete units, with the power to make their own strategic decisions — a model of coordinated decentralization that is entirely lost on those looking for leaders and puppet masters. For instance, at the spokes council meetings before the anti-FTAA protests in Quebec City, Jaggi Singh acted only as facilitator — a glorified note-taker, keeping track of all the autonomous actions planned: one group announced they would form a marching band, another planned to wrap the security fence in toilet paper, another planned to throw hundreds of paper air planes through the chain link, another — a group of Harvard grad students — planned to read Foucault to the police. Those with more confrontational plans stayed silent and met only in the relative safety of their own affinity groups.

On the ground, the results of these miniature protests converging is either frighteningly chaotic or inspiringly poetic — or both. Rather than presenting a unified front, small units of activists surround their target from all directions. And rather than build elaborate national or international bureaucracies, temporary structures are thrown up instead: empty buildings are hastily turned into 'convergence centres', and independent media producers assemble impromptu activist news centres. The ad hoc coalitions behind these demonstrations are frequently named after the date of the planned event — J18, N30, A16, S11, S26 — and when the date is passed, they leave virtually no trace behind, save for an archived website.

The hubs and spokes model is more than a tactic used at protests; the protests are themselves made up of 'coalitions of coalitions', to borrow a phrase from Kevin Danaher of Global Exchange. Each anti-corporate campaign is comprised of many groups, mostly NGOs, labour unions, students and anarchists. They use the Internet and regular international conference calls, as well as face-to-face meetings, to do everything from cataloguing the latest transgressions of the World Bank to bombarding Shell Oil with faxes and e-mails to distributing ready-to-download anti-sweatshop leaflets for protests at Nike Town. The groups remain autonomous, but their international coordination is deft and, to their targets, frequently devastating.

The charge that the anti-corporate movement lacks 'vision' falls apart when looked at in the context of these campaigns. It's true that, to a casual observer, the mass protests in Seattle, Washington, D.C., Prague and Quebec City can, in their hodgepodge of slogans and causes, seem simply like colourful parades of complaints. But in trying to find coherence in these large-scale shows of strength, observers may be confusing the outward demonstrations of the movement with the thing itself — missing the forest for the people dressed as trees. This movement *is* its spokes, and in the spokes there is no shortage of vision.

The student anti-sweatshop movement, for instance, has rapidly moved from simply criticizing companies and campus administrators to drafting alternate codes of conduct and building its own quasi-regulatory body, the Worker Rights Consortium. More significantly, campus labour activists have been expanding their focus to include targets much closer to home: the caretakers and catering staff on their campuses, as well as the migrant farm workers supplying their cafeterias. The movement against genetically engineered and modified foods has leapt from one policy victory to the next, first getting many GM foods removed from the shelves of British supermarkets, then getting labelling laws passed in Europe, then making enormous strides with the Montreal Protocol on Biosafety. Meanwhile, opponents of the World Bank's and IMF's export-led development models have produced bookshelves' worth of resources on community-based development models, debt relief and reparations, as well as self-government principles.

Critics of the oil and mining industries are similarly overflowing with ideas for sustainable energy and responsible resource extraction — though they rarely get the chance to put their visions into practice. The growing movement against Big Pharma has plenty of ideas about how to get affordable AIDS drugs to those living with the disease, it's just that they keep getting dragged into trade court for their trouble. The Zapatistas, meanwhile, have gone from saying 'Ya Basta' to Nafta, to being at the forefront of a movement for radical democratic reform within Mexico, playing a major role in toppling the corrupt seventy-one-year reign of the Institutional Revolutionary Party, and placing indigenous rights at the centre of the Mexican political agenda.

The fact that these campaigns are decentralized is not a source of incoherence and fragmentation. Rather, it is a reasonable, even ingenious adaptation both to pre-existing fragmentation within progressive networks and to changes in the broader culture. The traditional institutions that once organized citizens into neat, structured groups are all in decline: unions, religions, political parties. Yet something is propelling tens of thousands of individuals onto the streets anyway — an intuition, a gut instinct, perhaps just the profoundly human desire to be part of something larger than oneself. What but this web could catch them all?

The structure of the movement is also a by-product of the explosion of NGOs, which, since the Rio Summit in 1992, have been gaining power and prominence. There are so many NGOs involved in anti-corporate campaigns that nothing but the hubs and spokes model could possibly accommodate all their different styles, tactics and goals. Like the Internet itself, both the NGO and the affinity group networks are indefinitely expandable systems. If somebody doesn't feel like they quite fit in to one of the 30,000 or so NGOs or thousands of affinity groups out there, they can just start their own and link up.

For some, this surfer's appeal to activism is an abomination. But whether or not one agrees with the model, there is no doubt that one of its great strengths is that it has proven extraordinarily difficult to control, largely because it is so different from the organizing principles of the institutions and corporations it targets. It responds to corporate concentration with a maze of fragmentation, to centralization with its own kind of localization, to power consolidation with radical power dispersal.

Once again, this strategy has been employed most deftly by the Zapatistas. Rather than barricading themselves, from the first communiqué they flung open the doors and invited the world 'to watch over and regulate our battles'.[8] The summer after the uprising, the Zapatistas hosted a National Democratic Convention in the jungle; 6,000 people attended, most from Mexico. In 1996, they hosted the first Encuentro For Humanity And Against Neo-Liberalism. Some 3,000 activists travelled to Chiapas to meet with others from around the world. These networks, many of them informal, made the Zapatista struggle impossible to contain.

Joshua Karliner of the Transnational Resource and Action Center calls this web-like system 'an unintentionally brilliant response to globalization'. And because it was unintentional, we still lack even the vocabulary to describe it, which may be why a rather amusing metaphor industry has evolved to fill the gap. I'm throwing my lot in with 'hubs and spokes', but Maude Barlow of the Council of Canadians says, '[w]e are up against a boulder. We can't remove it so we try to go underneath it, to go around it and over it.' Britain's John Jordan, one of the founders of Reclaim the Streets, puts it this way: 'transnationals are like giant tankers, and we are like a school of fish. We can respond quickly; they can't.' The US-based Free Burma Coalition talks of a network of 'spiders', spinning a web strong enough to tie down the most powerful multinationals.

At almost all the global protests, this non-strategy baffled even the most outra-geously over-prepared security forces: not only did it delay the opening of the World Trade Organization in Seattle, but a similar strategy saw protesters dressed as 'pink fairies' dancing on the walls of the convention centre during the World Bank/IMF meeting in Prague and saw large portions of the security fence taken down during the Summit of the Americas in Quebec City. Charles Ramsey, Washington DC's police chief, explains what the web looks like from a security point of view. 'You have to experience it to fully appreciate just how well orga-nized they are, how many different ways they can come at you', he said on the second day of the World Bank protests in his city, sounding a little like General Custer describing the wily tactics of the Sioux in 1876.[9]

Fittingly, it's a US military report about the Zapatista uprising that provides the most comprehensive take on these 'network wars'. According to a study produced by RAND, the Zapatistas waged 'a war of the flea' that, thanks to the Internet, the *encuentros*, and the global NGO network, turned into a 'war of the swarm'.[10]

The military challenge of a war of the swarm, the researchers noted, is that it has no 'central leadership or command structure; it is multiheaded, impossible to decapitate'.[11]

Of course, this multiheaded system has its weaknesses too, and they were on full display on the streets of Washington during the anti-World Bank/IMF protests. At around noon on April 16, the day of the largest protest, a spokes council meeting was convened for the affinity groups that were in the midst of blocking all the street intersections surrounding the headquarters of the World Bank and the IMF. The intersections had been blocked since 6 a.m., but the meeting delegates, the protesters had just learned, had slipped inside the police barricades before 5 a.m.

Given this new information, most of the spokespeople felt it was time to give up the intersections and join the official march at the Ellipse. The problem was that not everyone agreed: a handful of affinity groups wanted to see if they could block the delegates on their way out of their meetings. The compromise the council came up with was telling. 'OK, everybody listen up', Kevin Danaher shouted into a megaphone. 'Each intersection has autonomy. If the intersection wants to stay locked down, that's cool. If it wants to come to the Ellipse, that's cool too. It's up to you.' This was impeccably fair and democratic, but there was just one problem — it made absolutely no sense. Sealing off the access points had been a coordinated action. If some intersections now opened up and other, rebel-camp intersections stayed occupied, delegates on their way out of the meeting could just hang a right instead of a left, and they would be home free. Which, of course, is precisely what happened.

As I watched clusters of protesters get up and wander off while others stayed seated, defiantly guarding — well, nothing — it struck me as an apt metaphor for the strengths and weaknesses of this nascent activist network. There is no question that the communication culture that reigns on the Net is better at speed and volume than at synthesis. It is capable of getting tens of thousands of people to meet on the same street corner, placards in hand, but is far less adept at helping those same people to agree on what they are really asking for before they get to the barricades — or after they leave. Perhaps that's why a certain repetitive quality has set in at these large demonstrations: from smashed McDonald's windows to giant puppets, they can begin to look a little like McProtests. The Net made them possible, but it's not proving particularly helpful in taking them to a deeper stage.

For this reason and others, many in the movement have become increasingly critical of 'summit hopping', and generally agree that there needs to be more structure between mass protests. Clearly, far too much expectation is being placed on these large demonstrations: the organizers of the Washington DC demo, for instance, announced they would literally 'shut down' two $30 billion transnational institutions, at the same time as they attempted to convey sophisticated ideas about the fallacies of neoliberal economics to the stock-happy public. They simply couldn't do it; no single demo could, and it's only getting harder. Seattle's direct-action tactics worked as well as they did because they took the police by surprise. Now the police have subscribed to all the e-mail lists and have used the supposed threat posed by anarchists as giant fundraising schemes, allowing them to buy up all manner of new toys, from surveillance equipment to water cannons. More substantively, it was clear that by the time the protests in Prague rolled around in September 2000, the movement, no matter how decentralized, was in grave danger of seeming remote, cut off from the issues that affect people's day to day lives.

So the question is, if there is to be more structure, what kind should it be? An international political party that pushes to democratize world government? New national parties? How about a network of city and town councils each committed to introducing participatory democracy? Should it exist entirely outside of electoral politics and concentrate exclusively on creating counter-powers to the state?

These questions are more than tactical, they are strategic and often philosophical. Fundamentally, they hinge on how one defines that most slippery of terms: globalization. Is the problem with globalization simply that a good idea has been grabbed by the wrong hands, and the situation could be righted if only international institutions like the WTO were made democratic and accountable; if there were tough global rules protecting the environment, taxing financial transactions, and upholding labour standards? Or is globalization, at its core, a crisis of representative democracy in which power and decision-making are delegated to points further and further away from the places where the effects of those decisions are felt — until representative democracy means voting for politicians every few years who use that mandate to transfer national powers to the WTO and the IMF? Is this a movement trying to impose its own, more humane brand of globalization, or is it a movement against centralization and the delegation of power *on principle*, one as critical of left-wing, one-size-fits-all ideology as of the neoliberal recipe for McGovernment?

While there is near consensus on the need to sit down and start sorting through these questions, there is precious little on the next set of obvious questions: at whose table? And who gets to decide? The World Social Forum was by the far the most ambitious attempt so far to get this process under way, drawing a remarkable 10,000 delegates. Few of them, however, seemed to know what to expect: a model UN? A giant teach-in? A mock parliament? A party? It turned out that the organizational structure of the forum was so opaque that it was nearly impossible to figure out how decisions were made or to find ways to question those decisions. There were no open plenaries and no chance to vote on the structure of future events.

Though the Forum was billed as a break in the protests, by the third day frustrated delegates began to do what they do best: they protested. There were marches and manifestos — a half-dozen at least. Beleaguered forum organizers found themselves charged with everything from reformism to sexism, not to mention ignoring the African continent. The Anti-Capitalist Youth contingent accused them of ignoring the important role direct action played in building the movement. Their manifesto condemned the conference as 'a ruse' using the mushy language of democracy to avoid a more divisive discussion of class. The PSTU, a breakaway faction of the Workers Party, began interrupting speeches about the possibility of another world with loud chants of: 'Another world is not possible, unless you smash capitalism and bring in socialism!' (It sounded much better in Portuguese.)

Some of this criticism was unfair. The forum accommodated an extraordinary range of views, and it was precisely this diversity that made conflicts inevitable. But much of the criticism was legitimate and has implications that reach far beyond a one-week conference. How *are* decisions made in this movement of movements? On the anarchist side, all the talk of radical decentralization often conceals a very real hierarchy based on who owns, understands and controls the computer networks linking the activists to one another — what Jesse Hirsh, one of the founders of the anarchist computer network Tao Communications, calls 'a geek adhocracy'. And on the NGO side, who decides which 'civil society representatives' go behind the fence in Davos or Quebec City — while protesters outside are held back with water cannons and tear gas? There is no consensus among protest organizers about participating in these negotiations, and, more to the point, there is no truly representative process in place to make these decisions: no mechanism to select acceptable members of an activist delegation and no agreed-upon set of goals by which to measure the benefits and pitfalls of taking part.

And yet with a sweeping new round of WTO negotiations set for the fall of 2001, and the Free Trade Area of the Americas negotiation on-going, these questions about process were and are urgent. How do we determine whether the goal is to push for 'social clauses' on labour and environmental issues in international agreements, or to take whole sections — like food safety and agriculture — out of the agreements, or to try to shoot these agreements down altogether?

There are serious debates to be had over strategy and process, but it's difficult to see how they will unfold without bogging down a movement whose greatest strength so far has been its agility. Part of the problem is structural. Among most anarchists, who are doing a great deal of the grassroots organizing, direct democracy, transparency and community self-determination are not lofty political goals, they are fundamental tenets governing their own organizations. But although fanatical about process, anarchists tend to resist efforts to structure or centralize the movement. In contrast, many of the key NGOs, though they may share the anarchists' ideas about democracy in theory, are themselves organized as traditional hierarchies. They are run by charismatic leaders and executive boards, while their members send them money and cheer from the sidelines. The International Forum on Globalization — the brain trust of the North American side of the movement — lacks transparency in its decision-making and isn't accountable to a broad membership. Meanwhile, traditional membership-based structures like political parties and unions have been reduced to bit players in these wide webs of activism.

Perhaps the real lesson of Porto Alegre is that democracy and accountability need to be worked out first on more manageable scales — within local communities and coalitions and inside individual organizations, then broadened out. Without this foundation, there's not much hope for a satisfying democratic process when 10,000 activists from wildly different backgrounds are thrown in a room together.

For a model of how to extract coherence from a movement whose greatest tactical strength so far has been its similarity to a swarm of mosquitoes, it's useful to turn, once again, to the closest thing this movement has to a leader: a mask, two eyes and a pipe — a.k.a. Subcomandante Marcos. Marcos's own story is of a man who came to his leadership not through swaggering certainty, but by coming to terms with political uncertainty, by learning to follow. Though there is no confirmation of Marcos's real identity, the most repeated legend that surrounds him goes like this: an urban Marxist intellectual and activist, Marcos was wanted by the state and was no longer safe in the cities. He fled to the mountains of Chiapas in southeast Mexico filled with revolutionary rhetoric and certainty, there to convert the poor indigenous masses to the cause of armed proletarian revolution against the bourgeoisie. He said the workers of the world must unite, and the Mayans just stared at him. They said they weren't workers and, besides, land wasn't property but the heart of their communities. Having failed as a Marxist missionary, Marcos immersed himself in Mayan culture. The more he learned, the less he knew.

Out of this process, a new kind of army emerged, the EZLN defined itself in terms of not being controlled by an elite of guerrilla commanders but by the communities themselves, through clandestine councils and open assemblies. 'Our army', says Marcos, 'became scandalously Indian.'[12] That meant that he wasn't a commander barking orders, but a subcomandante, a conduit for the will of the councils. His first words said in the new persona were: '[t]hrough me speaks the will of the Zapatista National Liberation Army.'[13]

It's tempting to dismiss the Zapatista model as only being applicable to Indigenous struggles, but that is to miss the point entirely. The reason why there are there are now 45,000 Zapatista-related websites, why Marcos's communiqués are available in at least fourteen languages, and why twenty-two Zapatista books have been written and twelve documentaries made, is that there is something about the theory of Zapatismo that reaches far beyond Chiapas. It has to do, I think, with the very definition of revolution — and where power should truly rest. A few years ago, the idea of the Zapatista command travelling to Mexico City to address the congress would have been impossible to imagine. The prospect of masked guerrillas (even masked guerrillas who have left their arms at home) entering a hall of political power signals one thing: revolution. But when the Zapatistas travelled to Mexico City in March 2001, they weren't interested in overthrowing the state or naming their leader as president. In fact, when they finally gained entrance to the Congress, they left Marcos outside.

If anything, in their demands for control over land, direct political representation, and the right to protect their language and culture, the Zapatistas are demanding *less* state power over their lives, not more. What sets the Zapatistas apart from typical Marxist guerrilla insurgents is that their goal is not to win control, but to seize and build autonomous spaces where 'democracy, liberty and justice' can thrive. This is intimately linked with an organizing model that doesn't compartmentalize communities into workers, warriors, farmers and students, but instead seeks to organize communities whole, across sectors and across generations, creating genuine 'social movements'. For the Zapatistas, creating these autonomous zones isn't a recipe for dropping out of the capitalist economy, but a base from which to confront it. Marcos is convinced that these free spaces, created from reclaimed land, communal agriculture and resistance to privatization, will eventually create counter-powers to the state.

This organizing model has spread throughout Latin America, and the world. You can see it in the anarchist squats of Italy (called 'social centres') and in the Landless Peasants' Movement of Brazil, which seizes tracts of unused farmland and uses them for sustainable agriculture, markets and schools under the slogan 'Ocupar, Resistir, Producir' (Occupy, Resist, Produce). These same ideas were forcefully expressed by the students of the National Autonomous University of Mexico during the long and militant occupation of their campus. Zapata once said the land belongs to those who work it, their banners blared, WE SAY THAT THE UNIVERSITY BELONGS TO THOSE WHO STUDY IN IT.

What seemed to be emerging organically is not a movement for a single global government but a vision for an increasingly connected international network of very local initiatives, each built on direct democracy.

When critics say that the protesters lack vision, what they are really saying is that they lack an overarching revolutionary philosophy — like Marxism, deep ecology or social anarchy — on which they all agree. That is absolutely true, and for this we should be extraordinarily thankful. At the moment, the anti-corporate street activists are ringed by would-be leaders, anxious for the opportunity to enlist them as foot soldiers. At one end there is the Socialist Workers Party, waiting to welcome all that inchoate energy in Seattle and Washington inside its own sectarian, evangelical framework. On the other, there is John Zerzan in Eugene, Oregon, who sees the rioting and property destruction as the first step toward the collapse of industrialization and a return to pre-lapsarian 'anarcho-primitivism' — a kind of hunter-gatherer utopia.

It is to this young movement's credit that it has as yet fended off all of these agendas and has rejected everyone's generously donated manifesto, holding out for an acceptably democratic, representative process to take its resistance to the next stage. Will it be a ten-point plan? A new political doctrine? Maybe not. Maybe out of the chaotic network of hubs and spokes, something else will emerge: not a blueprint for some utopian new world, but a plan to protect the possibility of many worlds — 'a world', as the Zapatistas say, 'with many worlds in it'.[14]

Maybe instead of meeting the proponents of neoliberalism head on, this movement of movements will surround them from all directions.

NOTES

Portions of this essay first appeared in *The Nation*, *The Guardian* and *The Globe and Mail*.

1   In cases where no specific source is referred to, quotations and information are based on personal observation or communication.
2   *Newsweek*, 13 December 1999, p 36.
3   Mark Steyn, 'Zealots' Only Concrete Argument: They Grasp Their Projectiles; Less So Their Principles', *National Post*, 23 April 2001.
4   Subcomandante Marcos quoted in Robert Collier, 'Commander Marcos Identifies With All', *San Francisco Chronicle*, 13 June 1994.
5   Subcomandante Marcos, *First Declaration of La Realidad For Humanity Against Neoliberalism*, by the Clandestine Indigenous Revolutionary Committee General Command of the Zapatista Army of National Liberation, Mexico, January 1996. Available at http://www.ezln.org/documentos/1996/19960130.en.htm.
6   Subcomandante Marcos in Juana Ponce de Leon, ed., *Our Word Is Our Weapon*, Toronto: Seven Stories Press, 2001.
7   TeleGeography Inc, *Hubs and Spokes: A TeleGeography Internet Reader*, Washington, D.C.: TeleGeography, 2000, p. 9.
8   Subcomandante Marcos, *EZLN's Declaration of War: Today We Say Enough Is Enough (Ya Basta!)*, General command of the EZLN, 1993.
9   Charles H. Ramsey during a press conference, Washington, DC, 17 April

2000. Bob Dart and Alec Schultz report Ramsey to have said that '[t]hey are very very organized' ('Protests Shut Parts of Capital: Meetings Go On; Bankers Vow Reform', *The Palm Beach Post*, 17 April 2000).

10   David F. Ronfeldt, John Arquilla, Graham E. Fuller, Melissa Fuller, *The Zapatista Social Netwar in Mexico*, Los Angeles: Rand, 1998, p. 50.
11   Ibid., p. 119.
12   Marcos in Ponce de Leon, ed., *Our Word Is Our Weapon*.
13   Ibid.
14   For the quote 'a world made of many worlds', see Zapatista Army of National Liberation (read by Subcomandante Marcos), *Second Declaration of La Realidad* at the closing act of the First Intercontinental Encounter for Humanity and Against Neoliberalism, August 1996.

QUÉBEC CITY 2001 AND THE MAKING OF TRANSNATIONAL SUBJECTS

ANDRÉ C. DRAINVILLE

In the last two decades, the organizations which are dedicated to managing the world economy, and the social forces wanting to reform or revolutionize it, have both made global politics seem a cosmopolitan affair. Borrowing the inclusive language of city-builders, the World Bank *et al.* have invited selected NGOs and other would-be representatives of 'global civil society' to gather together, think civic thoughts and define the conditions of global civility. In tune, transnational social forces have defined themselves with reference to cosmopolitan *proxies* ('global civil society' here too, 'humanity', 'the peoples of the earth', 'the women — or the workers, or the poor — of the world') and have let themselves be drawn into a variety of scenarios (ranging from the civic schemes of the World Bank to reformist plans for a 'Tobin Tax' or a people's UN assembly, to ideas for global social contracts) that all end with the settling of global social relations.[1]

Though these scenarios may look like radical strategies for bringing transnational capital under social control — and thus seem like important breaches in the global order of things — they actually underestimate what might be born of the global meeting of social forces. Puffed up and ensconced in reverent absolutes, the peoples (or the women, or the workers, or the poor) of the world will not struggle for themselves or establish and sustain positions against transnational power. Cut off from any real social context, these cosmopolitan ghosts are fated to settle for a mollifying consensus from which might — perhaps — be found ways to humanize global capitalism, but nothing to challenge or revolutionize it. We need to reason from concrete, contingent, practices, in specific locations, at critical moments when broad political considerations — always the stuff of cosmopolitan planning — get turned into questions of strategy.[2] Rather than take cosmopolitan subjects for granted, we need to inquire into their making. Only thus can we look beyond ways to humanize global capitalism, and think about ways to revolutionize it.

In Québec City, where this article was written, the 'Summit of the Americas' was held between 20 April and 22 April 2001. A polycentric gathering of would-be hemispheric actors — from globalizing elites intent on making a 'Free Trade Area of the Americas' (FTAA), to sundry 'Peoples of the Americas' collected in a parallel summit, to a saturnalia of protests at the periphery of both events — it was a privileged occasion on which to think critically about the political construction of transnational subjects. This essay begins with a brief survey of the places where the events related to the Summit of the Americas were held. In the second part, these places and what was made in them are related to broader processes of order and change in the world economy.

QUÉBEC CITY 2001

The Summit of the Americas

At the centre of happenings in Québec City was the 'Summit of the Americas', hosted by the 'Bureau of the Summit of the Americas', a concern of Canada's Department of Foreign Affairs and International Trade (DFAIT). After Miami (1994) and Santiago (1998), this was the third official gathering of heads of states of the hemisphere since George Bush launched the 'Enterprise for the Americas Initiative' (EAI, 1991) to 'unify the Americas from Anchorage to Tierra Del Fuego in the world's biggest free trade pact'.[3]

Housed in the *Centre des Congrès*, on René Lévesque Boulevard, near the provincial parliament, shielded behind a 3.5 kilometres long, three-metres high fence establishing a 'security perimeter' defended by a united front of municipal, provincial and federal police, the Summit was a political enigma cloaked in a security spectacle: inside, thirty-four national delegations — 9,000 delegates — worked for the first time with a complete draft of the FTAA (Free Trade Area of the Americas; in French, Zone de Libre Échange des Amériques, or ZLEA) agreement. Yet, what would be discussed was not made public before the summit, in spite of considerable public pressure; nor was what would be discussed between them and the corporate patrons who sponsored various get-togethers (*inside* the security perimeter).

Also organized by the DFAIT's Bureau were song-and-dance celebrations of hemispheric peoples and cultures. Starting in the fall, *Voix des Amériques* concerts were held at Le Capitole, the permanent venue for *The Elvis Story* (in English on the marquise), a hyper-real revue (a 'real copy' in Umberto Eco's term, a perfect substitute for reality) that draws much of its clientele from the tourist trade and the suburbs, whose producers have spearheaded attempts to commodify *Place d'Youville*, a former market place that serves as a gathering place for youths and, sometimes, a starting point for urban riots.[4] The last concert in the *Voix* series, held days before the Summit, was the *Tropicalia* review, that promised 'all the *joie de vivre*, all the colours of Brazil ... a trip south through the samba and the bossa nova'. At the end of the Summit, DFAIT sponsored an extravaganza of 600 artists, later televised by the Canadian Broadcasting Corporation, the official broadcaster of the Summit.

Other DFAIT-sponsored events included a Summit school (to encourage young reporters to inquire into 'the realities of the Americas'), a Youth Forum ('Emotion, authenticity and cultural diversity') that produced a 'practical, realistic, report', later circulated amongst official delegations; a picture-drawing contest; a cooking festival ('Savouring the Americas'); a 'Writers of the Americas' Summit; a film festival; and a book fair (the 'Library of the Americas'). An 'Inter-American Cooperation Beyond Free Trade' colloquium focusing on the 'wealth and complexity of interamerican cooperation' was hosted by Laval University's *Institut Québécois des Hautes Études Internationales* (a privileged partner of both DFAIT and Canada's Department of Defense).[5]

Implicating academics, representatives of government-created and sponsored NGOs as well as members of national and global governing agencies, it was a model of partnership between academia and governing institutions. It ended on Friday April 20, as the heads of states' Summit began, by making policy recommendations that were, conveniently, a faithful match for the 'Summit of the Americas Declaration and Plan of Action', released as the Summit ended on Sunday April 22.[6]

The People's Summit

Well removed from the security perimeter — in a tent in the old harbour in Lower Town, beside picturesque old Québec — was the second 'Peoples' Summit of the Americas', that had for its theme: 'Resisting. Proposing. Together.' Organized by the *Réseau Québécois d'intégration continentale* (RQIC), and Common Frontiers — respectively Québec's and Canada's link to the Hemispheric Social Alliance (HSA) — the Peoples' summit was itself largely funded and, literally, *placed* by Canada's DFAIT's and Québec's Ministry of External Affairs.[7]

In keeping with the heads of states' summit, the People's Summit was a mix of the purposeful and the festive. From Monday through Thursday, policy forums — involving, for the most part, duly registered representatives of 'civil society' — dealt with issues outlined in the latest draft of the 'People's Hemispheric Agreement' (PHA) on 'women and globalization', 'education', 'labour', 'agriculture', 'communications', 'human rights', the 'environment', and so on. In the evening, plenary sessions were held to find ways to aggregate demands and reach a consensus that could later be incorporated in the next draft of the PHA. On Friday, teach-ins were organized.

On Saturday, the People's work was done and a People's March was held. A first group — roughly 10,000 — gathered on the Plains of Abraham (in Upper Town, near the security perimeter); another, larger, group — estimates vary from 30,000 to 50,000 — gathered in Lower Town near the People's tent. When they met — at the corner of Charest Boulevard and rue de la Couronne in Lower Town, a short walk away from the security perimeter — they formed the largest crowd ever assembled in Québec history (save for that which heard young Céline

Dion sing for Pope John–Paul II). But immediately the march split into two, very unequal, groups. Shepherded by 1,500 marshals from the *Fédération des Travailleurs du Québec*, upwards of sixty thousand marched not towards but away from the perimeter to the Parc de l'exposition, where the People were assembled in a parking lot, between a shopping centre and the Pepsi coliseum, to listen to speeches from their representatives.[8] A much smaller group — perhaps 1,000 — broke away from the People's March and walked back uptown to support direct actions against the security perimeter. When they reached the fence, the *Funk Fighting Unaccountable Naughty Korporations* tried, but failed, to organize a sit-in.

Protests: teach-ins, demonstrations and other carnivalesque happenings

In already tried fashion (although only a few years old, anti–summit protests have already established set ways), the Summit of the Americas also occasioned a saturnalia of protests, teach-ins, direct actions and street theatre, organized for the most part either by *Opération Québec Printemps 2001* (OQP 2001), a broad coalition of local community and student groups, or by the *Comité d'acceuil du Sommet des Amériques* (CASA) working with the *Convergence des Luttes Anti-Capitalistes* (CLAC), both anarchist groups, the former from Québec city, the latter from Montréal.[9]

Some teach-ins and conferences were held in what was termed the 'solidarity perimeter', in the Limoilou neighbourhood (further removed than even the People's Summit from the security perimeter). Drawing on militants and experts from such nodes of anti-globalization activity as the International Forum on Globalization, the Third World Network, or *L'observatoire sur la Mondialisation*, they focused on a wide variety of political issues related to globalization in general and to the FTAA in particular: the privatization of water, the clear-cutting of forests, union history, human rights, health care, art and activism, education, the Tobin tax, etc. Workshops on interacting with the media, legal rights, direct actions and ways of conducting civil disobedience were also held inside the 'solidarity perimeter'.

On Friday the 20th, a 'Carnaval anti-capitaliste' was organized by the CASA/CLAC. At 1p.m., a crowd of some 5,000 gathered at Laval University in the suburbs where people joined either a green bloc (peaceful and festive), a yellow bloc (obstructive and defensive) or a red bloc (intent on disturbance and direct actions). Greens went either to the Ilôt Fleuri (a wasteland in Lower Town underneath a highway, remade into a post-industrial happening place: think Blade Runner meets travellers' festivals), or to the Faubourg Saint-Jean Baptiste uptown where the local *Comité populaire* had organized a peaceful occupation of the neighbourhood.[10]

Yellows and reds, along with a small 'black block' assembled by the ad *hoc* Autonomous Organizing Collective of Anti-Authoritarians from the Mid-West, Northeast, Montréal and Québec, marched to the security perimeter. They arrived in the middle of the afternoon. A catapult brought from the Ottawa region by the *Deconstructionist Institute for Surreal Topology* (self-described *Lanarkists*) tried to launch stuffed toy-animals into the security perimeter, while those who had received training in civil disobedience tried to organized a sit-in. Quickly, both were overtaken by events: a segment of the fence was brought down, police fired tear gas and the already familiar to-and-fro of anti-summit protest began.

Giving colour and context to events were theatre groups — some linked to OQP, others to the *CASA*, or from outside Québec — working to foster what the historical avant-garde (Futurists, Dada, the surrealists, etc.) would have recognized as a radically creative ambiance. The best, most derisive, action was in the Saint-Jean Baptiste neighbourhood, where a section of the fence was decorated with bras and girdles, some inscribed with slogans ('My mother is not for sale'), others with bilingual anti-FTAA/anti-*ZLÉA* slogans (English on one cup, French on the other, with more equanimity than is usually found in the politics of language in Québec).

Feeding mainstream and alternative newspapers and working to facilitate links with other events elsewhere in the hemisphere was the *Centre des Médias Alternatifs-Québec 2001* (the CMAQ), Québec's link to the IndyMedia (independent media) family. Set up in the fall of 2000 by *Alternatives* (a DFAIT-funded NGO), officially launched at parties in Québec City (on 25 January) and in Montréal (on 1 February), the CMAQ was headquartered in the Méduse art complex, on côte d'Abraham, a short walk — but more than a stone's throw — away from the security perimeter, but within range of the policemen's gas. There were also housed medics, who helped those harmed by tear gas and rubber bullets.

Matters of security

The separation between the heads of states' summit and other events was as definite and spectacular as it has ever been in the short history of counter-summit protests. To serve the needs of official delegates and protect their intimacy there were more than 6,000 policemen and women, working for all the police corps with some kind of authority in the region: the Québec City municipal police (circulation, perimeter security), the Sainte-Foy municipal police (airport security), the *Sureté du Québec* (crowd control, criminal activities) and the Royal Canadian Mounted police (internal passports, logistics, perimeter security). They were aided in their work by more than 1,200 soldiers and student volunteers from local police colleges, who were stool-pigeons among the protesters.

Giving weight and significance to the police and soldiers was a spectacle of authority that had been under construction for several months, with the help of police forces from Seattle, Prague, Washington and other sites of anti-summit protests. The first move in the construction of the spectacle of authority — a symbolic move, targeted at what police have come to associate with anti-globalization activities — was the Internet publication in August 2000 of the Canadian Security Intelligence Service's report on 'Anti-Globalization protests'. This was a perfectly banal document that revealed nothing about security arrangements but did signal CSIS's intent to monitor all forms of communication.[11]

In real life, the spectacular build-up of authority started on the first of November, when a press conference was held during which the Québec Minister of Public Security Serge Ménard and Québec city police spokesman Gaétan Labbé, backed up by representatives of other police corps, unveiled what they called security measures 'unprecedented in Canadian history'.[12] Afterward, every detail of security arrangements (the number of hotel rooms and apartments rented by the RCMP, the kind of assault vehicles and plastic bullets the SQ might use, the breadth of the security perimeter and the depth of police infiltration of anti-globalization groups, etc.) were similarly unveiled at press conferences by a row of senior police officers. On February 4th, three CASA protesters who were distributing anti-FTAA leaflets to tourists in town for the Winter Carnival (the most media-saturated event in Québec City) were arrested at lunch-time on the most central intersection in the city. They refused to identify themselves and were later released. Two weeks later, the city of Ste-Foy declared (in a by-law later revoked) that the wearing of scarves and balaclavas would be forbidden between 1 April and 2 May, in order, as they openly put it, not to 'interfere with repressive measures' (a direct echo of what the Philadelphia police did before the Republican convention in July 2000).

THE MAKING OF TRANSNATIONAL SUBJECTS

Summit happenings are frequently analyzed in the narrow terms of who stood or fought with whom, did what when, won or lost which battle, or what was won or lost in it, but they also need to be related to broader and more diffused processes of order and change in the post-Bretton Woods world economy. Specifically, they can be understood to be part of the making of new transnational subjects.

Consensus and neoliberal governance

Driving attempts to redefine the terms of global order in the post-Bretton Woods period have been what Stephen Gill has termed globalizing elites, gathering 'at the apex of social hierarchies in the emerging world order', in places increasingly detached from national social formations, working with relatively coherent purpose and ideology.[13] In the immediate wake of the Bretton Woods crisis, globalizing elites either gathered in institutions inherited from the Bretton Woods period (the International Monetary Fund, the World Bank, the Bank for International Settlements (BIS), the Organisation for Economic Cooperation and Development) but made more relevant and autonomous by the context of crisis, or they established new forums (the Trilateral Commission, the World Economic Forum in Davos, G7 summits, etc.).

What was done in these exclusive — indeed almost clandestine — gatherings could sometimes be defined in concrete, immediate, terms. Monetarist targeting, for instance — a key neoliberal 'concept of control' and a central component of neoliberal policies in all advanced capitalist countries in the latter half of the 1970s — was born in the BIS and in still more discreet places, such as the Brunner-Meltzer conferences in Konztanz, the bi-annual Carnegie/Rochester Conferences, or the meetings of the Mont Pélerin Society.[14]

More broadly, meetings of global elites served to nurture what the OECD called the 'collegial management of the developed world's interests' and the G7, a 'sense of common purpose and vision'.[15] Thus they were key to defining the terms of neoliberal regulation, arguably the first mode of regulation born in the world economy itself.

Early in the post-Bretton Woods period, neoliberal concepts of control were impressed — by means of structural adjustment plans and monetarist regulation — on debtor countries that faced monetary or balance-of-payment crises, whether at the centre of the world economy (Britain in 1976) or at the periphery (Chile, Argentina or Peru). Echoing what *haute finance* had dreamed of in the age of the *Pax Britannica*, globalizing elites tried to 'impos[e] upon society ... the concept of the self-regulating market'.[16] The attempt to regulate the world economy authoritatively — by domination rather than hegemonic leadership, to borrow a distinction dear to contemporary political economy — has remained an integral part of neoliberal ordering. The Multilateral Agreement on Investment (MAI), which tried to install investors as privileged subjects in international law, was the latest and most explicit example.

Beginning in the 1980s, however, political events (IMF riots in Caracas, Warsaw, Buenos Aires, Abidjan and Libreville, the popular removal from office of neoliberal presidents in Brazil, Venezuela and Guatemala), as well as structural rigidities (Fordist mechanisms at the centre of the world economy, state planning in socialist economies, weak or nonexistent mechanisms of financial surveillance at the periphery) exposed the economic costs and political fragility of global over-determination.[17]

To increase the efficiency of adjustment and solidify the political foundations of neoliberalism, global regulatory agencies began to concern themselves with political and social processes beyond crude pressure, and to structure their relationship with NGOs and other would-be representatives of global civil society.[18]

It is this concern that defines 'global governance', the political adjunct to global neoliberalism.

'Global governance' is an attempt to invent a political interlocutor with whom globalizing elites might negotiate sustainable terms for global accumulation: a 'real copy', a perfectly fabricated and perfectly acceptable substitute for global civil society. This absolutely crucial attempt is what sets governance apart from previous modes of global regulation: 'mercantile sponsoring' in the seventeenth and eighteenth century, 'free-trade liberalism' in the nineteenth century, 'embedded liberalism' after the Second World War, 'neoliberalism' after the Bretton Woods crisis. Where these all relied for their political sustenance on a relatively exclusive coalition of globalizing elites working in association with a global patchwork of local and nationally-constituted elites (even 'embedded liberalism' was embedded not in the world economy itself, but in national social formations), 'global governance' tries to assemble a broad-based, possibly sustainable, global constituency to bolster and stabilize global order. This constituency, we can think of as a 'global growth machine': a 'broad coalition of social forces that share an apolitical, ostensibly "value-free" understanding of economic growth', and have moved 'beyond opposition to proposition' to define a consensual path for capitalist growth.[19]

Whether it will succeed in moving global neoliberalism beyond mere domination towards something like hegemony will depend on the outcome of political struggles.

The most spectacular places to see governance's growth machine at work are, precisely, 'global summits'. These are to global governance what universal exhibits were to free-trade internationalism in the age of *Pax Britannica*: idealized representations of order. Where, as Charlotte Brontë put it, universal exhibits gathered a 'unique assemblage of all things' promised by free-trade capitalism, global conferences are gatherings of what appears as a model citizenry, ideally bound to find the best — most efficient, most portable and sustainable — solutions to global problems: of development, at the United Nations Conference on Environment and Development in Rio, June 1992; of human rights, in Vienna a year later; of population growth, in Cairo in September 1994; of social development, in Copenhagen in March 1995; of housing, in Istanbul in June 1996; of variformed challenges to the reform of the United Nations, at the 'We the Peoples' Millennium Forum in New York in May 2000; of the production of wealth, social reproduction and related issues at the 'World Social Forum' in Porto Alegre in January 2001.[20]

Exhibited at global conferences, governance solutions get synthesized into blueprints and forward-looking plans of action — Rio's 'Agenda 21', Cairo's 'Programme of Action', Copenhagen's 'World Social Charter', 'Istanbul's 'Habitat Agenda', New York's 'Declaration and Agenda for Action', Porto Alegre's 'Manifest'. These visible artefacts of a broad division of political labours are made elsewhere and imported into global conferences. To inquire into how and by whom they are made is to begin looking into 'governance' as an attempt to construct transnational subjects.

In the last two decades the regulatory agencies of the world economy have broadened and structured their relationship with would-be representatives of global civil society. At the World Bank, for instance, a concerted effort began in the early 1980s to involve NGOs more closely in policy-making (what is termed the 'mainstreaming' and 'upstreaming' of NGOs): new institutional points of contact were created, new funding windows and lending facilities were opened, and new operational directives were issued that defined the terms of NGO-World Bank collaboration. The proportion of projects involving NGO participation — less than 6 per cent between 1973-88 — grew to almost 50 per cent by the mid-1990s.[21]

In like manner, the OECD made 'a political virtue of the necessity to increase economic efficiency' and started in the early 1980s to mix 'good development policy [with] good politics' by folding development aid into national strategies drawn up in collaboration with representative coalitions of local NGOs and social elites.[22]

Here as well, new funding windows were opened and the relationship with NGOs, GONGOs, GOINGOs, QUANGOs and other would-be representatives of global civil society was further structured.[23] At the World Trade Organization, an NGO ombudsman was put in place and a 'Citizen's Summit' was called for the Seattle Ministerial meeting, that was to serve as a background to the official launch of the *Millennium Round* of negotiations before street protests overtook planned events.[24] Even the World Economic Forum in Davos, a quintessential elite place, has opened itself up somewhat: in 2001, Lori Wallach, Director of Global Tradewatch and a key figure of Seattle protests, addressed delegates at the personal invitation of the Forum's founder Klaus Schwab, who thinks of himself as something of a radical amongst the company he keeps.[25]

At a time when governance agencies are working to 'provide security, prosperity, coherence, order and continuity to the [global] system', Québec's Summit of the Americas can be situated in relation both to the making of neoliberal concepts of control, and to efforts to assemble a global civil society acceptable to globalizing elites.[26] About the importance of the Summit of the Americas in this process little can be said for the moment, except that it was an occasion for hemispheric elites to further define the terms of the 'neo-liberal conditioning framework' in the Americas begun by the North American Free Trade Agreement.[27] In marked contrast to the WTO summit in Seattle — 'the first big negotiation on world trade for over five years' — the Québec summit was not defined in relation to any objectives that might give protesters a measure of their success.[28]

About the making of a global growth machine, it needs be said that this has been an integral part of neoliberal integration in the Americas since its inception. George Bush's 'Enterprise for the Americas' speech made explicit reference to the need to 'strengthen hemispheric democratization', a wish later operationalized by the Miami 'Plan of Action' that explicitly instructed governments to 'review the regulatory framework for non-governmental actors with a view to facilitating their operation and promoting their ability to receive funds', with a view to 'giv[ing] depth and durability to democracy'.[29]

Key here is the Inter-American Development Bank (IDB), which has worked — in tune with other regional affiliates of the World Bank — to foster participatory development and to structure relationships with NGOs, 'stakeholders' and other civic partners of globalizing elites. In 'governance' fashion, there have been grand civic gatherings and new sources of funding. The first notable gatherings were IDB conferences held in September 1994 on 'Strengthening Civil Society' and 'Civic Participation and Socioeconomic Participation'.[30] Also in 1994, the IDB held an hemispheric forum on 'Women in the Americas: Participation and Development' from which was born the Oaxaca Initiative ('A Framework for Equitable and Sustainable Development in the Americas'). At the March 1998 IDB Annual Meeting in Cartageana, Executive Vice-President Nancy Birdsall and Edmundo Jarquin, of the newly-created 'State and Civil Society Division', addressed participants at the 'Social Programs, Poverty and Citizen Involvement' seminar, to tell them about the 'inevitability of citizens' involvement in sustainable development'. The two-day seminar concluded on an indisputable 'governance' note: '*[c]itizen participation, properly channeled, generates savings, mobilized additional financial and human resources, promotes equity and makes a decisive contribution to the strengthening of society and the democratic system*'.[31]

In January 1999 the IDB co-sponsored a 'Global Meeting of Generations', in Washington, DC in collaboration with the 'International Association of Students in Economics and Management', 'Youth for Development and Cooperation', the UNDP and the 'International Development Conference'. There, 'one hundred young social entrepreneurs from around the world' sat with 'global, national and grassroots development organizations', to 'discuss key issues and opportunities facing humanity in the 21st century', and to draw up civic blueprints.

Beyond summitry, the IDB has also worked to broaden and structure its relationship with would-be representatives of civil society. Before 'governance', only the 'Small Project Program' (1979) provided a structured, sustained, link between NGOs and the IDB. Back then, representatives of civil society were only involved with the IDB in exceptional circumstances — and then only in a service-delivery capacity.[32] In the last decade, however, the IDB has conducted what Nancy Birdsall called a 'diagnostic survey of the present status of civil society in the region' and, as a result, it set up a variety of outreach and consultation programs for NGOs.[33]

As well, new funding windows and 'social investment funds' were opened to encourage and structure NGO participation: in 1987, a 'Social Investment Fund' was established that was explicitly demand-driven and aimed at fostering the active involvement of community organizations and NGOs in all stages of the project cycle. In 1991, the Indigenous Peoples Fund (IPF) was set up. To 'promote the long-term and sustainable development of the native peoples of Latin America and the Caribbean', the IPF encouraged consultations of all sorts — from information-sharing to decision-making in project-identification and design — between native leaderships and the IDB. In the same spirit, the Multilateral Investment Fund (1992) has concerned itself with building partnerships between NGOs and private voluntary organizations, particularly those representing people usually left out of the economic mainstream. The three investment 'windows' of the MIF — the 'Technical Cooperation Facility', the 'Human Resources Facility' and the 'Small Enterprise Development Facility' — all provide services to build knowledge, encourage economic empowerment and involve women and youth in the 'enterprise economy'.

The IDB has also worked to 'mainstream' and 'upstream' representatives of hemispheric civil society, and to further participatory development, 'defined in broad terms as the process through which people with a legitimate interest (stakeholders) influence and share control over development initiatives, and the decisions and resources which affect them'. In true 'governance' spirit, the IDB has sought efficiency, both political and economic: '*[p]articipation improves project design by reducing the cost of obtaining accurate and site-specific data on environmental, social and cultural factors as well as stakeholders' felt needs and priorities. Also, project managers can get input from all groups, including people often marginalized in the development process*'. [34]

As the political contours of regional integration were taking shape in the early 1990s the IDB set up a 'State and Civil Society Division' and a 'Social Programs and Sustainable Development Department'.[35] As well, a Women in Development (WID) unit was created in 1994 that begat a 'Fund for Women's Leadership and Representation' to direct funds to organizations that promote women's participation and leadership at national, regional, and local levels, in the economic, political and social spheres.[36]

Until very recently, the Organization of American States had played a minor role in the construction of a hemispheric growth machine (though sometimes it did act as a secretariat for hemispheric integration — as it did in Lima in June 1997, when OAS Ministers of Foreign relations set the agenda for the Santiago Summit of the Americas).[37] After Santiago, however, a 'Unit for the Promotion of Democracy' was created that has worked, modestly, through state institutions, 'to consolidate both civic practices and mechanisms of participation in the political process'.[38] In June 1999 a 'Committee on Civil Society Participation' was created 'to establish clear, transparent, modern procedures for interaction between civil society and the political organs of the OAS'.[39] These procedures allowed the Committee to consult with more than 900 organizations and to assemble a stock of policy proposals. At the 'Hemispheric Meeting' (Miami, 18–20 January 2001), these proposals were synthesized into the 'Final Document: Recommendations by Civil Society Organizations' that will, in all likelihood, have been part of what was discussed in Québec City.[40]

As well as the IDB and the OAS, other governing agencies have also worked to define efficient and sustainable terms of hemispheric social relations by hosting meetings with designated representatives of civil society. At their fourth meeting in San José (Costa Rica) in March 1998, trade ministers established the 'Committee of Government representatives on the Participation of Civil Society'. In November, this Committee issued an 'Open Invitation to Civil Society' that detailed both its desire to work with civil society representatives and the terms of collaboration. The Committee met twice in the summer of 1999. On November 4, 1999, during the fifth meeting of the trade ministers of the Americas in Toronto, the Committee's report was made public.[41]

In the spring of 2000 a second 'Open Invitation to Civil Society' was extended, in preparation for Québec's Summit of the Americas, arguably the most important gathering yet of the hemispheric growth machine, both quantitatively and in terms of policy-readiness: never did so many gather with such defined purpose or with, in the background, such a decorous, 'colourful tapestry of cultures, values and traditions'.[42]

Standing at the apex of another transnational hierarchy that has taken shape in the last decade, the People's Summit was the other part of the hemispheric growth machine that met in Québec City. For a decade between the mid-eighties and mid-nineties social forces opposed to neoliberal integration in the Americas organized summits, gatherings and *encuentros*. In North America, the FTA and NAFTA negotiations occasioned a veritable explosion of trans-border summits between the Action Canada Network (ACN), the American Fair Trade Campaign (FTC) and the *Red Mexicana de Acción Frente Libre Comercio* (RMAFLC).[43]

Amongst notable summits were: the ACN-RMLAC *Encuentro* (Mexico, October 1990), the ACN-RMAFLC-FTC summit (Mexico, April 1991), the San Ygnacio *encuentro* of environmental groups (April 1991), the Zacatenas meeting (October 1991), the Trinational Working Women's conference (Valle de Bravo, February 1992) and the tri-national cross-border meeting between representatives of the ACN, the RMAFLC, the CTC and the American Alliance for Responsible Trade (Niagara Falls, October 1993). This was the last tri-national summit before the NAFTA came into effect on January 1994. After NAFTA, two *Encuentros por la Humanidad y contra el Neoliberalismo* were organized in Mexico by the *Ejército Zapatista de Liberación National* (EZLN): the first took place in Chiapas in July–August 1996, the second in *Belem do Para*, 6 to 11 December 1999.

In the same period, trans-border summits were also being organized nearer Brazil, another pole of transnational integration. The Sao Paulo Forum was founded in 1990 by Brazil's *Partido Dos Trabalhadores* (PT) and representatives from left organizations and movements, including the Sandinista National Liberation Front of Nicaragua, the Farabundo Marti National Liberation Front of EL Salvador, the Broad Front of Uruguay, Bolivia's Free Bolivar Movement, Peru's United Left and the Cuban Communist Party.[44]

The second meeting of the Sao Paulo Forum was held in Mexico City in June 1991; the third in Managua in July 1992, the fourth in Havana in July 1993 and the last in Montevideo in 1995. A gathering of more than two hundred left movements, parties and organizations, it was hailed by Libya's Mu'ammar al-Qadhafi as the embryo of a 'Popular World Front'.[45]

But fronts born of popular summitry did not hold up. Less than four years after Niagara Falls and two after Montevideo, popular summits were already being folded into the process of hemispheric governance. In 1997, the *Nossa América* popular forum was held in Belo Horizonte, alongside the 'Third Summit Meeting of Ministers for Commerce' and the 'Third Business Forum of the Americas'. In true 'governance' fashion, it both gave birth to a new transnational subject (the 'Hemispheric Social Alliance') and, on its behalf, produced a syncretic, reformist, agenda accepting of what Michel Chossudovsky has called the 'dominant counter-discourse', which presses for the inclusion of environmental, labour and human rights clauses within trade agreements, and pushes for poverty alleviation schemes and institutional reforms.[46]

In April 1998, the First Peoples' Summit, convened by the Hemispheric Social Alliance, was held in Santiago, alongside the second Summit of the Americas.[47] 'Two thousand delegates met in twelve sectoral forums, workshopping ideas for an alternative social and economic model in the hemisphere.' Then was drafted the first People's Hemispheric Agreement' (PHA), entitled 'Alternatives for the Americas'. Key to it was the People's acceptance of free trade and foreign investments as privileged 'instruments for achieving just and sustainable development'.[48] The HSA campaign continued in March 1999 in Costa Rica, where a Coordinating Group was chosen — that included Common Frontiers and the RQIC — to pilot the PHA push for inclusion and reform. A further draft of the PHA was prepared at a 'civil society meeting' in Rio in June 1999 (held in parallel with the meeting of heads of states from the European Union, Latin Americas and the Caribbean). And during the 'citizens' forum' held prior to the fourth summit of Trade Ministers of the Hemisphere (Toronto, November 1999) the PHA draft was prepared that was discussed and updated when 'hemispheric civil society' reconvened for the Second People's Summit in Québec city.

Thus was being constructed a 'hemispheric growth machine' that operates mainly as a problem-solving body working to define terms for sustainable accumulation. The heads of states' Summits and the People's Summits, of course, are not reducible to one another. In terms of their political origins, as well as in feeling and intent, they are relatively distinct entities. And if there was nothing more to neoliberalism than concepts of control coercively imposed — what global neoliberalism was before the mid-eighties — then the People's Summit would be a radical event indeed. But in the age of governance, when global regulatory agencies are trying to move neoliberal regulation beyond coercion towards consensus, the attempt to create a responsible hemispheric civil society and the People's' move from 'Resisting' to 'Proposing' should be seen as twinned enterprises, both parts of the making of a 'hemispheric growth machine'.

Protest and resistance

The political dynamics of the post-Bretton Woods period opened room not only for transnational concepts of control and governance-defined civility, but also for forms of oppositional politics. To describe it, some have written of 'new left internationalism', others of 'global contention', of 'global social movements', or of 'global resistance'.[49] By many accounts, what is most distinctive about this new kind of global politics — in relation both to the inherited ways of left internationalism and to 'governance' — is how it creates, at the point of contact with global power (where strategic courses meet) what Michel Foucault would have recognized as 'communities of resistance'.[50]

Lately, the best places to observe transnational communities of resistance in action have been protests against gatherings of globalizing elites. Most famously, fifty thousand met in Seattle on 30 November 1999 to force the closing of the second ministerial conference of the World Trade Organization. On 16 April 2000, eight thousand protested the annual meeting of World Bank and IMF in Washington. In September, fifteen thousand were in Prague to protest the 55th annual WB/IMF summit — the first such event to be held in a former East-block country.[51] A few months later, a few hundred were in Davos to protest the opening of the 31st World Economic Summit.[52] Brought together by organizations with an acute sense of the marvellous and the sensational (the Ruckus Society, the Direct Action Network, Reclaim the Streets, Mobilization for

Global Justice, etc.), often coloured wondrously (in Prague, yellows were 'ecolos', pinks reds of all sorts, blues anarchists and anti-fascists), fused by tactical preoccupations readily dramatized by journalistic accounts, their carnivalesque aesthetics and sense of happening contrasting markedly with 'governance's' dutiful greys and decorous fêtes (this year at Davos, Youssou N'Dour sang and danced for the globalizing elites), summit protesters are certainly most spectacular communities of resistance.

Less sensational, but more significant, are the transnational communities of resistance being born in countless campaigns against the ways and consequences of globalization: union busting and gender exploitation in export zones (in Saipan, Mexico's *maquilladoras*, Guatemala, etc.), brand-name exploitation (by GAP, General Electric, Guess, Mitsubishi, Nike, Reebok, Suzuki and others), sexual tourism (in South-East Asia and Europe), the ecological impact of structural reforms, the imprisonment of notable labour leaders or social activists (Ken Saro-Wiwa, Mumia Abu-Jamal, Wei Jingsheng, Wariebi K. Agamene, A. Aidelomon, Frank O. Kokori and others), undemocratic transnational policies (the Multilateral Agreement on Investment, for instance). Organized by a diffused *'nébuleuse'* of relatively new international organizations, documentation and research centres, these campaigns have brought social forces directly onto the terrain of the world economy, not as a severed and regimented lot of problem-solvers, nor as the obligatory agents of cosmopolitan *proxies*, but as rooted and indefinite communities of struggle. Elsewhere, I have called this the radical, ordinary, new internationalism of social movements:

> not radical because it represents a leap of consciousness, because it proclaims ex cathedra its anti-capitalism, or because it invents new and broader solidarities, but because it is an increasingly ordinary, everyday expression of the deep fellowship of the moved and the shaken of the world economy [and] because it expresses a shared marginalization that is more deeply rooted materially than that projected by cosmopolitan projects of the 19th century or desired by Internationals. This is not the crystalline internationalism of those who share a similar position in the mathematical equations explaining the capitalist accumulation process, but the cloudy internationalism of those who live in a capitalist world economy, and who resist global capitalism as an historically specific and contingent mode of social organization.[53]

Transnational campaigns tend to be tied to particular issues, and are dismissed for their 'economic-corporatist' consciousness and their inability to tell us 'what they are fighting for' and what 'they care about.' Although less political than strategic, and certainly lacking in programmatic coherence, they may nonetheless be having a structuring impact on the world economy as a place of politics.[54] Dragging context and politics with them to the world economy, at once global and radically grounded, transnational communities of resistance may be transforming the world economy into a place where ideas and modes of organizations as well as ways of life and struggle become relatively autonomous from individual agency. Charged by contextualized struggles, the world economy may be becoming a conductor, or even a catalyst. This we may take as a guiding hypothesis, as we turn our attention back to Québec's Summit of the Americas.

QUÉBEC CITY AND THE MAKING OF TRANSNATIONAL SUBJECTS

The protests in Québec City, of course, neither rose in the sky like the sun at an appointed time, nor were they simply induced by some kind of global ambience (or by what Edward Said has called a 'global oppositional mood'[55]). They were made not by cosmopolitan ghosts but by actually-existing groups. Between June 2000 (when SalAMI's first training camp was held in Val Cartier) and the beginning of the Summit, some fifty *formations* (training courses, from prepared kits) were given near and around the city by *formateurs* and *formatrices*, to a medley of groups (union locals, community groups, nuns, students and women's groups), on a variety of issues related to neoliberal globalization (and, in the case of CMAQ's *Ateliers de formations,* on the manufacturing and dissemination of dissenting news).[56]

In that period there were also teach-ins and *formations* in Montréal, two CLAC/CASA *consultas* in Québec City (the first, in February, brought together between three and four hundred anarchist sympathizers; the second, in March, was open only to group representatives but still gathered about one hundred people); several meetings of the *Université populaire* and *Alternative*-linked radio shows (on CKIA, *Radio Basse-ville*); truly innumerable conferences on globalization-related issues (organized by such diverse groups as the *Table de concertation contre la pauvreté de Sainte Foy-Sillery*, the Ontario Coalition Against Poverty, *Droit de Parole, Communication Basse-ville,* the Shakti women of colour collective, the Immigrant Workers' Centre, etc.); at least one workshop on legal rights (organized by the *Ligue des Droits et Libertés*); as well as numerous anti-capitalist activities and spectacles (in Québec city anti-capitalist music may be becoming a genre of its own). Between mid-January and March, a CASA caravan also reached two dozen cities in the Canadian Maritimes and in the North-East United States. During the protests OQP and CASA committees, in collaboration with others, organized food, housing (the equivalent of 300 hotels were set up in a couple weeks, with volunteer labour, no money, while dealing with police harassment) as well as medical assistance and legal aid for those who were injured or arrested (at the time of writing, OQP and the CASA were working with the *Travailleurs Canadiens de l'Automobile* and others to set up a *Comité Légal de soutien* for prisoners).[57]

The protests in Québec City were also made internationally, sometimes by the very groups and people that had organized counter-summit protests elsewhere. Reasoning like a policeman, looking for a confederacy of anti-globalization forces, we could follow trails of personal and political contacts, some open and institutional, others clandestine, both in 'real' life and on-line. Connecting dots, we could show that, indeed, the making of protests in Québec City was linked to like happenings elsewhere, by specific people and organizations who shape the aesthetics of anti-summit protests (anti-capitalist carnivals too are made, by such groups as the Ruckus Society or Reclaim the Streets), give them their language, tactics (lock-downs, street parties, property destruction, affinity groups, civil disobedience, etc.) and a measure of political coherence.

But beyond what was constructed in the most voluntarist sense of the term, the protests in Québec City were also charged by a more abstract — but no less determining — sense of context. Were references to the works of Louis Althusser not so out of fashion as to have become nearly indecipherable we could write of the making of the protests in Québec as having been 'overdetermined' by the global level.[58] Short of that, we can more modestly suggest that protests were more than what could have been made in a vacuum, and, perhaps, more politically significant than what a policeman could see.

A good measure of the significance of a global sense of place to the making of protests in Québec City is how groups and people involved were 'practically conscious' (to borrow Anthony Giddens' term) of happenings elsewhere on the terrain of the world economy, and how their politics were being defined not just locally, but also in answer to what was done elsewhere, in other circumstances.[59] Especially revealing here is how issues inherited from the very short history of summit protests became structuring concerns in preparation for Québec's Summit of the Americas.[60]

Early summit protests were events unto themselves. Sure of their contrapuntal unity, radically defiant of political intent and instrumental thinking, participants subsumed political differences under strategic concerns: 'how to climb trees, block roads, lock down on doors, eat and shit in extreme situations, scale buildings, deal with cops, minister to the injured, show solidarity and survive in jail', how to 'hold ... the space, wait ..., [and] make ... the point that we have a right to be here.'[61] When the 'Peoples' Global Action Against Free Trade and the World Trade Organisation' (PGA) held what was arguably the first contemporary anti-summit protest in Geneva in May 1998, diversity of politics and tactics reigned, with radically little concern for common programs: *the people came with the banners of all kinds of struggles against some aspect of globalization: local unions fighting privatizations or austerity, groups of solidarity with the south, squatters, plus many personal banners, musicians, and the caravan tractors towing a huge sound system'.*[62]

A year later in Prague, a simple colour scheme sufficed to articulate different positions, and 'despite tactical and strategic differences between protesters, most agreed that their action had been effective in ... shutting down the summit and bringing the destructive policies of the World Bank and IMF to the attention of the world'.[63] But in Seattle — the first significant anti-globalization protest held in the United States and a crucial moment in many respects — the nature of protest changed. Though there were moments of broad collaboration ('Teamsters and Turtles Together at Last'), the Seattle protests are most remembered — and most significantly by militants involved in making the protests in Québec — for a sharp division between street protests and the orderly politics of trade unions wanting to get 'labour a seat at the table' to make globalization work for workers.[64] Tellingly, twenty city blocks separated union workers gathered in a football stadium at the foot of the Space Needle to hear speeches and wave banners 'under the indulgent eyes of the Seattle constabulary', and the convention centre where 'protesters on the front line were taking their stand'. When the divide could have been closed (as the union crowd left the stadium), 'the marshals for the union march steered the big crowds away from the action'.[65]

In that context, the subjective sense of totality that had prevailed earlier disintegrated into the political settling of scores: *in situ* no more, protests became objectivized and politicized. In what must be one of the more curious moments of anti-summit protest, Medea Benjamin and her colleagues from the San Francisco-based Global Exchange, which had waged a four year campaign against Nike, stood on the steps of Nike Town and other sweatshop outlets in downtown Seattle to defend them against anarchists and other trouble-makers, calling on the police to identify and arrest them.[66]

After Seattle, anti-summit protests became remarkably less about themselves, more reflexive and politically deliberate, and more divided. This was evident, for instance, on 16 April 2000, when eight thousand demonstrators met in Washington for the annual meeting of World Bank and IMF (unsupported by organized labour), and in Nice in December when thousands of activists gathered against the summit of European Union heads of state. In both cases, anti-summit protesters were cut off from local political issues and there were sharp conflicts between political affiliations and tendencies.[67]

More explicitly political than Geneva's PGA or Prague's Initiative Against Economic Globalization (INPERG), Québec's OQP was, from the beginning, a more intent host. While the former groups were lithe organizations that functioned as technical links between movements, rather than centres of political power (more like corresponding societies than the Comintern), the OQP made itself into something that resembled an executive committee and it spent almost the whole year preceding the Summit of the Americas wading through broad ideological debates: are 'we' to define ourselves as 'citizens', 'the people' or 'the proletariat'? Are 'we' against 'capitalism', 'neoliberalism', 'globalization' or 'capital'? Are 'we' for 'reform' or 'revolution'? It also tried to settle on a correct plan of action to match its political aims and to draw up an 'invincible, credible, legitimate' political programme that would be 'understandable by all and absolutely realist.'[68]

Not before its *Manifeste* was finally drawn up in February 2001 did OQP put aside political differences with the CASA/CLAC to coordinate housing and food distribution initiatives.[69] Three weeks before the Summit, the immense task of finding housing for out-of-city militants had barely begun, teach-ins and demonstrations to take place in the 'solidarity perimeter' had not yet been planned, and medical and legal assistance services were still divided along broad political lines. The CMAQ — arguably the most politically committed of all

IndyMedia outfits — was still working on ways to reconcile the IndyMedia 'open publishing' tradition with its desire for relevant, properly contextualized and informed reporting.

In the weeks, days and hours before the Summit, amazing energy was expended and protests did emerge from having been nearly buried in globally-reflexive politics. Protesters were fed and housed (some at Laval University or in local colleges, others in private homes), an indisputable sense of place and event was created and, again *in situ*, protesters did create a radical presence that challenged both the will-to-order of the heads of states summit and the apolitical reformism of the People's Summit. But still, so animated were protests by global reflexivity (and by the anticipation of tourists, in the majority everywhere, including among the police) that the patient politics of civil disobedience and the fragile ambience of anti-summit protests were rapidly overtaken by more animated and confrontational ways of politics, especially near the security perimeter. In spite of considerable efforts invested in civil disobedience (by one estimate, a third of the people who participated in Friday's CASA/CLAC march had received some form of legal or political training), protests did not shape up at all as planned (or as they did in the student occupation movement of May 1968 in Paris — the first global anti-systemic movement, a generation ago, before global reflexivity).[70]

Reacting to events from Seattle and elsewhere, dynamized by a globally-inflated sense of predetermination, all those involved were looking for a more definite and quicker resolution than they would have otherwise. Thus did cosmopolitan ghosts come back into the picture, carried by global reflexivity: spectres confronting spectres, everyone in Québec acted with more abandon, fighting what the *Economist* had called — before Seattle — the 'fight for globalization'.[71]

In the end, the police ran out of tear-gas and took to using rubber bullets more offensively than they had planned.[72] Carnivalesque happenings — the most fragile indicators of a sense of place and event — were swept away: the *Funk Fighting Unaccountable Naughty Korporations* were gassed out of their efforts to reclaim the streets, the *Lanarkists* were not given much time to catapult stuffed toy-animals into the security perimeter, the Ilôt Fleuri was charged by police and the Saint-Jean Baptiste neighbourhood — a green zone no more, as of Saturday — was inundated with tear-gas. The only puppets seen were on the People's march as it walked away from the security perimeter.

Also significant were local links made in the process of what was, in essence, a globally-situated event. Some years ago, writing about anti-NAFTA campaigns in Canada, Mexico and the United States, I suggested that transnational activism did not just transcend locality but was also constitutive of it.[73] This was seen in the *Red Mexicana de Acción Frente Libre Comercio* socializing the politics of opposition to the PRI; and in the role played by the Action Canada Network in the broadening of what was then being celebrated as 'coalition politics' (a part of which has since moved, gingerly, toward a 'structured movement, something transitional that is more than a coalition and less than a party', intent on 'changing how we think about politics, extending the range of what's possible, and considering a fundamental challenge to capitalism').[74]

In Québec, opposition to free trade with the United States and Mexico in the 1980s did not have a similar impact, largely because of the hegemony of neoliberal nationalism, that defined Free Trade as an opportunity for Québec's bourgeoisie. But popular opposition to the Summit of the Americas did encourage new links between local social movements. In the year that preceded the Summit, two corporatist student bodies (the *Fédération des étudiants(es) Universitaire du Québec* and the *Fédération des étudiants(es) des CEGEPS du Québec*), were openly challenged by the new *Association solidaire pour un syndicalisme étudiant*, remarkably more militant, and intimately involved in anti-Summit politics. In like manner, the regrouping of community and alternative media — under the *Altermédia* banner — was closely linked to the creation of the CMAQ (born at the *Colloque des médias alternatifs québécois* in November 2000 in Drummondville). In the Mercier riding in Montréal — held continuously by the *Parti Québécois* since the radical poet Gérald Godin defeated Liberal Premier Robert Bourassa in 1976 — a provincial by-election was held on 9 April contested by the first united left candidate in Québec history.[75]

All this entered into the politics of opposition to the Summit of the Americas.

Four hundred and sixty people were arrested in Québec city during the Summit of the Americas and charged with the habitual menu of offences against the State: assault against a policeman, unlawful assembly, causing a disturbance, riot. Crimes of presence, they signal the limits of neoliberal civility. A dozen protesters were kept in jail in the week that followed. Most notable was the CLAC's Jaggi Singh, who was, for seventeen days, Québec's Mumia Abu-Jamal. To support him and others the OQP and the CASA (now the *Comité d'adieu au Sommet des Amériques*) organized demonstrations at the Orsainville penitentiary in Charlesbourg and at the Palais de Justice in Lower Town, a short walk from the now-empty site of the People's Summit. On 1 May the CASA organized a support march for political prisoners that started at the Parc de l'Amérique française, near where the security perimeter had been, and ended at the Palais de Justice.

Thus was a community of resistance made in Québec City in the months that preceded the Summit of the Americas. Determinedly about itself, radically unbound by the exigencies of problem-solving politics, entirely *in situ*, evanescent where global civility tends to immanence, this community was markedly different from the twinned summits of the hemispheric growth machine. Were terms of this kind not so out of date, we would raise the hypothesis of a 'revolutionary rupture' with existing forms of power.[76]

CONCLUSION

For three days in April, Québec city was part of what Saskia Sassen calls the 'world-wide grid of strategic places'.[77] Like other places in that grid, it was a contested terrain.

To raise critical awareness of the kind of politics being made in the post-Bretton Woods world economy, I have emphasized differences between two relatively coherent ensembles: i) a hemispheric growth machine gathered to settle social relations in conformity with neoliberal values and perspectives, and ii) a community of resistance charging the world economy with politics.

What actually happened, of course, did not entirely conform to this distinction. Some groups involved in Summit politics — *Alternatives* and *OQP*, for example — did cross the divide between ghosts and resistants; the People's tent was more open to protestors that had originally been planned, though for a fee, and only after organizers realized that fewer delegates had shown up than had registered; some unionists did join the CASA/CLAC march on Friday; and a few who started Saturday's march away from the security perimeter did double back towards it, to support direct action (in spite of the remarkably police-like efforts of FTQ's marshals). Some attended the People's Summit from Monday to Thursday and then went to the solidarity perimeter, to the Ilôt Fleurit, or to protests near the security perimeter on Friday and Saturday. After the Summit, the *Travailleurs Canadiens de l'Automobile*, the Québec branch of the Canadian Auto Workers, did help organize legal support for political prisoners, and some of the People's representatives, most notably Françoise David of the *Fédération des femmes du Québec*, did express sympathy for political prisoners, though all the media, including the CBC, had only run human-interest stories on Jaggi Singh. At the level of tactics, there was not, as Thomas Walkom put it, 'a straightforward fissure between young anarchists who advocate so-called direct action — a phrase that covers everything from sit-ins to rock throwing — and those committed to peaceful protest'.[78]

At the level of discourse and in political programmes, those who gathered in the People's summit and those who occupied places near the security perimeter still had more in common with one another than they did with the globalizing elites on whose part no significant divide-crossing was recorded — though we all saw Summit delegates take their tags off, not to join the protests, but to walk about unfenced parts of the old city.

On the whole, though, groups and popular movements opposed to the ways of neoliberal integration in the Americas were configured as argued above — parties to the hemispheric growth machine on one side, resistants on another — not showing what they had in common and amounting to less than they could have. This, undoubtedly, was a political failure. Had the People's tent been more open from the beginning, then something more political than yet another collection of near-parliamentary briefs could have come out of the People's Summit; had 60,000 people walked to the security perimeter on Saturday, a more meaningful occupation of the place could have been organized; or, alternatively, had direct action resisters marched with the People they would have had a less insignificant afternoon.

Looking toward the future, this raises the crucial question of the articulation between parts of what could be, but is not yet, a global movement against neoliberalism. In their optimism, slogans heard in Québec City during the Summit of the Americas — '*L'Union fait la force*', '*À qui la rue? À nous*', '*Pueblo unido, jamas sera vencido*' — gave a misleading sense of the ease with which joint actions can be organized by disparate groups.[79]

But, as Althusser suggested in one of his rare political interventions, only in concrete actions can social movements be fused into more than they are individually, to take advantage of moments of revolutionary rupture.[80] In the present context, gatherings of globalizing elites provide excellent occasions for such concrete actions. Properly constructed, organized protests can then provide, as John Berger wrote of mass demonstrations, necessary 'rehearsals of revolutionary awareness'.[81]

The next Summit of the Americas will be held in Buenos Aires.

NOTES

I would like to thank the following, who generously shared thoughts and information: Pierre Beaudet, Sébastien Bouchard, Sacha Alcide Calixte, Sam Gindin, Robert Jasmin, Michel Lambert, Leo Panitch, Évelyne Pedneault, Véronica Rioux.

1   André C. Drainville, 'Of Social Spaces, Citizenship, and the Nature of Power in the World Economy', *Alternatives, 20,* Spring 1995; André C. Drainville, 'The Fetishism of Global Civil Society: Global Governance, Transnational Urbanism and Sustainable Capitalism in the World Economy', *Comparative Urban and Community Research*, no. 6, 1999 (1998). On scenarios for settling social relations, see for instance: William P. Kreml and Charles W. Kegley Jr., 'A Global Political Party: The Next Step', *Alternatives*, January–March 1996; Daniele Archibugi and David Held, eds., *Cosmopolitan Democracy: An Agenda for a New World Order*, London: Polity Press, 1995; Richard Falk, *On Humane Governance: Towards a New Global Politics*, University Park, Pennsylvania: The Pennsylvania State University Press/ World Order Models Project, 1995; and Ricardo Petrella, *Écueils de la mondialisation: Urgence d'un nouveau contrat social*, Montréal: Fides, 1997.
2   Robert W. Cox, *Production, Power and World Order: Social Forces in the Making of History*, New York: Columbia University Press, 1987.
3   For the complete text of the EAI announcement, see *Public Papers of the Presidents of the United States, George Bush: January 1 to June 30, 1990*, Washington: United States Government Printing Office, 1991, pp. 873-7.
4   Umberto Eco, 'Travels in Hyperreality', in *Travels in Hyperreality: Essays*, San Diego: Harcourt Brace Jovanovich, 1986, pp. 3-58. Between 1996 and 1997, *Place d'Youville* was the starting point of riots on *St-Jean Baptiste* day, Québec's national holiday.
5   Details of DFAIT events can be found at http://www.holaquebec.ca.
6   In the spirit of inter-agency collaboration the *Institut* also served as a DFAIT

temp agency, recruiting *agents et agentes de liaison* and other support staff for the Summit of the Americas, and it was host to several Summit officials, including, thrice, Marc Lortie, the Prime Minister's sherpa. A press release detailing the Conclusions of the colloqium can be found at the Institut's web site: http://www.ulaval.ca/scom/Communiques.de.presse/2001/avril/IQHEIzlea.

7   Founded in 1994, the RQIC is under the hegemonic guidance of Québec's main union confederations (the *Confédération des Syndicat Nationaux*, the *Centrale des enseignants du Québec* and the *Fédération des travailleurs et travailleuses du Québec*). Its membership also includes another, much smaller, union confederation (the *Centrale des syndicats du Québec*,), union-made or union-funded NGOs (most notably the *Centre international de solidarité ouvrière* and *Solidarité populaire Québec*), a professional appendage of the union movement (the *Association canadienne des avocats du mouvement syndical*), two state-funded NGO's (the *Association québécoise des organismes de coopération internationale* and the *Fédération des femmes du Québec*) and two research centres based in Montréal universities that are also close to unions (McGill's *Centre d'études sur les régions en développement* and UQUAM's RQIC).

8   On 'protest pits' and anti-summit movements, see Alexander Cockburn, Jeffrey St.Clair, and Allan Sekula, *5 Days that Shook the World: Seattle and Beyond*, London: Verso, 2000, p. 19.

9   Members of OQP included one neighbourhood committee (the *Comité populaire Saint-Jean Baptiste*), several student associations (the *Comité de mobilisation de l'Association étudiante du CEGEP de F-X Garneau* , the *Comité de mobilisation de l'Association étudiante du CEGEP de Saint-Foy*, the *Coalition de l'Université Laval sur le libre-échange dans les Amériques*,), left parties and NGOs (the *Parti pour la Démocratie Socialiste*, *ATTAC*, the Rassemblement pour une Alternative Populaire, the *Parti Communiste du Québec*, *Alternatives*), locally-based unions (the *Syndicat des Employés de la Fonction Publique*, the *Syndicats des professeurs du CEGEP de Sainte-Foy*) as well as solidarity NGOs (*Carrefour Tiers-Monde*, *Casa latino Americaine de Québec*, *Plan Nagua*).

10   N.d., 'Sommet des Amériques: ne nous laissons pas intimider. Occupons notre quartier', *L'Info-bourg*, 1, 2001.

11   Canadian Security Intelligence Service, 'Anti-Globalization — A Spreading Phenomenon', Ottawa: CSIS, 2000.

12   CIEPAC, 'Seattle: The World Mobilization of the Century Against Globalization', Chiapas: Centro de Investigaciones Economicas y politicas de Accion Comunitaria, 1999; Claudette Samson, 'Il faudra 3.8 kms de clôture', *Le Soleil*, 2 November 2000, A-3; Claudette Samson, 'Un sommet de sécurité', *Le Soleil*, 2 November 2000, A-1, A-2.

13   Stephen Gill, 'Structural Change and Global Political Economy: Globalizing élites and the emerging world order', in Yoshikazu Sakamoto, ed., *Global Transformation: Challenges to the State System*, Tokyo: United Nations University Press, 1994. On this, see also Robert W. Cox, *Production, Power and World Order: Social Forces in the Making of History*, New York: Columbia

University Press, 1987, pp. 250-65.

14   On the neoliberal concept of control, see Peter Burnham, 'Neo-Gramscian Hegemony and International Order', *Capital and Class*, 45, Fall 1991; Henk Overbeek, *Global Capitalism and National Decline*, London: Unwin Hyman, 1990. About the global construction of monetarism, see André C. Drainville, 'Monetarism in Canada and the World Economy', *Studies in Political Economy* , no. 46, Spring 1995.

15   Peter Hajnal, *The Seven Powers Summit: Documents from the Summits of Industrialized Countries*, New York: Kraus International Publications, 1989. OECD, *Facing the Future: Mastering the Probable and Managing the Unpredictable*, Paris: OECD, 1979, p. 78.

16   Karl Polanyi's *Great Transformation*, cited in Robert W. Cox, 'Structural Issues of Global Governance: Implications for Europe', in Stephen Gill, ed., *Gramsci, Historical Materialism and International Relation*, Cambridge: Cambridge University Press, 1993, p. 261.

17   Rutherford M. Poats, ed., *Twenty-Five Years of Development Co-operation: A Review*, Paris: Organization for Economic Cooperation and Development (Development Assistance Committee), 1985. On IMF riots and early resistance to neoliberal regulation, see also Didier Bigo, 'Contestations populaires et émeutes urbaines; les jeux du politique et de la transnationalité', *Cultures et contacts* numéro spécial sur les émeutes urbaines, 1992; John Walton, 'Urban Protests and the Global Political Economy: The IMF Riots', in Michael Peter Smith and Joe R. Feagin, eds., *The Capitalist City: Global Restructuring and Community Politics*, Basil Blackwell, 1987.

18   See Peter B. Kenen, 'The Use of IMF Credit', in Cathcrine Gwin *et al.*, eds., *The International Monetary Fund in a Multipolar World: Pulling Together*, Washington: Overseas Development Council, 1989, p. 69. On the changing relationship between the World Bank and developing countries and on the Social Dimensions of Adjustment program, administered by the World Bank in cooperation with the United Nations Development Program, see *Making Adjustment Work for the Poor*, Washington: World Bank, 1990.

19   André C. Drainville, *Ways of Global Politics*, Routledge, forthcoming; Harvey Molotch, 'The City as Growth Machine', *American Journal of Sociology*, 82, no. 2, 1976.

20   Charlotte Brönte cited in Carl Malamud, *A World's Fair for the Global Village*, Cambridge: The MIT Press, 1997. The Porto Alegre 'World Social Forum' was divided into four themes: 'The production of wealth and social reproduction', 'Access to wealth and sustainability', 'Civil society and the public arena' and 'Political Power and ethics in the new society'.

21   Alexandre Marc and Mary Schmidt, *Participation and Social Funds*, ed. Environment Department, vol. 4, *Participation Series*, Washington DC: The World Bank, 1995.

22   Rutherford M. Poats, 'Crisis-Driven Reform', in Poats, *Twenty-Five Years*

of Development Co-operation, pp. 59-64.

23   In their introduction to *NGOs, the UN & Global Governance*, Leon Gordenker and Thomas G. Weiss distinguished between NGOs (Non Governmental Organisations), GONGOs (Government Organized Non-Government Organisations (that belonged principally to the cold war period) and QUANGOs (Quasi-Nongovernmental Organisations such as the International Committee of the Red Cross). In World Bank vernacular CBOs are Community-Based Organizations. GOINGOs are Government Induced Non-Governmental Organizations.

24   Michel Chossudovsky, 'Seattle and Beyond: Disarming the New World order', Transnational Foundation for Peace and Future Research, http://www.transnational.org/forum/meetéseattle.html., 2000).

25   Pierre Hazan, 'Riche Idée', *Libération*, 26 January 2001, p. 56.

26   James N. Roseneau, 'Governance in the Twenty-first Century', *Global Governance*, Winter 1995.

27   Ricardo Grinspun and Maxwell A. Cameron, *The Political Economy of North American Free Trade*, Montréal/Kingston/London: Mc Gill-Queen's University Press, 1993.

28   'The Battle in Seattle', *The Economist*, 27 November 1999, pp. 21-23.

29   The Miami 'Plan of Action' is quoted from Thomas Risse-Kappen, ed., *Bringing Transnational Relations Back In: Non-State Actors, Domestic Structures and International Institutions*, Cambridge: Cambridge University Press, 1995.

30   IDB, 'From Grassroots to Government', *The IDB extra (Inter-American Development Bank)*, 1994, pp. 8-9.

31   IDB, 'Citizens Participation Increases Efficiency of Development', Washington D.C./Cartagena: Inter-American Development Bank, 1998 (emphasis added).

32   IDB, 'Echoes of Forging Links with NGOs', Washington D.C.: Inter-American Development Bank, 1997; Leslie M. Fox, 'Sustaining Civil Society', Washington: Civicus (The International Task Force on Enhancing the Resource Base of Civil Society), 1996.

33   Roger Hamilton, 'Turning Residents into Citizens: Latin America's reform bandwagon needs more drivers — lots more', *The IDB (Inter-American Development Bank)*, November 1994, pp. 6-7.

34   IDB, 'Echoes of Forging Links with NGOs' (emphasis added).

35   The FTA came into effect on January 1, 1989; NAFTA in 1994; Mercosur and the 'Group of Three' accord between Columbia, Mexico and Venezuela in 1995; the Adean Community Pact in 1997.

36   Editors, 'Citizens of the Rain Forest', *The IDB (Inter-American Development Bank)*, August 1993, 3; IDB, 'From Grassroots to Government', *The IDB extra (Inter-American Development Bank)*, 1994, pp. 8-9; IDB, 'How we put it all together', *IDB Extra 'Urban Renaissance' (Inter-American Development Bank)*, 1997, p. 8; IDB, 'IDB Women', 1996.

37   On the OAS's turn to participatory development, see OAS, *Inter-American*

Strategy for Public Participation in Environment and Sustainable Development: Decision Making in the Americas, Washington: Organization of American States, 1996.

38   The Santiago Plan of Action designated the OAS as a privileged forum for 'the exchange of experience and information amongst civil society organizations'. On this, see Organization of American States, *Work Plan of the Unit for the Promotion of Democracy*, cited in Guy Gosselin and Jean-Philippe Thérien, 'The Organization of American States and Hemispheric Regionalism', in Gordon Mace and Luyis Bélanger, ed., *The Americas in Transition: The Contours of Regionalism*, Boulder: Lynne Rienner, 1999.

39   See http://www.civil-society.oas.org.

40   The document is available at http://www.summmit-americas.org/documents.

41   Comité de représentants gouvernementaux sur la participation de la société civile, 'Invitation ouverte à la société civile dans les pays de la ZLÉA', http://www.ftaa-alca.org/spcomm/soc2_f.asp, 2000.

42   Translated from http://www.holaquebec.ca/bienvenue/intro_e.htlm

43   Thalia Kidder and Mary McGinn, 'In the Wake of NAFTA: Transnational Workers Networks', *Social Policy*, Summer 1995.

44   William I. Robinson, 'The Sao Paulo Forum: Is There a New Latin American Left?', *Monthly Review*, no. 44, December, 1992, pp. 1-12. On the Sao Paulo Forum, see also 'Left to start work on alternative: Sao Paulo Forum Offers Few Hints Regarding Content', *Latin America Weekly Report*, 15 June, 1995, pp. 258-259; Raul Ronzoni 'Latin America: The Left Meets to Discuss its Role and Integration', *Inter Press Service*, 25 May 1995.

45   BBC Summary of World Broadcasts, Wednesday, 31 May 1995.

46   Michel Chossudovsky, 'Seattle and Beyond: Disarming the New World order', Transnational Foundation for Peace and Future Research, http://www.transnational.org/forum/meetéseattle.html, 2000. According to Julio Turra, of the United Workers Federation of Brazil, 'the whole idea of incorporating social clauses or social charters into these 'free trade' pacts … was really projected at the 1995 Social Summit in Copenhagen. The goal of integrating trade unions internationally into the whole apparatus of globalization was made explicit at that summit' ('Leader of the Brazilian United Workers Federation (CUT) describes labour summit organized to respond to the extension of NAFTA throughout the Americas', http://www.igc.apc.org/workers/cut.html.)

47   Richard Feinberg and Robin Rosenberg, eds., *Civil Society and the Summit of the Americas: The 1998 Santiago Summit*, Boulder: Lynne Rienner, 1999.

48   Alliance for Responsible Trade *et al.*, 'Alternatives for the Americas: Building a People's Hemispheric Agreement', 1998.

49   Reviews of relevant literature can be found in André C. Drainville, 'Left Internationalism and the Politics of Resistance in the New World Order', in David Smith and Jósef Böröcz, eds., *A New World Order: Global*

Transformations in the Late Twentieth Century, Westport: Praeger, 1995; André C. Drainville, *Ways of Global Politics*. See also Jeffrey M. Ayres, *Defying Conventional Wisdom*, Toronto: University of Toronto Press, 1998; Robin Cohen and Shirin M. Rai, eds., *Global Social Movements*, London: Athlone Press, 2000; and Saskia Sassen, Globalization and Its Discontents New York: The New Press, 1998.

50   Michel Foucault, 'Le sujet et le pouvoir', in *Dits et écrits (1954-1988)*, Paris: Gallimard, 1994, pp. 227-243. See also C. Gordon, ed., *Power/Knowledge: Michel Foucault*, New York: Pantheon Books, 1980.

51   Robin Hahnel, 'Speaking Truth to Power: Speaking Truth to Ourselves', *Z*, June 2000 pp. 44-51.

52   Nicole Pénicaut and Christian Dutilleux, 'Davos et Potrto Alegre, deux sommets du monde', *Libération*, 26 January 2001; Nicole Pénicaut, 'Combler le fossé', *Libération*, 26 January 2001.

53   Drainville, 'Left Internationalism and the Politics of Resistance'.

54   Cited from *Z* staff, 'This Yawning Emptiness', *Z*, June 2000, pp. 4-5.

55   Edward Said, *Representations of the Intellectual*, New York: Pantheon Books, 1994.

56   At the June 2000 camp, formateurs and formatrices were given a broad general Cahier de formation as well as several thematic kits (on 'éducation et mondialisation', 'écologie et mondialisation', 'programmes sociaux', 'droits de la personne', 'femmes et mondialisation', 'droits du travail', etc.)

57   OQP2001, 'Communiqué de Presse', Opération Québec Printemps 2001, 2001.

58   On overdetermination, see Louis Althusser, 'Contradiction et surdetermination', in *Pour Marx*, Fondations, Paris: La Découverte, 1986, pp. 85-129.

59   Anthony Giddens, *The Constitution of Society*, Berkeley: University of California Press, 1984.

60   It is a measure of the shortness of this history that Québec's bid to host the Summit of the Americas was presented to the federal government in April 1999, six months before the Seattle WTO summit. See Robert Fleury, 'L'Allier nuance ses propos', *Le Soleil*, 27 March 2001, A3.

61   Citations are, in order, from Cockburn, St.Clair, and Sekula, *5 Days that Shook the World*, and Adam Sternbergh, 'The Dirty Kids who Show up for the Gathering', *This Magazine*, November/December 1998.

62   http://www.agp.org/agp/en/PGAInfos/bulletin2/bulletin2b.html (emphasis added).

63   NEFAC, 'Anti-capitalist Resistance in the Streets of Prague', *The Northeastern Anarchist*, February 2001; Vittorio de Philippis and Christian Losson, 'Assemblées annuelles du FMI et de la Banque mondiale', *Libération*, 27 September 2000, pp. 26-7.

64   Teamster's leader James Hoffa jr, cited in Cockburn, St.Clair, and Sekula, *5 Days that Shook the World*. On 'the myth of Seattle', see for instance: n.d., 'Sommet des Amériques: construction et impact d'une situation', *Le*

Maquis, 2001, pp. 3-4.

65   Cockburn, St.Clair, and Sekula, *5 Days that Shook the World*.

66   Alex Cockburn, 'So Who Did Win in Seattle? Liberals Rewrite History', http://www.antenna.nl/~waterman/cockburn.html: Global Solidarity Dialogue, 2000.

67   Robin Hahnel, 'Speaking Truth to Power: Speaking Truth to Ourselves', *Z*, June 2000.

68   SalAMI, 'Mobilisations et résistances civiles contre le Sommet des Amériques et le projet de Zone de libre-échange des Amériques: Plan d'action et propositions de SalAMI', http://www.alternatives.ca/salami/html/zlea.html: SalAMi, 2000.

69   The *Manifeste contre le Sommet des Amériques et la Zone de libre-échange des Amériques* was made public on March 20th, a month before the summit. See Jean-Simon Gagné, 'Sommet des Amériques: Un manifeste percutant contre la ZLÉA', *Le Soleil*, 21 March 2001, A12.

70   Immanuel Wallerstein, '1968: Révolution dans le système mondial', *Les temps modernes* pp. 514-5, May-June 1989.

71   After Seattle, where 'the fight for globalization' had been lost by the WTO, *The Economist* took to accusing protestors of having fomented it. See 'Countdown to ruckus', *The Economist*, 4 December 1999, and 'The Battle in Seattle', *The Economist*, 27 November 1999.

72   The SQ alone fired more than 300 plastic bullets at individuals and 1700 *bombes fumigènes* into the crowd. François Cardinal, 'Pleins Gaz à Québec!', *Le Devoir*, 26 April 2001, A2. At the time of writing, reports from other police corps had not yet been presented.

73   André C. Drainville, 'Social Movements in the Americas: Regionalism from Below', in Gordon Mace and Luyis Bélanger, eds., *The Americas in Transition: The Contours of Regionalism*, Boulder: Lynne Rienner, 1999.

74   On the 'Rebuilding the Left' movement, see Sam Gindin, 'Toward a Structured Anti-Capitalist Movement', *Canadian Dimension*, January/February 2001. On Canadian links between global capitalism, local struggles and the 'new spirit of resistance to global capitalism', see David McNally, 'Rebuilding the Left', *Canadian Dimension*, September/October 2000; Harman Rosenfeld and Jayme Gianola, 'Prospects for a New Left? A Report on the Rebuilding the Left Conference', *Canadian Dimension*, January/February 2001.

75   Running as an Independent, Paul Cliche received a quarter of votes, and finished a close third behind the *Libéral* and *Parti Québécois* candidates (Kathleen Levesque, 'Banc d'essai pour la gauche', *Le Devoir*, 15 March 2001, A1–A8).

76   Althusser, 'Contradiction et surdetermination'.

77   Saskia Sassen, *Globalization and its Discontents*, New York: The New Press, 1998.

78   Thomas Walkom, 'Mélange of Quebec protesters united in rethinking

strategy', *The Toronto Star*, 29 April 2001.

79   Malcom Reid, *What I Saw*, Québec: Malcom Reid, 2001.

80   See Althusser, 'Contradiction et surdetermination'.

81   John Berger, 'The Nature of Mass Demonstrations', *New Society*, 23 May 1968, pp. 754-5.

THE NATURE AND CONTRADICTIONS OF NEOLIBERALISM

GÉRARD DUMÉNIL AND DOMINIQUE LÉVY

A sudden change in the rules governing the functioning of capitalism occurred at the end of the 1970s. This change can only be understood in relation to the deterioration in the economic performance of the major capitalist countries during the 1970s, and the failure of the initial set of policies which had been adopted in order to stem the deterioration. The slowdown in the growth of labour productivity, lower accumulation and growth rates, rising unemployment, inflation, and the increased macro-instability (booms and recessions) marked the contours of what can retrospectively be called *the structural crisis of the 1970s and 1980s*. The Keynesian policies which had contributed to the prosperity of the 1960s were tried again at first, but accelerating inflation undermined them. At the same time, the growing difficulties of the so-called socialist countries freed the ruling classes of capitalist countries from a fundamental political concern. These developments created the conditions for a sharp reversal of policies which occurred at the end of the 1970s. A prominent element in this transformation was the change in monetary policy in 1979, the dramatic rise of interest rates in the last year of the Carter Administration, that we denote as *the 1979 coup*. Rapidly, with the election of Margaret Thatcher in the United Kingdom and Ronald Reagan in the USA, the overall political import of the new course became clear: repression of workers' claims for better living standards and working conditions, an attack on the welfare state, acceptance of unemployment, deregulation (especially of financial activities), etc. More than 'policies' in the narrow sense of the term were at issue. This new framework of rules to which the functioning of capitalism was subjected, is now known as neoliberalism, a return to liberalism in a new configuration.

After twenty years of neoliberalism, how should its performance be assessed? The costs of neoliberalism in terms of unemployment were huge. Initially, it prolonged the effects of the structural crisis. In the USA the unemployment rate peaked in the mid-1980s; in Europe an even more lasting wave of unemployment developed. The Third World was devastated by the debt crisis; monetary and financial institutions were shaken even in the USA; large monetary and financial crises signalled a new financial instability in the world economy. Speculation grew in the stock markets of large capitalist countries, adding to the threat of financial collapse. But today, inflation is down. The unemployment rate declined gradually in the USA, until it returned to the levels of the 1960s, and over the last few years a similar decrease has been under way in Europe. Despite the threat of recession, by the turn of the century growth was an object of pride in the USA and the envy of other countries. The speculative bubble was shrinking and the threat of a major collapse had so far not materialized.

In the overall assessment of neoliberalism, much complexity is created by the differences between the performance of various countries — notably the USA, Europe, Japan, and the periphery. Why was unemployment more severe in Europe than in the USA? In the growth of the US economy during the second half of the 1990s, what is most significant: the virtues of neoliberalism, or US hegemony? Or to frame the question differently: can the 'performance' of the USA be generalized to a broader set of countries?

This essay concerns neoliberalism, neoliberalism under US hegemony: its place in the history of capitalism, the social significance of the new rules that it imposes, its social costs and associated risks, its *future*. We have already discussed elsewhere the costs and benefits of neoliberalism.[1] Its resilience is certainly the most difficult issue to tackle. Can we detect within neoliberalism *internal contradictions* that cast doubt on its ability to survive, both economically and politically? In other words, what is the nature of the new order of capitalism: a mere transition made possible by the crisis and the defeat of the labour movement, or a new era? These questions raise the issue of the interpretation of Keynesianism. Were the Keynesian years an exception following the Great Depression, or did they suggest the possible contours of another capitalism, or even a first step of capitalism beyond its own rules? Thus the definitions of capitalism, of Keynesianism and of neoliberalism are all at stake in this discussion.

This essay should, then, be understood as a contribution to a broad, very ambitious, debate. It addresses two types of issues. The first section is devoted to explaining the dynamics of capitalism, its periodization, and the interpretation of neoliberalism. The perspective is that of the Marxist analysis of history, what used to be called historical materialism (relations of production and productive forces, classes and class struggle, and the state), and Marx's economic analysis in *Capital* (historical tendencies, crises, money and finance, etc.). The periodization of capitalism underlying this investigation combines three levels of analysis: (1) the transformation of the relations of production (the ownership and control of the means of production); (2) the historical tendencies of technology and distribution (notably trends in the profit rate); (3) the succession of specific power configurations (the domination of various fractions of the ruling classes and their compromises with other classes). We broadly characterize neoliberalism as a specific power configuration, the reassertion of the power of capitalist owners, after years of controls on finance: a new discipline imposed on all other classes (on managerial and clerical personnel as well as productive workers), and an attempt, or set of attempts, to implement a new social compromise.

The second section discusses various fields in which the long-run sustainability of the neoliberal order may be questioned, depending on neoliberalism's ability to: (1) establish a new social compromise in an environment of rising inequality (associating broader social strata to the growing prosperity of the few, really or fictitiously); (2) ensure the stability of the economy (avoiding various forms of crisis: recession, and monetary and financial crises); (3) ensure significant accumulation and growth. In the last of these is implied the ability to finance sufficient accumulation, in a system where profits are largely distributed to rich households (*via* interests payments and dividends) and, to date, are not ploughed back into non-financial corporations; to spread the benefits of the new social order outside of the USA, at least minimally (to prove that these benefits are not exclusively the result of the USA's global hegemony); and to maintain a steady growth rate (beyond the gradual deflation or bursting of the 1990s financial bubble). The long-run sustainability of the neoliberal order also depends (4) on prolonging the more favourable trends of technical change that have been apparent since the mid-1980s.

A concluding section briefly outlines the possible future of neoliberalism: the more or less likely forms of its perpetuation and possible alternatives — conditions which might lead to its gradual or sudden disappearance; and the compatibility of neoliberalism with the continuing transformation of the relations of production.

Despite its broad perspective, the paper should not be understood as a *thorough* critique of capitalism. Its scope is still limited. We do not relate the pursuit of growth and technical change to the preservation of the planet, or rule by the owners of capital to the misery of many countries of the periphery, to gender and race exploitation, or to the gradual assertion and diffusion of ways of life and ideologies along lines which will be extremely difficult to reverse.

I A HISTORICAL PERSPECTIVE[2]

1.1 *A Marxist framework of analysis*

At the centre of Marx's and Engels' interpretation of history in the *Communist Manifesto* are the fundamental dialectics of productive forces and relations of production. Relations of production may stimulate or inhibit the development of the productive forces, and the development of the productive forces creates the conditions for the transformation of the relations of production. This framework is applied twice: first to the transition between feudalism and capitalism, and then to the development of capitalism itself (heralding the transition to socialism).

Each configuration of relations of production corresponds to a specific class pattern. This is obviously true in the comparison between feudalism and capitalism, but also holds during the various phases of a given mode of production. For example, the rise of the banking system and, more generally, of financial capital, is reflected in the maturation of a specific fraction of the ruling classes.

This division of the ruling classes into various fractions is particularly clear in *The 18th Brumaire*. There, Marx distinguishes between *landowners*, *the aristocracy of finance*, and *large industrialists*. Together, they govern under various *regimes*, which we call *power configurations*: the Restoration, the Monarchy of July, the Republic, or the Empire. They can rule jointly (as in the Republic or Empire) and possess a larger (as in the Republic) or narrower (as in the Empire) degree of freedom to openly express their internal contradictions. The hegemony of one specific group can be more (as in the Restoration and Monarchy of July) or less clear. More generally, because of the always gradual character of the transitions between various modes of production (such as between feudalism and capitalism), the ruling classes of successive modes of production may coexist (as they did under the Old Regime). In such configurations, the nature of the various groups is always evolving and hybrid forms may exist.

In these historical dynamics *class struggle* is crucial. In the broad sense of the term, it includes both the opposition between ruling classes and dominated classes, and the tensions between the various fractions of the ruling classes. The state is the organized expression of the power configurations, the locus of their formation and preservation, and the instrument of coercion that goes with this power.

Concerning the economics of capitalism, Marx developed in *Capital* the thesis that under capitalism technical and distributional changes tend to follow specific patterns of evolution, which we call *trajectories à la Marx*. These trajectories combine: (1) the growth of output, capital, and employment; (2) the rise of labour productivity, the real wage, the capital-labour ratio (various *compositions of capital*), and the decline of the profit rate. These tendencies express the difficulty of sustaining the growth of labour productivity without resorting to increased amounts of capital investment (what we call the *difficulty of innovation*). The decline of the profit rate creates the conditions for large crises: recessions, unemployment, speculation, etc.[3]

This economic framework of analysis is closely related to the above historical framework. Although Marx had not developed these tools when he wrote the *Communist Manifesto* with Engels, it is the existence of these historical tendencies which accounts for the recurrent structural crises and business-cycle fluctuations characteristic of capitalism. In various respects, Marx's *Capital* makes explicit the basic insights of the *Manifesto*, and its assessment of capitalism's catastrophic future.

1.2 *The dynamics of capitalism*

1.2.1 *The ownership of the means of production, management, and modern finance*

Central to capitalist relations of production is the *private ownership of the means of production*. This includes simultaneously: (1) ownership in the narrow sense of the term — the power to purchase and sell means of production, including labour power, and (2) the right and the ability to manage them. This fundamental relationship was profoundly altered at the end of the nineteenth century. The main development, whose early forms had already been analyzed by Marx, was the separation between ownership and management (the two above components), and the concentration of ownership within financial institutions. These transformations cannot be separated from the emergence of modern finance.

These transformations of capitalist ownership reached new heights in the USA in the wake of the structural crisis of the 1890s. The crisis followed a period of decline in the profit rate. It degenerated into a crisis of competition, with enterprises attempting to stem the collapse of their profit rate by various forms of horizontal alliances. This was the period of cartels and trusts. Antitrust legislation forbade any form of agreement in which firms were preserved as independent entities sharing, for example, markets or profits. Simultaneously, company law was enacted allowing mergers and the formation of holding companies. A huge merger wave followed at the turn of the century, known in the USA as the *corporate revolution*.

Within corporations, management was delegated to large pyramidal structures of managerial and clerical personnel. They undertook what Marx used to call the *functions of the functioning capitalist* — i.e., in contemporary terminology, *management* in a rather broad sense of the term (actually, all unproductive labour). These functions are those required in order to maximize the profit rate. This second transformation is known as the *managerial revolution*.

Large corporations were formed under the control of finance, whose modern configuration — consisting of financial institutions tightly linked to non-financial corporations — was simultaneously emerging.[4] It was accompanied by a dramatic development of financial mechanisms, a huge wave of 'financial innovation'. Paralleling the rise of credit mechanisms, and beyond the mere financing of transactions, the amount of money increased tremendously, especially in bank accounts.[5] Although the term is not used, one could call this a *financial revolution*.

This new configuration of twentieth century capitalism represented a considerable transformation of capitalist relations of production, a new aspect of what Marx had called the *socialization* of production (in contrast to production relations adequately embodied in individuals, such as the individual owner-manager). This social trait of capitalism was constantly reinforced during the twentieth century. Under neoliberalism it reached new heights with the development of huge financial institutions, such as mutual and pensions funds, and the transfer of still more capitalist tasks to salaried personnel. The managerial revolution has now reached the core of the capitalist system — i.e., finance.

1.2.2 *Accumulation, the purchase of labour power, and the macro-economy*

In addition to ownership (in the juridical sense of the term) and management, there are also 'macro-economic' components to the capitalist exercise of the private ownership of the means of production. Two major aspects must be identified. (1) In a capitalist economy, capital accumulation may require savings from profits, but capital can also be 'created' by the banking system, *via* credit mechanisms and the issue of money. The total amount of this creation is crucial, since inflation may result from excess credit, and capital in the form of securities and cash may be devalued.[6] More generally, independent of its destination, accumulation or consumption, excess credit poses a threat to previously accumulated capital, both by inflation and by the possible destabilization of financial institutions. (2) In controlling the valorization process of capital (a component of management), the purchase of labour power is of particular importance. As analyzed by Marx, the *periodic replenishment of the reserve army of labour* plays a central role in the determination of the cost of labour, and hence of profits, periodically imposing strong pressures on wages, pressures which tend to compensate for the rise of wages during periods of overheating (*overaccumulation*).

Capitalism gradually developed centralized institutions and mechanisms charged with the control of the macro-economy, with major consequences for the issuing of money, the level of activity, and employment. As in the case of the juridical forms of ownership and management, *centralized* macro-economic policies actually modified the exercise of the private ownership of the means of production, in the direction of an increased *socialization*. The emergence of such mechanisms actually raises the issue of their *aims*. In whose interests do they work?

In the late nineteenth century, this control was ensured by large private financial institutions (in the USA, mostly large New York banks in the *National Banking System*). The main concern was the stability of the purchasing power of money in terms of gold, and the stability of the financial system.[7] The stabilization of the macro-economy gradually became an objective *per se*. The shock of the Great Depression and World War II inaugurated the era of Keynesianism with the involvement of the state (the central bank) and new aims. The capitalist class saw this as an encroachment on its power, since these aims included full employment and affected price stability (the preservation of accumulated capital). The recognition of the right to work and the establishment of the welfare state after World War II considerably modified the wage relation, as labour power was gradually treated less and less as an ordinary commodity. Under neoliberalism, however, the earlier objectives of finance were restored, with a renewed contempt for the problem of unemployment and an overriding concern for price stability. There has been and there will be no reversal of this 'macro-economic' component of the private ownership of the means of production; only the specific macro-economic targets set within it are at issue.

1.2.3 *Maximizing the profit rate*

The profit rate is a key variable in the functioning of capitalism and the mechanisms involved undergo significant transformations. The *maximizing of the profit rate* performs, in its own way, a number of necessary economic tasks. It determines the efficient use of inputs and resources; it guides the selection of the most efficient techniques and the choice between various fields of investment (among firms and industries). It also drives the efforts made by individual firms to stimulate demand.

There is an important political component embedded in the undertaking of these functions. In particular, the first function (economizing in the use of resources) implies: (1) the forms and degrees of the pressure exercised on workers, given their resistance and the existing set of regulations; and (2) a similar impact on the environment, on the rules regulating its preservation (given the resistance of various fractions of the population). There is obviously an international aspect to this search for profits too, which accounts for the *imperialist* features of the leading capitalist countries (their rivalry and their domination over the periphery).

The maximizing of the profit rate is an expression of the capitalist nature of the relations of production, but this capitalist feature also depends on: (1) the contours of various fields partially insulated from the profitability criterion (e.g. defence, education, health, research); (2) the private appropriation of the surplus as the income of a class of owners; (3) the concentration of wealth among the few; (4) the effects of regulations and policies (as particular components of the general functions of the state), macro-economic policies, taxation (the taxation of firms and upper income brackets), etc.

1.2.4 Classes and power configurations

The transformation of relations of production described in the previous three sections is connected to the parallel evolution of class patterns.

The managerial revolution resulted in the rise of the so-called *new intermediary classes* of managerial and clerical personnel, distinct from the traditional petty bourgeoisie. The transfer of the capitalist functions to salaried workers was, however, realized in a highly 'polarized' fashion, with the concentration of conception, initiative, and authority at the top of the hierarchy (managerial personnel), and execution of tasks at the bottom (clerical personnel). *This polarization represents a new class relation.* This opposition is distinct from the separation of the capitalist owner from the productive worker in Marx's analytical framework in *Capital*. The position of the productive worker vis-à-vis the means of production was also modified. As the delegation of capitalist functions progressed, the control of the productive worker over the labour process was further diminished.

The complexity of the contemporary class pattern of capitalism is an expression of the coexistence of these fundamental class contradictions: (1) between capitalists and productive workers — the traditional capitalist relation; (2) between managers and all categories of 'managed' workers, productive and unproductive — a new class contradiction.[8]

Thus, two fractions of the ruling classes coexist (cooperate but also fight, to various degrees). At the top of the social hierarchy are capitalist owners and managers, just like the aristocracy and bourgeoisie in the Old Regime described by Marx.

The power of the ruling classes is usually tempered by compromises. Two aspects can be distinguished within such compromises. One concerns the content and extension of cooperation among the fractions of the ruling classes, such as management and capitalists, within various state or parastatal institutions. There is an *interface* between these classes, the world of boards of directors where owners still engaged in some form of management collaborate with top managers, who are also owners to a certain extent. This interface is crucial to the preservation of a type of capitalism where ownership and management are basically separated. The other aspect concerns compromise with broader fractions of the population. At issue are the participation of larger sections of salaried workers in prosperity, when it exists, and the stringency of the discipline recurrently imposed on these groups, etc.

As recalled in section 1.1, the state is the locus of the formation and preservation of power configurations. This is true of the cooperation between the fractions of the ruling classes, as well as of the compromise with broader segments of the population.

The degrees of *hegemony* and *compromise* exercised by capitalist owners are of primary importance in the definition of power configurations. Since the beginning of the twentieth century, with the emergence of modern finance and the delegation of management to salaried personnel, the hegemony of capitalist owners can be described as that of *finance*, meaning by this, financial institutions and individuals holding large portfolios of financial securities.[9] This hegemony is always tempered by the alliance with top management, but during such a hegemony the rules of the owners are basically endorsed by top management. Schematically, two such periods of hegemony have existed, one at the beginning of the century and another since the 1980s. They were separated by the *Keynesian compromise*, in which finance was 'repressed' to a certain extent, and in which top management, in its private and public components, was 'reunited' to some extent with the other fractions of management. Keynesianism limited the prerogatives of finance concerning what we called above the 'macro-economic' facet of capitalist ownership; it encouraged sectional behaviour by managers and established a rather broad compromise among wage-earners; it extended the field of activities freed from the necessity to maximize the profit rate (i.e. 'the market').[10]

Actually, the emergence and stabilization of neoliberalism would have been impossible without the convergence of top management and capitalist owners, a modification in the content of the compromise characteristic of the interface. The *right turn* of the 1980s, analyzed by Thomas Ferguson and Joel Rogers[11], and the consolidation of neoliberalism, cannot be reduced to the rise of the reactionary forces which originally backed Ronald Reagan. President Reagan simply adjusted his policies in line with other business groups.

1.2.5 *Historical tendencies and crises*

A central component of Marx's analysis in Volume III of *Capital* is the description of the patterns of evolution which in section 1.1 we called *trajectories à la Marx*, whose central feature is a declining profit rate. Such declines lead to structural crises. In our opinion, this framework of analysis is still very relevant to the study of capitalism, with the proviso that structural crises failed to cause the collapse of capitalism but instead stimulated its transformation, making possible fresh upswings in the profit rate.[12]

As shown in Figure 1, the succession of various phases in the USA since the Civil War is particularly evident in the profile of the *productivity of capital*. The dotted line represents the trend characteristic of the average technology, abstracting from the effects of the business cycle. The fluctuations around this trend mirror the movements of the average level of activity. Note the fall into the Great Depression, and the levels reached during World War II. Unless otherwise specified, the series in the figures are the results of authors' computations on the basis of national accounting frameworks.[13] A first phase of decline is apparent in the late nineteenth century leading to the structural crisis of the 1890s;

Figure 1: Secular trends of capital productivity (dollars of product per dollar of fixed capital): USA (private economy)

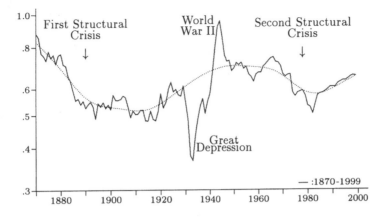

a gradual recovery is observed, evident from the 1920s; the Great Depression apparently interrupted this movement as a result of the sharp and lasting contraction of the activity, but actually accelerated the elimination of the backward fractions of the productive system; a second period *à la Marx* is observed during the second half of the 1960s, 1970s, and early 1980s; the trough was attained during the great recession of 1982; eventually there is a new trend upward.

These movements are related to the transformations in the relations of production described earlier. We interpret the upswing in the first half of the century as an effect of the *managerial revolution*, which resulted in increased efficiency in the use of capital (in all components of activity: within the workshop, with Taylorism and the assembly line, but also in commercial activities, and in inventory and liquidity management). In our opinion, a new revolution in management is presently under way, whose effects have become apparent since the mid-1980s. The 'marginal efficiency' of managerial innovation was probably declining, because of its costs. The new revolution can be described as a revolution within management itself. Information technology allows for gradual improvements in efficiency and diminishing costs, but it is clear that other organizational elements are also involved. More and more sophisticated management must avoid any bureaucratic bias.

1.2.6 *Imperialism and US hegemony*

In our opinion, *imperialism* has been, to various degrees and under various forms, a permanent feature of capitalism. A chronology of its successive stages should be established. Since the 1960s and 1970s, and the dissolution of the colonial empires, it survives in the collective dominance of the major capitalist countries. Among these countries, one is dominant: the United States. The notion of *US hegemony*, as we use it, refers to this configuration: the imperial collective domination of the major capitalist countries of the centre over the periphery under US leadership.

1.2.7 *Periodizing capitalism in the twentieth century*

A basic problem in the periodization of capitalism is the existence of various competing criteria.[14] The transformations of relations of production (with their multiple elements), class patterns, power configurations, technical trends and crises, as well as stages of imperialism, all are potential alternative criteria.

These alternative criteria are linked in many respects, but they also possess a significant degree of autonomy concerning both the mechanisms involved and the timing. For example, the transformations in macro-policies and the establishment of the Keynesian compromise, following the Great Depression and World War II, occurred during a period of continuing favourable trends in technology and distribution (see above, section 1.2.5); the depression resulted in part from the rapidity of technical change, but also from the slow adjustment of macro-policies and institutions. The various criteria delineate different periods, and their combination easily degenerates into the multiplication of sub-periods. Structural crises and wars are convenient markers.

1.3 *Neoliberalism and the new capitalism*

How can neoliberalism be interpreted in the context of capitalist transformation?

Before entering into a more technical analysis, the following general comments may be made concerning the nature and content of neoliberalism.[15] (1) Concerning the relations of production, neoliberalism cannot be analyzed as a movement away from the overall process of socialization and the delegation of management to salaried personnel. It actually accelerated this transformation in some respects, while blocking it in others. What is at issue is only the modification of earlier trends. First, as in the first period of the hegemony of finance, in the early twentieth century, neoliberalism strengthened the separation between ownership and management. It accelerated the development of large non-financial corporations managed by business staffs; salaried management grew within financial institutions (like mutual and pension funds). The new pro-merger attitude of the government helped this development. Second, the behavioural 'bias' of managers and public officials is important here. This is what is key in the new pro-finance model of corporate governance, regulations, and policies: moving away from managerial autonomy within corporations, and away from the Keynesian compromise and the state. Neoliberalism meant the unambiguous reassertion of the maximization of the profit rate in every dimension of activity (see above, section 1.2.1). (2) In spite of the rise of managerial and clerical personnel engaged in financial activity, neoliberalism cannot be defined in terms of specific class patterns. This general observation must, however, be qualified in some respects. An important point is that there will be no 'euthanasia of the rentier' (if such a process was ever underway). In addition, reliance on extreme social inequality may prolong or extend the most acute forms of exploitation for a fraction of productive workers, and simultaneously enlarge the proportion of personnel engaged in personal services. Neoliberalism reinforces the tendency of capitalism to keep the lower strata of wage workers where they are, rather than advance them into the upper strata. (3) Unemployment will be used, as was traditional in capitalism, as a lever to control labour costs and to discipline wage workers. The stability of prices will ensure the preservation of the wealth of the holders of monetary and financial assets. Neoliberalism is thus a form of 'aggressive' capitalism. (4) The new more favourable patterns of technical change of recent decades, if maintained, might open a new path for capitalism. These trends became apparent under neoliberalism but they are not intrinsically characteristic of it. They are, to a large extent, managerial achievements. Their sustainability is an issue. Moreover, neoliberal or not, the capitalism of the future is not immune to new trajectories à la Marx and the accompanying structural crises. This point is politically important because of the way propaganda tends to classify all 'favourable' aspects of contemporary capitalism as features of neoliberalism. (This underlines the importance of a careful approach to periodization.)

Two definitions of neoliberalism can, then, be given. (1) In a narrow sense, the term *neoliberalism* can be used to designate a course of events, a set of 'policies', that occurred during the 1980s and 1990s, with the potential to lead to a new phase of development. It can be interpreted *as an attempt, in the 1980s, by a class of capitalist owners, to restore, in alliance with top management, its power and income after a setback of several decades.* Some of the features recalled above are analogous to nineteenth century capitalism, but it goes without saying that the notion of restoration does not imply that the new course of capitalism is identical to any events experienced in the past. (2) In a broader sense, the term *neoliberalism* can be used to designate a new capitalism, with certain characteristics of sustainability: *the historical outcome of the restoration of the power and income of a class of capitalist owners in the context of advanced managerial capitalism.*

The difference between the two patterns could be significant. It could even be so large that the term *neoliberalism* comes to appear inappropriate to designate longer-term developments.

II CONTRADICTIONS?

Do any of the traits of the last twenty years put in question the sustainability of neoliberal capitalism? Can we detect any internal contradictions? In this second section, we basically consider the US economy, which we compare with the average of three European countries (France, Germany, and the United Kingdom),[16] and with France alone.[17] (Japan should obviously be considered in a more extensive study.)

2.1 *Ruling and compromising*

2.1.1 *The wealth of the wealthiest*

Rising inequality has often been described as a characteristic of neoliberalism. There is obviously an international component to this feature, and the gap between the most advanced countries and the poorer countries of the periphery is well known.[18]

Even at the centre of the capitalist world economy, the lower fractions of the population were injured by neoliberalism. Unemployment reached double-digit

Figure 2: Share of total wealth held by the top 1% of wealth holders (%): USA, households

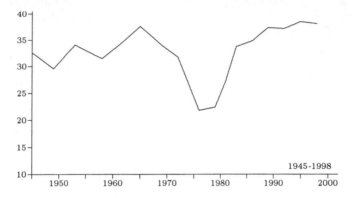

Wealth includes real estate (housing), securities and cash, and consumer durables.
Source: the data are from E. Wolff, *Top Heavy*, The New Press: New York, 1996, supple-
mented by more recent estimates.

levels, briefly in the USA after the change in monetary policy, and remained close
to such levels in Europe for fifteen years. Simultaneously, the wealthiest fraction
significantly improved its income and wealth.

There is a specifically *financial* aspect to these flows of income and wealth
toward the richest. It is clearly apparent in the large amounts of interest and dividends paid by non-financial enterprises, one set of households and the state, to
financial institutions and, basically, another set of households. The dramatic rise
of the stock market from the mid–1980s added to this increasingly unequal distribution of wealth.[19] The astounding 'compensation' of top managers has also been
frequently emphasized.

This rise in the income and wealth of the wealthiest part of the US population
followed a period of real setback and can to some extent be described as a
recovery. During the first phase of the structural crisis of the 1970s low profits, low
distributions of dividends and low interest rates, combined with large inflation
rates, had considerably reduced the income of the ruling classes. As shown in
Figure 2, the fraction of the total wealth in the USA, held by the richest 1% among
households, fluctuated between 30 and 35% during the first decades after World
War II. This percentage declined to 22% in 1976. Neoliberalism reversed this.

These observations illustrate a few aspects of the notion of 'aggressive capitalism' introduced earlier. Confronting the decline of their income and wealth,
the ruling classes politically modified the course of capitalism. From the mid–
1980s onwards they were able to impose tight controls on the growth of wage
costs and to enlarge, to an astonishing extent, their own 'siphoning off' of profits.
They restored their position dramatically, even *prior to* the appearance of the new
upward trend in the profit rate.

One may question the sustainability of this course of development in the long
run. In the first place, the stagnation of wages (manifested in the increasing share

of profits despite the slow growth of labour productivity) has played an important role in the recent recovery of the profit rate, and the growth of the cost of workers' benefits has been gradually reduced. Two basic trade-offs are involved, between: (1) wage costs and profits; and (2) income transfers favourable to finance and accumulation.

Secondly, the struggle of wage-earners for better working conditions and living standards suffered a double blow: its defeat during the structural crisis and the assertion of neoliberalism; and the collapse of any alternative to capitalism in the 'socialist' countries (actually a long history of gradual disillusionment), and the failure of all social-democratic or Keynesian reformist ways out. The discouraging consequences of these setbacks will not last for ever. Unless the present technological advance is prolonged, creating durable conditions for a relaxation of these trade-offs, it will become more and more difficult to repress labour.

In order to preserve their privileges, the ruling classes have two options: either the establishment of a new social compromise of their own (to align larger segments of the population with the prosperity of the wealthiest), or a shift towards a more and more authoritarian regime.[20]

2.1.2 'All capitalists'

Neoliberalism broke the solidarity of wage-earners and destroyed the compromise which had set limits to the power of finance, which had characterized the Keynesian years. The leading social role in the old power configuration had been played by managerial personnel (managers, engineers, professionals) within both private corporations and state and parastatal administration. The arrangement affected wage-earners in general *via* the commitment to full-employment, larger access to education, and the welfare state in general. In spite of the controls over finance, the relationship with finance was also one of compromise. The primary limitation to the earlier pre-eminence of finance concerned the control of credit, by regulations and new monetary policy targets (see above, section 1.2.2), while other aspects of financial activity (notably the allocation of capital) were less affected, notwithstanding the limits placed on horizontal mergers and restrictions on the financial activities of the commercial banks, and on international movements of capital. This raises the question of what new compromise might be substituted for that which prevailed during the Keynesian years.

It is easy to understand that crucial to the neoliberal program of restoring the power and income of capitalist owners within advanced managerial capitalism is their relationship with management. A key element is *top management*, beginning with what we call the *interface* between ownership and management. As already mentioned, the reliance on top management has been a prominent feature of neoliberalism from its inception, and it was strongly associated with the new flow of income toward finance. This feature is so congenial to neoliberalism that it can hardly even be described as a social compromise. Such a 'compromise' would, in any event, belong to the first category outlined above in section 1.2.4: cooperation between the various fractions of the ruling classes.

But the establishment of a broader compromise, including the middle classes,

Figure 3: FDIC-insured commercial banks (—) and savings and loans institutions (---) that were closed or received FDIC assistance: USA

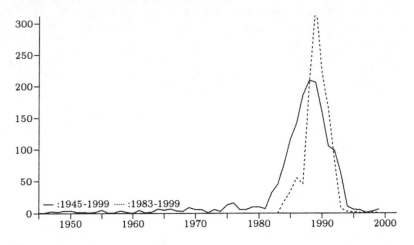

FDIC: Federal Deposit Insurance Corporation

is crucial to the survival of neoliberalism. The slogan is 'everyone is a capitalist'. Its main practical components are: (1) the distribution of shares to wage-earners, as a supplement to their wages; (2) stock options; and (3) pension funds. The effectiveness of these devices is increased by tax incentives. Institutions such as pension and mutual funds, which developed before neoliberalism, expanded to unprecedented levels and will remain a central element in the neoliberal edifice, associating the upper half of households with the fate of capital. In the establishment of this compromise, the dramatic rise of the stock market from the mid-1980s onwards acted like a bonanza. The middle classes who had some financial assets actually subscribed to the view that the most lax capitalist rules increased their living standards, and that class barriers could be gradually overcome. This favourable period is over.

2.2 *(De)Stabilizing the economy*

The purpose of this section is to discuss the (in)stability of capitalism dominated by neoliberalism. Is neoliberalism a system especially prone to monetary and financial crises? Does such a propensity put its survival in question? In this discussion, we will distinguish between domestic and international issues.

2.2.1 *Domestic issues: financial crisis and macro-stability*

In the USA the rise of neoliberalism created a significant financial crisis during the 1980s. It is not the purpose of the present study to recount the development and various phases of this crisis.[21] The amplitude of the event is illustrated in Figure 3, which shows the number of banks and savings associations which failed or were rescued. The figures speak for themselves. The crisis resulted from the sharp rise of real interest rates in the early 1980s, deregulation, and defaults. The feedback effect on American banks of the crisis of the debt of the so-called *Less*

Figure 4: Yearly growth rate of output for each quarter (%): USA

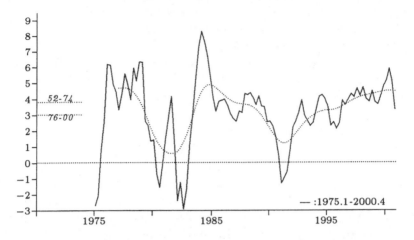

The variable depicted is the growth rate of each quarter in comparison to the same quarter one year earlier. The dotted line is a trend line abstracting from shorter-term fluctuations. The short horizontal segments describe the average growth rates for the two periods 1952-74 and 1976-2000.

Developed Countries was considerable. Most other advanced capitalist countries were also affected to various degrees. This financial crisis was an expression of the deepening of the structural crisis and the implementation of neoliberalism, and can be interpreted as a transitional phenomenon. A primary lesson is that after the early reluctance to act by the Reagan administration, which claimed that the 'market' would take care of the situation, the US government and monetary policy did much to stop the problems of the financial system spreading to the real economy.

This sharp disturbance of the working of financial institutions at the centre must be contrasted with the relative stability of the macro-economy (a rather stable rate of growth) from the mid–1980s onwards. Figure 4 depicts the yearly growth rate of output for each quarter since 1975 in the USA. One can see in this figure the negative growth rates of output in the recessions of 1980 and 1982, and the peak in 1983, which coincided with the emergence of neoliberalism. But growth was markedly stable during the rest of the period, with the exception of the 1993 recession. Thus, beyond the initial period of dramatic disturbance (the transition years), neoliberalism can claim to have made a contribution to macro-economic stability. Despite the decline which began in 2000, this is an object of pride in the USA.[22]

The analysis of these developments refers to basic macro-economic mechanisms. The crucial issue, in these respects, is one of stability (see Box overleaf).

It is important to keep in mind that, despite the abandonment of some of the rules established after the Great Depression, the transformation of the institutional framework in the early 1980s *strengthened* the power of the central bank. As indi-

---

BUSINESS-CYCLE FLUCTUATIONS
MONETARY AND FINANCIAL (IN)STABILITY

Under 'ordinary' conditions, i.e., in the absence of exceptional shocks and destabilization of monetary and financial institutions, demand levels, in contemporary capitalism, are controlled, during the phases of the business cycle, by monetary policy (in particular, in the USA, by mortgage credit for housing purchases).[23] The stability of the general level of activity shows that these mechanisms are still very powerful, perhaps more efficient than ever. There is little inflation and capacity utilization rates are, in the average, 'normal' (i.e., fluctuating around a figure slightly above 80%). One may say, more technically, that *local stability* is generally ensured.

'Ordinary' conditions are not always present. A sudden and large shock, such as a collapse of the stock market and the accumulation of defaults on bad debts, could *destabilize* the economy, affecting the demand behaviour of households and the supply and demand behaviour of firms. A recession may follow, destabilizing demand and output levels. As was the case in the USA during the 1930s and the early 1980s (during the monetary and financial crisis), and as is presently the case in Japan, such shocks affect the functioning of the banking system, a key driver in the mechanisms of monetary policy. This may render monetary policy inefficient for some time and be manifested in sharp fluctuations upward and downward, or a collapse of activity. In the latter case, a public deficit (borrowings by the government, one channel in the issue of money) is required, though not necessarily sufficient.

---

cated in its name, there were two facets to the US *Deregulation and Monetary Control Act* of 1980. New prerogatives were given to the central bank, which were required by the need to exercise strong pressure on the economy, targeted at the elimination of inflation. The commitment to intervention under more dramatic circumstances also remains strong (as shown by the government's reaction to the banking and savings and loans associations crises in the 1980s). *With respect to macro-policy, neoliberalism did not destroy but reinforced the institutions of Keynesianism, except that the targets were changed — price stability rather than full employment.*[24]

Overall, the comparison between the two periods of financial hegemony is telling. There is continuity in the targets: (1) the stability and survival of monetary and financial institutions, and (2) the stability of the general level of prices. The major difference is that during the second, neoliberal, hegemony, the tools of Keynesian macro-economic policy were inherited and effectively used by and for finance.

2.2.2 *International issues: instability and US hegemony*

The most dramatic crises of neoliberalism were the international monetary and financial crises of the 1980s and 1990s, beginning with the debt crisis of the *Less Developed Countries* in 1982; then the crisis of the Mexican economy in 1994, those of South-East Asia in 1997, of South America and Russia in 1998, and most recently of Turkey in 2000-01. Independently of the rise of real interest rates, the central *financial and monetary* factors of the crises of the 1990s were: (1) the international mobility of capital, which was gradually established as a prominent component of the new neoliberal order; and (2) flexible exchange rates and the strange combination of flexibility and rigidity (the pegging of some currencies to the dollar) prevailing on international currency markets.

The international institutions of Keynesianism, the IMF and the World Bank, also survived the transition to neoliberalism, but, like the central banks of capitalist countries, the targets of their activity were redirected. They became the agents of the diffusion of the neoliberal order throughout the planet, with the additional concern that regional perturbations should not jeopardize stability at the centre.

Already, the Bretton Woods agreements had failed to create a genuine international bank, with its own, independent, currency. A special role had been given in the final agreement to currencies potentially 'as good as gold', i.e., the dollar. When the dominance of the USA was undermined for the first time at the end of the 1960s, the rules established at Bretton Woods began to unravel. The so-called 'crisis of the dollar' did not undo the dollar's pre-eminence.[25] On the contrary, its hegemony was maintained in a new institutional context, that of flexible exchange rates and gradually liberated flows of capital. Indeed the most conspicuous, almost caricatural form, of US hegemony is the gradual dollarization of the world economy.

In spite of this similarity the situation is in important respects different from that prevailing domestically within the major capitalist countries, particularly the USA. Contrary to what occurred domestically, no strong framework has emerged with responsibility for maintaining the international monetary and financial stability of the world economy. Regardless of the class content of the reasons for this, it poses an important threat to international stability. It is a serious contradiction within neoliberalism, linked to the transition away from many of the components of the Bretton Woods agreements (periodically adjustable rates of exchange, limitations on the mobility of capital during periods of crisis, etc.). Its most threatening aspect is the failure to impose a regulatory framework limiting the movement of capital whenever and wherever necessary, and, more generally, to regulate international financial and monetary institutions and mechanisms.

A major reason for this failure to establish an independent set of international institutions was the USA's determination to preserve its hegemony. There are strong similarities between the resistance of private finance in the early twentieth century to the emergence of adequate mechanisms for macro-economic stabilization, and the resistance of the USA both to the establishment of such an international framework after World War II and to the transformation of monetary and financial institutions in the wake of the crisis of the dollar.

Figure 5: Rate of accumulation (%): France, Germany, and United Kingdom (– • –), and the USA (—)

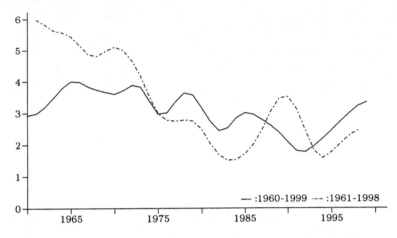

The unit of analysis is the total private economy. The accumulation rate is the growth rate of the fixed capital stock, net of depreciation. The series has been slightly smoothened to abstract from short-term fluctuations.

2.3 *Accumulating capital*

2.3.1 *Slow accumulation*

The accumulation of capital under neoliberalism is slow, and the transfer of income to finance is threatened by this sluggishness. This is the conclusion which follows from a quantitative analysis of growth rates within the major capitalist countries, and it raises the question of the compatibility between rapid accumulation and the large transfers of income toward financial institutions and rich households that are characteristic of neoliberalism. Note that the contrary view is presently dominant. The neoliberal creed is: (1) the USA is the leading neoliberal country; (2) its economic growth is rapid, faster than in other advanced capitalist countries; therefore (3) neoliberalism means investment (capital accumulation) and growth. In Europe, an additional proposition is: (4) Europe must emulate the USA.

But basic observations contradict this dogma. Figure 5 shows the rate of accumulation in the USA and the average of three European countries since the 1960s. The two curves show a declining trend, and the different patterns of evolution in Europe and in the USA, especially since the mid-1980s. Despite the fluctuation upward in the 1990s in the USA there is no neoliberal miracle guiding accumulation. The rate of accumulation moves cyclically: most likely, the last points in the series for the USA will appear as a peak, and it is not yet possible to detect the trend upward which should follow from the rise in the profit rate. Figure 6 shows the rate of net investment in the USA. It shows that investment only recovered to its pre-neoliberal levels in the late 1990s.[26]

It is a common feature of neoliberalism, in both the USA and Europe, that very large fractions of profits are paid in interest and dividends. Consequently,

Figure 6: Rates of net savings (——) and net investment (- - -) (%): USA

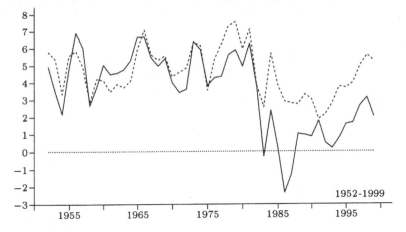

Investment is that of enterprises. In this context, net means after subtracting the depreciation of fixed capital. Savings are the difference between the total net product and all purchases of goods and services (including the purchase of residential capital by households) other than the investment by enterprises. (Capital gains are not counted as a component of income.)

despite the restoration of the profit rate since the mid-1980s, the rate of retained profits (after all payments, including interest and dividends) remains low, as does the accumulation rate (which is tightly linked to the rate of retained profits). This is illustrated in Figure 7, in the case of France. One can note: (1) the strong recovery of the profit rate prior to the payment of interest and dividends, significantly above its levels of the early 1970s; (2) the rising rate of transfer of profits to finance, with the effect that the rate of retained profits remains below the level of the 1970s; (3) the close correlation between the rate of retained profits and the rate of accumulation.[27] A central feature of neoliberalism is that the investment of non-financial corporations is self-financed. In the USA this has been the case since World War II, and continues to be so. In France heavy reliance on borrowing disappeared with neoliberalism. Whatever the complexity of the actual channels, things unfold within neoliberalism as if the profits pumped out of the productive sector of the economy do not return to it. This is a central contradiction of 'actually existing neoliberalism': its inability to promote strong accumulation. This does not deny, however, the role of finance in the allocation of capital among various activities (its propensity to finance promising innovations, possibly beyond what is appropriate).

This feature of neoliberalism is puzzling. It is certainly possible to imagine a configuration of capitalism in which large flows of profits are transferred to capitalist owners, *via* the payment of interest and dividends, and then returned to the non-financial sector in the form of new loans and newly issued shares. But this has not been the case so far. It is rather intuitive that high real interest rates

Figure 7: Rate of profit before the payment of interest and dividends (—), rate of retained profits (after these payments) (---), and accumulation rate (·····) (%): France, non-financial corporations

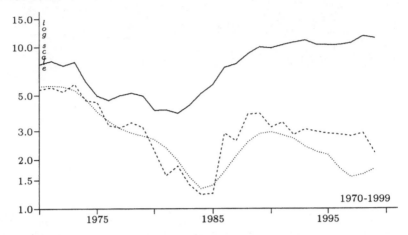

The accumulation rate is the growth rate of the stock of fixed capital, net of depreciation. Profits, in both definitions of the profit rates, are divided by net worth. This figure uses a logarithmic scale on the vertical axis, and the distance between the curves are, thus, proportional to the ratios among the various rates. The burden of interest and dividends payments is measured by the distance between the two series (---) and (—).

discourage borrowing, but these trends suggest, more surprisingly, that in the relationship between the productive sector and the stock market *maximizing the market price of corporations* has been more important, or at least more successful, than relying on financial markets to finance accumulation. (The repurchase of their own shares by corporations is, of course, negative accumulation.) No other feature of neoliberalism shows so clearly that its ruling classes are parasitic, and the capability of neoliberalism to meet the requirements of accumulation will be crucial in the long run.[28]

2.3.2 *Advanced capitalist countries: Growth under US hegemony*

A basic flaw in the neoliberal creed (see section 2.3.1 above) is the second proposition in the neoliberal mantra: the growth differential between the USA and Europe and Japan. Attributing this to the beneficial effects of neoliberalism overlooks the advantages of the USA's hegemony, in particular the pre-eminence of the dollar, its so-called *seignorage*.[29]

As is well known, US accumulation was not financed, after the beginning of the 1980s, by domestic savings but by foreign savings. As shown in Figure 6, the rate of savings of all agents in the USA dropped suddenly in those years to about zero, exactly at the inception of neoliberalism. No other country could have afforded the external deficits (and the corresponding imports of capital) resulting from the gap between domestic investment and savings.[30]

It is difficult to balance US domestic factors and international determinants in explaining this unusual situation. On average, profit rates do not appear larger in the USA than in Europe,[31] and it is not clear that foreign capital was attracted by larger profitability levels in the USA. Capital flows to the USA seem to be more a consequence of US domestic policy, given the attraction of the privileges attached to hegemony.

One specific domestic feature of the US economy is that credits to households continued to rise throughout the 1990s.[32] This is certainly a crucial factor in the explanation of the very high spending levels (consumption plus purchases of residential capital by households) in the USA, and hence the very low levels of domestic savings. This is where the absence of external constraint and reliance on external deficits is crucial.

Thus neoliberalism, when assessed from the viewpoint of major capitalist countries (without bringing the periphery into the picture), already appears to be a very hierarchical system. The lesson that the USA, as the leading example of neoliberalism, is supposed to teach seems quite dependent on the USA's hegemony. A new balance of power, in favour of Japan and, to a lesser extent, Europe, would fundamentally challenge the alleged virtues of neoliberalism in relation to accumulation and growth. The US example does not demonstrate the ability of neoliberalism to achieve growth, first, because US accumulation is not strong (see section 2.3.1 above) and, second, because much of the USA's superior performance can be imputed to their world hegemony rather than to their comparative advance along the neoliberal route.

2.3.3 *Prosperity and the bubble*

In the analysis of the growth of the economy an important role is often attributed to the stock market rise of the late 1990s, in particular in the USA,[33] and this could be seen as grounds for questioning the ability of neoliberalism to maintain continuously growing levels of demand.[34] If this view were sound it would indeed signal a significant contradiction in the functioning of capitalism under neoliberalism.

The parallel between the last two decades and the beginning of the twentieth century, and the occurrence of the Great Depression, plays an important role here. The 1920s and the last fifteen years of the twentieth century have much in common: (1) new trends in technology and distribution; (2) audacious monetary and financial innovations; (3) a merger wave; and, probably not coincidentally, (4) a sharp rise in stock market indices. Keynesian economists see a connection between demand and stock indices in relation to the Depression, contending that a contraction of demand followed from Wall Street's collapse at the end of 1929.[35] This line of argument implies that activity had been previously stimulated by the rise of the stock market (as a result of a *wealth effect*).[36] The same would presumably be true of the recent prosperity in the USA, at least during the 1990s.

A preliminary difficulty with this interpretation of contemporary spending levels in the USA is that the speculative boom was common to most advanced capitalist countries, with the obvious exception of Japan, and was not stronger in the USA than in Europe. For example, a bubble of exactly the same amplitude and timing existed in France, and demand was not stimulated to the same extent as in the USA. But our disagreement is even more fundamental.

There is no questioning the fact that the rise of the value of the portfolio of shares held by a fraction of households affects their spending and borrowing behaviour, but monetary policy is still powerful (see section 2.2.1 above, and Box) and can adjust the levels of demand against the pressure of other determinants (i.e., ex post). In the absence of a rise of the stock market, monetary policy could have performed its tasks even more easily. The same will be true after the current market adjustment, provided that the monetary and financial framework is not unsettled in the process.

Much confusion is created by the coexistence in the USA of the stock market bubble, the rise of household credit, and external deficits. A quite unusual chain of events has been at work: (1) loans stimulate the spending of households (consumption and purchase of housing) — possibly, for a fraction of the population, through the inducement of the rising stock market; (2) the additional total spending (i.e., spending of households plus investment by firms) is purchased from abroad without significant inflationary consequences for domestic prices; (3) the normal utilization of productive capacity, *via* the control of price stability, is assured with great care by monetary policy.

Overall, it appears that a speculative bubble is a predictable development in the context of a merger wave, the recovery of the profitability in a segment of the economy, and deregulation of financial mechanisms. But we do not believe it is a necessary component of the formation of demand in general, or under neoliberalism in particular. A large crisis could follow from the bursting of the bubble if the necessary macro-policies were not implemented — if the shock radically destabilized the banking system, or if the crisis reached cumulative international proportions — but such developments are distinct from the mechanisms which govern the formation of demand when the conditions for stability are ensured, as was the case during the second half of the 1990s. The bubble is not a condition for the survival of neoliberalism. Quite the contrary, a 'soft landing' may be a condition for the continuation of the new course of capitalism. Without the bubble, neoliberalism would be neither more nor less apt to secure accumulation and growth.

2.4 *Improving technology*

It becomes more and more clear that about in the mid-1980s a period characterized by more favourable conditions of technical change began (see section 1.2.5). In Europe as in the USA the declining trend of the productivity of capital was not only interrupted but reversed (see Figure 1), and profit rates tended to rise. The prevalence and prolongation of these trends is crucial to neoliberalism and the future of capitalism in general. A gradually more efficient technology is a necessary condition for steady and lasting growth, together with its international diffusion (obviously with the limitations inherent to capitalism), and the implementation of a new social compromise. The question must, therefore, be posed of a possible link between neoliberalism and the features of technical change.[37]

We believe that a deep-seated transformation of management is presently underway, as in the early twentieth century, once again in the wake of a structural crisis (see section 1.2.5). The similarity between these two episodes is large. The managerial revolution of the early twentieth century was tightly linked to the preceding merger wave (the 'corporate revolution'); both finance and management were involved (in the context of the separation between ownership and management). The same is true of the transformations of the last two or three decades of the twentieth century. Obviously, the new technologies benefited from earlier R & D, and appear basically to have been a managerial achievement, the work of engineers and specialists. The previous merger wave, the *conglomerate* wave, had managerial features, related to the prevailing antitrust legislation, but under neoliberalism finance changed the rules and a pro-merger attitude was adopted.[38] Finance allowed for the restructuring of the economy, modifying the juridical framework and its application, and provided the necessary coordination and funding; and it imposed stricter profitability criteria. As is typical in capitalism, the task was undertaken under the pressure of a profitability crisis, i.e., ex post, with high costs for large segments of the population, but finance can claim to have made a contribution.

That finance played a role in the restructuring of the economy during the crisis of the 1970s and 1980s does not imply that it possesses the ability to prolong these trends. Their continuation is, however, crucial to the future of neoliberalism and capitalism in general. We have no prognosis to offer in this respect. The pattern of events in the twentieth century suggests only that specific risks accompany rapid technical change, as shown by the Great Depression, while on the other hand the benefits of a technical and organizational revolution may last several decades.

III BEYOND NEOLIBERALISM?

This last section uses the basic distinctions introduced in this study — between the transformation of relations of production, tendencies and crises, and power configurations — to discuss the future of neoliberalism.

3.1 Tendencies and crises

A common feature of all significant changes in the period covered in this essay is their relation to crises. This basic function of economic 'violence' remains a core feature of capitalism.

A first, very dramatic, development, which might contradict the neoliberal dream, would be that *history repeats itself*. This first transition scenario is that of great *instability*. The favourable course of technical change, opening a new phase of capitalism and financial hegemony, as in the beginning of the twentieth century, is suddenly and provisionally interrupted by a major depression, like that of the 1930s. The Great Depression was the *crisis of the recovery from the structural crisis of the late nineteenth century under financial hegemony*, with a significant mone-

tary and financial component. The entire sequence of events could be reproduced: (1) structural crisis (that of the 1970s); (2) new favourable trends
(presently underway), and a new hegemony of finance (as is also the case now);
(3) a major crisis (recurrently announced); (4) a second period of controls on
finance and a new social compromise.

If the path of technical change is less rapid, or if the favourable trends observed
during the last fifteen years come to an end or are reversed, difficulties will be felt
via 'significant' crises. They will be aggravated by social tensions (caused, for
example, by stagnating wages or the difficulty of financing retirement plans) and
international confrontations (which may impose new monetary and financial
rules). Instead of maintaining its prerogatives, finance will have to gradually
retreat. The transfer of profits in its favour will be limited and new regulations
will be imposed. Neoliberalism faces this potential scenario in the medium run.

A spectacular development would be the occurrence of a new structural crisis
(such as that of the 1890s and 1970s). History would then repeat itself yet again
and a new power configuration would be imposed in the wake of such a crisis
(as was the case in the transition between the 1970s and 1980s), but the new
element would be that finance would be in command, instead of repressed.

3.2 Relations of production

At an even more profound level of analysis, the crucial issue is one of relations
of production. The history of capitalism reveals their gradual transformation in the
direction of an increased socialization: (1) the growing size and a larger interde-
pendency of individual units of production, the central coordination of
macro-policies and the definition of regulatory frameworks, the concentration of
ownership and allocation of capital, the social control of education, research, etc.;
(2) the delegation of the functions implied by the accomplishment of these tasks
to specialists within non-financial corporations and financial institutions.
Neoliberalism was possible, because it did not interrupt these developments but
strengthened them. In all instances, the issue was the definition of *targets*:
managing *firms* and the *macro-economy* in the interest of the owners, with much
contempt for the costs borne by other classes or countries.

It is not clear that neoliberalism can measure up to the task of furthering this
socialization in all of its components, as listed above. The question is, therefore,
posed, whether there is a fundamental contradiction between this historical task
and the narrow perspective of the interests of the owners. This essay set out a
number of significant limitations. (1) The current forms of capital ownership still
guarantee a large degree of initiative for finance which is incompatible with the
quest for monetary and financial stability. First, they still allow the collective
retreat of financial investors whenever they are confronted by potential losses (as
manifested in international financial crises and collapses of the stock market).
Macro-policies are only efficient under 'ordinary' conditions, and monetary and
financial disturbances jeopardize their effectiveness. Second, the other facet of
ownership — the allocation of capital among industries and firms — is still largely
subject to the very volatile expectations of major financial institutions, such as

pension and insurance funds, motivated solely by the interests of their customers, again with potentially negative macro-consequences. (2) Despite the involvement of finance in the definition of the new more favourable course of technical change in its first stages, neoliberalism has not resolved one of the major contradictions of capitalism: the capability to maintain a steady course of technical change. This would require new levels of the socialization of R & D and the implementation of innovation, i.e., a more profound transformation of relations of production beyond the basic profit-maximizing requirements of individual firms or corporate alliances.

3.3 Power configurations: alternative issues

3.3.1 Neoliberalism: the end of history?

Some of the contours of the capitalist dream of the ruling classes under neoliberalism are easy to infer from the events of the last two decades and the associated propaganda. Capitalism is the end of history. The owners of capital consolidate their position and income, and govern in close collaboration with top management. A broader compromise is established with the upper middle classes, who benefit from slowly rising purchasing power, health insurance, and pension funds; they share the benefits of a rising stock market (after a 'soft landing') and high interest rates. Accumulation rates are reasonable and crises are limited in extent. This is made possible by the continuing favourable shape of technical change. The hierarchy of wage-earners remains strong, but the situation is under control. Thanks to the export of capital to peripheral countries, segments of the population in the periphery are gradually moving toward a status similar to that of the lower income brackets of the centre; small elites collaborate with the ruling groups of the major capitalist countries. The USA leads the way, followed by Europe and Japan (finally adjusted to the benefits of neoliberalism), and, at some distance, by the more cooperative other countries.

A more conflictual course of events is, however, more likely, and probably foreseen by the shrewdest advocates of neoliberalism. Distributional tensions will remain significant, and social conflicts will have to be confronted. The rivalry among major capitalist countries and anti-imperialist struggles by forces in the periphery will remain significant. Stability will be basically ensured, but at the cost of recurrent crises. Capitalism must transform itself, but the fundamental features of the power configuration will be preserved. The problem will be to lead the international race and ensure the continuing pre-eminence of the ruling classes.

3.3.2 Beyond neoliberalism: the pursuit of history?

An alternative outcome is that the neoliberal power configuration will be destabilized, following one of the alternative scenarios outlined earlier. Just as the structural crisis of the 1970s paved the way for the come-back of capitalist owners, a logical consequence of our analysis is that a new compromise will then have to be struck between the leading managerial classes and the rest of the labour force (or at least some fractions of it). Depending on the form and extent of class struggles, the managerial and popular components of the configuration of power will be more or less accentuated — anywhere from a new form of Keynesianism to some more radical transformation.

Regardless of its precise social content, there are certain tasks essential to capitalism that any new compromise will have to carry out. The first historical setback to finance introduced the socialization of the *control of the macro-economy*, in the broad sense of the term (stabilizing business fluctuations and ensuring the stability of financial mechanisms and institutions). Redirecting these tools toward new (to some extent 'earlier') targets will not be the most difficult task to achieve. On the agenda for 'post-neoliberalism' are new degrees of socialization to achieve more efficient technical progress and accumulation. (Possible directions for this were suggested during the decades of the Keynesian compromise, but none of them was successfully implemented, neither the preservation of the favourable path of technical change, nor strong accumulation — hence inflation, hence unemployment.) The economics of a new compromise will be largely determined by its politics. Capitalism is not the end of history.

NOTES

1   G. Duménil, D. Lévy, 2001, 'Costs and Benefits of Neoliberalism. A class analysis', forthcoming in *Review of International Political Economy*, 8.4.2000, *Crise et sortie de crise. Ordre et désordres néolibéraux*, Presses Universitaires de France, Paris.

2   A more detailed analysis can be found in G. Duménil & D. Lévy, 'Periodizing Capitalism. Technology, Institutions, and Relations of Production', in R. Albritton, M. Itoh, R. Westra, A. Zuege, *Phases of Capitalist Development: Booms, Crises, and Globalization*, London: Palgrave, 2001.

3   We analyzed these mechanisms, in particular the patterns of technical change and the relationship between declining profit rates and crises in previous works (G. Duménil & D. Lévy, *The Economics of the Profit Rate: Competition, Crises, and Historical Tendencies in Capitalism*, Aldershot: Edward Elgar, 1993, 'Technology and Distribution: Historical Trajectories à la Marx', *Journal of Economic Behavior and Organization*, 2000 (forthcoming)). See also: D. Foley, 2000, 'Endogenous Technical Change with Externalities in a Classical Growth Model', Department of Economics, Graduate Faculty, New School University, New York, forthcoming in *Journal of Economic Behavior and Organization*.

4   Hilferding analyzed one of its possible configurations (R. Hilferding, *Finance Capital: A study of the Latest Phase of Capitalist Development*, London & Boston: Routledge and Kegan Paul, [1910] 1981).

5   G. Duménil & D. Lévy, *La dynamique du capital. Un siècle d'économie américaine*, Paris: Presses Universitaires de France, 1996 ch.22.

6   There is also a problem concerning the allocation of this capital among capitalists.

7   To avoid bankruptcies, financial panics, and the suspensions of payments.

8   Our reference to a *Marxist framework of analysis* can be seen as a combination of *fundamentalism* and *revisionism*. The consideration of new class patterns is a central element of this revisionism. The analysis of exploitation and the relationship between productive and clerical workers is typical of the problems faced by contemporary Marxism. Two basic attitudes can be distinguished: (1) a strict adherence to Marx's framework — surplus-value is extracted from productive workers (when this difficulty is not simply ignored, other groups are classified as *petty bourgeois*); (2) an implicit revision — a new proletarian or working class is defined including production and clerical workers. Our viewpoint is closer to this second attitude, but we make explicit the conceptual leap that it implies.

9   This is an 'institutional' definition of *finance*. It can also be defined in the strict sense as a class. The notion of *finance capital*, meaning a tight and hierarchical relationship between industrial capital and banking capital, is usually attributed to Rudolf Hilferding (*Finance Capital*). American sociologists attempted to identify among capitalists (shareholders and members of boards of directors), in the postwar US society, a specific subset of *financial capitalists*, whose ownership and power span financial and non-financial corporations (M. Soref & M. Zeitlin, 'Finance Capital and the Internal Structure of the Capitalist Class in the United States', in M. Mizruchi & M. Schwartz, *Intercorporate Relations. The Structural Analysis of Business*, Cambridge: Cambridge University Press, 1987. See also K. van der Pijl, *The Making of an Atlantic Ruling Class*, London & New York: Verso, 1984.

10 In some countries large segments of the productive system were placed under the control of state officials.

11 T. Ferguson & J. Rogers, 1986, *Right Turn. The Democrats and the Decline of American Politics*, New York: Hill and Wang, 1986.

12 This is a second illustration of the combination of *fundamentalism* (in the reference to the tendency for the profit rate to fall) and *revisionism* (in the identification of phases of restoration). We share this view with Ernest Mandel, (*Long Waves of Capitalist Development. The Marxist Interpretation*, Cambridge and Paris: Cambridge University Press & Éditions de la Maison des Sciences de l'Homme, 1980).

13 A recent description of the series can be found in G. Duménil & D. Lévy, *Crise et sortie de crise. Ordre et désordres néolibéraux*, Paris: Presses Universitaires de France, 2000.

14 The paper excludes phenomena which are often used as markers in the periodization of capitalism, such as the transformations of *competition*, notably the notions of competitive and monopoly capitalism. This choice is deliberate since we question the relevance of this distinction. The transformations of competition can be considered in combination with other phenomena, as in Lenin's analysis of imperialism, or in isolation.

15 The notion of 'liberalism' itself is already quite ambiguous. See, for example,

the introduction to J. Weinstein, *The Corporate Ideal in the Liberal State, 1900-1918*, Boston: Beacon Press, 1968.

16   In 1995, the output of these three countries represented 70% of that of the USA.

17   This analysis borrows from Duménil & Lévy, 'Costs and Benefits of Neoliberalism'; *Crise et sortie de crise*, 2001

18   UNPD, *Human Development Report*, Bruxelles: De Boeck, 1999.

19   In the measurement of financial income (interest and dividends received plus capital gains), it is important to correct for the impact of inflation.

20   Immanuel Wallerstein sees in the growing demand for democratization one of the contradictions (in addition to the exhaustion of the reserves in cheap labour and ecological resources), which will provoke the final outbreak of capitalism, presently on the verge of entering its last Kondratieff cycle (I. Wallerstein, 'Globalization or the Age of Transition? A Long-Term View of the Trajectory of the World-System', *International Sociology*, Vol. XV(2), 2000).

21   Federal Deposit Insurance Corporation, *History of the Eighties. Lessons for the Future*, Washington: FDIC, 1997

22   We abstract from the slowdown of the US economy which began in 2000 (figure 4). Independently of other more dramatic developments (always possible in the present context of threatening financial instability and which would affect the world economy), the USA could enter a new recession (while Europe has not to date).

23   A theoretical exposition and modeling can be found in the third part of G. Duménil & D. Lévy, *La dynamique du capital. Un siècle d'économie américaine*, Paris: Presses Universitaires de France, 1996.

24   The balance of external accounts is a target to be taken into account in Europe, but not in the USA (section 2.3.2).

25   L. Panitch, 'The New Imperial State', *New Left Review*, March–April 2000.

26   Because of the shortening of the service life of fixed capital, it is necessary to consider the rate of *net* investment, and not of *gross* investment as is often done.

27   The small gap during the 1990s reflects the desperate attempt by firms to get out of debt, manifested in rates of self-financing larger than 100%.

28   It is important to keep in mind that the financing of future retirement plans depends on growth (and technical progress), not on its institutional form, redistribution among wage earners or pension funds. Pension funds could only contribute to the solution of this problem, if they led to larger savings and growth rates, which is not presently the case. What is at stake in the alternative between redistribution and funds is a more or less egalitarian framework.

29   P. Gowan, *The Global Gamble. Washington's Faustian Bid for World Dominance*, London: Verso, 1999. We will abstract in this section from other aspects of the dominance of the USA, such as its position in trade or financial international agreements, political pressure or military intervention.

30 Obviously, the rate of exchange of the dollar is also at issue. With the exception of the sharp fluctuation upward in the early 1980s, the real exchange rate of the dollar remained comparatively low, in particular with respect to the yen, but this weakness did not offset the trade deficit.

31 Labour costs remain higher in the USA than in Europe, and available measures contradict the view that a technical gap could offset these differences.

32 The comparison with France shows the significant difference in the patterns of evolution. During the 1970s and the first half of the 1980s, the ratio of the total debt of households to their disposable income fluctuated in both countries between 60% and 70%. This rate of indebtedness grew in 1990, but while it declined during the following years in France, it went on rising in the USA, reaching the unprecedented level of 95%.

33 R.J. Gordon, 'Technology and Economic Performance in the American Economy', Working Paper, Conference of the *Centre Saint-Gobain pour la Recherche en Économie*, 2000.

34 F. Chesnais, 'La "nouvelle économie": Une conjoncture propre à la puissance hégémonique américaine', in Séminaire Marxiste, *Une nouvelle phase du capitalisme?*, Paris: Syllepse, 2001.

35 In our opinion, this interpretation is dubious: (1) The stock market fell after industrial production; (2) the depression continued well after the restoration of the stock market.

36 In such models, the wealth of final consumers is a variable in their demand function, besides their income.

37 At issue here is the degree of autonomy of the various levels of analysis: relations of production, tendencies and crises, and power configurations.

38 G. Duménil, M. Glick, & D. Lévy, 'The History of Competition Policy as Economic History', *The Antitrust Bulletin*, Vol. XLII(2), 1997. The basic characteristic of conglomerates was *diversification*, as the law limited mergers of firms engaged in the same activity.

THE GROWTH OBSESSION

ELMAR ALTVATER

In pre-capitalist and pre-industrial times economic growth was dependent on population growth which, in turn, depended on the supply of goods and services for subsistence and reproduction. But since the Industrial Revolution GDP growth has been propelled by the dynamic development of the productive forces, i.e. by increased (labour) productivity. From the second half of the nineteenth century, average growth rates increased remarkably. This growth, however, has been extremely uneven over time and in space, and has failed to narrow the inequalities between peoples and regions in a globalizing world.

Ignoring all evidence to the contrary, a recent World Bank report reached the remarkable conclusion that 'growth is good for the poor', i.e. that faster growth is not widening but closing the gap between rich and poor — and, moreover, not as the effect of a 'trickle-down' process; the report alleges the existence of a '1-to-1-relation' between growth and poverty-reduction.[1] The World Bank report is thus very optimistic with regard to the distributional effects of economic growth.[2] Yet even this bizarre (and strongly contested) conclusion does not touch upon the all-important question of whether economic growth is sustainable, economically as well as socially and ecologically. The essay by Paul Cammack in this volume exclusively examines the World Bank's project of 'making poverty work'. This essay discusses the economic, ecological and financial limits to growth and address the question of why quantitative growth is so crucial for the capitalist system.

1 GROWTH TRIUMPHANT?

In the history of industrial capitalism, and in particular during the second half of the twentieth century under the rule of 'Fordism', economic growth can be said to have been 'triumphant'[3] — owing to the ever more efficient mobilization of productive resources. Between 1950 and 1973 (the year of the collapse of the Bretton Woods system and the 'oil crisis'), nearly everywhere in the world growth rates reached levels unprecedented in human history, tempting Richard Easterlin to predict that '[t]he future ... to which the epoch of modern economic growth is leading is one of never ending economic growth, a world in which ever growing abundance is matched by ever rising aspirations'.[4] Yet the assumption that physical inputs can expand indefinitely and produce an ever growing real output is, as McMichael says, 'ecological nonsense — nothing physical can grow indefinitely'.[5] The statement 'growth forever' therefore only makes sense if the growth that Easterlin and other growth-enthusiasts have in mind is mere monetary growth (known as inflation), or a purely virtual 'new' economy (without transportation, material production, and physical consumption of resources). And indeed these notions are often invoked in arguments that try to reconcile ecological sustainability with the requirements of a capitalist growth economy.[6]

Yet in both recent economic history and contemporary economic theory enthusiasm for growth is anything but a marginal phenomenon. For one thing, it follows from the 'Eurocentric logic'[7] of quantitative growth, i.e. of an acceleration in time and expansion in space ('time-space-compression', as David Harvey calls it)[8] that is responsible for the contemporary process of globalization. It is important to note, however, that in this line of thought it is not simply 'growth' that matters but *efficient* growth. Capital does not like disorderly growth; it needs growth which serves the end of profitability. Conversely, profitability is the motor of growth. Therefore, not only the growth rate of GDP counts but also the profit rate and the accumulation rate. This raises complicated theoretical and methodological questions, especially in the era of globalization when it is no longer the national economy (or a given sector, such as manufacturing) which defines the arena for the formation of an average rate of profit.[9] Since surplus profits can be generated by both advanced productivity and low labour costs, the same profit rate may result from very different constellations of productivity, wages, and capital-labour relations. The social implications of 'growth' become indeterminate under these conditions.

Furthermore, in this line of thought the performance of the 'real economy' is usually interpreted without reference to financial globalization. This approach is seriously flawed because monetary capital is more mobile and flexible than ever before. Investment decisions (and therefore also growth rates) are not only determined by (industrial) profit rates but also by the global interest rates on financial assets. Since under conditions of financial globalization accumulation no longer necessarily takes place in the real economy, the relation between surplus value, profits, accumulation and real GDP-growth has become much looser. Under certain circumstances it is now more profitable to accumulate financial assets than to invest in real projects. Thus, prices of financial assets are inflated whereas commodity-prices (in particular in manufacturing, as shown by Duménil and Lévy)[10] are deflated — at least relative to the price-index of GDP. The broken link between real and monetary accumulation manifests itself as a paradoxical 'inflationary deflation'.[11]

A second general reason why most social scientists and politicians obsessively preach the ideology of triumphant growth is the idea that economic growth increases employment, incomes and taxes, and in this way provides resources for the alleviation of social conflicts, the expansion of development assistance, the eradication of poverty, the implementation of environmental standards, and so on. Steady growth was indeed the backbone of the corporatist 'Keynesian class compromise' associated with the 'Fordist' mode of regulation that characterized developed capitalism during the postwar period; and it is also assumed to offer a remedy for backwardness in the less-developed world — the argument of 'modernization' theory. Thus a recent article dedicated to the benefits of the 'Washington Consensus' declares: 'Without investment there is no economic growth, and without economic growth there is no sustainable economic policy …'[12]. The idea that there could be a mode of social cohesion other than the capitalist one based on high economic growth is, naturally, not considered.

Given these two mutually reinforcing general reasons for the obsession with growth, it is not surprising that disseminating policy proposals for the stimulation of growth is a common preoccupation of economists, whether they work within the Keynesian tradition or are of a more neoclassical and neoliberal persuasion.[13] Even many ecological economists also believe that it is not economic growth, but economic *stagnation*, that harms the environment.[14] This may not be entirely false with respect to 'dirty', i.e. visible and perceptible, pollution. However, 'clean' life style-pollution, e.g. the emission of greenhouse gases or the 'externalization' of ecologically destructive effects into remote areas or into the far future (nuclear waste), is without doubt also a side-effect of growth and welfare creation.[15]

In addition, as Immanuel Wallerstein has pointed out, growth-mania is of a systemic nature. It is enshrined in the institutions which allow the system to function as a 'totality': 'Capitalism as a historical system is defined by the fact that it makes structurally central and primary the endless accumulation of capital. This means that the institutions which constitute its framework reward those who pursue the endless accumulation of capital and penalize those who don't.'[16] Since the accumulation of capital is driven on by (the anticipation of) profits, Wallerstein's statement really summarizes the 'grand narrative' of the modern capitalist system: the processes of profit-making, accumulation, and institutional regulation, which give a degree of security to the system, simultaneously produce insecurity on all levels of social and individual life.

Wallerstein is confident that the contemporary long cycle of accumulation which has lasted for over a century will soon come to an end, and that capitalism will then enter a stage of systemic crisis. It is true that growth mania has no real ground in the real economy. But the continued construction of institutions that emphasize growth and further instil the profit motive in individual capitalists needs to be understood as an attempt to maintain social, economic and social stability and avoid a radical, 'paradigmatic' change. Whether it is dressed up as 'modernity' or 'post-modernity', whether it appeals to a 'Third Way' or a 'new economy', or as a rationale for overcoming backwardness, growth mania is nothing but a conservative reaction to the tendency to 'systemic crisis' identified by Wallerstein.

2 DISEMBEDDING

The transition to a 'growth economy' in the nineteenth century was just one aspect of the ongoing 'great transformation' of pre-capitalist social forms into a capitalist market economy.[17] The combination of commodification processes, the circulation-facilitating function of money and the ready availability of fuels formed a perfect 'trinity' that sparked capital's acceleration in time and expansion in space, i.e. accumulation and growth.[18] Markets have existed ever since people began to exchange products, but until the capitalist mode of production emerged markets remained 'slow' and growth rates low. Capitalism established a social, economic, political, cultural foundation, and the requisite sources of energy, which allowed for the mobilization and development of productive forces on a hitherto unknown scale. In the course of the 'primitive accumulation of capital', economic growth emancipated itself from the limited energy supply afforded by living labour. Thereafter, throughout the history of capitalism, workers have been replaced by means of production fuelled by (mainly) fossil energy. This process has been analyzed as the 'real subsumption of labour' or the 'production of relative surplus value'.[19] Capital and its institutions went through a process of 'autonomization' ('*Verselbständigung*') vis-à-vis society (e.g. popula-tion growth, human needs) and social control. This was the process conceptualized by Polanyi as the 'disembedding' of the market from the social system;[20] the former then imposed its logic — i.e. the rule of commodities, money and capital — on the latter.

Today, we have to be aware that, firstly, the process of disembedding was by no means an event unique to the nineteenth century; and, secondly, that the continuing process of disembedding embraces money in its many different forms and functions. Money not only circulates goods and services in 'ordinary markets'; as credit it obeys not only the rules of the real economy but also the 'logic' of a disembedded financial system operating on a global scale, partially disconnected from the real economy and increasingly serving to finance not only real (domestic and foreign) investment but also speculation.

Modern financial instruments are almost entirely disconnected from the real economy. As a result, it is possible for growth rates of turnover of financial assets to be many times higher than the growth of any indicator of 'real' activity. However, the disembedded financial sphere has certainly not become irrelevant to the functioning of the real economy or society. On the contrary, globally formed interest rates on financial assets require matching real growth rates and in this way exert a severe pressure on the real economy. This sets new *economic* limits to growth.

3 ECONOMIC LIMITS TO GROWTH

Economic growth is the result of a process of the transformation of energy and matter. In Marxian terms this is the concrete and use value aspect of growth. From this perspective, it should be evident that growth has its limits. After all, planet Earth's stocks of energy and matter are limited. We will discuss this in the next section. But economic growth is also the outcome of a social production process ruled by money (through the interest rate) and capital (through the profit rate). In the long run, capital requires a 'geometric' growth of inputs in order to maintain stable (relative) growth rates. Because the long-run geometric growth of absolute quantities is an absurd idea, high rates of (real) economic growth can only be sustained for a certain period of time. Nevertheless, the maintenance of high interest rates requires nothing less than the realization of precisely this absurdity and the dominant growth discourse presents it as a socially and economically feasible objective.

Statistical evidence (see Table 1) shows that (a) the absolute increases of GDP in highly developed countries remained positive and rather stable since the beginning of the 1960s (with merely cyclical fluctuations); and that (b) in the 1990s real increases were not only smaller in absolute terms, but were also achieved on the basis of an already higher level of real GDP. Growth rates inevitably declined.

Table 1: Absolute increases of real GDP (1991 prices) in billions of national currency, annual averages

Period and Country (Currency)	1960-69	1970-79	1980-89	1990-96	1960-96
USA (US$)	110.05	120	140.83	120.13	122.72
Japan (YEN)	11.98	9.68	12.18	7.02	11.27
Germany (DM)	46.92	45.52	36.64	76.3**	46.15*
France (FF)	140.1	139.31	123.3	68.35	134.19
Great Britain (BP)	8.26	8.85	13.37	6.88	9.56
Italy (LIT)	29.94	29.61	24.97	9.13	28.25

* 1960-1989 only
** Since 1990 unified Germany; Germany until 1989 West Germany only; Italy: 1000 bn Lira; Japan: 100 bn Yen

Source: Council of Economic Advisers (Sachverständigenrat zur Begutachtung der gesamtwirtschaftlichen Entwicklung, Jahresgutachten 1997/98, table 3*; author's calculations)

In Germany the highest increase in real GDP occurred in 1968, after the 'small' crisis of 1966-67; DM 102 billions translated into a real growth rate of GDP of 7.46%. In 1988 the same absolute increase would have produced a growth rate of only 4.43%. The increase actually achieved in that year equalled no more than DM 83.4 billions. The real growth rate was 3.62%, still rather high by historical standards. In the USA, the highest absolute increase in GDP (US$ 327.4 billion) during the period under investigation occurred in 1983; the real rate of growth for that year was 7.00%. In 1996 the same real increase would have produced a growth rate of 4.99%. In reality, GDP in that year grew only by a (still respectable) 2.76%.

In his long-term analysis of economic growth, Angus Maddison has measured the impact of labour productivity, hours worked and capital productivity on the annual average compounded growth rate. He shows that 'over the long term, working hours of the average person fell by half; labour input increased less than population…'. His findings clearly underline the positive relation between labour productivity and economic growth. '[L]abour productivity', he continues, 'rose a good deal faster than GDP per capita. From 1820 to 1992 Japanese labour productivity rose 46-fold compared with a 28-fold increase in per capital GDP'.[21]

But although labour productivity has obviously been the main motor of growth in the last century, a look at the growth figures since 1950 reveals that (1) total factor productivity fell in all countries under consideration, that (2) the capital-labour ratio increased until the mid-1970s and has decreased since then, and that (3) the capital coefficient increased (i.e. 'capital productivity' declined remarkably). The impact of the factors mentioned on the profit rate is negative. For the profit rate depends positively (1) on a distribution of income in favour of capital, i.e. on low real wages per worker; (2) on an increase in labour productivity; and negatively (3) on a growing capital-labour ratio (which, in value terms, indicates the rising organic composition of capital). In the long run, the profit rate tends to decline (as Marx showed), but of course this decline is cyclically modified. Therefore, during the last decade of wild deregulation, flexibilization and mobilization of all factors of production (i.e. of high pressures on individual and social wages, a redistribution of income in favour of capital, and decreasing costs of constant capital (especially of raw materials)), the profit rate went up sharply. Nevertheless, Wallerstein's expectation of a 'global profit squeeze'[22] is plausible in the long run.

Since the 1960s, in the industrialized countries rates of productivity growth, although declining, have still been higher than the rate of growth of manufacturing output.[23] The consequence has been the dismissal of workers and the emergence of an 'employment gap'. Growth tends to become 'jobless growth' — a development that can only be counteracted by a reduction of working time or the creation of jobs in the public and non-manufacturing private sector. The historical reduction of working hours per person described by Maddison reduces society's growth potential, but at the same time it provides a partial solution to the problem of the 'employment gap'. In Europe between 1973 and 1992 the number of people in employment rose from 138 to 148 million, while there was a 5% *decrease* in the number of hours worked — from 242 to 232 billion.[24]

Table 2: Annual percentage changes of output per hour and output in manufacturing in 10 industrialized countries, 1979-1995

Country	USA	Can	Japan	Bel	Fr	Ger	It	NL	Swe	GB
Manufacturing output	2.1	1.7	3.4	2.0	0.7	0.4	2.3	2.0	2.1	0.7
Output per hour	2.6	1.7	3.4	3.9	3.1	2.2	3.8	3.3	3.3	4.2

Source: Christopher Sparks and Mary Greiner, 'U.S. and foreign productivity and labor costs', *Monthly Labor Review*, February 1997, p. 29.

Table 2 summarizes the long-term development of productivity (output per hour worked) and growth (output in manufacturing). From the end of the 1970s until the mid-1990s, only Japan and Canada achieved an output-growth equal to productivity-growth; all other industrialized countries display the pattern which Maddison discovered as a long-term tendency from the early nineteenth century until the 1990s. The picture, however, changes when long-term GDP-growth is compared with growth rates of GDP per person employed, because the growth rate of labour productivity in services as compared with manufacturing is generally lower. The growth of 'unproductive labour'[25] has the effect of diminished productivity increases. Owing in particular to the growing weight of financial services in production and sales (for instance in the motor-car industry it has reached about 70%), 'unproductive' labour partly offsets the productivity increases achieved by 'productive' labour[26] and hence also the resulting widening employment gap. But because of the introduction of new communication-technologies into the service sector, this sector is likely to display higher rates of productivity growth in the future — a scenario already announced by the advocates of the 'new economy' — so there are no guarantees that the service sector's capacity to absorb a substantial part of the labour force can be sustained in the long run.

There are no easy solutions for the employment gap in dynamic capitalist societies. That is, structural unemployment must be considered an inevitable consequence of a strongly-performing economy. It is not, however, a state of affairs that people happily and voluntarily resign themselves to. The Left has always pursued 'alternative' (i.e. non-market) policies for achieving full employment. As the space for such alternative projects has sharply contracted, increasingly often the only remaining choice is for people to 'exit' from the system of paid employment. This can take the form of a passive acceptance of unemployment and its consequences or the active organization of new forms of labour. The latter way out refers to nothing but the 'informal sector' which is growing in all parts of the world and thus reducing the employment gap. The ILO notes that more than 80% of new jobs created in Latin America and Africa in recent years have been in the informal economy.[27] We return to the 'informal sector' in section 5 below.

4 ECOLOGICAL LIMITS TO GROWTH AND PRODUCTIVITY

High productivity increases constitute one of the basic features of industrial capitalism in general and of the Fordist system in particular. For this reason, productivity growth forms the starting point of Adam Smith's analysis of the 'origins of the wealth of nations': specialization and a deepening of the division of labour help to increase the output per working hour, and this causes income and wealth to rise.[28] David Ricardo extended the argument to the international division of labour, based on free trade. His 'law of comparative advantage' still serves as one of the most important theoretical foundations of modern economics, and is even enthusiastically embraced by the modern, Eurocentric globalization literature.[29]

Leaving aside the effects of efficiency gains, productivity can only be increased by putting more fixed capital into circulation and by consuming ever larger quantities of matter and energy.[30] Of course, the reproduction of capital(ism) as a whole remains crucially dependent on (surplus) value which can only be produced by labour. But capital's attempt to emancipate itself from its dependence on living labour by substituting the latter with fossil energy and machinery, establishes a new relationship to nature. Fordism, too, cannot be understood as a mere technical and social innovation. It also includes a new relationship to nature, for both the system of production and consumption and the mode of social regulation are heavily based on the use of fossil energy.[31]

It is clear that the material preconditions of the 'Western life style' cannot be established in all societies on earth without destroying nature to the point where human life on earth is jeopardized.[32] One of the first signs that the limits of environmental space have been reached is that the goods needed for production and consumption become 'oligarchic', i.e. reserved for an oligarchy able to secure its access to these resources with monetary claims. Those who do not possess monetary wealth are increasingly excluded from the consumption of goods and services. Consequently the number of poor people in the world is rising; in 1998 the World Bank counted 2.8 billion human beings living below the international poverty line of $2 per capita per day.[33]

But there are also absolute limits, not all of whose effects can be so easily avoided by the rich. Serious studies of the carrying capacity of global ecosystems and on the concept of 'environmental space' have demonstrated that these set objective limits to the process of economic growth.[34] By now (since the Rio Conference of 1992) it has become common sense that fossil resources are not only limited, but that their excessive use is responsible for the greenhouse effect and other ecological evils. It is in this way that the question of ecological sustainability asserts itself and reshapes the discourse of the social sciences in general and that of the economics of growth in particular. This should be sufficient reason to jettison any illusions concerning the benign nature of economic and financial globalization. Moreover, Western liberal (formal) democracy could only be globalized if the 'Western way of life' itself could be globalized.

But a situation of genuine globality, i.e. a world society based on equality and reciprocity (if not on solidarity), will never be achieved through *capitalist* globalization.

5 FINANCIAL LIMITS TO GROWTH

The interest rate constitutes a benchmark ('hard budget constraint')[35] for any economic undertaking. If capitalists fail to make a profit at least equal to the prevailing interest rate, their capital will be classified as non-profitable and loans made to them will be termed non-performing. As long as the real interest rate is lower than the real growth rate of GDP and of the 'marginal efficiency of capital' (i.e. the profit rate), returns from productive investments will exceed the monetary price of capital, and therefore borrowers in financial markets are likely to invest their loans in the real economy. This 'Keynesian state of affairs' came to an end, however, at the same time as the 'golden age' of Fordist expansion, namely in the course of the 1970s. Since the beginning of the 1980s, the real interest rates on global financial markets have by far exceeded the average real growth rate of GDP.[36] The real economy is 'depressed' by the financial system. The OECD gives three reasons for this configuration of finance and production: first, the growing fiscal deficits and the accumulation of public debt in the highly developed countries; second, higher inflationary risks and consequently a greater weight of risk factors in the formation of interest rates; and third, the globalization of financial markets since the second half of the 1970s, with the result that deregulated market mechanisms rather than public interventions began to exercise the function of credit allocation.[37] The political project of deregulation, liberalization, flexibilization and privatization has thus intensified global competition with regard to the stability of currencies and profitability of assets. The growing opportunities of exploiting interplace-differentials of profitability on a global scale, together with technical (information and communication technologies) and financial innovations (from hedge funds to derivatives and offshore financial centres), can be considered as the main impulse of globalization.

There is, however, a fourth reason for the high real interest rates that have prevailed since the beginning of the 1980s which is not recognized by the OECD: the crisis of American hegemony. The US trade balance deficit existing since 1971 (due to the outflow of capital) and the deterioration of the current account since the mid-1970s, together with the breakdown of the fixed exchange rate system of Bretton Woods, exerted downward pressure on the exchange rate of the US dollar, and spurred on inflation. A further deterioration of the (still hegemonic) dollar could only be prevented by means of an increase in US interest rates.[38] The period of high interest rates began in 1979 under the Carter administration and was rigorously continued by the Reagan administration. Its effects on the US exchange rate were positive, but proved devastating for debtors — in the USA (e.g. the Savings & Loans crisis), but above all in the Third World. The combination of high interest rates, rising oil prices and declining commodity prices triggered a Third World debt crisis which has not yet been overcome twenty years later. Table 3 shows the relation between real long-term interest rates and real growth of GDP in highly developed countries.

Table 3: Real growth rates and long term real interest rates in industrialized countries, 1960-1995

	Real GDP (annual growth rates in percent)				Real Long Term Interest Rates (percent per annum)			
	60-73	74-79	80-89	90-95	60-73	74-79	80-89	90-95
USA	4.0	2.6	2.4	1.9	1.5	-0.5	4.9	4.4
Japan	9.7	3.5	3.8	1.9	..	-0.2	4.3	3.9
Germany	4.3	2.4	2.0	2.0	2.6	3.1	4.8	3.8
France	5.4	2.7	2.1	1.3	1.9	-0.3	4.7	5.9
GB	3.1	1.5	2.4	1.0	..	-2.0	3.5	4.7

Source: OECD, *Historical Statistics 1960-1995*, Paris, 1997, p. 50 and p. 108.

According to the traditional Keynesian paradigm, the accumulation of capital is financed with loans provided by 'monetary wealth owners', i.e. by banks and institutional investors. The interest rate compels industrial capitalists to produce a profit that is large enough to service their loans as well as to fulfil their own accumulation requirements. In this way, the interest rate is linked to profits, employment and real capital accumulation, i.e. to the social organization of the accumulation regime and its political regulation. The interest rate itself is subject to regulation by (national) monetary authorities, above all the Central Bank. Although it is still a central premise of Keynesian theory, globalization has by now significantly eroded the ability of national monetary authorities to determine interest rates which are nowadays formed on global financial markets. On the one hand, *arbitrage* between different markets equalizes interest rate (and exchange rate) differentials; on the other hand, the differentials (calculated in 'basis points') are continuously recreated, which triggers new rounds of speculation.

Those who lend out monetary wealth (e.g. shares in firms or funds, or government bonds) thereby become *claim holders*. The international financial system works as a very powerful device for channelling surplus produced anywhere in the world to financial claim holders in the big financial centres. As a result, inequality is rising drastically. However, there are so many intermediaries in the chain between monetary claims, debt service and surplus transfer in real terms that under normal conditions these links are rarely visible for people and become recognizable only in times of a crisis. The financial system seems to be a 'virtual world' without any influence on production and reproduction, i.e. on people's living conditions and the natural environment. It is also often regarded as a kind of 'zero sum game' among players in the virtual world of the stock market: some lose what others gain and vice versa, and nothing real is happening. In reality it is another mechanism whereby financial asset holders gain at the expense of those who do not belong to this enviable species. US figures indicate that between 1989 and 1997, 86% of stock market gains went to the top 10% of households, while between 1983 and 1995 the bottom 40% of households lost 80% of their net worth.[39] These facts are in stark contrast with the World Bank's claim that there is a positive '1-to-1-relation' between growth and poverty alleviation. The 'post-modern' understanding of the financial system as de-linked from the real world of production and distribution is completely inadequate for grasping the contradictions and crisis tendencies generated by the global financial system. Some of these tendencies are addressed briefly here.

(1) Although global markets rely in principle on private initiative, the role of the state is indispensable for the working of the system. Of course, nation-states as well as international institutions provide the framework for the social and economic (world) order. With respect to global finance, however, the role of the state, as a public debtor vis-à-vis private monetary wealth owners, is that of a direct participant. The private financial system is fundamentally flawed because wealth owners (and claim holders) are private agents, whereas debtors in most cases are public institutions — or they become public ones when private debtors default. The debt crisis of the 1980s was, above all, caused by the default on public debt, whereas the debt crisis of the 1990s was one of private debt default. This change was an outcome of the policies of deregulation and privatization which have been pursued by international institutions and national governments alike. The Keynesian (as well as Marxian) notion of debtors as private (industrial) capitalists who service their debt by extracting and realizing surplus value has lost its validity in the era of global financial speculation. The debt service of private monetary claims has become 'socialized': governments are made to pass on the costs to their citizens. This is the reason why public debt has increased so remarkably in nearly all countries during the last twenty years. Where neither private debtors nor national states are in a position to service private debt, international institutions (notably the IMF) provide new credits on condition that the country in question adopts a policy package of structural adjustment. The primary aim of debt crisis management is to safeguard the assets of claim-holders from industrialized countries, and thus to prevent a 'systemic crisis'. In the medium and long term, these policies channel resources from the citizens of the indebted country to claim-holders in other countries. Thus the redistribution of real wealth (surplus value) between creditors and debtors is organized by official institutions, not just by the market. This is one of the ways in which capitalism contradicts 'free market' ideology; the latter's presentation of capitalist reality contrasts ever more sharply with people's experience of it.

(2) In most cases, so-called 'emerging markets' are characterized by high real growth rates and/or high nominal interest rates, both serving to attract foreign capital. When the growth rate declines or the currency is expected to depreciate, foreign capital immediately exits the 'emerging market' in order not to 'submerge'. The result of such capital flight is a further depreciation of the currency. In the cases of the Asian countries, Mexico, Brazil and Russia, curren-

cies depreciated between 50 and 80%. For several reasons, the effects were devastating: (a) the foreign debt to be serviced, which is denominated in foreign currency, shot up; (b) higher export volumes were required in order to earn constant export revenues; (c) higher import prices put an inflationary pressure on the economy; (d) for those who had hard currency at their disposal, whether citizens or foreigners, asset prices fell. The global extension of financial claims thus turns out to be a much more efficient device for the transfer of real value and the intensification of exploitation than, for instance, the plundering activities conducted under colonial rule from the sixteenth century onwards. The operating mode of the global credit system annihilates the potential comparative cost advantages of free trade. It follows yet again that the 1-to-1-relation between growth and poverty eradication, posited by the World Bank, is false.

(3) While on the one hand financial capital exerts *deflationary* pressures on the prices of commodities, on the other hand it produces an *inflation* of asset prices. This paradoxical situation of an '*inflationary deflation*'[40] is an indicator of the extent to which the global financial system has become disconnected from the real economy. A financial boom takes place alongside overproduction and overcapacity in the real economy: 'There is too much of everything. From cashmere to blue jeans, silver jewellery to aluminium cans ... Asia is the epicenter of the problem. Massive investment made on the assumption of continued high rates of growth resulted in broad overcapacity...'.[41] The postwar configuration of international institutions was tailored for a world of constant and moderate rates of inflation; it was designed to counter the deflationary pressures which had proved so destructive after the great crisis of 1929. During the 1930s, deflationary tendencies had resulted in a nearly complete collapse of the world market and nation-states' subsequent resort to protectionist measures and aggressively autarchic policies. Low nominal interest rates cause stock market quotations to rise.

However, in connection with the deflationary tendencies of product prices and real growth rates, even low real interest rates do not trigger new investment in the real economy because of its low profitability, as the case of Japan shows. Japan 'built massive industrial capacity at home and abroad throughout the 1980s, encouraged by low interest rates. In the late 1980s, Japanese monetary authorities lowered real interest rates to virtually nothing to help Japanese exporters survive a drastic strengthening of the yen in 1986. That policy fuelled a huge stock-market bubble...'.[42] However, the low real interest rates were still too high in relation to the expected profit rate. Overproduction or overaccumulation of capital triggered a crisis which had its origins in the 'real' sphere of the economy but first surfaced in the monetary sphere — as a stock market crisis in Japan and as a financial crisis in Asia, Russia and Brazil.

A situation characterized by these tendencies is extremely unstable and may cause the collapse of companies which suddenly find themselves in deep debt. This is the situation which Keynes referred to as a 'liquidity trap': although nominal interest rates are low, even near zero, nobody borrows because investments are not even expected to produce the minimum profit rate. Under such circumstances, it makes sense for individuals to transfer their liquid funds to places where they can earn higher short-term profits.

Nowadays, owners of monetary wealth, rather than 'traditional' industrial capitalists, determine the process of global accumulation. The real rate of return on capital is of less relevance for investment decisions than monetary interest rates. But the process of disembedding and de-linking have not created a completely autonomous financial sphere. The effects of the global financial system constitute the lived experience of people in countries hit by financial crises. The government of Indonesia speaks of at least 30 million people living below the poverty line. In Thailand poverty and informalization are growing visibly. In Russia hunger and malnutrition have returned on a broad scale. In large parts of the country money has disappeared and a pre-modern barter economy is on the rise — a different kind of 'virtual economy'.[43] Although the empirical data are better for some cases than for others, the tendency in other countries hit by the crisis is basically the same. All this points to the fact that the financial system continues to have a profound impact on real accumulation, labour and political regulation.

6 CONCLUSION:
GROWTH, NATURE, EMPLOYMENT AND MONEY

The problems discussed above arise because for decades both productivity growth and real interest rates have been considerably higher than real growth rates. These are expressions of the declining profit rate on capital in most parts of the world.[44] Unemployment and inequality are increasing on a global scale. For many, the most obvious and convenient way out of this precarious situation appears to be the stimulation of economic growth. In most policy proposals of national governments, international institutions such as the IMF or the World Bank, research institutes or the media, the stimulation of growth is understood as a panacea capable of resolving each and every global problem. But not only are there economic obstacles to an increase of real growth rates, there are also serious ecological limits to further quantitative growth (which, to be sure, also make themselves felt in economic and social terms). The question then becomes: is it possible to reduce the real interest rate or to curb the growth of labour productivity, rather than to continue to stimulate the real growth rate of GDP?

Lowering the interest rate was Keynes' proposal for the creation of new jobs. If the marginal efficiency of capital (the profit rate) could not be increased, the interest rate should be decreased (the 'euthanasia of the rentier').[45] However, this remedy is premised on the sovereignty of the monetary authorities with regard to the determination of the interest rate. As a result of market deregulation, exchange rate liberalization, and financial innovations, the formation of the interest rate on global financial markets can no longer be significantly influenced by national central banks. And global institutions with an adequate control over financial markets do not exist. Even the reform proposals developed after the Asian crisis of 1997 (e.g. by the 'Global Financial Stability Forum' — see the essay by Soederberg in this volume) do not go beyond recommendations for more transparency, prudent behaviour, improved surveillance, monitoring and safe-guards; there is no suggestion for interventions into the working of financial markets.

Germany's former finance minister, Oskar Lafontaine, tried to establish a degree of political control over global interest rates (by capping them) and exchange rates (by introducing target zones). He was well aware that such a project could only be realized in cooperation with the European Central Bank and in coordination with the other G7 (G8)-governments. But Lafontaine's proposals were indignantly rejected by 'the markets', the big TNCs, the 'inde-pendent' central bankers, public opinion, members of his own government, and — last but not least — leading mainstream economists. Lafontaine's project was the last attempt to break out of the dominant growth discourse and to reconquer economic policy sovereignty from 'the global markets'.

There is a third possible solution: reducing the rate of productivity growth. However, economic growth takes place through competition and is thus based on individual countries' efforts to improve their competitive position; this, in turn, requires increases in productivity. This means that the discourse of global-ization and competitiveness inevitably relies on productivity and the conditions required to improve it. This view was very clearly expressed by the Brazilian President Fernando Enrique Cardoso:

> Globalisation means competition founded on higher levels of productivity. That is to say more output per unit of labour. Unemployment has there-fore resulted from the very reason that makes an economy successfully competitive ... Flexibility of labour relations should also result in lower costs for the hiring of workers... In countries with large populations such as Brazil and India consideration must also be given to the operation of the so-called informal economy as far as job creation is concerned ...[46]

The consequence of 'successful' adjustment to the challenges of globalization is thus the creation of a dual economy: a formal part, competitive and highly productive, and an informal part that serves to absorb dismissed workers precisely because it is in general less productive than the formal one.[47] The rise of the informal economy obviously provides a 'solution' for the problem of growing unemployment. Its detrimental effects on labour conditions, wages, social security, health conditions and so on become virtues in the era of global-ization and under an accumulation regime or growth model which excludes growing parts of the global labour force from the formal employment system. The percentages of informal labour in total employment in 'Third World' countries range from 30% in Chile to 84% in Uganda.[48] In Latin America, between 1990 and 1996 the share of informal employment in non-agricultural sectors increased from 51.6% in 1990 to 57.4% in 1996.[49] In rural areas the percentage of informal work was even higher; the Brazilian Institute for Geography and Statistics (IBGE) considers as much as 90% of the labour force as informal. In Central and Eastern

Europe, too, the transition to a market economy and the crisis of 1997 pushed many workers out of the formal into the informal sector, and even in highly developed European countries, informal labour is also becoming more and more important. The percentage of people employed in the so-called 'shadow economy' constitutes between 7% and 16%, depending on the measure used, not counting the roughly 15% of the labour force which is self-employed.[50]

Informal labour, although normally less productive than formal labour, does not have to be unproductive in the Marxian sense. Therefore, the tendency of informalization may be a (partial) solution to the employment problem which does not exert pressure on the average profit rate. In fact, since wage costs in the formal sector are also influenced by the low level of pay for informal labour, the effect on the average profit rate is in all likelihood positive, particularly in those industries where big corporations take advantage of the informal labour of local suppliers.[51] We need to consider the possibility that globalization offers new opportunities for capital to bully working people. On the one hand, capital will try to increase the profit rate and boost productivity by the continued forced flexibilization of labour and wages. On the other hand, it will push redundant workers into the informal sector where they supply low-paid labour, engage in self-employment for local and regional markets, or organize services compensating for the functions that the welfare state has abandoned under pressure from capital.

The growth of the informal sector thus seems to offer a partial solution to the problem of unemployment. Much, though, depends on the measure of productivity that is applied. Normally, this is labour input (in hours worked) against saleable output. This measure is not arbitrary; it is an outcome of 'occidental rationality', the prevailing definitions of property rights, and the associated tendency to compare competitiveness in highly integrated world markets in monetary terms. Nevertheless, there is another measure that would make sense: labour input over the whole life cycle of a product including repairing, tuning and updating the product, and including the *non-traded outputs* of production, i.e. externalized pollution. A procedure of this kind could extend the rules of 'least cost planning' already used in energy markets to the markets for other products. Unfortunately, this measure would not be voluntarily accepted by 'the markets'. Markets and competition enforce acceleration, whereas environmental sustainability requires a policy of deceleration, i.e. restraining productivity increases.

Since the stimulation of growth fails to address the problems of unemployment, inequality and economic instability, a more viable solution could be provided by a combination of new forms of regulation of global financial markets in order to reduce the real interest rate, and a deceleration of productivity growth by means of an expansion of informal sectors and/or a transition to ecologically more sustainable production (and consumption) patterns (and lifestyles). Public awareness of the economic, financial, ecological, and social problems raised by globalization and possible solutions to them still has to be created — e.g. by social movements and NGOs. Without it, the illusory faith in 'growth triumphant' is

bound to live on and fuel further deregulation measures — while failing to overcome the crisis. At the end of the day, growth will stagnate or decline, the
environment will deteriorate further and the poor will remain poor and grow
ever more numerous — all because of the simple-minded notion that growth
rates can be advanced even while the limits of the environmental space have been
reached and the real economy is depressed by real interest rates higher than the
sustainable rate of real GDP growth. In an era of globalization, the conventional
paradigm of economic policy is in need of radical rethinking. Such a paradigmatic
shift, however, will necessarily have to be accompanied by practical efforts to re-
embed the global economic system in qualitatively new social relations and forms
of political regulation, on both local and global levels. It is to a transformation of
this kind that the movements against de-civilized capitalism, from Seattle to
Genoa, aspire.

NOTES

1   David Dollar and Aart Kraay, *Growth is Good for the Poor*, Development
     Research Group of the World Bank, http://worldbank.org/research, down-
     loaded June 2000.
2   This position has been quoted broadly by newspapers, underlining the neces-
     sity of economic growth as a solution for everything. For instance: 'there is
     no getting around the fact that economic growth must be the point of depar-
     ture for all improvements in living standards...' (Maza Livanos Cattaui,
     'Globalization Holds the Key to Ending World Poverty', *International
     Herald Tribune*, 30 June 2000). Similarly, the argument of Keith Marsden,
     published in *The Wall Street Journal Europe* (19 July 2000): 'To reduce
     poverty, grow the economy.' Not everybody in the World Bank shares the
     view outlined by Dollar and Kraay and supported by the new chief econo-
     mist Nicholas Stern. The editor responsible for the World Development
     Report 2000 Ravi Kanbur resigned from his office because he could not
     agree with the optimistic (and in many ways opportunistic) interpretation of
     Dollar and Kraay (Alan Beattle, 'World Bank Stages Intellectual Battle over
     Globalisation', *Financial Times*, 30 June 2000).
3   Richard A. Easterlin, *Growth Triumphant: The Twenty-first Century in
     Historical Perspective*, Ann Arbor: The University of Michigan Press, 1998.
4   Ibid., p.153. This statement seems to be a repetition of quite similar futur-
     ological predictions of perennial growth by Herman Kahn and his Hudson
     Institute in the 1960s (Fred Moseley, 'The United States Economy at the
     Turn of the Century: Entering a New Era of Prosperity?', *Capital and Class*,
     No 67, Spring 1999, p.26). The emphasis on the desirability and feasibility
     of growth is an essential aspect of the affirmative discourse of modernity
     because one of the most important features of modernity is its quantitative
     expansion in time and space.
5   Philip McMichael, quoted by John Bellamy Foster, 'The Crisis of the Earth.

Marx's Theory of Ecological Sustainability as Nature-Imposed Necessity for Human Production', *Organization & Environment*, Vol. 10, No. 3 (September), 1997, p. 126.

6   Paul Ekins and Michael Jacobs, 'Environmental Sustainability and the Growth of GDP: Conditions for Compatibility', in V. Bhaskar and A. Glyn., eds., *The North, The South and the Environment. Ecological Constraints and the Global Economy*, London: Earthscan, 1995.

7   Enrique Dussel, 'Beyond Eurocentrism: The World-System and the Limits of Modernity', in Frederic Jameson and Masao Miyosh, eds., *The Cultures of Globalization*, Durham and London: Duke University Press, 1998, p. 3 passim.

8   David Harvey, *Justice, Nature & the Geography of Difference*, Cambridge, Mass./ Oxford: Blackwell, 1996.

9   This has to be understood as a statement about the main trend in economic development. There are also counter-tendencies, such as protectionism between trading blocks, and the great divide between those parts of the world captured by the dynamics of globalization and the parts excluded from these.

10   Gérard Duménil and Dominique Lévy, 'Brenner on Distribution', *Historical Materialism*, 4 (summer), 1999.

11   Paul Mattick 'Die deflationäre Inflation', in Elmar Altvater, Volkhard Brandes, and Jochen Reiche, eds., *Inflation — Akkumulation — Krise, I, Handbuch 3*, Frankfurt-Main/ Köln: Europäische Verlagsanstalt, 1976.

12   Moisés Naím, 'Washington Consensus or Washington Confusion?', *Foreign Policy*, Spring, 2000, p. 96.

13   For example, World Bank, *World Development Report 2000/2001: Attacking Poverty*, Washington D.C., 2000.

14   Jügen Blazejczak, ed., *Zukunftsgestaltung ohne Wirtschaftswachstum? — Ergebnisse eines Workshops des DIW im Auftrag von Greenpeace Deutschland*, DIW — Diskussionspapier Nr. 168, Berlin, May 1998; Andrew Glyn, 'Northern Growth and Environmental Constraints', in V. Bhaskar and Andrew Glyn, eds., *The North The South and the Environment. Ecological Constraints and the Global Economy*, London: Earthscan, 1995.

15   For the distinction between 'clean' and 'dirty' pollution, see Elmar Altvater and Birgit Mahnkopf, *Grenzen der Globalisierung. Ökonomie, Politik, Ökologie in der Weltgesellschaft*, Münster: Westfälisches Dampfboot, 1999.

16   Immanuel Wallerstein, 'A Left Politics for the 21st Century? Or, Theory and Praxis Once Again', *New Political Science*, Vol. 22, Number 2, 2000.

17   Karl Polanyi, *The Great Transformation*, Frankfurt am Main: Suhrkamp, 1978.

18   The question of whether this process began, as Polanyi assumes, in the eighteenth and nineteenth century or much earlier, in the course of the long sixteenth century, is an important one; however, this question cannot be answered here.

19   Karl Marx, *Das Kapital*, Marx-Engels Werke 23, Vol. 1, chapter 14.

20 Polanyi, *The Great Transformation*; Anthony Giddens, *Konsequenzen der Moderne*, Frankfurt/M.: Suhrkamp, 1995; Altvater and Mahnkopf, *Grenzen der Globalisierung*, chapter 3, pp. 90-123.

21 Angus Maddison, *Monitoring the World Economy 1820-1992*, Paris: OECD, 1995, p. 40. Data presented and interpreted by Crafts support Maddison's statement; see Crafts, *Globalization and Growth*.

22 Wallerstein, 'A Left Politics for the 21st Century?', p. 147.

23 The German Institute for Economic Research (DIW) calculated an annual average increase of production value in German manufacturing of 1.7% and an average increase of labour productivity (production value per person employed) of 3.7% from 1991 to 1999 (Deutsches Institut für Wirtschaftsforschung, Wochenbericht 14/2000).

24 Mario Pianta, 'Trasformazioni del lavoro: il "terzo settore"', *Parolechiave*, 14/15 dicembre 1997, Roma: Dozelli editore, 1998.

25 For the USA, see Fred Moseley, 'The United States Economy at the Turn of the Century: Entering a New Era of Prosperity?', *Capital and Class*, 67, Spring 1999, pp. 28-9.

26 This is not the place to discuss the Marxist concepts of productive and unproductive labour. For Marx, a worker is productive insofar as he (she) produces surplus value. Unproductive labour, by contrast, does not produce, but merely consumes surplus value. This does not mean that it is useless. Unproductive labour is often necessary in order to sustain a social process of reproduction. The distinction between productive and unproductive labour is not coterminous with that between production and services, or with that between material and immaterial labour. It is, however, obvious that productivity increases can be 'consumed' by unproductive workers, so that there is some margin for the creation of jobs outside the 'productive' sector.

27 Paul E. Bangasser, *The ILO and the Informal Sector: an Institutional History*, Geneva: ILO, 2000 (http://www.ilo.org/public/english/employment/strat/publ/ep00-9.htm, downloaded 24 October 2000); Victor Tokman, 'La informilidad en los anos noventa: situatción actual y perspectivas', in Jorge Carpio and Irene Novacovsky, eds., *De igual a igual. El desafío del Estado ante los nuevos problemas sociales*, Buenos Aires: Siempro, FLACSO, 1999. For European countries, see Sergio Bologna and Andrea Fumagalli, eds., *Il Lavoro Autionomo di Seconda Generazione. Scenari del Postfordismo in Italia*, Milano: Feltrinelli, 1997; Friedrich Schneider and Dominik Enste, *Schattenwirtschaft und Schwarzarbeit. Umfang, Ursachen, Wirkungen und wirtschaftspolitische Empfehlungen*, München und Wien: R. Oldenbourg, 2000.

28 Adam Smith, *An Inquiry into the Nature and Causes of The Wealth of Nations*, Chicago: The University of Michigan Press, 1976 [1776].

29 David Held, Anthony McGrew, David Goldblatt and Jonathan Perraton, *Global Transformations. Politics, Economics and Culture*, Cambridge: Polity Press, 1999.

30 In any given production process, the material content of a unit of output may

decrease. But in the long run, and on a society-wide scale, the consumption of energy and matter is increasing so rapidly that the carrying capacity of ecosystems has become overstretched. If it were possible to reduce the consumption of matter and energy by simple technical measures, many difficulties during climate and water negotiations would not arise.

31 Elmar Altvater, *Der Preis des Wohlstands*, Münster: Westfälisches Dampfboot, 1992; Elmar Altvater, *The Future of the Market*, London: Verso, 1993.

32 Robert Goodland, Herman Daly, and Serafy El, *Nach dem Brundtland-Bericht: Umweltverträgliche wirtschaftliche Entwicklung*, Bonn: Deutsche UNESCO-Kommission, 1992.

33 World Bank et. al, *Global Poverty Report*.

34 Wuppertal Institut für Klima, Umwelt, Energie, *Zukunftsfähiges Deutschland. Ein Beitrag zu einer global nachhaltigen Entwicklung*, ed. by BUND and Misereor, Basel/Boston/Berlin: (Birkhäuser), 1996; annual reports of the Worldwatch Institute Report (1984 etc.): Lester R. Brown et al., *State of the World*, New York/ London: W.W. Norton.

35 János Kornai, 'The Soft Budget Constraint', *Kyklos*, vol. 39, No. 1, 1986.

36 OECD, *Economic Outlook*, June 1993, Paris.

37 Ibid., pp.29-31.

38 The macro-economic policy trilemma first articulated by Mundell (that a government can achieve only two of the following three objectives — a fixed or at least stable exchange rate, the free movement of capital, and an independent monetary policy) has been resolved by using high interest rates to protect the exchange rate in the face of a more and more deregulated financial market (i.e. independent monetary policy has been sacrificed).

39 Gates, 'People-ized Ownership Patterns', p. 437.

40 Mattick, 'Die deflationäre Inflation'.

41 Jonathan Friedland and Leslie Chang, 'Spreading Fat Slows Global Economy', *Wall Street Journal*, 30 November 1998. The authors continue their argument by pointing to the fact that China and other new competitors have been throwing masses of cheap goods on already satiated markets. But the main culprit of global overproduction is Japan.

42 Ibid.

43 Clifford G. Gaddy and Barry W. Ickes, 'Russia's Virtual Economy', *Foreign Affairs*, September/ October 1998.

44 Robert Brenner, 'The Economics of Global Turbulence', *New Left Review*, No 229.

45 John M. Keynes, *The General Theory of Employment, Interest and Money*, London/Melbourne/Toronto: Macmillan, 1964 [1936].

46 The text of the speech can be accessed on the Internet: http://www.brasil.emb.nw.dc.us/fpst06gl.htm; downloaded 24 January 1999; in Portuguese: Folha de Sao Paulo, 28 January 1996.

47 ILO, *Employment, Incomes and Equality*, Geneva: ILO, 1972; Alejandro Portes, 'The Informal Economy. Perspectives from Latin America', in Susan

Pozo, ed., *Exploring the Underground Economy, Studies of Illegal and Unreported Activity*, Michigan: W.E. Upjohn Institute for Employment Research, 1996.

48   See http://www.ilo.org/public/spanish/region...temas/worker/doc/otros/iv/ii/i/index.htm

49   Victor Tokman, 'La informilidad en los anos noventa: situatción actual y perspectivas', in: Jorge Carpio/ Irene Novacovsky, eds., *De igual a igual. El desafío del Estado ante los nuevos problemas sociales*, Buenos Aires: Siempro, FLACSO, p. 82.

50   Paolo Perulli, 'Die Bedeutung der informellen Arbeit im postindustriellen Europa', in Elmar Altvater and Birgit Mahnkopf, coord., *Die Ökonomie eines friedlichen Europa, Ziele — Hindernisse — Wege*, Münster: Agenda-Verlag, 2000.

51   This is the theme of a growing number of books, e.g. Kathryn Ward, ed., *Women Workers and Global Restructuring*, Ithaka N.Y: ILR Press., 1990; Altvater and Mahnkopf, *Grenzen der Globalisierung*.

THE ART OF RENT:
GLOBALIZATION, MONOPOLY AND THE
COMMODIFICATION OF CULTURE

DAVID HARVEY

That culture has become a commodity of some sort is undeniable. Yet there is also a widespread belief that there is something so special about certain cultural products and events (be they in the arts, theatre, music, cinema, architecture or more broadly in localized ways of life, heritage, collective memories and affective communities) as to set them apart from ordinary commodities like shirts and shoes. While the boundary between the two sorts of commodities is highly porous (perhaps increasingly so) there are still grounds for maintaining an analytic separation. It may be, of course, that we distinguish cultural artefacts and events because we cannot bear to think of them as anything other than authentically different, existing on some higher plane of human creativity and meaning than that located in the factories of mass production and consumption. But even when we strip away all residues of wishful thinking (often backed by powerful ideologies) we are still left with something very special about those products designated as 'cultural'. How, then, can the commodity status of so many of these phenomena be reconciled with their special character?

Furthermore, the conditions of labour and the class positionality of the increasing number of workers engaged in cultural activities and production (more than 150,000 'artists' were registered in the New York metropolitan region in the early 1980s and that number may well have risen to more than 250,000 by now) is worthy of consideration. They form the creative core of what Daniel Bell calls 'the cultural mass' (defined as not the creators but the transmitters of culture in the media and elsewhere).[1] The political stance of this creative core as well as of the cultural mass is not inconsequential. In the 1960s, recall, the art colleges were hot-beds of radical discussion. Their subsequent pacification and professionalization has seriously diminished agitational politics. Revitalizing such institutions as centres of political engagement and mobilizing the political and agitational powers of cultural producers is surely a worthwhile objective for the left even if it takes some special adjustments in socialist strategy and thinking to do so. A critical examination of the relations between culture, capital and socialist alternatives can here be helpful as a prelude to mobilizing what has always been a powerful voice in revolutionary politics.

1. MONOPOLY RENT AND COMPETITION

I begin with some reflections on the significance of monopoly rents to understanding how contemporary processes of economic globalization relate to localities and cultural forms. The category of 'monopoly rent' is an abstraction drawn from the language of political economy.[2] To the cultural producers themselves, usually more interested in affairs of aesthetics (sometimes even dedicated to ideals of art for art's sake), of affective values, of social life and of the heart, such a term might appear far too technical and arid to bear much weight beyond the possible calculi of the financier, the developer, the real estate speculator and the landlord. But I hope to show that it has a much grander purchase: that properly constructed it can generate rich interpretations of the many practical and personal dilemmas arising in the nexus between capitalist globalization, local political-economic developments and the evolution of cultural meanings and aesthetic values.

All rent is based on the monopoly power of private owners of certain portions of the globe. Monopoly rent arises because social actors can realize an enhanced income stream over an extended time by virtue of their exclusive control over some directly or indirectly tradable item which is in some crucial respects unique and non-replicable. There are two situations in which the category of monopoly rent comes to the fore. The first arises because social actors control some special quality resource, commodity or location which, in relation to a certain kind of activity, enables them to extract monopoly rents from those desiring to use it. In the realm of production, Marx argues, the most obvious example is the vineyard producing wine of extraordinary quality that can be sold at a monopoly price. In this circumstance 'the monopoly price creates the rent'.[3] The locational version would be centrality (for the commercial capitalist) relative to, say, the transport and communications network or proximity (for the hotel chain) to some highly concentrated activity (such as a financial centre). The commercial capitalist and the hotelier are willing to pay a premium for the land because of accessibility. These are the indirect cases of monopoly rent. It is not the land, resource or location of unique qualities which is traded but the commodity or service produced through their use. In the second case, the land or resource is directly traded upon (as when vineyards or prime real estate sites are sold to multinational capitalists and financiers for speculative purposes). Scarcity can be created by withholding the land or resource from current uses and speculating on future values.

Monopoly rent of this sort can be extended to ownership of works of art (such as a Rodin or a Picasso) which can be (and increasingly are) bought and sold as investments. It is the uniqueness of the Picasso or the site which here forms the basis for the monopoly price.

The two forms of monopoly rent often intersect. A vineyard (with its unique Chateau and beautiful physical setting) renowned for its wines can be traded at a monopoly price directly as can the uniquely flavoured wines produced on that land. A Picasso can be purchased for capital gain and then leased to someone else who puts it on view for a monopoly price. The proximity to a financial centre can be traded directly as well as indirectly to, say, the hotel chain that uses it for its own purposes. But the difference between the two rental forms is important. It is unlikely (though not impossible), for example, that Westminster Abbey and Buckingham Palace will be traded directly (even the most ardent privatizers might balk at that). But they can be and plainly are traded *upon* through the marketing practices of the tourist industry (or in the case of Buckingham Palace, by the Queen).

Two contradictions attach to the category of monopoly rent. Both of them are important to the argument that follows. First, while uniqueness and particularity are crucial to the definition of 'special qualities', the requirement of tradability means that no item can be so unique or so special as to be entirely outside the monetary calculus. The Picasso has to have a money value as does the Monet, the Manet, the aboriginal art, the archaeological artefacts, the historic buildings, the ancient monuments, the Buddhist temples, and the experience of rafting down the Colorado, being in Istanbul or on top of Everest. There is, as is evident from such a list, a certain difficulty of 'market formation' here. For while markets have formed around works of art and, to some degree around archaeological artefacts (there are some well-documented cases, as with Australian Aboriginal art, of what happens when some art form gets drawn into the market sphere) there are plainly several items on this list that are hard to incorporate directly into a market (this is the problem with Westminster Abbey). Many items may not even be easy to trade upon indirectly. The contradiction here is that the more easily marketable such items become the less unique and special they appear. In some instances the marketing itself tends to destroy the unique qualities (particularly if these depend on qualities such as wilderness, remoteness, the purity of some aesthetic experience, and the like). More generally, to the degree that such items or events are easily marketable (and subject to replication by forgeries, fakes, imitations or simulacra) the less they provide a basis for monopoly rent. I am put in mind here of the student who complained about how inferior her experience of Europe was compared to Disney World:

> At Disney World all the countries are much closer together, and they show you the best of each country. Europe is boring. People talk strange languages and things are dirty. Sometimes you don't see anything interesting in Europe for days, but at Disney World something different happens all the time and people are happy. It's much more fun. It's well designed.[4]

While this sounds a laughable judgement it is sobering to reflect on how much Europe is attempting to redesign itself to Disney standards (and not only for the benefit of American tourists). But, and here is the heart of the contradiction, the more Europe becomes Disneyfied, the less unique and special it becomes. The bland homogeneity that goes with pure commodification erases monopoly advantages. Cultural products become no different from commodities in general. 'The advanced transformation of consumer goods into corporate products or "trade mark articles" that hold a monopoly on aesthetic value', writes Wolfgang Haug, 'has by and large replaced the elementary or "generic" products', so that 'commodity aesthetics' extends its border 'further and further into the realm of cultural industries'.[5] Conversely, every capitalist seeks to persuade consumers of the unique and non-replicable qualities of their commodities (hence name-brands, advertising, and the like). Pressures from both sides threaten to squeeze out the unique qualities that underlie monopoly rents. If the latter are to be sustained and realized, therefore, some way has to be found to keep some commodities or places unique and particular *enough* (and I will later reflect on what this might mean) to maintain a monopolistic edge in an otherwise commodified and often fiercely competitive economy.

But why, in a neoliberal world where competitive markets are supposedly dominant, would monopoly of any sort be tolerated let alone be seen as desirable? We here encounter the second contradiction which, at root, turns out to be a mirror image of the first. Competition, as Marx long ago observed, always tends towards monopoly (or oligopoly) simply because the survival of the fittest in the war of all against all eliminates the weaker firms.[6] The fiercer the competition the faster the trend towards oligopoly if not monopoly. It is therefore no accident that the liberalization of markets and the celebration of market competition in recent years has produced incredible centralization of capital (Microsoft, Rupert Murdoch, Bertelsmann, financial services, and a wave of takeovers, mergers and consolidations in airlines, retailing and even in older industries like automobiles, petroleum, and the like). This tendency has long been recognized as a troublesome feature of capitalist dynamics, hence the anti-trust legislation in the United States and the work of the monopolies and mergers commissions in Europe. But these are weak defences against an over-whelming force.

This structural dynamic would not have the importance it does were it not for the fact that capitalists actively cultivate monopoly powers. They thereby realize far-reaching control over production and marketing and hence stabilize their business environment to allow for rational calculation and long-term planning, the reduction of risk and uncertainty, and more generally guarantee themselves a relatively peaceful and untroubled existence. The visible hand of the corporation, as Alfred Chandler terms it, has consequently been of far greater importance to capitalist historical geography than the invisible hand of the market made so much of by Adam Smith and paraded ad nauseam before us in recent years as the guiding power in the neoliberal ideology of contemporary globalization.[7]

But it is here that the mirror image of the first contradiction comes most clearly into view: market processes crucially depend upon the individual monopoly of capitalists (of all sorts) over ownership of the means of production including finance and land. All rent, recall, is a return to the monopoly power of private ownership of any portion of the globe. The monopoly power of private property is, therefore, both the beginning point and the end point of all capitalist activity. A non-tradable juridical right exists at the very foundation of all capitalist trade, making the option of non-trading (hoarding, withholding, miserly behaviour) an important problem in capitalist markets. Pure market competition, free commodity exchange and perfect market rationality are, therefore, rather rare and chronically unstable devices for coordinating production and consumption decisions. The problem is to keep economic relations competitive *enough* while sustaining the individual and class monopoly privileges of private property that are the foundation of capitalism as a political-economic system.

This last point demands one further elaboration to bring us closer to the topic at hand. It is widely but erroneously assumed that monopoly power of the grand and culminating sort is most clearly signalled by the centralization and concentration of capital in mega-corporations. Conversely, small firm size is widely assumed, again erroneously, to be a sign of a competitive market situation. By this measure, a once competitive capitalism has become increasingly monopolized over time. The error arises in part because of a rather too facile application of Marx's arguments concerning the 'law of the tendency for the centralization of capital', ignoring his counter-argument that centralization 'would soon bring about the collapse of capitalist production if it were not for counteracting tendencies, which have a continuous decentralizing effect'.[8] But it is also supported by an economic theory of the firm that generally ignores its spatial and locational context, even though it does accept (on those rare occasions where it deigns to consider the matter) that locational advantage involves 'monopolistic competition'. In the nineteenth century, for example, the brewer, the baker and the candlestick maker were all protected to considerable degree from competition in local markets by the high cost of transportation. Local monopoly powers were omnipresent (even though firms were small in size), and very hard to break, in everything from energy to food supply. By this measure nineteenth century capitalism was far less competitive than now.

It is at this point that the changing conditions of transport and communications enter in as crucial determining variables. As spatial barriers diminished through the capitalist penchant for 'the annihilation of space through time', many local industries and services lost their local protections and monopoly privileges.[9] They were forced into competition with producers in other locations, at first relatively close by, but then with producers much further away. The historical geography of the brewing trade is very instructive in this regard. In the nineteenth century most people drank local brew because they had no choice. By the end of the nineteenth century beer production and consumption in Britain had been regionalized to a considerable degree and remained so until the 1960s (foreign imports, with the exception of Guinness, were unheard of). But then the market became national (Newcastle Brown and Scottish Youngers appeared in London and the South) before becoming international (imports suddenly became all the rage). If one drinks local brew now it is by choice, usually out of some mix of principled attachment to locality or because of some special quality of the beer (based on the technique, the water, or whatever) that differentiates it from others. Plainly, the economic space of competition has changed in both form and scale over time.

The recent bout of globalization has significantly diminished the monopoly protections given historically by high transport and communications costs while the removal of institutional barriers to trade (protectionism) has likewise diminished the monopoly rents to be procured by that means. But capitalism cannot do without monopoly powers and craves means to assemble them. So the question upon the agenda is how to assemble monopoly powers in a situation where the protections afforded by the so-called 'natural monopolies' of space and location, and the political protections of national boundaries and tariffs, have been seriously diminished if not eliminated.

The obvious answer is to centralize capital in mega-corporations or to set up looser alliances (as in airlines and automobiles) that dominate markets. And we have seen plenty of that. The second path is to secure ever more firmly the monopoly rights of private property through international commercial laws that regulate all global trade. Patents and so-called 'intellectual property rights' have consequently become a major field of struggle through which monopoly powers more generally get asserted. The pharmaceutical industry, to take a paradigmatic example, has acquired extraordinary monopoly powers in part through massive centralizations of capital and in part through the protection of patents and licensing agreements. And it is hungrily pursuing even more monopoly powers as it seeks to establish property rights over genetic materials of all sorts (including those of rare plants in tropical rain forests traditionally collected by indigenous inhabitants). As monopoly privileges from one source diminish so we witness a variety of attempts to preserve and assemble them by other means.

I cannot possibly review all of these tendencies here. I do want, however, to look more closely at those aspects of this process that impinge most directly upon the problems of local development and cultural activities. I wish to show first, that there are continuing struggles over the definition of the monopoly powers that might be accorded to location and localities and that the idea of 'culture' is more and more entangled with attempts to reassert such monopoly powers precisely because claims to uniqueness and authenticity can best be articulated as distinctive and non-replicable cultural claims. I begin with the most obvious example of monopoly rent given by 'the vineyard producing wine of extraordinary quality that can be sold at a monopoly price'.

2. ADVENTURES IN THE WINE TRADE

The wine trade, like brewing, has become more and more international over the last thirty years and the stresses of international competition have produced some curious effects. Under pressure from the European Community, for example, international wine producers have agreed (after long legal battles and intense negotiations) to phase out the use of 'traditional expressions' on wine labels, which could eventually include terms like 'Chateau' and 'domaine' as well as generic terms like 'champagne', 'burgundy', 'chablis' or 'sauterne'. In this way the European wine industry, led by the French, seeks to preserve monopoly rents by insisting upon the unique virtues of land, climate and tradition (lumped together under the French term 'terroir') and the distinctiveness of its product certified by a name. Reinforced by institutional controls like 'appellation controlée' the French wine trade insists upon the authenticity and originality of its product which grounds the uniqueness upon which monopoly rent can be based.

Australia is one of the countries that agreed to this move. Chateau Tahbilk in Victoria obliged by dropping the 'Chateau' from its label, airily pronouncing that 'we are proudly Australian with no need to use terms inherited from other countries and cultures of bygone days'. To compensate, they identified two factors which, when combined, 'give us a unique position in the world of wine'. Theirs is one of only six worldwide wine regions where the meso-climate is dramatically influenced by inland water mass (the numerous lakes and local lagoons moderate and cool the climate). Their soil is of a unique type (found in only one other location in Victoria) described as red/sandy loam coloured by a very high Ferric-oxide content, which 'has a positive effect on grape quality and adds a certain distinctive regional character to our wines'. These two factors are brought together to define 'Nagambie Lakes' as a unique Viticultural Region (to be authenticated, presumably, by the Australian Wine and Brandy Corporation's Geographical Indications Committee, set up to identify Viticultural regions throughout Australia). Tahbilk thereby establishes a counter-claim to monopoly rents on the grounds of the unique mix of environmental conditions in the region where it is situated. It does so in a way that parallels and competes with the uniqueness claims of 'terroir' and 'domaine' pressed by French wine producers.[10]

But we then encounter the first contradiction. All wine is tradable and therefore in some sense comparable no matter where it is from. Enter Robert Parker and the *Wine Advocate* which he publishes regularly. Parker evaluates wines for their taste and pays no particular mind to 'terroir' or any other cultural-historical claims. He is notoriously independent (most other guides are supported by influential sectors of the wine industry). He ranks wines on a scale according to his own distinctive taste. He has an extensive following in the United States, a major market. If he rates a Chateau wine from Bordeaux 65 pts and an Australian wine 95 pts then prices are affected. The Bordeaux wine producers are terrified of him. They have sued him, denigrated him, abused him and even physically assaulted him. He challenges the bases of their monopoly rents.[11]

Monopoly claims, we can conclude, are as much 'an effect of discourse' and an outcome of struggle as they are a reflection of the qualities of the product. But if the language of 'terroir' and tradition is to be abandoned then what kind of discourse can be put in its place? Parker and many others in the wine trade have in recent years invented a language in which wines are described in terms such as 'flavor of peach and plum, with a hint of thyme and gooseberry'. The language sounds bizarre but this discursive shift, which corresponds to rising international competition and globalization in the wine trade, takes on a distinctive role, reflecting the commodification of wine consumption along standardized lines.

But wine consumption has many dimensions that open paths to profitable exploitation. For many it is an aesthetic experience. Beyond the sheer pleasure (for some) of a fine wine with the right food, there lie all sorts of other referents within the Western tradition that track back to mythology (Dionysus and Bacchus), religion (the blood of Jesus and communion rituals) and traditions celebrated in festivals, poetry, song and literature. Knowledge of wines and 'proper' appreciation is often a sign of class and is analyzable as a form of 'cultural' capital (as Bourdieu would put it). Getting the wine right may have helped to seal more than a few major business deals (would you trust someone who did not know how to select a wine?). Style of wine is related to regional cuisines and thereby embedded in those practices that turn regionality into a way of life marked by distinctive structures of feeling (it is hard to imagine Zorba the Greek drinking Mondavi Californian jug wine, even though the latter is sold in Athens airport).

The wine trade is about money and profit but it is also about culture in all of its senses (from the culture of the product to the cultural practices that surround its consumption and the cultural capital that can evolve alongside among both producers and consumers). The perpetual search for monopoly rents entails seeking out criteria of speciality, uniqueness, originality and authenticity in each of these realms. If uniqueness cannot be established by appeal to 'terroir' and tradition, or by straight description of flavour, then other modes of distinction must be invoked to establish monopoly claims and discourses devised to guarantee the truth of those claims (the wine that guarantees seduction or the wine that goes with nostalgia and the log fire, are current advertising tropes in the USA). In practice what we find within the wine trade is a host of competing discourses, all with different truth claims about the uniqueness of the product. But, and here I go back to my starting point, all of these discursive shifts and swayings, as well as many of the shifts and turns that have occurred in the strategies for commanding the international market in wine, have at their root not only the search for profit but also the search for monopoly rents. In this the language of authenticity, originality, uniqueness, and special unreplicable qualities looms large. The generality of a globalized market produces, in a manner consistent with the second contradiction I earlier identified, a powerful force seeking to guarantee not only the continuing monopoly privileges of private property but the monopoly rents that derive from depicting commodities as incomparable.

3. URBAN ENTREPRENEURIALISM, MONOPOLY RENT AND GLOBAL FORMS

Recent struggles within the wine trade provide a useful model for understanding a wide range of phenomena within the contemporary phase of globalization. They have particular relevance to understanding how local cultural developments and traditions get absorbed within the calculi of political economy through attempts to garner monopoly rents. It also poses the question of how much the current interest in local cultural innovation and the resurrection and invention of local traditions attaches to the desire to extract and appropriate such rents. Since capitalists of all sorts (including the most exuberant of international financiers) are easily seduced by the lucrative prospects of monopoly powers, we immediately discern a third contradiction: that the most avid globalizers will support local developments that have the potential to yield monopoly rents even if the effect of such support is to produce a local political climate antagonistic to globalization! Emphasizing the uniqueness and purity of local Balinese culture may be vital to the hotel, airline and tourist industry, but what happens when this encourages a Balinese movement that violently resists the 'impurity' of commercialization? The Basque country may appear a potentially valuable cultural configuration precisely because of its uniqueness, but ETA with its demand for autonomy and preparedness to take violent action is not amenable to commercialization. Let us probe a little more deeply into this contradiction as it impinges upon urban development politics. To do so requires, however, briefly situating that politics in relation to globalization.

Urban entrepreneurialism has become important both nationally and internationally in recent decades. By this I mean that pattern of behaviour within urban governance that mixes together state powers (local, metropolitan, regional, national or supranational) and a wide array of organizational forms in civil society (chambers of commerce, unions, churches, educational and research institutions, community groups, NGOs, etc.) and private interests (corporate and individual) to form coalitions to promote or manage urban/regional development of some sort or other. There is now an extensive literature on this topic which shows that the forms, activities and goals of these governance systems (variously known as 'urban regimes', 'growth machines' or 'regional growth coalitions') vary widely depending upon local conditions and the mix of forces at work within them.[12]

The role of this urban entrepreneurialism in relation to the neoliberal form of globalization has also been scrutinized at length, most usually under the rubric of local-global relations and the so-called 'space-place dialectic'. Most geographers who have looked into the problem have rightly concluded that it is a categorical error to view globalization as a causal force in relation to local development. What is at stake here, they rightly argue, is a rather more complicated relationship across scales in which local initiatives can percolate upwards to a global scale and vice versa at the same time as processes within a particular definition of scale — interurban and interregional competition being the most obvious examples — can rework the local/regional configurations of what globalization is about.

Globalization should not be seen, therefore, as an undifferentiated unity but as a geographically articulated patterning of global capitalist activities and relations.[13]

But what, exactly, does it mean to speak of 'a geographically articulated patterning'? There is, of course, plenty of evidence of uneven geographical development (at a variety of scales) and at least some cogent theorizing to understand its capitalistic logic. Some of it can be understood in conventional terms as a search on the part of mobile capitals (with financial, commercial and production capital having different capacities in this regard) to gain advantages in the production and appropriation of surplus values by moving around. Trends can indeed be identified which fit with simple models of 'a race to the bottom' in which the cheapest and most easily exploited labour power becomes the guiding beacon for capital mobility and investment decisions. But there is plenty of countervailing evidence to suggest that this is a gross oversimplification when projected as a monocausal explanation of the dynamics of uneven geographical development. Capital in general just as easily flows into high wage regions as into low and often seems to be geographically guided by quite different criteria to those conventionally set out in both bourgeois and Marxist political economy.

The problem in part (but not wholly) derives from the habit of ignoring the category of landed capital and the considerable importance of long-term investments in the built environment which are by definition geographically immobile (except in the relative accessibility sense). Such investments, particularly when they are of a speculative sort, invariably call for even further waves of investments if the first wave is to prove profitable (to fill the convention centre we need the hotels which require better transport and communications, which calls for an expansion of the convention centre…). So there is an element of circular and cumulative causation at work in the dynamics of metropolitan area investments (look, for example, at the whole Docklands redevelopment in London and the financial viability of Canary Wharf which pivots on further investments both public and private). This is what urban growth machines are often all about: the orchestration of investment process dynamics and the provision of key public investments at the right place and time to promote success in inter-urban and inter-regional competition.

But this would not be as attractive as it is were it not for the ways in which monopoly rents might also be captured. A well-known strategy of developers, for example, is to reserve the choicest and most rentable piece of land in some development in order to extract monopoly rent from it after the rest of the project is realized. Savvy governments with the requisite powers can engage in the same practices. The government of Hong Kong, as I understand it, is largely financed by controlled sales of public domain land for development at very high monopoly prices. This converts, in turn, into monopoly rents on properties which makes Hong Kong very attractive to international financial investment capital working through property markets. Of course, Hong Kong has other uniqueness claims, given its location, upon which it can also trade very vigorously in offering monopoly advantages. Singapore, incidentally, set out to capture monopoly rents and was highly successful in so doing in somewhat similar fashion, though by very different political-economic means.

Urban governance of this sort is mostly oriented to constructing patterns of local investments not only in physical infrastructures such as transport and communications, port facilities, sewage and water, but also in the social infrastructures of education, technology and science, social control, culture and living quality. The aim is to create sufficient synergy within the urbanization process for monopoly rents to be created and realized by both private interests and state powers. Not all such efforts are successful, of course, but even the unsuccessful examples can partly or largely be understood in terms of their failure to realize monopoly rents. But the search for monopoly rents is not confined to the practices of real estate development, economic initiatives and government finance. It has a far wider application.

4. COLLECTIVE SYMBOLIC CAPITAL, MARKS OF DISTINCTION AND MONOPOLY RENTS

If claims to uniqueness, authenticity, particularity and speciality underlie the ability to capture monopoly rents, then on what better terrain is it possible to make such claims than in the field of historically constituted cultural artefacts and practices and special environmental characteristics (including, of course, the built, social and cultural environments)? All such claims are, as in the wine trade, as much an outcome of discursive constructions and struggles as they are grounded in material fact. Many rest upon historical narratives, interpretations and meanings of collective memories, significations of cultural practices, and the like: there is always a strong social and discursive element at work in the construction of such claims. Once established, however, such claims can be pressed home hard in the cause of extracting monopoly rents since there will be, in many people's minds at least, no other place than London, Cairo, Barcelona, Milan, Istanbul, San Francisco or wherever, in which to gain access to whatever it is that is supposedly unique to such places.

The most obvious example is contemporary tourism, but I think it would be a mistake to let the matter rest there. For what is at stake here is the power of collective symbolic capital, of special marks of distinction that attach to some place, which have a significant drawing power upon the flows of capital more generally. Bourdieu, to whom we owe the general usage of these terms, unfortunately restricts them to individuals (rather like atoms floating in a sea of structured aesthetic judgements) when it seems to me that the collective forms (and the relation of individuals to those collective forms) might be of even greater interest.[14] The collective symbolic capital which attaches to names and places like Paris, Athens, New York, Rio de Janeiro, Berlin and Rome is of great import and gives such places great economic advantages relative to, say, Baltimore, Liverpool, Essen, Lille and Glasgow. The problem for these latter places is to raise their quotient of symbolic capital and to increase their marks of distinction so as to better ground their claims to the uniqueness that yields monopoly rent. Given the general loss of other monopoly powers through easier transport and communications and the reduction of other barriers to trade, the struggle for collective symbolic capital becomes even more important as a basis for monopoly rents. How else can we explain the splash made by the Guggenheim Museum in Bilbao with its signature Gehry architecture? And how else can we explain the willingness of major financial institutions, with considerable international interests, to finance such a signature project?

The rise of Barcelona to prominence within the European system of cities, to take another example, has in part been based on its steady amassing of symbolic capital and its accumulating marks of distinction. In this the excavation of a distinctively Catalan history and tradition, the marketing of its strong artistic accomplishments and architectural heritage (Gaudi, of course) and its distinctive marks of lifestyle and literary traditions, have loomed large, backed by a deluge of books, exhibitions, and cultural events that celebrate distinctiveness. This has all been show-cased with new signature architectural embellishments (Norman Foster's radio communications tower and Meier's gleaming white Museum of Modern Art in the midst of the somewhat degraded fabric of the old city) and a whole host of investments to open up the harbour and the beach, reclaim derelict lands for the Olympic Village (with cute reference to the utopianism of the Icarians) and turn what was once a rather murky and even dangerous nightlife into an open panorama of urban spectacle. All of this was helped on by the Olympic Games which opened up huge opportunities to garner monopoly rents (Samaranch, President of the International Olympic Committee, just happened to have large real estate interests in Barcelona).[15]

But Barcelona's initial success appears headed deep into the first contradiction. As opportunities to pocket monopoly rents galore present themselves on the basis of the collective symbolic capital of Barcelona as a city (property prices have skyrocketed as the Royal Institute of British Architects awards the whole city its medal for architectural accomplishments), so their irresistible lure draws more and more homogenizing multinational commodification in its wake. The later phases of waterfront development look exactly like every other in the western world, the stupefying congestion of the traffic leads to pressures to put boulevards through parts of the old city, multinational stores replace local shops, gentrification removes long-term residential populations and destroys older urban fabric, and Barcelona loses some of its marks of distinction. There are even unsubtle signs of Disneyfication. This contradiction is marked by questions and resistance. Whose collective memory is to be celebrated here (the anarchists like the Icarians who played such an important role in Barcelona's history, the republicans who fought so fiercely against Franco, the Catalan nationalists, immigrants from Andalusia, or a long-time Franco ally like Samaranch)? Whose aesthetics really count (the famously powerful architects of Barcelona like Bohigas)? Why accept Disneyfication of any sort?

Debates of this sort cannot easily be stilled precisely because it is clear to all that the collective symbolic capital that Barcelona has accumulated depends upon values of authenticity, uniqueness and particular non-replicable qualities. Such marks of local distinction are hard to accumulate without raising the issue of local empowerment, even of popular and oppositional movements. At that point, of course, the guardians of collective symbolic and cultural capital (the museums, the universities, the class of benefactors, and the state apparatus) typically close their doors and insist upon keeping the riff-raff out (though in Barcelona the Museum of Modern Art, unlike most institutions of its kind, has remained amazingly and constructively open to popular sensibilities). And if that fails, then the state can step in with anything from something like the 'decency committee' set up by Mayor Giuliani to monitor cultural taste in New York City to outright police repression. Nevertheless, the stakes here are of significance. It is a matter of determining which segments of the population are to benefit most from the collective symbolic capital to which everyone has, in their own distinctive ways, contributed both now and in the past. Why let the monopoly rent attached to that symbolic capital be captured only by the multinationals or by a small powerful segment of the local bourgeoisie? Even Singapore, which created and appropriated monopoly rents so ruthlessly and so successfully (mainly out of its locational and political advantage) over the years, saw to it that the benefits were widely distributed through housing, health care and education.

For the sorts of reasons that the recent history of Barcelona exemplifies, the knowledge and heritage industries, the vitality and ferment of cultural production, signature architecture and the cultivation of distinctive aesthetic judgements have become powerful constitutive elements in the politics of urban entrepreneurialism in many places (particularly in Europe). The struggle to accumulate marks of distinction and collective symbolic capital in a highly competitive world is on. But this entrains in its wake all of the localized questions about whose collective memory, whose aesthetics, and who benefits. Neighbourhood movements in Barcelona make claims for recognition and empowerment on the basis of symbolic capital and can assert a political presence in the city as a result. The initial erasure of all mention of the slave trade in the reconstruction of Albert Dock in Liverpool generated protests on the part of the excluded population of Caribbean background and produced new political solidarities among a marginalized population. The holocaust memorial in Berlin has sparked long-drawn out controversies. Even ancient monuments such as the Acropolis, whose meaning one would have thought by now would be well-settled, are subject to contestation.[16] Such contestations can have widespread, even if indirect, political implications. The amassing of collective symbolic capital, the mobilization of collective memories and mythologies and appeals to specific cultural traditions are important facets to all forms of political action (both left and right).

Consider, for example, the arguments that have swirled around the reconstruction of Berlin after German reunification. All manner of divergent forces are colliding there as the struggle to define Berlin's symbolic capital unfolds. Berlin, rather obviously, can stake a claim to uniqueness on the basis of its potential to mediate between east and west. Its strategic position in relation to the uneven geographical development of contemporary capitalism (with the opening up of the ex-Soviet Union) confers obvious advantages. But there is also another kind of battle for identity being waged which invokes collective memories, mythologies, history, culture, aesthetics and tradition. I take up just one particularly troubling dimension of this struggle, one that is not necessarily dominant and whose capacity to ground claims to monopoly rent under global competition is not at all clear or certain.

A faction of local architects and planners (with the support of certain parts of the local state apparatus) seeks to revalidate the architectural forms of eighteenth and nineteenth century Berlin and in particular to highlight the architectural tradition of Schinkel, to the exclusion of much else. This might be seen as a simple matter of elitist aesthetic preference, but it is freighted with a whole range of meanings that have to do with collective memories, monumentality, the power of history and political identity in the city. It is also associated with that climate of opinion (articulated in a variety of discourses) which defines who is or is not a Berliner and who has a right to the city in narrowly defined terms of pedigree or adhesion to particular values and beliefs. It excavates a local history and an architectural heritage that is charged with nationalist and romanticist connotations. In a context where the ill-treatment of and violence against immigrants is widespread, it may even offer tacit legitimation to such actions. The Turkish population (many of whom are now Berlin-born) have suffered many indignities and have largely been forced out from the city centre. Their contribution to Berlin as a city is ignored. Furthermore, this romanticist/nationalist architectural style fits with a traditional approach to monumentality that broadly replicates in contemporary plans (though without specific reference and maybe even without knowing it) Albert Speer's plans (drawn up for Hitler in the 1930s) for a monumental foreground to the Reichstag.

This is not, fortunately, all that is going on in the search for collective symbolic capital in Berlin. Norman Foster's reconstruction of the Reichstag, for example, or the collection of international modernist architects brought in by the multinationals (largely in opposition to local architects) to dominate the Potsdamer Platz, are hardly consistent with it. And the local romanticist response to the threat of multinational domination could, of course, merely end up being an innocent element of interest in a complex achievement of diverse marks of distinction for the city (Schinkel, after all, has considerable architectural merit and a rebuilt eighteenth century castle could easily lend itself to Disneyfication). But the potential downside of the story is of interest because it highlights how the contradictions of monopoly rent can all too easily play out. Were these narrower plans and exclusionary aesthetics and discursive practices to become dominant, then the collective symbolic capital created would be hard to trade freely upon because its very special qualities would position it largely outside globalization and inside an exclusionary political culture that rejects much of what globalization is about. The collective monopoly powers that urban governance can command can be directed towards opposition to the banal cosmopolitanism of multinational globalization but in so doing ground localized nationalism.

The dilemma — veering so close into pure commercialization as to lose the marks of distinction that underlie monopoly rents or constructing marks of distinction that are so special as to be very hard to trade upon — is perpetually present. But, as in the wine trade, there are always strong discursive gambits involved in defining what is or is not so special about a product, a place, a cultural form, a tradition, an architectural heritage. Discursive battles become part of the game and advocates (in the media and academia, for example) gain their audience as well as their financial support in relation to these processes. There is much to achieve, for example, by appeals to fashion (interestingly, being a centre of fashion is one way for cities to accumulate considerable collective symbolic capital). Capitalists are well-aware of this and must therefore wade into the culture wars, as well as into the thickets of multiculturalism, fashion and aesthetics, because it is precisely through such means that monopoly rents stand to be gained, if only for a while. And if, as I claim, monopoly rent is always an object of capitalist desire, then the means of gaining it through interventions in the field of culture, history, heritage, aesthetics and meanings must necessarily be of great import for capitalists of any sort. The question then arises as to how these cultural interventions can themselves become a potent weapon of class struggle.

5. MONOPOLY RENT AND SPACES OF HOPE

By now critics will complain at the seeming economic reductionism of the argument. I make it seem, they will say, as if capitalism produces local cultures, shapes aesthetic meanings and so dominates local initiatives as to preclude the development of any kind of difference that is not directly subsumed within the circulation of capital. I cannot prevent such a reading, but this would be a perversion of my message. For what I hope to have shown, by invoking the concept of monopoly rent within the logic of capital accumulation, is that capital has ways to appropriate and extract surpluses from local differences, local cultural variations and aesthetic meanings of no matter what origin. European tourists can now get commercialized tours of New York's Harlem (with a gospel choir thrown in). The music industry in the United States succeeds brilliantly in appropriating the incredible grass roots and localized creativity of musicians of all stripes (almost invariably to the benefit of the industry rather than the musicians). Even politically explicit music which speaks to the long history of oppression (as with some forms of rap and Jamaican reggae and Kingston Dance Hall music) gets commodified and circulated widely throughout the world. The shameless commodification and commercialization of everything is, after all, one of the hallmarks of our times.

But monopoly rent is a contradictory form. The search for it leads global capital to value distinctive local initiatives (and in certain respects the more distinctive and, in these times, the more transgressive the initiative the better). It also leads to the valuation of uniqueness, authenticity, particularity, originality and all manner of other dimensions to social life that are inconsistent with the homogeneity presupposed by commodity production. And if capital is not to totally destroy the uniqueness that is the basis for the appropriation of monopoly rents (and there are many circumstances where it has done just that and been roundly condemned for so doing) then it must support a form of differentiation and allow of divergent and to some degree uncontrollable local cultural developments that can be antagonistic to its own smooth functioning. It can even support (though cautiously and often nervously) all manner of 'transgressive' cultural practices precisely because this is one way in which to be original, creative and authentic as well as unique.

It is within such spaces that all manner of oppositional movements can form even presupposing, as is often the case, that oppositional movements are not already firmly entrenched there. The problem for capital is to find ways to co-opt, subsume, commodify and monetize such cultural differences just enough to be able to appropriate monopoly rents therefrom. In so doing, capital often produces widespread alienation and resentment among the cultural producers who experience first-hand the appropriation and exploitation of their creativity for the economic benefit of others, in much the same way that whole populations can resent having their histories and cultures exploited through commodification. The problem for oppositional movements is to speak to this widespread alienation and exploitation and to use the validation of particularity, uniqueness, authenticity, culture and aesthetic meanings in ways that open up new possibilities and alternatives. At the very minimum this means resistance to the idea that authenticity, creativity and originality are an exclusive product of bourgeois rather than working class, peasant or other non-capitalistic historical geographies, and that they are there merely to create a more fertile terrain from which monopoly rents can be extracted by those who have both the power and the compulsive inclination to do so. It also entails trying to persuade contemporary cultural producers to redirect their anger towards commodification, market domination and the capitalistic system more generally. It is, for example, one thing to be transgressive about sexuality, religion, social mores and artistic conventions, but quite another to be transgressive in relation to the institutions and practices of capitalist domination. The widespread though usually fragmented struggles that exist between capitalistic appropriation and past and present cultural creativity can lead a segment of the community concerned with cultural matters to side with a politics opposed to multinational capitalism and in favour of some more compelling alternative based on different kinds of social and ecological relations.

It is by no means certain, however, that attachment to 'pure' values of authenticity, originality and an aesthetic of particularity of culture is an adequate foundation for a progressive oppositional politics. It can all too easily veer into local, regional or nationalist identity politics of the neofascist sort of which there are already far too many troubling signs throughout much of Europe as well as elsewhere. This is a central contradiction with which the left must in turn wrestle. The spaces for transformational politics are there because capital can never afford to close them down. They provide opportunities for socialist opposition. They

can be the *locus* of exploration of alternative life-styles or even of social philosophies (much as Curitiba in Brazil has pioneered ideas of urban ecological
sustainability to the point of reaping considerable fame from its initiatives). They
can, as in the Paris Commune of 1871 or in the numerous urban-based political
movements around the world in 1968, be a central element in that revolutionary
ferment that Lenin long ago called 'the festival of the people'. The fragmented
oppositional movements to neoliberal globalization as manifest in Seattle,
Prague, Melbourne, Bangkok and Nice and then more constructively, as the
2001 World Social Forum in Porto Alegre (in opposition to the annual meetings
of the business elites and government leaders in Davos), indicate such an alternative politics. It is not wholly antagonistic to globalization but wants it on very
different terms. The striving for a certain kind of cultural autonomy and support
for cultural creativity and differentiation is a powerful constitutive element in
these political movements.

It is no accident, of course, that it is Porto Alegre rather than Barcelona, Berlin,
San Francisco or Milan that has opened itself to such oppositional initiatives.[17] For
in that city, the forces of culture and of history are being mobilized by a political movement (led by the Brazilian Workers' Party) in a quite different way,
seeking a different kind of collective symbolic capital to that flaunted in the
Guggenheim Museum in Bilbao or the extension to the Tate Gallery in London.
The marks of distinction being accumulated in Porto Alegre derive from its
struggle to fashion an alternative to globalization that does not trade on
monopoly rents in particular or cave in to multinational capitalism in general. In
focusing on popular mobilization it is actively constructing new cultural forms
and new definitions of authenticity, originality and tradition. That is a hard path
to follow, as previous examples such as the remarkable experiments in Red
Bologna in the 1960s and 1970s show. Socialism in one city is not a viable
concept. But then it is quite clear that no alternative to the contemporary form
of globalization will be delivered to us from on high either. It will have to come
from within multiple local spaces conjoining into a broader movement.

It is here that the contradictions faced by capitalists as they search for monopoly
rent assume a certain structural significance. By seeking to trade on values of
authenticity, locality, history, culture, collective memories and tradition they
open a space for political thought and action within which socialist alternatives
can be both devised and pursued. That space deserves intense exploration and
cultivation by oppositional movements that embrace cultural producers and
cultural production as a key element in their political strategy. There are abundant historical precedents for mobilizing the forces of culture in this way (the role
of constructivism in the creative years of the Russian Revolution from 1918-26
is just one of many historical examples to be learned from). Here lies one of the
key spaces of hope for the construction of an alternative kind of globalization.
One in which the progressive forces of culture can seek to appropriate and undermine those of capital rather than the other way round.

NOTES

1   Daniel Bell, *The Cultural Contradictions of Capitalism*, New York: Basic Books 1978, p. 20; David Harvey, *The condition of postmodernity*, Oxford: Basil Blackwell, 1989, pp. 290-1; 347-9; Brandon Taylor, *Modernism, post-modernism, realism: a critical perspective for art*, Winchester: Winchester School of Art Press, 1987, p. 77.

2   The general theory of rent to which I am appealing is presented in David Harvey, *The limits to capital*, Oxford: Basil Blackwell, 1982, chapter 11.

3   Karl Marx, *Capital, vol. 3*, New York: International Publishers, 1967, pp. 774-5.

4   Cited in Douglas Kelbaugh, *Common Place*, Seattle: University of Washington Press, 1997, p. 51.

5   Wolfgang Haug, 'Commodity aesthetics', *Working Papers Series*, Department of Comparative American Cultures, Washington State University, 2000, p. 13.

6   I have summarized Marx's views on monopoly in Harvey, *The Limits to Capital*, chapter 5.

7   Alfred Chandler, *The Visible Hand: The Managerial Revolution in American Business*, Cambridge, Mass.: Harvard University Press, 1977.

8   Marx, *Capital vol. 3*, p.246. See also Harvey, *The Limits to Capital*, chapter 5.

9   Karl Marx, *Grundrisse*, Harmondsworth, Middlesex: Penguin, 1973, pp. 524-39. For a general expansion of this argument see Harvey, *The Limits to Capital*, chapter 12; *The Condition of Postmodernity*, part 3 and for a specific application of the concept see William Cronon, *Nature's Metropolis*, New York, Norton, 1991.

10   Tahbilk Wine Club, *Wine Club Circular*, Issue 15, June 2000, Tahbilk Winery and Vineyard, Tahbilk, Victoria, Australia

11   William Langewiesche, 'The million dollar nose', *Atlantic Monthly*, vol. 286, No. 6, December 2000, pp. 11-22.

12   Bob Jessop, 'An entrepreneurial city in action: Hong Kong's emerging strategies in preparation for (inter) urban competition', *Urban Studies*, 37 (12), 2000, pp. 2287-2313 and David Harvey, 'From managerialism to entrepreneurialism: the transformation of urban governance in late capitalism', *Geografiska Annaler*, 71B, 1989, pp. 3-17.

13   See Kevin Cox, ed., *Spaces of Globalization: Reasserting the Power of the Local*, New York: Guilford Press, 1997.

14   Pierre Bourdieu, *Distinction: A Social Critique of the Judgement of Taste*, London: Routledge and Kegan Paul, 1984.

15   Donald McNeill, *Tales from the New Barcelona: Urban Change and the European Left*, New York: Routledge, 1999.

16   Argyro Loukaki, 'Whose genius loci: contrasting interpretations of the Sacred Rock of the Athenian Acropolis', *Annals of the Association of American Geographers*, 87 (2), 1997, pp. 306-29.

17   Rebecca Abers, 'Practicing radical democracy: lessons from Brazil', *Plurimondi*, 1 (2) 1999, 67-82; and Ignacio Ramonet, 'Porto Alegre', *Le Monde Diplomatique*, No. 562, 1, January 2001.

DIGITAL POSSIBILITIES, MARKET REALITIES: THE CONTRADICTIONS OF COMMUNICATIONS CONVERGENCE

GRAHAM MURDOCK AND PETER GOLDING

CONVERGED MEDIA, ERODED CITIZENSHIP

Advances in communications technology over the last forty years have generated considerable rhetoric and hyperbole about the transformations in social relationships they would both enable and compel. In particular, the emergence of the computer as a tool for storing and rapidly manipulating increasingly large sets of data, and its convergence with telecommunications systems providing the means for swift and extensive transmission and carriage, has been the root of endless discussion about the presumed arrival of an 'information society'.[1] The convergence of these developments, both technologically and organizationally, with the broadcasting industry has completed a fusion offering genuinely massive transformations in the worlds of work and leisure.

The technological core of these developments, digitization, involves the common transformation of a variety of modes of communication — print, speech, audio-visual materials, raw data — into a common form as electronic binary digits. This allows each form to be readily transmuted into any of the others, and for all of them to be stored, retrieved, manipulated, and distributed with unprecedented facility through the merged apparatuses of computing and telecommunications. Our concern here is not with the arguments about whether or not these innovations permit us to diagnose a transformation into a new kind of society. Suffice to say we understand them to have made major impacts on the relations between human beings and their environments, and between differing groups and social sectors, but in ways that largely enhance or recompose existing relationships. In short, the political economy of these changes will identify shifts in the structuring of late modernity and of contemporary capitalism, but nothing more epochal.

Three contradictions arising from current changes are of significance here.[2] First, the massively increased efficiency by which information (a term used here generically) can be produced and distributed allows a substantial reduction in unit costs which could, in principle, create major enhancements in aggregate consumption and thus of standards of living and welfare. In practice, however, there is a strong correlation between those societies in which digitization — the 'information revolution' — is most advanced, and those with rising inequalities of condition.

Secondly, new means of accessing and producing information appear to lower the entry costs for new producers. On the internet anyone can be an author. The distinction between producer and consumer becomes malleable, and the power of the consumer in the ideal market, based on perfect knowledge of price and product choices, is substantially, indeed unprecedentedly, realizable. At the same time, however, distribution systems, not least the internet itself, have become enmeshed in the same convergence — economic rather than technological — that has transformed it increasingly into the model of older communication forms. They have become vehicles for the promotion and marketing of branded goods, and of the communication services themselves, as they become rapidly incorporated into the ownership of major communication multinationals.

Thirdly, the rise of faster, simpler, and more mobile forms of communication, and their diffusion to large sections of the population of richer societies, either through individual or civic access, opens visions of 'cyberdemocracy', the Jeffersonian ideal of direct citizen-government dialogue in which communication both comprehensively reveals the process and substance of government to the citizen, and also reconstructs the methods of accountability of elected representatives and public officials to the population, and the demand for it. At the same time the emergence of the 'public relations state', and widespread concern about the apparent torpor and disenchantment of electorates in many western countries with the mainstream political apparatus, suggest a less healthy set of consequences. Thus, while the widespread use and availability of new forms of political communication have set in place the possibility of radical transformations of organization and mobilization, they also facilitate considerable centralization of political control, and the further migration of power from the civic political to the private corporate sector.

As soon as a modern market-based media system emerged in the second half of the nineteenth century, critics identified a fundamental contradiction between the requirements of democracy and the logic of capitalist enterprise. The ideal of citizenship promised everyone the right to participate fully and equally in contemporary social life and to help determine the forms it might take in the future. Commentators rightly saw that this promise could only be made good if access to the basic material and symbolic resources required by participation was universalized. In the cultural sphere, this meant guaranteeing access to the widest possible range of (1) the information required to make considered personal and political decisions, (2) frameworks of interpretation, explanation and evaluation and debates over their relative strengths and limits, (3) representations of coexisting and competing aspirations and ways of life, and (4) opportunities for active participation in shaping debates and representations. Many observers argued that the capitalist cultural industries failed to fulfil these conditions due to the endemic tensions between a conception of citizenship rooted in a vision of the common good and the private interests of owners and advertisers.

These deficits were addressed by a prolonged struggle to institutionalize the public interest within the communications system. This took two main forms, regulation and public subsidy. These devices assumed many of their modern characteristics in the inter-war period with the coincidental emergence of the two dominant forms of modern communications — mass broadcasting and domestic telecommunications connections — and the consolidation of a mass democratic system based (albeit incompletely) on universal suffrage. Regulation, the preferred choice in the United States, set out, firstly, to ring-fence the scope of capital by imposing restrictions on ownership and advertising, and secondly, to promote the public interest by requiring companies to forego some opportunities for profit maximization and deliver certain basic cultural resources for citizenship. These included minimal or zero domestic telephone call charges, broadcast programmes for unprofitable minorities, and air-time for rights of reply. In contrast, European societies sought to provide cultural resources for citizenship by operating both broadcasting and telecommunications organizations as public utilities funded out of taxation.

This dual system, in which public sector broadcasting and telecommunications corporations coexisted with commercial print, film, and music industries, survived, with modifications (such as the introduction of a strongly regulated commercial television system in Britain in the mid-1950s), until the late 1970s. From that point on, the communications landscape has been transformed by an accelerating process of marketization. This is the essential context within which convergence must be viewed.

The central dynamic of convergence is economic not technological. The development of fixed and mobile devices that combine the present functions of the television set, desktop computer and telephone/fax machine is not the main story. Instead of asking, as many techno-enthusiasts do, 'What can digital technologies do and where might they take us?', we need to ask 'How is the political economy of the communications system shifting under the impact of market-led convergence and what are the consequences of this movement for patterns of corporate control and popular use? Will fatter communications companies mean a thinning out of citizenship?'

THE FORWARD MARCH OF MARKETS ACCELERATED

Marketization is both an institutional and ideological intervention. It entails three analytically distinct processes. Firstly, the size and operating scope of the market sector is progressively increased by colonizing space previously occupied by public sector institutions and by relaxing or removing the public interest requirements of regulation. Secondly, market criteria of success — cost-saving, commercial revenue generation, and customer maximization — are established as the primary yardsticks against which the performance of all organizations, including those still formally in the public sector, are evaluated. Thirdly, audiences and users of communications facilities are addressed primarily as consumers with a sovereign right to have their personal needs met, rather than as citizens whose right to full social participation carries with it an obligation to recognize and respect the needs and aspirations of others. By linking demands for expression and satisfaction to the logic of purchase and possession, marketization promotes consumerism as the meta-ideology of the age.

Institutionally, marketization is propelled by four basic dynamics.

1. **Privatization**. The sale of strategic public assets to private investors and the reconstitution of public enterprises as profit-seeking corporations, as in the transfer of the telecommunications business of Britain's state owned PTT (post, telegraph and telephone utility) to a new commercial concern, British Telecom.

2. **Liberalization**. Opening up monopoly or restricted markets to competition. Significant examples include the final liberalization in 1998 of the telecommunications markets in the member states of the European Union previously controlled by PTTs , and the introduction of commercial cable and satellite television services into European television markets historically dominated by either a single public broadcasting organization (as in Norway and Sweden) or by a strongly regulated public/commercial duopoly (as in the UK).

These two processes, taken together, have massively increased the scale and scope of corporate reach in key communications sectors. Corporations' room for manoeuvre within this enlarged space has been significantly extended by a third process.

3. **The reorientation of regulation** from underwriting the public interest to securing a business environment that gives major corporations maximum scope for action. The celebration of enterprise and commercial innovation that underpins this shift also extends to the public sector, producing a fourth dynamic:

4. **Corporatization**, whereby public sector organizations are encouraged and/or compelled (through cuts to their core public funding) to pursue commercial opportunities more aggressively and to adopt corporate forms of organization.

The onward institutional and ideological march of these core elements of marketization has been propelled by the relentless rise of variants of neoliberal economic thinking. Faced with increased popular and elite disillusion with the performance of public enterprises and dirigiste policies, governments throughout the capitalist world in the late 1970s began to listen more attentively to the siren song of the new marketers. The conservative governments of President Reagan in the United States and Mrs Thatcher in Britain became emblematic of the emerging market orthodoxy, though it was arguably the 1984 (Labour) government in New Zealand — the country that had established the first modern welfare state — that insisted most zealously that there was 'no alternative' to comprehensive marketization.[3] Nor was structural readjustment confined to mature capitalist economies. It was globalized, firstly by the conditions attached to loans to developing countries, and secondly by shifts in the policy regimes of the world's three most populous societies — China, India and Russia. As a result of the pro-market reforms initiated by Deng in China and Rajiv Ghandi and his successors in India, and the collapse of the Soviet regime, by the end of the end of 1980s all three regions were integrated to varying degrees into the new marketized world order.

This redrawing of the global map has established a new economic playing field for the major corporations. The aim now is to re-write the rules to confer additional advantages on leading players. As capitalism's centre of gravity moves from manufacturing to services, so these sectors account for an increasing share of economic activity. Historically under welfare capitalist regimes, however, key services have tended to be operated primarily as public enterprises. In some countries (including the UK) some sectors such as water, gas, and voice telephony have been privatized (by selling state assets to private investors) and liberalized (by allowing competition in supply), but in other major areas, notably education, health and some cultural services, public sector enterprises retain a substantial and often a dominant presence. Corporate awareness of the untapped potential for profits in these sectors has made the service industries a major target for further marketization, spearheaded by the General Agreement on Trade in Services (GATS) being promoted by the World Trade Organization (WTO). The GATS was originally introduced in 1994 but is currently being renegotiated with the aim of extending its scope and closing loop-holes for non-compliance.

The GATS, as the WTO's Secretariat points out, 'is the first multilateral agreement to provide legally enforceable rights to trade in all services' supported by 'a built-in commitment to continuous liberalisation through periodic negotiations'.[4] Embedded in this sentence are two key propositions. Firstly, the agreement will cover all services. The WTO classification lists twelve main areas. Subdivision 2, 'Communications Services', includes telecommunications services, radio and television services, sound recording, and motion picture production. Subdivision 10, 'Recreational, Cultural and Sporting Services', includes news agency services, theatres and music performances, together with libraries, museums and 'other cultural services'. Taken together, these categories embrace most of the key industries producing and distributing the informational and symbolic resources that support the cultural rights of citizenship. Secondly, the agreement stretches the established definition of 'trade' to include services provided 'by a service supplier of one Member, through commercial presence in the territory of any other Member'.[5] The clear intention is to open up the full range of services previously administered by national governments to international competition and to exert continuous pressure on governments to establish full liberalization in all relevant sectors. Once implemented the aim is to make all such moves irreversible. As the Secretariat noted, 'bindings undertaken in the GATS have the effect of protecting liberalization policies, regardless of their underlying rationale, from slippages and reversals'.[6]

Supporters of the GATS have sought to answer critics by drawing attention to two provisions in the draft agreement. Firstly they point out that it excludes services provided solely by government. It does, but this caveat does not apply to services supplied in competition with the private sector, which would cover most public services (including public broadcasting services) in most 'restructured' capitalist economies . Secondly, they argue that countries will be able to choose which sectors they want to open up. This is misleading. The draft 'general oblig-ations' place the onus on governments to justify their existing regulatory regimes. Article VI.4 of the GATS specifies that these should be 'no more burdensome than necessary to ensure the quality of the service'.[7] The Working Party on Domestic Regulation is currently urging that this should be interpreted as requiring governments to demonstrate that no less 'trade restrictive' option was available to them. If a government set a goal of facilitating universal internet access for example, it could be argued that instead of providing communal points of access in libraries, schools and community centres it would be less 'trade restric-tive' to give low income families vouchers to spend in the marketplace.

Whether or not all the proposals currently on the table are incorporated into the revised version of the GATS, the marketized world view that underpins them is already firmly entrenched. The history of communications liberalization in the European Union, for example, can be read as a steady march across rough terrain (in which public interest arguments have precipitated frequent landslips and blockages) towards a regulatory regime oriented around corporate requirements. Surveying the final liberalization of voice telephony services in the EU in 1998, the then Deputy Director General of the competition directorate greeted the move as a very welcome step towards 'open and competitive structures in the telecoms and media sectors' in which these services' 'high growth potential' could be pursued unimpeded.[8] The previous year, a position paper on the convergence of the telecommunications, computing and audio-visual industries had argued strongly that 'in principle 'there should 'be no restrictions on business activities 'and that companies should be allowed to supply any service over any network to any users.[9] This was modified in redrafting, but the revised version remained firmly committed to minimizing barriers to corporate action, arguing in almost identical terms to the GATS that 'regulation should be limited to what is strictly necessary to achieve clearly defined objectives' and be deployed 'simply as a tool, alongside the use of market forces'.[10] This argument is illustrative of the funda-mental rethinking of the role of regulation now in process.

RETREATING FROM REGULATION

As indicated above, marketization entails moving the underlying rationale of regulation from defending the public interest to advancing business interests. This shift is institutionalized by transferring key areas of allocative and operational deci-sion-making to corporations, and redefining the proper province of public regulation as keeping a general watching brief on corporate performance and intervening only where absolutely necessary.

Historically regulators would allocate key communicative resources, such as broadcasting franchises and radio spectrum space, on the basis of a so-called 'beauty contest' in which applicants would be judged against a range of criteria, including their contribution to the public good (however defined). In a number of countries, this system is now in the process of being displaced by competitive auctions in which strategic resources go the highest bidder. This favours players who are already well resourced and established. The recent auction of spectrum capacity for the third generation of mobile telephones, instituted by the 'New Labour' government in Britain in 2000, is a particularly dramatic example. The funds this exercise raised for the Treasury outstripped initial projections by a considerable margin, but left successful bidders with far less development money than they had originally calculated. They are now seeking partnerships to spread the costs, a process that will further consolidate the market power of the players with the deepest pockets.

Regulators are also progressively withdrawing from intensive oversight of corporate operational performance, preferring a 'light touch' to a 'heavy hand' and transferring responsibility for compliance to the corporations themselves, backed by annual or periodic regulatory audits. The promotion of self-regulation is at the heart of the British government's proposals to dissolve the current regulatory bodies responsible for overseeing broadcasting and telecommunications and to create a new body, OFCOM (analogous to the FCC in the United States), charged with ensuring that Britain takes maximum advantage of the business opportunities offered by a converged media environment.[11]

There is a fundamental contradiction in the emerging regulatory regime of marketization. On the one hand, open competition is being promoted as the most effective way to secure the core public interest criteria of diversity of service and universal access. On the other hand, governments wish to ensure that they can field national contenders with the critical mass to compete effectively with the major players in a converged international marketplace. This tension between promoting competition and creating national champions is being rapidly resolved in favour of the largest corporations.

CONSOLIDATING CORPORATE POWER

The last five years have seen an unprecedented wave of mergers and acquisitions in the communications industries as the major players have moved to take maximum advantage of the new market environment opened up by privatization, liberalization and the relaxation of ownership regulations, and the new opportunities presented by convergence. Much of this activity has been driven by three main ambitions; to establish a significant presence across the full range of core areas of cultural production and content; to control distribution as well as production through vertical integration; and to integrate emerging media sectors into established nodes of media power.

Digitization significantly increases both the number and scope of distribution channels. Digital compression means that many more broadcast channels can be carried in the spectrum space or cable networks now occupied by relatively bulky analogue signals, while increasing versatility at the point of delivery allows key technologies to become multi-functional. Mobile telephones can be used for text messaging and accessing still images and video, for example. This rapid proliferation and extension of carriage and delivery has not been matched by a concomitant increase in original production, however. Converging communications is conduit-rich but content-poor. Consequently, control of content remains a pivotal source of competitive advantage. To remain a major player in public communications it is therefore necessary to have significant holdings in all three of the major media sectors — print, recorded music, and the moving image industries. The German-based concern, Bertelsmann AG (the third largest global media operator), illustrates the emerging structure of multimedia conglomeration very well. Originating as a print-based company with significant interests in books, newspapers and magazines (which now include eighty magazine titles published worldwide and the US-based publisher, Random House), it is now a major presence in both European television (through CLT-UFA, which operates the well-established RTL network) and the international music industry, with holdings that include the RCA Victor label and Napster's recently acquired online business, whose free distribution policy had previously been seen as a substantial threat to the entrenched power of the record majors.

As the Napster example demonstrates, the advantages of control over strategic content are further consolidated if some control can also be exercised over carriage and delivery. This has led companies to take full advantage of the opportunities for vertical integration opened up by changes in the US regulatory regime, and in particular the chance to combine the production facilities of the Hollywood studios with the distribution reach of the US television and cable networks. In 1995 the Walt Disney Company bought the broadcasting network operated by Capital Cities/ABC for $19 billion; and in 1999 Viacom, which controlled the old Paramount Pictures studio, merged with the CBS network. Both consolidated corporations also have extensive transnational interests in cable television. In addition to the flagship Disney Channel, Disney operates the world's most successful network of sports channels, ESPN, with a presence in 165 countries, while Viacom controls the MTV music network and the Nickelodeon film channel. The former reaches 342 million households worldwide; the latter, over 300 million.

In October 2000, the purchase of another major Hollywood studio, Universal, by the French-based concern, Vivendi, was approved by the EU Competition Commissioner, Mario Monti. This brought together Universal's production capacity, and Europe's largest pay television operator, Canal Plus, which reaches fourteen million subscribers in eleven European countries, with one of the continent's major forces in cinema exhibition. But this integration of key audio-visual resources was only one element in a much more ambitious game plan. Indeed, Vivendi's rapid rise encapsulates many of the core processes of marketization. It began as a utility company taking advantage of moves towards privatization within Europe to supply water and other services (including rail travel). The profits from these activities provided a 'war chest' that could be used to expand into key areas of communications. The aim was to make convergence a paying proposition by combining strategic holdings in both established and emerging media. In addition to the film and television interests, these now include: the sixty publishing houses grouped under the Havas division, selling 80 million books a year; the substantial Universal music interests (which account for 22 per cent of the global market and now include the MP3.com internet music distributor, bought in May 2001); Vizzavi, an internet portal operated in partnership with Europe's biggest mobile phone operator, Vodaphone; and Viventures, a venture capital fund with investments in over fifty internet companies on both sides of the Atlantic. As the company chairman, Jean-Marie Messier, pointed out at the time of the MP3.com purchase, the expertise offered by these strategic stakes in digital media 'will be a tremendous advantage, especially in the digital distribution of all Vivendi Universal content and the creation of common technology platforms'.[12]

The only other corporation to match the scope of Vivendi Universal's operations so far is AOL Time-Warner, formed in January 2000 and finally approved by the European Commission in October 2000, within days of the final clearance of the Vivendi Universal tie-up. Time-Warner, itself the product of a series of earlier acquisitions which brought together substantial holdings in the audio-visual industries based on the Warner Brothers' Hollywood studios and music interests, Ted Turner's CNN satellite news system, and the publishing interests developed from the success of *Time* and *Life* magazines, was already the world's leading 'old' media corporation at the time of the amalgamation with AOL. This latest merger offers access to some of the best known on-line service providers including America Online (with over 22 million subscribers), AOL International (with 4.4 million subscribers in fourteen countries), CompuServe Interactive Services, and the Netscape internet browser.

The formation of Vivendi Universal and AOL Time-Warner, and their successful clearance of the relevant regulatory hurdles in both the US and the EU, with requests for only very modest concessions, suggests that the future shape of the converging media marketplace will be determined primarily by transnational corporations with significant stakes across the whole range of 'old' and 'new' production and distribution systems. The emergence of these integrated communications corporations not only changes the terms of competition, making it increasingly difficult for new entrants to establish a viable presence. It also obliges national regulators to recognize and accept the commercial 'realities' of transnational convergence. This in turn puts additional pressure on publicly-funded media organizations which have traditionally seen their primary role as providing cultural resources for citizenship.

INCORPORATING PUBLIC COMMUNICATIONS

One of the central features of marketization is the progressive application of corporate institutional models and rationales to organizations still formally in the public sector. This drive to corporatize public communications was pursued most forcefully in New Zealand where the public broadcaster, Television New

Zealand, was converted from a licence-funded organization to a State Owned Enterprise with a statutory duty to maximize the returns it made to the Treasury. The licence fee continued to be levied but the monies raised were put into a general production fund, New Zealand On Air, designed to support national programme-making. However, awards were conditional on the applicant demonstrating that one of the major channels has agreed to air the programme. As a consequence ultimate editorial control lay with the channel schedulers rather than with the NZOA panel, allowing significant sums of public subsidy to be directed to projects endorsed by commercial channels.[13]

Governments in other mature capitalist economies have pursued corporatization somewhat less literally, preferring to promote change by creating conditions that pointed insistently towards commercial solutions. This was most often achieved by reducing the real value of public subsidy at precisely the time when public media organizations were facing intensified competition for both core production resources and audiences. These shortfalls were addressed in three main ways. Firstly, production costs could be cut by scaling down in-house facilities and 'outsourcing' projects to independent producers, or by introducing internal markets in which creative teams within the organization bid against external suppliers for project commissions, as in the BBC's 'Producer Choice' initiative. Secondly, costs could be spread by entering into public-private partnerships. In May 2001 for example, the BBC signed a three-year deal with the Cobalt Media Group to develop major feature films, entitling both partners to a 50 per cent share of any net profits from joint projects. This was the latest in a lengthening line of partnership agreements that the Corporation has signed, including a major deal with the Discovery Channel. Critics of these arrangements have argued that whilst they help to sustain the BBC's ability to launch big budget projects, they raise awkward questions about the locus of editorial control and the criteria underpinning decisions to back one project rather than another. A third way to address the escalating costs of production is to maximize the income generated by sales in overseas and secondary markets and by merchandising and ancillary products, from magazines to toys. Again, the BBC has pursued these options with considerable vigour, and has been in the forefront of exploiting the commercial possibilities of moving onto the internet through its commercial subsidiary Beeb.com.

These initiatives may be successful in their immediate aim of generating more income for domestic production but they generate several deep-seated contradictions. Firstly, the more successful a public corporation is in raising commercial revenues the weaker its case for continuing to receive earmarked public subsidies, in the form of either a licence fee or a block grant. Secondly, the more successfully it competes in the marketplace the more vociferously commercial actors are likely to raise questions of unfair competition on the grounds that decades of public subsidy have enabled organizations like the BBC to build a valued brand with worldwide recognition without the cost of transnational advertising, and that the licence fee continues to confer an unwarranted advantage. As one disgruntled competitor put it: '[i]f its job is to compete in the new media arena then [the BBC] must lose the licence fee, because if it's competing aggressively with everyone else, there's no reason why it should get a licence fee and we shouldn't'.[14] Thirdly, it is likely to be increasingly difficult to maintain the 'Chinese Walls' that currently separate the public service side of the BBC's operations from commercial operations already thoroughly imbued with the practices and rhetorics of corporate life. In order to attract the best qualified staff to join its commercial internet venture, Beeb.com, for example, the BBC recently offered new recruits 'phantom' share options with values tied to the overall valuation of the business. As a Corporation spokesperson explained at the time, 'Beeb Ventures needs to be in tune with the marketplace'.[15] The declared rationale for this rush to embrace corporate strategies is that the returns from these enterprises help ensure that the BBC can continue to provide the widest possible range of services, both over air and on the internet, free at the point of use. But the more insistently corporate language, practices and 'targets' are adopted the more likely they are to tunnel under the Chinese Walls and find their way into the mainstream of the Corporation's rhetoric and strategies.

Arguably, the need for publicly-funded communications organizations committed to resourcing citizenship is greater than ever at a time when the onward march of marketization has increasingly converted information and communication goods into commodities and tied access ever more securely to ability to pay. This is particularly so now, when inequalities of income and condition are increasing in a number of key economies and transnationally.

SOCIAL DIVISIONS AND DIGITAL DIVIDES

The widening of social divisions that has been endemic in many Western societies in recent years is reflected in ownership of and access to new information resources. The cliché of the 'digital divide' is, like most clichés, well founded in empirical reality. In the UK the wealthiest 1 per cent own between a fifth and a quarter of total household wealth; half the population own just 6 per cent of total wealth. The gap between household incomes is nearly as stark.[16] The earnings of the poorest tenth of male workers as a proportion of the top tenth fell from 43 per cent to 30 per cent between 1979 and 2000.[17] The number of people in poverty increased from 9 per cent to 25 per cent of the population between 1979 and 1999, an increase that included an additional 3.1 million children.[18] Household expenditure matches these inequalities. Lower income groups spend a higher proportion of their income on essentials. While the poorest twenty percent spend 22 per cent of their income on food and non-alcoholic drink, for the top fifth the figure is 13 per cent (of a figure itself roughly double the disposable income of the poorest fifth). [19]

This inequality readily appears in the ownership and use of communication goods and facilities, as we have explained in a number of analyses elsewhere.[20] Unequal access to the internet is an important indicator here, since it illustrates some key features of the digital divide. In the UK, while headline figures constantly trumpet the growing number of households who have accessed the internet recently, or who now have home access, 60 per cent had still not accessed the internet by the end of 2000. In early 2001, while 78 per cent of professional households had used the internet, only 27 per cent of those in homes with an unskilled head of household had done so, and the gradient from lowest to highest income groups remained steep, and had grown over the previous two years.[21] As market analysts Booz-Allen point out: 'as the online revolution runs its course, the divide looks set to grow worse ... far from evening out the emerging inequalities, the wave of growth is likely to exacerbate them in relative terms, leaving an unconnected or excluded group of over 20 million citizens'.[22]

The situation in the world's most advanced information economy is the same. The US National Telecommunications and Information Administration data show that, behind the apparent good news of rising access and gains among the digital 'have nots', only 19 per cent of people in households with annual incomes below $15,000 were internet users in 2000, contrasted with 70 per cent of those in households with incomes above $75,000. Single parent households are only half as likely to have access as two-parent households, while the gap between Hispanic groups and the remainder of the population did not diminish between 1998 and 2000.[23]

This pattern is sometimes regarded as an inevitable transition while the real costs of new forms of commodity and service, initially acquired by richer 'early adopters', reduce and are gradually diffused through the wider population. However, even if this were true of previous waves of consumer technologies, it is not happening with communication and information goods and services. The high initial capital costs act as a substantial barrier to low income groups. But even as they do reduce, the recurrent costs of unavoidable replacement of key items (as producer-enforced specifications are upgraded), the purchase of supplementary and increasingly essential associated equipment (modems, printers, scanners), and the cost of use (particularly online and subscription charges) all impose very high demands on consumer disposable income. In consequence ownership profiles are dissimilar to those of earlier generations of technology, creating two new forms of inequality. One simply demarcates the digital 'haves' from the 'have-nots', with a significant minority apparently permanently excluded from the new facilities. The second sees a major widening of the gap in the quality and capacity of the communication and information goods available to groups of differing spending power. Lower income groups, even where they are able to make an entry into the new marketplace, find themselves forced to manage with lower specification and limited capacity resources, which compromise fundamentally the more flamboyant claims of those who see the new technologies as 'democratizing enablers' which abolish social distinctions.

To meet this criticism governments have adopted two approaches. The first has been to seek to foster the growth of the information sector of the economy by the deregulation and quasi-subsidization of production. This has had special appeal to European governments anxious to confront competition from the US and Japan. The other approach has been to subsidize consumption, by incorporating information and communication goods into public provision. These initiatives have had their own difficulties.[24] In the UK the government has launched endless schemes to increase the use of new information and communication facilities by low income households. But these have mainly been conditionally linked to labour-market policy, imposing retraining and welfare benefits conditions, with very limited success even on their own terms. They also have the inevitable consequence of providing a 'hand-out' mode of distribution that places lower capacity resources into lower income homes, thus exacerbating the digital divide. An alternative to this approach offers collective forms of provision (for example in schools, public libraries, or community centres), which creates an additional contradiction, since the content providers (in the main private corporations) design their systems for the model of the individual household consumer market.

The divisions and inequities at the heart of the digital revolution within nations are inevitably replicated on a global scale. The availability of communications goods and services has perennially matched obstinate patterns of inequality in incomes and wealth between nations.[25] The availability of cheap, fast communication opens up possibilities for progressive social change in a variety of spheres, from health and education to the potential for liberatory networking between social movements with concerns and grievances that transcend the borders of nation states. Yet just as the contours of telecommunications mould onto the residual markings of empire, so the distribution patterns of new communications technologies match the global distribution and control of wealth.

With about 6 per cent of the world's population North America has about 41 per cent of the online population. Africa, by contrast, with nearly 10 per cent of the global population, has fewer than 1 per cent of the on-line population. There are more users online in Sweden than in the whole of sub-Saharan Africa. As Norris observes, '[t]he 29 OECD member states ... contain 97 per cent of all internet hosts, 92 per cent of the market in production and consumption of computer hardware, software and services, and 86 per cent of all internet users.'[26] The contradictory potential of the new communication technologies for poorer countries is intense. First, their growth enables new patterns of participation in the distribution of knowledge and competencies. Yet at the same time intellectual property regimes prevent poorer countries obtaining access to information of crucial use to them in technological development. This includes information about themselves, which often remains locked within the grasp of private and multinational users. Secondly, speed and cost advantages open up the entry of 'emerging market' economies into global commerce: a document sent between two African countries costs 200 times more to send by fax as by email, and 400 times more to dispatch by courier. Yet the control of available networks by global distributors of entertainment means that a set of contradictory forces is in play. Not surprisingly, agencies like the United Nations Development Programme see the third world cup as half empty, while the World Bank sees it as half full.[27] The gap in information and communication resources is both a consequence of global inequalities arising from the international economic order, and in turn becomes a reinforcing source of their perpetuation.

CITIZENS AND NETIZENS

The charge from the left has always, and rightly, been that the media's embrace by the corporate structure of capitalism has distorted their potential contribution to informing and empowering citizens in an effective democratic structure. The incorporation of the media into larger enterprises has resulted in three broad types of failure in this respect, the details of which we have catalogued elsewhere.[28] First, the range of voices available in the market place becomes determined not by political action or democratic entitlement, but by the combined forces of advertising, ownership, and market manipulation. Minority and weaker voices survive, but become marginalized and impoverished. Secondly, the ambitions and relevance of the media as contributors to popular enlightenment become muted, a charge most recently represented by the identification of 'tabloidization' in the 'quality press'; that is, the adoption by serious and information-oriented media of down-market efforts to entertain and expand their markets at the expense of their former broad and politically-significant content.[29] This latter charge has attracted a radical riposte; that it is itself rooted in an elitist and narrow notion of what it is to be 'relevant' and 'informative', and that the charge of 'dumbing down' is no more than a blinkered failure to acknowledge the widening of political discourse to embrace newer, more demotic, and possibly less gendered concerns.[30] It is hard, though, to recognize in the strident excesses of Jerry Springer or the UK *Sun* a welcome expansion of the imaginative breadth and popular liberation of political discourse. Thirdly, the media have been accused of narrowing their vision and conception of the world to represent an unchallenging consensus that conforms to the world view of the most powerful social groups. This view has underpinned much social research into the content of the media for several decades, in both particular areas of social affairs and in general.[31]

Yet all three charges are now challenged by the transformations being driven in communications by technological change. It is now argued that the massive expansion of channels for communication and information flow creates a landscape in which choice and abundance wholly compensate for, or indeed dissolve, these weaknesses in the media structures of modernity. First, there are no limits to the range of materials that can be made available. The internet, new and cheaper forms of information production and distribution, and the increased proportion of productive labour committed in advanced societies to information and communication activities, all combine to create a limitless cornucopia of diversity. Secondly, the very simplicity and availability of new communications forms lowers the entry threshold for oppositional forms of communication; the radical, progressive, and heterodox are as free to broadcast their voice or communicate among themselves as the previously powerful and dominant voices of yesterday's mediascape. The age of limitless information abundance, it is claimed, heralds the formation electronically of an agora without the ancient restrictions by wealth and gender.

There are a number of reasons to pause before applauding uncritically this apparent transformation. Debate about the potential and actual changes in political relations and communication consequent on new communication technologies is now voluminous. But a few brief contradictory pointers are of particular relevance here. First, it is important to recognize how frequently descriptions of new democratic communications focus on the apparent success of what might once have been termed prefigurative forms, that is anticipatory pioneers whose model could be seen to have potential for wider progressive application. A torrent of appreciative studies of newsgroups, email lists, electronic town meetings and the like has paid testimony to the potential liberatory character of the internet, in much the same terms as earlier writers celebrated citizens' band radio, guerrilla television and desktop publishing. But these acclamatory descriptions are almost invariably based on exceptional, wealthy, and demographically limited locations and populations, making their euphoric tone inappropriate and inapplicable to much of the rest of the world.

Second, as we have seen above, the facilities and networks that enable such new communicative democracy often bypass poorer sections of the population. As Wilhelm points out, '[p]rivate-sector investment in telecommunications infrastructure deployment in the largest metropolitan areas, such as fibre-optic networks built by competitive local exchange carriers, follows clear patterns of bypassing poor neighbourhoods and communities of colour in order to maximise profits'.[32]

Third, the 'new politics' underpinned by the direct electronic connection of government to governed, powerful to non-powerful, bypasses not just the poor but political organization and collectivity as well. There is here the potential for a fundamental individualization of politics. In cyberdemocracy the role of representative and intermediary organizations — trade unions, community groups, political parties, pressure groups — atrophies.

Fourth, digital democracy suggests a diffusion and distribution of power but, contradictorily, has exacerbated its concentration and centralization. This has two aspects. One is the transfer of effective power and control over major resources and strategic planning from the nation-state, imperfectly but nonetheless indubitably linked to a political system of accountability, to transnational corporations. The other is the 'concentration of politics in the registration, control and surveillance by states, corporations, and societies'.[33]

There are without question myriad examples of the politically progressive contribution of new communication and information technologies, from the emancipatory politics of the Zapatistas in Chiapas[34] to the international harrying of corporate giants like McDonalds.[35] But the very architecture and construction, as well as the political economy, of the new technologies, are liberatory in their potential but regressive in their contemporary reality.

CONSUMING CITIZENSHIP

The biases in the material organization of the new digital media are further reinforced by an insistent promotional rhetoric that has hollowed out the space previously available for the reconstruction and extension of citizenship, and refilled it with seductive promises of boundless consumption and personal satisfaction. Corporations entering the new media marketplace work with social maps on which affiliations are classified by life styles and leisure interests rather than by membership of moral communities. These market segments are then addressed by themed channels and internet sites. This produces a contradictory movement in which digital technologies facilitate 'the development of distinct groups organised around affinity and interest' while at the same time undermining the possibility of creating '*a* public — an active democratic encounter of citizens who reach across their differences to establish a common agenda of concern'.[36] This erosion of a communal public sphere is further accelerated by the emergence of personalized systems of delivery developing around the Personalized Video Recorder, which uses a programmable hard disk to track its users' particular interests across the range of channels and record the relevant programmes while filtering out the advertisements.

The arrival of these 'Me TV' systems exacerbates the problems advertisers have faced for some time, of viewers using their remote control consoles to zap away from advertising breaks. New technologies, however, offer several ways to reintegrate ads into the viewing experience. Advertisers can take up the option of 'brandcasting' and enter the marketplace with their own channels. They can incorporate products into the programmes through various forms of placement and encourage viewers to use the developing point-and-click technologies to order goods they have seen directly from the screen. They can use the wealth of socio-demographic and taste data generated by personalized viewing and interactivity to target ads more precisely so that viewers are only exposed to promotions for goods they are interested in. And they can follow viewers out of the house, using mobile phones as a marketing tool. As Charles Vallence of the WCRS agency notes, mobile telephony 'is the most personalised medium that has ever existed'.[37] The trick is to replace person-to-person calls with business-to-person traffic.

Historically the organization of an evening's viewing has resembled traditional cinema programming with a major feature (in the centre of prime time) surrounded by a news bulletin, second features, promotions and advertising. Viewing in the age of convergence is modelled on the shopping mall, in which the pleasures of looking are seamlessly combined with the pleasures of buying and possession. Broadcasting is no longer an event. It is an environment built around an ever-thickening network of connections between the television set and the internet. Within this space the 'mission to explain' and the obligation to represent yields to the drive to sell both the channel itself and the goods and services it promotes. Intimacy and interaction are enlisted in the service of marketing. As Jim Rudder, the director of interactive broadcasting at Rupert Murdoch's BskyB, candidly put it; '[i]t's about creating a close relation with the viewer. Once you have that relationship, the monetising is pretty predictable stuff. You will find opportunities all the way through.' [38]

The concerted 'monetizing' thrust of market-driven convergence has not gone unopposed, however. Despite the political and ideological battering they have received, many people working in public cultural organizations continue to view their productions as public goods rather than commodities and to argue forcefully that they should be available free of charge. The Massachusetts Institute of Technology's recent decision to make much of its course material available over the internet at no cost to users is a powerful restatement of this principle, particularly in a context where a number of other leading universities are developing commercially organized distance learning programmes. In addition, despite the rapid commercialization of the internet and the proliferation of subscription sites, a number of civil organizations still operate on the principle of reciprocity, posting material that others may find useful in the hope that they in turn will donate their own expertise and energy. These counter-moralities of exchange are fragile and continuously open to commodification, but they provide the only basis on which to build a digital commons that mobilizes emerging communications technologies in the service of an extended and cosmopolitan ethos of citizenship rather than consumption. Finding ways to develop this vision and construct an infrastructure to support it materially is the one of the greatest challenges facing democracy over the coming decades.

NOTES

1   See Peter Golding, 'Forthcoming Features: Information and Communications Technologies and the Sociology of the Future', *Sociology*, Volume 34 (1), 2000.

2   These are explained further in Peter Golding, 'World Wide Wedge: Division and Contradiction in the Global Information Infrastructure', in D.K. Thussu, ed., *Electronic Empires: Global Media and Local Resistance*, London: Arnold, 1988.

3   Jane Kelsey, *The New Zealand Experiment: A World Model for Structural Adjustment*, Auckland: University of Auckland Press, 1995.

4   *Trading into the Future*, available at the WTO website, http://www.wto.org.

5   *General Agreement on Trade in Services, Part 1 — Scope and definition, Article 1 (2c)*.

6   *Recent developments in services trade — overview and assessment*, Background note by the Secretariat for Trade in Services, World Trade Organization, 9 February 1999, (Document ref S/C/W/94).

7   *General Agreement on Trade in Services, Part 11 — General Obligations and disciplines, Article VI*.

8   J.F. Pons, *The Application of competition and antitrust policy in media and telecommunications in the European Union*: speech presented to the International Bar

Association, Vancouver, British Columbia, 14 September 1998, p. 10.

9   *Green Paper on the convergence of the telecommunications, audio-visual and information technology sectors , and their implications for regulation: Towards a common approach to information society services*. Brussels: European Commission: DG XIII, 1997, p. 14.

10   *Green Paper on the convergence of the telecommunications, media and information technology sectors, and the implications for regulation: Towards an information society approach*. Brussels: European Commission (COM(97)623) p. 40/24.

11   Peter Golding and Graham Murdock, 'Digital Divides: Communications policy and its contradictions', *New Economy*, Vol. 8 (2), 2001, pp.110-115.

12   Quoted in Nick Fletcher, 'Vivendi Universal snaps up MP3.com for $372m', *The Guardian*, 21 May 2001, p. 25.

13   See Graham Murdock, 'Public Broadcasting in Privatised Times: Rethinking the New Zealand Experiment', in Paul Norris and John Farnsworth, eds., *Keeping it Ours: Issues Of Television Broadcasting in New Zealand*, Christchurch: New Zealand Broadcasting School, 1998.

14   Quoted in Lucy Kung-Shankleman, *Inside the BBC and CNN: Managing Media Organizations,* London: Routledge, 2000, p. 181.

15   Quoted in David Teather, 'Beeb.com makes phantom offer', *The Guardian*, 2 February 2001, p. 29.

16   The Low Pay Unit's *New Review*, 68, March/April 2001, p. 18.

17   The Low Pay Unit's *New Review*, 66, November/December 2000, p. 7.

18   Jonathan Bradshaw, 'Child Poverty under Labour', in Geoff Fimister, ed., *Tackling Child Poverty in the UK: An End in Sight?*, London: CPAG, 2001, p. 10.

19   The Low Pay Unit's *New Review*, 68, March/April 2001, p. 18.

20   Peter Golding and Graham Murdock, 'Unequal information: access and exclusion in the new communications market place', in Marjorie Ferguson, ed., *New Communication Technologies and the Public Interest*, London: Sage Publications, 1986, pp. 76-81.

21   Office of National Statistics, *Internet Access*, London: HMSO, March 2001, p. 4.

22   Booz-Allen and Hamilton, *Achieving Universal Access*, London: Booz-Allen and Hamilton, 2000.

23   National Telecommunications and Information Administration, *Falling Through the Net: Toward Digital Inclusion*, October 2000, Figure II-3.

24   Golding and Murdock, 'Digital Divides'.

25   See Peter Golding and Phil Harris, eds., *Beyond Cultural Imperialism: Globalization, communication and the New International Order*, London: Sage Publications, 1997; Peter Golding, 'Global Village or Cultural Pillage? The unequal inheritance of the communications revolution', in R. McChesney, E. Meiksins Wood and J.B. Foster, eds., *Capitalism and the Information Age: The Political economy of the global communication revolution*, New York: Monthly Review Press, 1998.

26 Pippa Norris, 'The Worldwide Digital Divide: information poverty, the internet and development', Paper given at Political Studies Association of the UK, London, 12 April 2000, p. 3 (see http://www.Pippanorris.com).

27 United Nations Development Programme, *Human Development Report*, 1999, p. 58.

28 Peter Golding and Graham Murdock, 'Information poverty and political inequality: citizenship in the age of privatised communications', *Journal of Communication*, Vol. 39 (3), Summer 1989; 'Common Markets: Corporate Ambitions and Communication Trends in the UK and Europe', *Journal of Media Economics*, Vol. 12 (2), 1999. On the consequences for democratic information see Peter Golding, 'Telling Stories: Sociology, Journalism and the Informed Citizen', *European Journal of Communication*, Vol. 9 (4), 1994.

29 Peter Golding and Shelley McLachlan, 'Tabloidisation in the British Press: A quantitative investigation into changes in British Newspapers, 1952-1997', in C. Sparks and J. Tulloch, eds., *Tabloid Tales: Global Debates over Media Standards*, New York and Oxford: Rowman and Littlefield, 2000.

30 See Graeme Turner, 'Tabloidization, Journalism and the Possibility of Critique' *International Journal of Cultural Studies*, Vol. 2 (1), 1999.

31 For an early exploration of this thesis see Peter Golding and Graham Murdock, 'A Political Economy of Mass Communications', in *The Socialist Register*, London: Merlin Press, 1973.

32 Anthony Wilhelm, *Democracy in the Digital Age*, New York and London: Routledge, 2000, p. 151.

33 Kenneth Hacker and Jan van Dijk, eds., D*igital Democracy: Issues of Theory and Practice*, London: Sage, 2000, p. 210.

34 Judith Adler Hellman 'Real and Virtual Chiapas: Magic Realism and the Left' in Leo Panitch & Colin Leys, eds., *Socialist Register 2000: Necessary and Unnecessary Utopias*, London: Merlin Press, 2000.

35 www.mcspotlight.org/case/index.html.

36 See Todd Gitlin, 'Public sphere or public sphericles?', in Tamar Liebes and James Curran, eds., *Media, Ritual and Identity*, London: Routledge, 1998, p. 173.

37 Quoted in Julia Day, 'Hard sell in your hand', *Guardian New Media*, 19 March 2001, p. 50.

38 Quoted in David Teather, 'Now we have to show where the money is', *Guardian New Media,* 2 April 2001, p. 54.

THE DARK SIDE OF LIFE: GLOBALIZATION AND INTERNATIONAL ORGANIZED CRIME

REG WHITAKER

Economic globalization is a more complex concept than terms such as 'transnational corporations' and 'international finance' would immediately suggest. There is a licit global economy, but there is also an illicit global economy. The first is capitalist, the second is criminal. Moral critiques of capitalism aside, it is important to distinguish between the lawful and the unlawful, the licit and the illicit, because these differences have enormous consequences in the real world of wealth and power, especially for the emerging governance of the global economy.

THE BRIGHT SIDE AND THE DARK SIDE

Economic globalization has a public face, reflected in investment flows and currency exchanges, followed and publicized daily in the media, celebrated loudly by its impresarios and apologists, criticized by its detractors in public demonstrations. This is the open face, or what I will call the 'Bright Side' of globalization. I choose the word 'bright' both in a literal sense, reflecting the relative glare of publicity, and in the ironic sense that Monty Python closed *The Life of Brian* with the crucified singing a cheery chorus of 'Always look on the bright side of life'. The brightness apparently lies in the lack of obvious alternatives.

There is also a 'Dark Side', and here I am not referring to what globalization's critics point to as the underside of the promise, the exploitation and immiseration caused by rampant global capitalism. Rather I am referring to capitalism's dark *doppelgänger*, the criminal or illicit economy, which has always shadowed capitalism throughout its history, mimicking its methods, actively seeking the opportunities of markets not served by its legal counterparts, sometimes working in tacit alliance but more often in competition with its counterparts, sometimes passing in one or two generations from outlaws to in-laws of the legitimate order.

Organized crime was a presence in the era of national capitalist development. As capitalism's reach across national borders has accelerated, so too has the internationalization of criminal enterprise. The same technologies that have enabled cross-border capital flows in real time also facilitate cross-border criminal activity. Global financial mechanisms are shadowed by money laundering. Products proscribed by national laws, such as narcotics and prostitution, are provided by criminal organizations. In other cases, legal products are distributed by illegal means at lower prices (as with the global marketing of stolen automobiles). In other instances, legal products are provided by legal companies to illegal organizations who market them at lower prices through tax evasion (as with the collusion between cigarette manufacturers and smuggling networks). In other cases, products that are legally available to some customers are provided by criminal organizations to proscribed customers (as with illegal arms traffic). The combination of positive and negative inducements traditionally offered by capitalists to influence states that attempt to tax and regulate their activities (from political campaign funding to threats to pull out investment) are mirrored by a combination of bribery and intimidation used by criminal organizations on states interfering with their activities.

In December 2000 the United States government, at the direction of the President, produced an *International Crime Threat Assessment,* with the collaboration of all the major US security, intelligence, and law enforcement agencies.[1] This document begins its analysis of the growth of international criminal activity by painting the global landscape after the end of the Cold War. The breakdown of political and economic barriers with the collapse of the Soviet Bloc has encouraged an ever widening economic and trade liberalization, assisted by rapid technological advances in transportation and communication. The globalization of business and the explosion in international travel have contributed to an unprecedented freedom of movement of capital, goods, and services. All of these are of course welcomed and indeed heralded by the enthusiasts of capitalism, among whom the United States constitutes the vanguard. But the Bright Side's lustre glitters for a moment only to be shadowed by the Dark Side.

> The dynamics of globalization, however, particularly the reduction of barriers to the movement of people, goods, and financial transactions across borders, have enabled international crime groups to expand their global reach and criminal business interests. International organized crime groups are able to operate increasingly outside traditional parameters, take quick advantage of new opportunities, and move more rapidly into new geographic areas. The major international organized crime groups have become more global in their operations, while many smaller and more local crime groups have expanded beyond their country's borders to become regional crime threats.

Does this have a familiar ring to it? The eerie parallels with the Bright Side are developed further yet in the *International Crime Threat Assessment* document. Most organized criminal groups, the authors argue, have the following characteristics in common:

Seeking financial gain: '[g]reed and the quest for profits probably dictates more organized crime decisions than any other single motive. It is this consuming desire for money, and the power that typically goes with it, which drives and sustains organized crime.'

Member loyalty: through ethnicity and family considerations, most groups preferring their members to be of the same ethnic background: '[c]riminals generally believe they can better trust those people they know…Second, some of these groups originated from the pursuit of a common goal or scheme, whether economic, societal, or political.'

Pursuing corruption of government officials: '[m]ost organized crime groups have been enormously successful in their illegal ventures because they have successfully corrupted those persons charged with investigating and prosecuting them.'

Organizational maturity: '[o]rganized crime groups have some permanence and do not depend on the continuing participation of one or a few individuals for their existence.'

Hierarchical structure: with defined leadership-subordinate roles, through which the group's objectives are achieved.

Diversification: typically, groups engage in more than one kind of crime.

Multi-jurisdictional activities: groups operate over large areas of a region or countries.

Most of these attributes apply to licit business organizations. The ethnic base might seem at first glance peculiar to criminal groups, until one recalls that transnational corporations are not truly transnational, but are first and foremost American or Japanese or German or British. Of course they recruit managerial talent from outside their national base, but generally without losing their core national identity. The Mafia operating in America have Sicilian origins and strong Sicilian cultural discipline, but this has not prevented them from hiring non-Sicilian specialists to help run their operations from time to time. Globalization has not yet resulted in global organizations that transcend their national, or at best, regional, origins. Instead there are nationally or regionally based organizations that operate on a global scale. Criminal organizations perhaps differ from transnational corporations in the degree to which ethnicity defines membership in the inner core, a constraint made necessary by the greater secrecy in which they operate and the greater pressures to maintain loyalty and prevent penetration by police, as well as by rival criminal organizations.[2] It might be noted that ethnic/religious/kinship bonds have proved very useful as barriers to penetration among another set of internationally organized regional groups operating on the Dark Side, terrorist networks, although here ideology plays a decisive role as well.

A general principle regarding ethnicity can be derived: never absent entirely, ethnicity and national identity grow stronger as we move from the Bright to the Dark sides. Licit organizations that operate in the light of relatively high publicity and without the threat of police surveillance on a day-to-day basis can afford the luxury of extending the multinationality of their personnel. Indeed, a diverse workforce and even a diverse management structure are positive factors in expanding transnational penetration and exploitation of new regional markets. Criminal and other outlaw organization can afford this luxury less and require structural barriers against external scrutiny more. But all globalizing organizations still require to some degree a cultural matrix at their core.

With regard to corruption of government officials, at first blush this would seem to be a specific attribute of criminal organizations. Yet no honest observer who has witnessed the behaviour of corporations in creating favourable political and regulatory climates for themselves by the lavish use of their resources can let corporations off the hook so easily. The funding of political parties, for instance, describes an activity that, while usually although not always legal, is clearly moti-vated by the objective of buying priority access and influence with government officials. While criminal organizations may often have corrupted 'those persons charged with investigating and prosecuting them', there is a very old literature on how business organizations influence and even capture those bodies charged with regulating them. Corporations in the licit global economy also engage in bribery and corruption as a regular business practice, obviously and blatantly in the devel-oping and post-Communist countries, but in the Western world as well. 'If corruption is growing throughout the world, it is largely a result of the rapid privatization (and associated practices of contracting-out and concessions) of public enterprises worldwide.... Multinationals, supported by Western govern-ments and their agencies, are engaging in corruption on a vast scale in North and South alike.'[3]

However, even in the case of outright corruption, such practices in the licit economy can be identified as a problem that should be resolved by remedial action, a 'cost' that constitutes a 'diseconomy' and interference in the free market. With criminal organizations, corruption is a basic *modus operandi*. But the fact remains that despite differing styles of operation, both licit and illicit organizations systematically direct resources to act upon governments and government officials to encourage favourable results. At this game, it is the licit organizations that have been most successful — in on the ground floor, as it were, and with the law, by and large, on their side.

The parallels between the Dark and Bright sides of globalization are obvious to law enforcement and security forces, indeed, they serve to irritate and alarm them. The presidential *International Crime Threat Assessment*, for instance, is greatly annoyed by the way in which international criminal networks have 'taken advan-tage of the dramatic changes in technology, world politics, and the global economy to become more sophisticated and flexible in their operations'. With a few changes in terminology, the following words could almost sound like a left-wing diatribe against transnational globalization:

They have extensive worldwide networks and infrastructure to support their criminal operations; they are inherently flexible in their operations, adapting quickly to challenges from rivals and from law enforcement; they have tremendous financial resources to draw upon; and they are completely ruthless.

Are we talking about the Mafia or Microsoft? Much of this is perhaps in the eye of the beholder. But the adaptability of criminal organizations to the new economy goes further yet. The *Threat Assessment* laments the growing 'professionalization' of criminal operations. By employing individuals with specific expertise — specialists in transportation, and legal and financial experts ('some trained in the world's best business schools') — international criminal organizations are able to effectively manage information and 'quickly identify and adapt to market changes'. Worse, they are *networking*, enabling them to merge expertise and broaden the scope of their operations. 'Rather than treat each other as rivals, many criminal organizations are sharing information, services, resources, and market access according to the principle of comparative advantage'. In doing so, 'they reduce their risks and costs' and are better positioned to exploit opportunities. Although partnership ventures have so far been largely tactical, 'the potential for broader alliances to undertake more complex criminal schemes in an increasingly global economy is significant'. Not for nothing have criminal organizations hired advisers from the 'world's best business schools'. They offer textbook cases in management theory of how to be successful in the new global economy. In certain respects, criminal organizations even hold advantages over their Bright Side counterparts. In terms of flexibility and rapid response to market signals, illicit organizations are better adapted than their more elaborately structured licit counterparts who are encumbered with legal controls and more bureaucratized decision-making structures.

The managerial advantages are not all on the Dark Side, by any means. The economies of scale that have given such a competitive edge to transnational corporate organizations are not always available to their criminal counterparts. Federico Varese explains why 'unlike legitimate global businesses, Mafia firms find it hard to take advantage of the benefits of economy of scale. The bigger the organization, the harder it is to collect reliable information both on new recruits and local conditions. Moreover, the bigger the reach of the organization, the more likely it is that disputes will arise within it, and that criminal reputations will be faked, allowing police informants to penetrate the organization.'[4] So a mafia Microsoft is perhaps not so likely after all.

THE TWILIGHT ZONE

The parallels between the illicit and licit global economies are obvious: we are speaking broadly about markets, white, grey, and black, in capital, goods, services and people, each of which are manipulated differently on the Dark Side than on the Bright Side. But far from being sealed off from one another, the two sides are in symbiotic relationship. The Dark Side fastens upon and exploits the weaknesses and shortcomings of the Bright Side. It is not simply a matter of poverty 'causing' crime (the relationships here are much too complex to yield easy equations), nor is it simply the facile argument that law 'creates' crime, as with proscribing certain addictive drugs, or outlawing prostitution, or forcing economic migrants into the hands of criminal smugglers by barring their legal entry into wealthy countries. Of course, if cocaine, heroin, etc. were completely legal, criminal trafficking in drugs would dry up — by definition. However, the medical, social, and cultural problems that stem from drug abuse would hardly cease as a result. And the criminal trafficking networks would quite likely convert themselves into 'respectable' producers and suppliers for the legal market, just as some capitalist fortunes were built on alcohol smuggling during the Prohibition era in the USA. Anyone who thinks that such a process of rehabilitation would represent a net social benefit might take a close look at the tobacco companies which, along with the multi-national pharmaceutical corporations, conform more closely than perhaps any other actors in the licit economy to the corruption of governments and the intimidation of critics practised by criminal organizations on the Dark Side. Similarly, the idea that Western states could or would receive every migrant who might arrive from the Third World with no problems of political, cultural or economic absorption is a chimera — as much an illusion as the idea that Fortress Europe or Fortress North America can, by beefed-up security, interdict the entire flow of migration through, under, or over their gates. In short, the demands that give rise to criminal supply cannot be magically conjured away by simply declaring what was illegal to be legal.

There is a deeper sense in which states define and structure the scope of criminal activity. Citing the work of Janice Thomson,[5] H. Richard Friman and Peter Andreas[6] point to

> an important distinction between authority and control as two interrelated dimensions of state power. States claim metapolitical authority: the right to decide what is political and, as such, 'subject to state coercion'.... However, the authority to make rules differs from the ability to enforce them. The latter entails state power to control and is shaped by capabilities including police and security forces....
>
> [S]ome of the challenges to state controls over illegal transnational economic activities are, in a sense, self-produced. Criminalizing activities for which high market demand exists inflates their profitability and encourages new market entrants. An ironic symbiosis thus emerges between state control efforts and the proliferation of actors such as crime syndicates willing to circumvent them. *The gap between the state's metapolitical authority to pass prohibition laws and its ability to fully enforce such laws is the space where clandestine transnational actors operate. Indeed, the illicit global economy is defined by and depends on the state exercising metapolitical authority to criminalize without the full capacity to effectively enforce its criminal laws.* [emphasis added]

THE ECONOMY OF VIOLENCE

The 1920s Chicago gangster Al Capone is reputed to have once said that there are many things you can get with a smile and a gun that you can never get with a smile alone. He might just as well have been referring to the balance of legitimation and coercion practiced by his rival organization, and ultimate nemesis, the state. The latter finally put Capone behind bars, not for his organization's criminal activities, but for not paying taxes on them — an exemplary indication of which organization constituted the superior protection racket.

In his anti-Nazi play, *The Resistible Rise of Arturo Ui*, Brecht merged the figures of Capone and Hitler in the parable of the rise of the fascist gangster state. However tempting the image, it is important to understand that in liberal capitalist societies, violence is legitimately permitted only to the state. Where coercion is exercised by private associations, it is always limited and can only be legitimated by licensing or rule-based devolution by the state. Gated communities, shopping plazas, universities, and commercial plants and warehouses may employ private armed policing, but their authority to use force is legally delegated from the state through such devices as conferral of 'special constable' or 'deputy' status. The performance of such coercive delegates is normally subject to external review and discipline. There is, of course, a very good reason why market societies accept their states' monopoly over the legitimate exercise of coercion. It is the reason adduced by Hobbes in the seventeenth century for the state as Leviathan: the competitive state of nature is an intolerable state of insecurity, the war of all against all. In the age of globalization, this state of insecurity is reproduced on the terrain (Manuel Castells' 'space of flows'[7]) where transnational economic transactions escape national state controls. The primitive and chaotic nature of global governance is the reflection of the international state of nature, but the tools of governance vary strikingly as we move from the Bright to the Dark sides.

On the Bright Side, the tools of global governance are treaties, international agreements, cooperative regulation, exhortation, adjudication and arbitration (increasingly taking place outside legal jurisdictions through alternative dispute resolution mechanisms), and, occasionally, legal sanctions enforced by individual states in accordance with international agreements. On the Dark Side, the tools are policing and coercion: surveillance, intelligence collection, investigation, prosecution and punishment. Corporations by and large do not exercise direct coercion to advance their interests; they leave this to states. Criminal organizations do use direct violence, regularly, to manipulate markets — it is, indeed, a core part of their identity that distinguishes them from corporations. As violent organizations, they directly challenge states by threatening their monopoly over the legitimate exercise of force within a given territory. Internationally organized, transnational mafias not only exploit markets outside national jurisdictions, but they exploit spaces for coercive action not policed, or imperfectly policed, as a result of states' jurisdictional limitations within national boundaries. Thus international criminal organizations pose a particularly pointed challenge to state power in a globalized world. National states must either get their policing acts together or face the serious undermining of their legitimacy by antagonists who steal the very tools they claim to monopolize. This challenge also represents an opportunity for states to project their territorial-based power onto the broader global stage. As we shall see, it is not one that relatively powerful states — especially the only remaining superpower, the United States — are likely to pass up.

THE GLOBAL CRIMINAL *WHAT'S WHAT* AND *WHO'S WHO*

A quick inventory of international organized criminal activities might be in order. Lists vary, depending on which states or international organizations do the compiling, and whose ox is being gored, but the following is probably relatively non-controversial:

Contraband production and distribution: the global *drug trade* is the biggest item here, but there are many other contraband goods that move through criminal hands. A recent addition in this category are so-called '*intellectual property theft*' items, such as pirated videos and CDs. Of course there is nothing new about smuggling, perhaps the oldest form of 'international' criminal activity. What is different is the scale of operations, the sophisticated use of communications and transportation technology, and the emergence of globally organized networks and even cooperative ventures and strategic partnerships among rival networks.

Financial and commercial crime: the contemporary technologies of capitalist finance lend themselves to subversion by organized criminal groups able to hire and utilize business skills and technological savvy. The old criminal problem of *counterfeiting* has been globalized and made technically sophisticated, from fraudulent documentation to currency (phoney US $100 bills may now rival the real thing worldwide). *Financial fraud* is greatly assisted by globalization and the weakness of regulation. '*Cybercrime*' has become a major concern, as the computer technology that has permitted transnational capital flows in real time has come under systematic attack to a degree that is probably gravely underreported, given corporate reluctance to publicly admit to ineffective security. Organized *credit card fraud* is now a major international problem. Another aspect is *corruption* of business, where criminal elements systematically penetrate and gain control of licit organizations and activities, both as fronts for their criminal networks, and as a means of buying influence and protection.

Politically oriented criminal activity: this is a grab-bag category of activities that either directly target governments or have associations with politically motivated groups. The global market in the *illegal arms trade* serves not only the needs of criminal organizations themselves for state-of-the-art armament, but also 'rogue' states, or states under sanctions, or non-state 'terrorist' groups or insurgent forces. Illicit *technology transfers* and the smuggling of *weapons of mass destruction* (nuclear, biological, chemical) may find either state or non-state political actors as customers. There is also a considerable market for services associated with organized *sanctions violations*. Another growing problem is *environmental crime*, in which national or internationally agreed pollution controls are evaded, and hazardous wastes dumped surreptitiously. Criminal organizations offer opportunities for systematic *tax evasion* (as opposed to licit actors' tax avoidance) that denies states revenues. Systematic *corruption* of government officials fosters favourable environments for criminal activities. Finally, there is the question of direct connections between organized criminal networks and *terrorism*. The latter is probably exaggerated (the US no longer warns much about 'narco-terrorism', a Reagan-era formulation), apart from occasional tactical cooperation, and the tendency of some 'guerrilla' groups to degenerate into not much more than criminal protection and extortion rackets, including *kidnapping for ransom*. The key point here is that the political targets of organized criminal activity are chosen not with political or ideological objectives in mind, but purely as a means of increasing profits. From a policing and intelligence point of view, politically motivated non-state actors must be analytically separated from criminal organizations with monetary motivations.

Smuggling and trafficking in persons: globalization has greatly increased the flow of capital, goods and services, but the movement of people has been much more restricted, with growing state controls, whether over economic migrants or refugees and asylum seekers, being constructed in both Western Europe and North America. Not surprisingly, this has led to the increasing criminalization of illegal migration, and provision of *human smuggling* services by organized criminal networks. Many of those successfully smuggled become sources of virtual slave labour for criminal enterprises in host countries. Particularly odious is the supply of women and children for the global *sex trade*.

Money laundering: money laundering constitutes a separate category in the same way that international finance can be looked at separately from other forms of global capitalist activity. Money laundering is the means whereby the other forms of international criminal activity are financed, or, to put it differently, the means whereby criminal profits can be securely circulated and reinvested. Money laundering networks have become extremely sophisticated with the new technologies and financial expertise, which is to say that they have become extremely difficult to track and penetrate. Carefully constructed linkages to licit financial and commercial institutions compound the problem.

Turning to the major known criminal networks, the regional/ethnic basis of the global illicit economy is its most striking feature. The geography of criminal enterprise can be broken down into roughly eight bases, spanning all the continents of the globe.

Italian mafia: the oldest and best known of organized criminal groups, *Cosa Nostra* is based in Sicily, from whence it branched out first to North America with Italian immigration in the late nineteenth and early twentieth centuries, and more recently into global operations often in conjunction with other groups. Drugs and illegal arms traffic and recently environmental crimes feature heavily in Mafia activity. In its long history in Italy, the Mafia developed close relations with politicians and government officials, especially with the Christian Democrats during the long hegemony of the Right during the Cold War. Recently under attack from anti-corruption investigators, the Italian Mafia seems to have weathered the assaults.

Russia and former Soviet Bloc: the privatization of state-owned enterprises and political corruption in post-Communist governing structures has proved to be fertile ground for encouraging the growth of organized criminal networks (whose origins rest in Communist era black markets) that have now expanded well beyond their regional bases. The Russian financial sector has been a particular target for penetration, but other export-oriented economic sectors, such as oil and gas, and precious metals have also been deeply penetrated. Other parts of the former Soviet Bloc have generated their own specialties, such as the export of women and girls for the European and North American sex trade (the impoverished little pseudo-state of Moldova, which recently voted the Communist party back into power, has become one of the world's leading suppliers of virtually enslaved sex workers[8]). Other regional groupings are based in the Balkans. Criminal gangs specializing in drugs and other contraband dominate much of the Albanian countryside and extend as well into Kosovo, where the Kosovo Liberation Army obtained arms and ammunition via Albanian arms trafficking networks. Russian mafias have moved into North America via Russian expatriate communities. An ironic sidebar is the degree to which the 'save Soviet Jewry' campaigns of the 1970s and 1980s promoted the movement of Russian criminals abroad: a number were not actually Jews, but posed as such to gain immediate entry to Israel, which has continued as a base of operations since.

Triads and mainland Chinese gangs: the secretive Triad organizations that date back three centuries are particularly located in Hong King, Taiwan and ethnic Chinese overseas enclaves. Traditionally concerned with opium, gambling, prostitution, etc., and with close ties to the pre-Communist Kuomintang, Triads have been joined by mainland-based groups that have expanded into large-scale smuggling of people and lucrative financial crime, including credit-card fraud, intellectual property theft, and cybercrime. North America has become a focus for expansion. Canada, with its recent focus on encouraging entrepreneurial or business immigrants from Asia, acts as a useful gateway into the USA. Investment in legitimate businesses, both in Asia and North America, with associated influence on both the private and public sectors, has recently come to the fore.

Japanese Yakuza: deeply entrenched in Japanese society, the *Yakuza* hold a quasi-legitimate status.[9] Drugs, gambling, prostitution, arms, extortion and financial crime are staple activities. They too have been internationalizing their activities beyond Japan and the Japanese sphere in Asia, with limited direct presence in Hawaii and the west coast of the USA and strategic investments in real estate and money laundering through US financial institutions.

Latin American drug cartels: a natural monopoly in cocaine supply has made Latin

America a primary locus of the global drug trade. Centred in Columbia, the previously dominant Cali cartel suffered a number of reverses; a new generation of traffickers has followed with more diversified leadership.[10]

Activity has become more decentralized, with Mexico gaining in importance due to its proximity to the lucrative US market in narcotics, and its membership in NAFTA. The Caribbean is a major transit route. Throughout Latin American areas of criminal influence, corruption and intimidation of governments have been practised on a scale that has suggested to some observers the emergence of a new form of non-state authoritarianism.[11]

Shadowy links with American police and security forces have been strongly alleged in particular cases. Sometimes CIA and FBI assets become liabilities, however: the US invasion of Panama to imprison Manuel Noriega, former CIA asset and drug trafficker, is a prize example of a tactical alliance gone sour.

Nigerian criminal organizations: Africa has not been left off the global criminal map, and Nigerian criminal groups are at the apex of indigenous African organizations. Nigerian syndicates are especially internationalized, holding a strategic place in global drug trafficking routes, especially with Asian heroin and in transhipment of South American cocaine to Europe. They also specialize in middle-range financial fraud schemes targeting North American and European businesses and individuals. Nigerian groups benefit from a corrupt and authoritarian Nigerian state.

Middle and Near East: an ancient tradition of trade in contraband between South Asia, the Middle East and the Eastern Mediterranean continues today with criminal organizations centred in Turkey and Pakistan. Accusations that the pariah Taliban regime in Afghanistan permits a hard currency-earning opium poppy industry to supply up to nearly three-quarters of world production have recently been contradicted by that regime's apparent willingness to force opium fields out of production.[12]

North America: the heartland of global capitalism is obviously a focal point for international criminal activity. The US is the single largest market for illegal drugs. The highly deregulated US industrial and financial system offers numerous lucrative opportunities. And the relative lack of controls over the manufacture and sale of firearms makes the US a primary source for criminal groups engaged in the illegal arms trade. There is a tendency among American policymakers to view the US as a target of foreign organizations rather than as a home base for the operations of American criminal organizations. However, many of the 'ethnic' criminal organizations (like the 'Italian' Mafia) have long since been assimilated, like other immigrant groups, into the American melting pot; whatever their original cultural origins, they can now be considered good, or bad, Americans. More recent arrivals may still be primarily 'foreign' in orientation with stronger roots to their headquarters abroad, but in time many of these too may branch off as autonomous operations. Of course, there is political benefit to labelling criminal groups as foreign or 'other' and so we can expect that in official US anti-crime discourse, America will continue to be depicted as target rather than as source. Canada fits into this picture as well: with increasing economic integration under free trade and with relatively low levels of control over population mobility between Canada and the US, Canada is seen as a gateway for criminal entry into the US, as well as a target in itself.

The strongly regional and ethnic/cultural rootedness of global criminal organizations is a remarkable feature, worth further attention. Manuel Castells sees a direct link to the reassertion of the politics of identity in the information age.

> The more organized crime becomes global, the more its most important components emphasize their cultural identity, so as not to disappear in the whirlwind of the space of flows. In so doing, they preserve their ethnic, cultural, and, where possible, territorial bases. This is their strength. Criminal networks are probably in advance of multinational corporations in their decisive ability to combine cultural identity and global business.[13]

Castells goes on to point out that global criminal networks are also inducing a new culture, especially attractive to marginalized and alienated youth. The collective fascination of popular culture around the globe with action movies featuring protagonists from the criminal world 'may well indicate the cultural breakdown of the traditional moral order, and the implicit recognition of a new society, made up of communal identity and unruly competition, of which global crime is a condensed expression'.[14]

Whatever its cultural impact, there are still many questions about international organized crime's economic significance. Just how big a chunk of the global economy is represented by the Dark Side? What is the dollar value of criminal operations? There are no shortages of pat, but alarming, answers to these questions proffered by various 'authorities', official and unofficial. One oft-cited figure, stemming from a key 1994 UN Conference in Naples on international crime, was that the global drug trade amounted to $500 billion (US) per year. The American component of this trade has been variously estimated as anything from $20 billion to $200–300 billion. 'Experts' tracking global money laundering trails have estimated the global 'criminal product' as equal to $1 trillion.[15] The latter figure sounds highly alarming, but is just over half the cost of the tax cuts proposed by President George W. Bush to the US Congress in 2001 (and less than the counter-proposals by the Democrats). But how credible are such estimates in the first place? Peter Gill suggests that they 'must be taken with a large sack of salt'.[16] Obviously policing and security agencies have some organizational and budgetary stake in elaborating, if not exaggerating, the threat. They appear very much in the same guise as police chiefs appealing to local councils for more money. Such appeals are always and traditionally two-pronged: (1) 'we are doing a fine job of combating crime'; but (2), 'crime is increasing relentlessly and more resources are required to keep up the good work'. Nor is this inflationary tendency limited to the usual official suspects. There is a burgeoning field of private 'experts' who act as consultants and advisers to governments on crime policy who obviously have a stake in magnifying the threat (similar in motivation and effects to the counter-terrorism industry).

In point of fact, the criminal operations of the Dark Side defy measurement, by definition. How can police and 'experts' *know* the dollar value of operations, the trails of which are deliberately, and very professionally, covered up? If officials really knew as much as they profess to know about the value of criminal operations, they would know enough to shut them down.

That said, it is obvious that the global criminal economy is of a magnitude that does to a degree at least threaten the legitimacy of states and the profitability of corporations. Nor can there be much doubt about the social ravages of the drug and sex trades, or the corrosive political and human impact of illegal arms traffic, or the disastrous moral examples set by gangsters openly enjoying the proceeds of crime while intimidating and attacking critics with apparent impunity. Putting precise numbers on international crime is an inherently implausible enterprise, but even if the size of the problem cannot be accurately measured, there *is* a problem, and it is a *big* problem. As the Bright Side of globalization has grown by leaps and bounds, so too has its twin, the Dark Side.

THE SPECTRE: A NEW 'CRIMINTERN'?

In 1994 the Washington-based Centre for Strategic and International Studies sponsored a conference and subsequent book on global organized crime, titled *The New Empire of Evil*.[17] The echo from the rhetoric of Ronald Reagan's second Cold War was no accident. The conservative think tank featured a number of barely recycled Cold Warriors, as well as the Director of the CIA, to affirm that global mafias had in effect replaced the Soviet Union as the leading national security threat to the USA. One of the non-governmental participants in this symposium, journalist Claire Sterling (who in the Reagan era had advanced the thesis that international terrorism was all directed from Moscow) in the same year published a book that purported to describe a new international *Pax Mafiosa*.[18]

Despite the evident attraction in replacing the deposed Cold War enemy with another, equally nefarious Other, whose repellent characteristics could give good service in maintaining Cold War-level security budgets, this somewhat literal-minded transposition of one security paradigm to another, different, set of conditions has not maintained momentum into the decidedly post-Cold War twenty-first century. But this does not mean that international crime does not figure in the new dominant security paradigm. It does play a very important part, but as one (bad) actor among many, rather than as a new monolith.

In the new security paradigm, the centre no longer holds. While potentially hostile major powers like China, continue to cause concern, attention has shifted toward smaller, 'rogue' states like Iraq, Libya, and North Korea and toward regional security problems. Turbulent non-state actors are seen as particularly difficult to assess and counter, but even here, international criminal organizations often take an secondary billing to terrorist networks who represent more spectacular public threats to Western hegemony. The criminal threat does however interact with other diffuse threats in the present security paradigm in ways that have important implications for how security and policing will be deployed on a global scale in the years ahead.

The US *International Crime Threat Assessment* document defines international criminal organizations as posing 'significant' threats to 'democratic and free market systems, as well as vital US national interests', by

- increasing crime and societal problems;
- corrupting public officials;
- compromising the integrity of democratic institutions;
- penetrating the legitimate economy;
- damaging the credibility of banking and financial institutions;
- undermining support for democratic and free market reforms.

In short, the US views the criminal operations of the Dark Side as threats both to the state system and to the neoliberal agenda of global marketization. There are certain ironies inherent in this view. The very deepening of neoliberal globalization that the US seeks to promote will offer greater opportunities for sophisticated criminal groups to blend their international operations into the flows of legitimate commerce, making them less visible, as well as enhancing the volume, speed and efficiency of their operations. Moreover, as the Russian example has demonstrated, the rapid dissolution of illiberal command economies may pose more of a problem than a solution from a neoliberal perspective. As the *Threat Assessment* notes with admirable honesty, 'a radical breakdown of the Communist system in China could intensify the influence of Chinese criminal organizations within China's political and economic systems and provide a safe-haven for expanding criminal operations abroad'. Thus the Cold War security paradigm is turned on its head!

For the US, the worst case scenario for the next decade would see increasingly large, sophisticated, and well-armed criminal organizations forming effective strategic partnerships with one another and with other forces on the Dark Side, such as terrorist groups and rogue states, possibly even eventuating in the emergence of 'criminal states' that would not only serve to undermine the global financial and commercial system, but might adopt the anti-Western ideological agendas of terrorist groups, 'thereby weakening US political, economic, and security agendas around the world'. This does not add up to a new Crimintern, as such, but it is still a prospect menacing enough to trouble the dreams of American policy makers.

A NEW GLOBAL LEVIATHAN?

The Dark Side threat is, in the nature of these matters, also a considerable opportunity for US prospects of continuing global leadership. It is moreover part of a complex of issues surrounding globalization, on both the Dark and the Bright sides, that is preparing the ground for the return of the state after a series of retreats and setbacks it has suffered as a result of neoliberal globalization. The space of flows is largely unregulated and market mechanisms on their own are inherently insecure. Globalization has recreated the Hobbesian state of nature, this time writ large, with no Leviathan in sight — save that of the world's only superpower left standing, the United States. However, the US state is neither willing, for reasons of ideology, nor capable, for reasons of the limitations of even its power while acting alone, to take over the governance of the Bright Side. It is blatantly evident that unregulated market forces at work on a global scale are fostering catastrophic problems, of which environmental degradation is a particularly pressing example. Yet the US, under Bush, Jr., has unilaterally walked out of the Kyoto agreement on limiting greenhouse emissions. There is no reason to expect the US state to suddenly accept a calling to regulate and control the global state of nature when it continues to see the interests of American corporations and global economic liberalization as synonymous with its national interest. Nor does the US state, as a stand-alone entity, have the capacity to control the cyclonic space of flows, where national boundaries and national legal jurisdictions are blown away, sometimes leaving barely a trace. But it precisely here that the new security paradigm regarding the Dark Side offers a beachhead for the return of Leviathan, or at least Leviathan's children.

During Hobsbawm's 'Golden Age' of the twentieth century,[19] states continued to play a leading role, even as capitalism was extending its global base of operations. The Cold War was the key to the continued dominance of the state form. Even the continued quasi-Keynesian role of the state in the capitalist economy was in part predicated on the global contest with the Soviet Bloc (Keynes in khaki). State power could be extended internally, and projected externally, so long as national security, defined primarily in military and policing terms, could be plausibly invoked. Neoliberalism has undone much of this legitimation of state power, but the collapse of the Cold War enemy drastically undermined its ideological viability. Many on the left, hopeful of a 'peace dividend' and rightly suspicious of the repressive forms that state power had exhibited during the Cold war era, have subsequently ridiculed and warned against the post-Cold War identification by military, security, intelligence, and policing establishments of new enemies and new threats to replace the old. Yet in so doing, they miss the irony that it is precisely on the terrain of 'enemies' and 'threats' that the state, humiliated and routed by neoliberalism, is making a return. This is not perhaps the kind of reborn state that the left is likely to cherish, but it may be the only state we are likely to see with a fighting chance to restore some regulation to the global whirlwind.

If the borderless threats to national security emanating from the Dark Side are to be effectively contained ('contained' is carefully chosen, as crime has never, of course, been eradicated), it can only be as the result of two interrelated developments. The first is that states pool their limited national repressive resources and jurisdictional controls in a cooperative effort to counter borderless threats with what amounts to borderless policing. Secondly, and paradoxically, this can only be achieved if most national states, including the leading and more powerful ones, agree to accept the hegemonic leadership of the only remaining superpower state, the USA. In some sense, the limits of which will have to be painfully negotiated, borderless policing actually entails the *extension of borders*, namely the borders of US jurisdiction, as well as those of regional blocs under US influence, like Europe.

Early in 2001, the Director of the FBI, Louis Freeh told a gathering of business leaders at the World Economic Forum that the FBI was 'stretching its resources' to fight increasingly techno savvy criminals around the world. Because of the 'increasingly global nature of criminal activity', the FBI now has 'agents in at least 40 countries. It has also helped 26 countries train law enforcement agents'.[20] The old supranational policing structure, Interpol, is increasingly by-passed in favour of direct multilateral cooperation among police and security forces, to a considerable extent under US tutelage. There is a thickening web of police and security cooperation on the ground, as it were, with sharing of information, development of common databases, and even partnerships in action. A great deal of this goes on well below the level of elected politicians and senior bureaucrats. The so-called 'third pillar' of Maastricht (immigration, security, policing), for example, seems much less developed in terms of supranational institution building than the other two pillars. In fact, street level cooperation works so well that supranational institutions are less needed. And there is a reason for this: there is already an historical experience of direct cooperation across borders stemming from the years of the Cold War alliance.[21]

The emergence of an anti-money laundering regime offers a particularly intriguing example of how US-led transnational policing can work, and of its wider implications. Eric Helleiner points out that international tax evasion and capital flight have largely escaped liberal censure, both for ideological and technological reasons: some have sympathized with capital fleeing meddlesome governments, while others have argued that it is no longer technically possible to regulate the flow of capital across borders.[22] Helleiner points to the emerging anti-money laundering regime as evidence that reregulation is as much a feature of global finance as deregulation, and that the same technologies that have been said to erode state regulatory capacity may actually enhance it. US leadership has been a key factor here, as has the selective role of liberal ideology. As the US identified money laundering as a crucial element in tracking (and potentially disrupting) the global criminal economy, a very different approach was apparent than toward tax evasion and capital flight.[23]

The heart of the anti-money laundering regime is in the US Department of the Treasury, in a bureau known as the Financial Crimes Enforcement Network (FinCEN). FinCEN 'links the law enforcement, financial and regulatory communities together for the common purpose of preventing, detecting and prosecuting money laundering and other financial crimes'.[24] Its main tools are surveillance and analysis. First, a stiff reporting regime is encouraged for financial institutions around the world, and second, sophisticated 'artificial intelligence' software is deployed to sort the vast amount of data to detect anomalous patterns. When identified, such patterns can point to potential prosecutions, so long as the state with appropriate jurisdiction is willing to prosecute. Other states have been pressured to comply with beefed-up reporting requirements, and new more stringent local legislation has in many cases been passed at US behest. Nor has the financial sector been immune: traditionally secretive banking institutions have been encouraged to open up about their customers, at least to Uncle Sam.

The program remains to be proven, but it does highlight an exquisite irony: the very technologies that have facilitated instantaneous capital flows around the globe, and facilitated money laundering as the Dark Side shadowing of global finance, can also be turned into instruments of surveillance and intervention by states working together to monitor markets. In theory, every licit financial transaction on the globe can be tracked and with the appropriate software, sorted automatically to flag suspicious movements. FinCEN demonstrates that one of the ideological props of neoliberal globalization is a myth: cross-border flows can be checked, if the will exists to do so. In the case of money laundering, the will exists among the US government and its allies and to a degree in a private financial sector fearful of criminal threats to its operations. The same logic could be applied to the licit financial sector. That it has not been so applied is less a result of technological determinism than of ideology. Of course, financial institutions are ambivalent about these pressures to open their operations and their customer information to Big Brother in Washington DC. Many licit companies may be engaging in practices that will not stand close scrutiny. On the other hand, the depredations of the money launderers threaten to destabilize financial markets and undermine the legitimacy of respectable institutions. Perhaps at the end of the day, bankers are not nearly so powerful and invulnerable as their critics tend to depict them.

Under the new security paradigm, some quiet turf wars have broken out within state apparatuses. Security and intelligence agencies have been jostling for better position in relation to police agencies in combating international organized crime. This is particularly evident in the UK, where MI5, its heavy involvement in Northern Ireland apparently lessening with the onset of the peace process, has turned to global crime as a major target, thus stepping on some other jurisdictional toes. There are differences in approach between security and intelligence and law enforcement agencies. The former tend to be more interested in constructing the big picture and maintaining long-term penetrations of targeted organizations as useful intelligence assets; law enforcement agencies have traditionally been more interested in using sources in the shorter term to go for criminal prosecutions. Recently, a small scandal erupted in Canada when it was revealed in the press that a joint project on Chinese Triad penetration of Canada, involving investigators from the civilian security service, CSIS, and the national police agency, the RCMP, had come unstuck when CSIS brass torpedoed the project, and ordered copies of the draft report to be destroyed (the draft soon showed up on the internet). Turf wars are traditional in this area. More interesting is the contemporary trend described by Peter Gill to what he calls 'intelligence-led policing'. In the increasingly transnational world of policing, Gill argues, 'intelligence processes are absolutely central: networks of information exchange can develop *sub rosa* in a way that joint operations cannot.... Intelligence networks are always likely to be far in advance of operational networks and informal ones will always be far more extensive than formal ones.'[25]

Given a willingness to work together, states have at their disposal some awesome resources of surveillance to peer into the Dark Side. Recently, the European parliament has displayed some concern over the ECHELON system of communications interception carried out by the signatory countries to the UKUSA intelligence alliance (the USA, UK, Canada, Australia/New Zealand). The UKUSA network is equipped to intercept targeted communications throughout the world, specifically everything relayed via the communication satellite system — long distance telephone conversations, e-mail, etc. ECHELON describes a software 'dictionary' system for flagging key words and names and thus sorting 'signals' from the 'noise' that constitutes most everyday traffic. The FBI has a software program called CARNIVORE that is capable of trolling through the tide of e-mail communication to flag targeted subjects for closer scrutiny. Every web surfer knows how useful search engines can be in finding material of interest. ECHELON and CARNIVORE, and other less publicly known programs, indicate just how much more powerful technology can be when in the hands of states with virtually unlimited resources and motivation. In the battle against terrorists, criminals, and 'rogue' nations, the old Cold War alliance is still alive and kicking, reconstituted and rededicated to different purposes, expanded, and much more technologically sophisticated. The state may have retreated on some fronts, but on others it has been gathering its forces and focusing on new advances. What is different in the present era is that individual states, even the only superpower, cannot act effectively as stand-alone entities, but must always act in concert, albeit under firm American leadership. Might the rallying cry of the new security and policing Internationale not be 'Solidarity Forever'?

There are limits to state power. Some are political: even with American muscle being applied, cooperation is not always easy to achieve. The European restiveness about ECHELON seems in large part motivated by French suspicion of an 'Anglophone spy network' and fears about its alleged use to gather commercial intelligence on behalf of American transnational corporations (The French of course do the same thing, on a smaller scale — this has been dubbed 'FRENCHELON'). Some are technical: 128-bit encryption, which anyone can download free on the internet, and is the minimum standard for online financial transactions, has so far defied the best efforts of the biggest intelligence agencies like the American NSA or the British GCHQ at decryption. The FBI, having failed to achieve a 'key escrow' system by law, have raged impotently at the prospect that international terrorists and criminals are defeating their sophisticated interception efforts by using the same encryption programs that twelve year olds employ in playing online computer games with one another. Only in Tony Blair's UK has a government moved beyond festering frustration and taken the bull by the horns. The Regulation of Investigatory Powers (RIP) Act empowers law enforcement agencies to demand that persons who have engaged in encrypted communications suspected of relating to such matters as criminal activity, terrorism, or pornography, disclose their 'keys'. Failure to comply could lead to two years imprisonment.[26] At the same time, MI5 has set up a state-of-the-art centre to monitor all e-mail and online communication in and through the UK. The most telling criticism of the RIP act does not come from outraged civil libertarians but from powerful e-commerce interests who have threatened to take their operations offshore to escape a climate of insecurity for free enterprise. This is a serious contradiction in attempts to control the Dark Side. The facilitation of e-commerce via rapid and unregulated development of new information technologies (a key plank in the neoliberal agenda) runs up against law enforcement and security concerns, directed ironically at protecting the licit global economy.

Clearly, capitalism today faces once again the old Hobbesian dilemma, this time on a global, rather than a national, scale. Micro-rationality of economic actors leads to macro-irrationality. Security in the market state of nature can only be purchased at the cost of the transfer of power to Leviathan, this time an international Leviathan. But profit-maximizing economic actors who fear their competitors are also free market ideologues who greatly fear a new global Leviathan as a threat in and of itself. How this dilemma will fall out remains to be seen, but it is a reasonable conjecture that at the end of the day enlightened self-interest will outpace narrow greed. After all, the more global the operations of transnational corporations and finance become, the broader the picture available to capitalist decision makers and the better they will be able to appreciate the need for trade-offs and compromise in the name of long-term self-protection. On the other side, the new Leviathan is hardly motivated either by socialism or by power-seeking self-aggrandizement. Hobbes in the seventeenth century understood that Leviathan was all-powerful only for the purpose of enforcing contracts between private actors, not for performing the work of these actors. Nevertheless, to the extent that the new state security *entente* actually succeeds in enforcing effective controls over unruly criminal non-state actors, it will at the same time have shown that bureaucrats can compete on the same global terrain as capitalists, and that politics are, after all, as necessary as markets — indeed, necessary *for* markets. This may be no revolution in thinking, but it does modify the expansive claims of neoliberalism.

TAKING SIDES?

Both states and corporations are targeted and threatened by criminal organizations, and both have powerful stakes in combating and containing criminal activities. But if the clash of the big battalions on the global stage leaves many observers as emotionally unengaged as spectators at a battle of dinosaurs, one compelling truth about organized crime should not be obscured. Its real victims are ordinary people, aggressively exploited and destroyed for the enrichment of the rapacious and the savage. Critics of globalization may well cite the horrific human and ecological costs of licit capitalist profit-seeking behaviour, and the casual brutality of 'legitimate' state power in defence of capital. It takes nothing away from these critiques to grant that worse is done on the Dark Side, and with none of the liberal scruples that do intrude on the consciences of both the corporate and state elites, from time to time. And however great the democratic deficit may be, there is not even a shred of accountability that clings to the organizations of the Dark Side.

In the present political climate, contestation by 'civil society' of globalization and of the present instruments of global governance, such as they are, is increasingly at the centre of progressive politics. Unfortunately, the institutional objects of anti-globalization wrath, and in particular the policing and security forces that form the sharp edge of states in the street confrontations with protestors at Seattle, Prague, Quebec City and other sites for demonstrations, also happen to be the only forces that can seriously challenge the organized criminal groups that threaten to ravage civil society more ruthlessly and violently than the licit global economy. This is a central, but little noted, paradox of the present conjuncture: the legitimacy of state policing and security of the Bright Side is being undermined at the very moment when they are most needed to combat the multiple threats to global welfare posed by the organizations of the Dark Side.

NOTES

1   Available at http://www.fas.org/irp/threat/pub45270index.html.
2   Perhaps reflecting the relatively multicultural environment of the former Soviet Union, the Russian mafia operating in North America have been less ethnically exclusive in their recruitment than other organizations. While offering flexibility, this has also proved a problem: police penetration leading to some notable arrests has been based on planted non-Russian sources.
3   'Exporting corruption: privatisation, multinationals and bribery', The Corner House, *Briefing* 19, June 2000.
4   Federico Varese, 'There's no place like home: how the Mafia finds it difficult to expand from its geographical base', *Times Literary Supplement*, 23 February 2001, p. 4.
5   Janice Thomson, *Mercenaries, Pirates, and Sovereigns: State Building and Extraterritorial Violence in Early Modern Europe*, Princeton: Princeton University Press, 1994, and 'State sovereignty in international relations', *International Studies Quarterly*, 39:2, 1995.
6   H. Richard Friman & Peter Andreas, eds., *The Illicit Global Economy & State Power*, Lanham Md.: Rowman & Littlefield, 1999, 'Introduction', pp. 9–10.
7   Manuel Castells, *The Rise of the Network Society*, Oxford: Blackwell, 1996, pp. 376–428.
8   Martin A. Lee, 'The globalization of sexual slavery', *The San Francisco Bay Guardian*, 5 March 2001.

9   Bertell Ollman has argued that the *Yakuza* perform a crucial political role in legitimating the 'emperor-system' that is, in his opinion, the real basis of the Japanese regime: Ollman, 'The Emperor and the Yakuza', *New Left Review*, 2nd series: 8, March/April 2001.

10   Tom Farer, ed., *Transnational Crime in the Americas*, NY: Routledge, 1999.

11   Louise I. Shelley, 'Transnational organized crime: the new authoritarianism', in Friman & Andreas, *Illicit Global Economy*.

12   Barbara Crossette, 'Taliban's poppy ban seems to be a success, U.S. team says', *New York Times*, 20 May 2001.

13   Castells, *End of Millennium*, Oxford: Blackwell, 1998, p. 204.

14   *Ibid*, p. 205.

15   Figures cited in Peter Gill, *Rounding Up the Usual Suspects? Developments in Contemporary Law Enforcement Intelligence*, Aldershot: Ashgate 2000, p. 69.

16   *Ibid*.

17   Linnea P. Raine & Frank J. Cilluffo, eds., *Global Organized Crime: the New Empire of Evil*, CSIS: Washington, DC, 1994.

18   Claire Sterling, *Thieves' World: the Threat of the New Global Network of Organized Crime*, NY: Simon & Schuster, 1994.

19   Eric Hobsbawm, *Age of Extremes: the Short Twentieth Century, 1914-1991*, London: Abacus, 1995, pp. 225-402.

20   Agence France Presse, 5 April 2001.

21   Reg Whitaker, 'Refugees: the security dimension', *Citizenship Studies*, 2:3, November 1998.

22   Eric Helleiner, 'State power and the regulation of illicit activity on global finance', in Friman & Andreas, *Illicit Global Economy*.

23   Tom Naylor, who has produced some of the best and most critical writing on the global criminal economy, somewhat inexplicably derides the importance of tracking money laundering as a pointless enterprise. Naylor, 'Why Canada's new anti-money laundering bill is a washout', *The Globe & Mail*, 13 April 2000. On the contrary, money laundering provides the thread that, if unravelled, describes the ownership structure of the global criminal economy and can point to numerous trails of illicit activity. The US government is surely not wrong in concentrating its investigative resources on this target.

24   United States Department of the Treasury, Financial Crimes Enforcement Network, *Strategic Plan: 2000-2005*.

25   Gill, *Rounding Up the Usual Suspects?*, p. 54.

26   *Regulation of Investigatory Powers Act 2000*, Chapter 23, part III, ss. 49-53.

IMPERIALISM, DOLLARIZATION AND THE EURO

Guglielmo Carchedi

1. THE MYTHS OF GLOBALIZATION

In recent years, theories of imperialism have fallen into disgrace and have been replaced by more fashionable analyses in terms of globalization. This is regrettable. For while this term stresses real phenomena like the great upsurge in international capital mobility and the further extension of markets resulting from it, the analysis of these quantitative phenomena is often laden with ideological connotations. Very often these have to do with the triumph of capitalism over 'socialism' (e.g. Mitterand's programme commune) or 'communism' (the USSR, China, etc.) whereby capitalism's inner rationality allegedly displaces the irrationality and inefficiency of alternative systems, and brings in its wake not only democracy but also advanced technologies allowing men and women to become the arbiters of their own destiny. The implication of the confusion of analysis with ideology in the concept of globalization is that it is made to seem that not only competing systems but even class struggle must disappear. This makes it especially important to separate real phenomena from their ideological rendition. The Left's anti-capitalist struggles are invalidated if use is made of categories of analysis, like globalization, that are ideologically laden in favour of capital.

The failure to separate real phenomena from the ideological rendition may lead to ignoring the extent to which the limits of both social democracy and the communist regimes in the twentieth century were inextricably linked to their incorporation of fundamental elements of capitalist social relations. No less important, it may lead to implicitly accepting some basic tenets of orthodox economics. These tenets are all based on assuming that the basic unit, and thus the starting point, of analysis is the individual equipped with an inborn, a-historical, egoistic rationality; and that the free exercise of this rationality results in the economy either being in, or tending towards, equilibrium. But since it can be conclusively shown that these tenets do not fit empirical evidence, are marred both by logical inconsistencies and by circular reasoning, and are untestable in terms of neoclassical economics' own methodology,[1] it follows that there is no reason to assume that human nature is inherently egoistic and that any social system based on, say, altruism (socialism) is doomed to failure. No (theorization of a) social system radically alternative to capitalism can be based on the egoistic behaviour inherent in neoclassical economics.

The great(er) volume of capital moving across national frontiers in recent decades, which has nothing to do with the fall of the barriers posed by 'communism', has represented a situation whereby capital, unable to find a profitable outlet in the productive sphere, tries its luck in financial/speculative operations. Seen from this angle, the magnitude of (financial) capital movements, far from being the result of capitalism's greater freedom to express its rationality, is a sign of the limits capital imposes upon its own growth, upon itself. This is a sign that the present economic crisis is far from having been overcome. As for the further claim that ideologists of globalization advance, i.e., that thanks to globalization, democracy has extended to the former 'evil empire' as well as to other 'emerging' market economies, this is too blatantly false to deserve any serious consideration. Far from enjoying a 'peace dividend', those countries have sunk into unprecedented economic crises while substituting their traditional corrupted bureaucracies with an equally corrupted capitalist class. Moreover, it is a specific type of democracy, that which is functional for the development of capitalism, that is referred to, not the democracy upon which a socialist system should be based.[2]

Finally, empirical evidence gives the lie to the view that technological innovations allow people to shape their own destinies through the generalized cornucopia, higher employment, increasing skills and work satisfaction they allegedly bring. The empirical evidence brought to bear by Marxist value analysis shows that the introduction of technological innovations tendentially causes unemployment, decreasing real wages, de-qualification and de-skilling, new forms of labour's subordination to capital, and ultimately economic crises, while at the same time causing counter-tendencies.[3] It is true that privileged strata of the working class (mainly in some countries of the dominant block) can enjoy (temporarily) greater welfare as a result of technological innovations. But, on the whole, income disparities, poverty, unemployment and human degradation have never been so great as in this age of 'globalization'.

Far from illusions about 'the end of labour', the world proletariat not only obstinately refuses to disappear, it is in fact increasing in size. Indeed, by taking a global view, we may see that the world working class emerges more vividly than ever. This is obvious if the proletariat (collective worker) is defined in terms of production relations, as those who are directly or indirectly dependent for their livelihood on capital.[4] Even neoclassical economists should be able to understand that the greater capitalism's expansion, the larger the collective labourer. But they not only close their eyes to the spreading of capitalist production relations, they also manage to ignore the massive income differentials on a world scale (i.e. they consider them to be deviations from a model rather than features inherent in that model). Not surprisingly, they fail to see income differentials as a necessary result of class (production) relations. But, in face of the fact that a few hundreds super-billionaires own a wealth comparable to the income of 45% of the world population, how can they hold that the world working class is fading away? And even if one focuses on countries rather than on classes, copious statistical data on the 'rich countries' show that 'social exclusion' is spreading. It takes a fertile imag-ination (perhaps a necessary antidote to a barren theory) to hold onto the thesis that globalization tendentially brings with it a classless society.

The world proletariat cannot free itself of capital as long as it accepts its perspective. If the notion of globalization is as rich in ideological substance as it is poor in heuristic content, the analysis of the phenomena sketched above requires a different frame of analysis. This essay shall argue that the phenomena the theorists of globalization deal with should be seen from an opposite frame of analysis, one focusing on the world imperialist system and the new developments and contradictions within it. Elements of such an alternative view are submitted, even if in a necessarily sketchy form, in section 2. By way of example, section 3 focuses upon one aspect of this new imperialist dimension, that of international seigniorage and of the struggle between the dollar and the Euro as an aspect of inter imperialist rivalries. Finally, section 4 draws some conclusions on the class structure emerging from these developments.

2. THE REALITIES OF IMPERIALISM

From an economic standpoint, imperialism is *systematic* appropriation of inter national value, i.e. capitalist *enterprises* in the imperialist countries appropriate value systematically from *enterprises* (but also from 'independent' producers) in the dominated countries. While this requires both economic conditions (e.g. a specific structuring of the dominated countries' economies, as we shall see below) and non-economic ones (political, military, legal, institutional, etc.) for the continuation of that appropriation, what follows will focus principally on the former, the fundamental, aspect. The appropriation of value at the core of economic imperialism today happens in at least four ways: (a) repatriation of interests and profits on direct and indirect foreign investments; (b) payment of interests on foreign debts; (c) unequal exchange inherent in international trade; and (d) seigniorage, the advantage that accrues to the use of the hegemonic power's currency as the international currency. This essay will focus on seigniorage (in the next section) rather than on the other forms of value appro-priation. This is not due to the latter's necessarily greater importance in inter-imperialist relations. On the contrary, investments and foreign debt, as well as unequal exchange, play a much more visible role in shaping the internal struc-ture of the dominated countries. Especially foreign debt is a new phenomenon (relative to the old form of imperialism) whose importance goes further than being a source of interest payments. The debtor countries are actually at the mercy of the most powerful creditors who can impose upon the former the type of economic 'development' most consonant with their own interests (the infamous structural adjustment programs). Rather, the focus on seigniorage in this essay is meant to compensate for the disregard by official (and non-official) literature and to contribute to its theoretical elaboration.

Of course, imperialism is much more than value appropriation, but this systematic appropriation is the constant feature, although it manifests itself differently in imperialism's various phases. Currently, two differences stand out relative to traditional forms of imperialism. The first is that, alongside one imperialist nation extending its domination over the rest of the world (albeit not without differing forms of resistance), there exist also imperialist relations between two *blocks* of nations. One block is said to be the dominant, or imperialist, because it systematically appropriates international value from the other block, which is therefore said to be dominated. The *focus* here will be on those flows (appropriation) of international value which are *related to the existence of blocks* rather than of individual countries.

This appropriation is made possible by a series of international bodies, among which the IMF and the World Bank regulate international credit, the WTO international trade and patenting, NATO the control of natural resources (oil), and the UN inter-state contradictions, to the advantage of the imperialist countries as a whole (and of the hegemonic one in particular). The focus on inter-imperialist relations between blocks denies neither that national states have their own inter-imperialist relations aside from those between blocks nor that states retain much of their importance, as Leo Panitch correctly has insisted.[5] On the contrary, each imperialist country has its own imperialist relations with other, dominated, countries and each state still performs an economic, political, ideological and military role which is indispensable for the reproduction of capitalist relations (and thus for the operation of the multinational enterprises). However, besides nation-centred imperialist relations, there are also block-centred imperialist relations that are a new feature of imperialist development. The focus of this paper is on *these* relations.[6]

Also different from traditional analyses of imperialism is our understanding that this system structures not only the relations between the two blocks but also their internal composition. Let us begin with the dominant block. While all countries in this block participate, in different measure, in the appropriation of value, not all of them are imperialist. Three categories stand out within this block. The first is the US hegemon. Like all imperialist nations, it systematically appropriates international surplus value (in a variety of economic ways), but the US stands apart from the others as the hegemonic power for two interrelated reasons. Owing to its greater economic strength, it systematically appropriates *from the other imperialist countries* a part of the surplus value that has been either produced or appropriated by them. (Of crucial importance here, as section 3 of this essay shall argue, is seigniorage.) But in addition to this, the US can impose upon other

countries both the economic and the non-economic conditions for (the reproduction of) its hegemony. The economic conditions include not only 'the
Americanization ... of legal standards for regulating financial systems and
reporting information' and 'cross-border commercial arbitration and credit-rating
services' as Panitch suggests,[7] but also US management techniques and forms of
labour contracts. Paramount is the imposition upon other countries of an
economic structure functional for US interests — basically dependent development. The non-economic conditions are: (a) political preponderance, i.e. the US
is the constant reference point of any alliance within the dominant block (and
beyond); (b) military superiority, including through its dominance in military
organization with other major states; and (c) ideological power, whereby other
countries accept (each in its own way, in different measures, and with different
degrees of resistance depending on the circumstances) some of the cultural traits
functional for US economic domination.[8] Vital in all this is the control of the
institutes of education and of the means of (mass) communication. Hegemony in
one area, e.g. military, can be stronger than in another (e.g. ideological).
Hegemony in one area (e.g. economic) can be challenged more than in another
(e.g. military). It is *the whole* of these non-economic conditions that makes it
possible for the economic predominance to reproduce itself. This whole is not
only internally differentiated and contradictory but also subject to constant movement and change.

The second category of the dominant block is constituted by the other imperialist countries. On the one hand, they are on the same level as the US, and
compete against each other as well as the US both economically (e.g. by investing
in, and lending to, each other, i.e. by appropriating value in the form of profits
and interests from each other) and technologically, thus appropriating value
through unequal exchange. They also systematically appropriate international
surplus value from the dominated countries due to their greater economic
strength, and can impose upon the dominated countries the conditions of reproduction of that appropriation. These conditions can be both economic (like the
dumping of industrial waste and the shifting of pollution and environmental
damage to the dependent countries) and non-economic (along the dimensions
mentioned above). On the other hand, only the US is hegemonic, i.e. only it has
means for the systematic appropriation of value from both the other imperialist
countries and the dependent countries.

The third category comprises the dominated, non-imperialist, countries
within the dominant block. They participate, in virtue of their membership in that
block, in the appropriation of international surplus value without being themselves imperialist countries. They could not appropriate value systematically from
other countries if they were not members of the dominant block. Some of them
belong to the dominant block fully, and others only partially insofar as they do
not benefit from all aspects upon which domination is based. This distinction is
useful for an analysis of the EU. Germany, France, and the UK belong to the
imperialist core of the EU and of the dominant block while the other EU coun-

tries belong to the imperialist block without being themselves imperialist nations. These latter benefit in different degrees from that membership and are dependent upon the core countries. There is thus an internal hierarchy that reflects imperialist relations within the EU.

The dominant and dominated blocks can be further subdivided according to a number of criteria, such as economic development, structural differentiation, etc. They can also be subdivided into a number of smaller blocks, e.g. in terms of trade flows, economic cooperation or integration. They can be subdivided in geographical areas in which one or possibly two countries are predominant (Russia in Eurasia, Japan and China in East Asia, Brazil in Latin America, etc.). But, as far as an investigation of imperialism is concerned, it is from the above-mentioned categories that empirical analysis should begin. It should also be kept in mind that the distinction between the two blocks is analytical. In reality, not only can a country shift from one category to another, but also, for some countries it might not be clear-cut whether they belong to the imperialist group or not.

Consider now the dominated block. This structure is both the result of systematic appropriation of value in the past, and it remains the most important economic condition for the continuation of that appropriation. Currently, three possible realities define this block, varying according to the ability of the dominated countries to resist imperialist domination. First, the centre grows at the expense of the country of the dominated block to such an extent that local industry in the latter is not developed or is even destroyed. This is classic colonialism. Alternatively, some of the dominated countries can resist this process and set themselves on a path of dependent development. Or, by way of exception, a dominated country can break out of these relations of domination and join the imperialist centre. This change affects the internal composition of the two blocks but erases neither their existence nor their differences. Here too the distinction is analytical. In real life, countries can be hybrid (or transitional) forms in which some features are more pronounced than others.

Under colonialism, the colonies must deliver raw materials to, and import manufactured products from, the centre. Through the mechanism of unequal exchange inherent in international trade, the imperialist country robs the colonies of their raw materials and uses their markets as an outlet for its own (industrial) products. The colonies' resources are squeezed out and local industries (where they existed) attacked up to the point where they languish or disappear. At this point the colonies' capacity to absorb the centre's output is destroyed and they are abandoned to their fate. Even if local industries do survive, no substantial process of industrialization, capitalist development, and structural diversification takes place. In the dependent development type of imperialism, countries can achieve a degree of capitalist economic growth and diversification. However, capital in the dependent countries adjusts production and more generally its economic activity to the markets in the centre (export orientation) and diversifies its internal structure accordingly, rather than the other way around. Moreover, the centre exports to the dependent countries what these latter need (including capital as aid and infrastructures) for this process of dependence to continue. And finally, the dependent countries produce what the centre needs through the use of more labour-intensive techniques so as to ensure both a transfer of value to the centre and continued technological dependence.

In terms of the present discussion, international prices arise from inter-oligopolistic competition in the centre. They reflect structural technological (and thus efficiency) differentials between the imperialist countries and other countries. Therefore, the imperialist centre, and with it the dominant block, grows at the expense of the dominated block through the appropriation of value inherent in this system of prices. This appropriation is the origin, and in a subsequent period the outcome, of a cumulative process involving capital formation, investment in research and development, and technological innovations.[9]

3. DOLLARIZATION, SEIGNIORAGE AND THE EURO

A very important (but severely undertheorized) contemporary way in which international value is appropriated is US seigniorage.[10] This is an advantage accruing to the hegemonic power, due to the use of its currency as the international one. The economic literature distinguishes between (a) seigniorage as a stock (a one-time gain) and as a flow (a flow of revenue over time) and (b) national seigniorage (the appropriation of value by the state from its own subjects) and international seigniorage (appropriation from one state by another state).

The classic case is that of national seigniorage as a stock, i.e. that of the sovereign who holds the power to mint coins which cost him less than what he can purchase with them. As applied to modern conditions, 'A $1 bill costs about 3 cents to print, but the U.S. government can use it to buy $1 worth of goods'.[11] Each time a $1 bill is replaced, there is appropriation of value by the state of a value 33 times higher. The following data on the US monetary base give an idea of the magnitudes involved: $50bn in 1960, $81bn in 1970, $162bn in 1980, $314bn in 1990 and $608bn in 1999.[12] National seigniorage as a flow (of revenues), on the other hand, refers to interest paid by the Treasury to the Federal Reserve, roughly $25 billion a year, on U.S. Government securities that the Fed has acquired through open market operations.[13] However, when one branch of the state (the Treasury) pays interests to another branch of the state (the Fed), there is simply an internal transfer, a meaningless operation in terms of appropriation of value by the state from its subjects. The notion of national seigniorage as a flow of value is wrong.

When it comes to international seigniorage in relation to the dollar, i.e. the appropriation of value inherent in the use of the US dollar as the international currency, orthodox economics considers international seigniorage as interest paid by foreign central banks on US Treasuries. But this conflation of interest payments with seigniorage should be discarded. In fact, this would imply that the interests paid by the hegemonic country on the dominated countries' securities should be seen as seigniorage, thus attributing an imperialist role to the dominated countries. Seigniorage is properly understood, rather, in terms of the appropriation of value by the hegemonic country inherent in the use of its currency as the international currency. In what follows, therefore, we will consider international seigniorage as a stock. This presupposes that the notion of dollarization must first be introduced.

A distinction can be made among three types of dollarization.[14] Unofficial dollarization occurs when people hold their financial assets in dollars even if the dollar is not legal tender (or is legal tender but not for daily transactions). In semi-official dollarization, or officially bimonetary systems, countries allow a foreign currency as a second legal tender in everyday payments, even though the foreign currency plays a secondary role relative to the national currency. Finally, in offi-cial (or full) dollarization a country replaces its national currency with the US dollar. The national currency at most continues to exist in the form of coins having small value. That country becomes part of the US monetary system. Initially, its supply of money is determined by its monetary base (notes and coins both in circu-lation and as reserves) and by the conversion rate of the local currency into dollars. From that point on, it is determined by its balance of payments. The monetary base grows if exports are greater than imports and if capital inflows are greater than capital outflows, and it shrinks in the opposite cases.[15]

We can now consider the advantages of dollarization for the US. Let us start with unofficial dollarization. There are two advantages. The first is *trade-related international seigniorage*. If the US imports goods from a country, it gives dollars (paper that represents purchasing power but with practically no intrinsic value) and gets commodities with intrinsic value. If that country uses those dollars to import from the US, the US gives commodities with intrinsic value and gets back dollars with no intrinsic value.[16] However, if that country does not use those dollars to purchase back US goods (as it happens for other currencies) those dollars represent cost-free imports into the US. This is appropriation of value by the US due to the fact that it issues the world currency. According to one estimate, '[a]bout 55% to 70% of US dollars already circulate abroad, including about 75% of each year's new dollar issuance'.[17] This unofficial dollarization is a measure of US international seigniorage. The US can thus avoid doing what it preaches to other countries, i.e. to redress its trade deficit. The relation between national and international seigniorage is as follows. Each time the US government issues a $1 note, it appropriates commodities with an equal nominal value from the rest of society. In *nominal* terms, this loss is made good by importing commodities with the same nominal value *if* that dollar is kept abroad. In *real* terms, there is an added advantage due to unequal exchange.

It is true that if other countries did not import, US exporters would suffer. However, in terms of value appropriation, exports are a loss of value. At the limit, if the US were only to import and pay with practically worthless paper money, its exporters would go bankrupt but the US would live at the expense of the rest of the world. Why then the emphasis on exports? For two reasons. From the point of view of value realization, exports are of vital interest for imperialist nations in order to realize abroad that value which cannot be realized internally.

From the point of view of value appropriation, a developed capitalist system is not based on overt robbery. Instead, value is appropriated through less visible means, including the unequal exchange inherent in international commerce (and thus on imports and exports). Every time the US exports, the conditions are re-created for a further appropriation of value through imports, due to unequal exchange, since without exports imports would not be possible.

The second advantage of unofficial dollarization is *debt-related international seigniorage*. The US, thanks to the dollar's role as the world currency, can pay for its debts (if it does) with its own currency. Every time the dollar depreciates, the creditor countries lose value to the US and the latter's debt (in real, value, terms) diminishes. And, besides being the hegemonic power, the US is also the world's major debtor country, a fact which increases the importance of debt-related seigniorage. Consequently, foreign central banks hold huge dollar reserves, thus acting as the bank of last resort for the US. The danger is of course that foreign central banks might cease to play this role.

As for official dollarization, the advantages for the US can be summarized as follows. First, by making devaluation impossible, dollarization deprives the dollar-ized countries of one basic instrument of international competition vis-à-vis the US. Second, dollarization strengthens trade between the dollarized countries and the US. As a result, unequal exchange grows. Third, US productive and finan-cial investments in that area might also rise (due, for example, to the disappearance of the currency risk or to the further fall in real wages). Excess capital in the US is reduced and the repatriation of profits and of interest on finan-cial investments increases. Fourth, if a country lacks the necessary funds to dollarize, it will have to procure them through international debt. As long as the debt is not redeemed, the outflow of interest will tend to keep the country in a state of either colonialism or dependent development. Lastly, and most impor-tantly, a vastly increased dollar area constitutes a novel strategy to counter the challenge of the Euro. As US senator Chuck Hagel put it, '[i]f dollarization proved to be successful, the U.S. dollar could become the Western Hemisphere's version of the Euro'.[18] It is this factor that explains why dollarization became a real option for the US in the 1990s.

In spite of these advantages, up to now the US has displayed a cautious attitude towards dollarization. There are several reasons for this. First, dollarization could be seen as the antechamber of a monetary union. This would put pressure on the Fed to take the monetary interests of those countries into consideration, especially if they are important US trade partners.[19] Second, even without a monetary union, a major wave of dollarization would put the same pressure on the Fed. This would probably weaken the confidence in the soundness of the dollar.[20] Third, the issue of seigniorage sharing would be 'pretty hard to explain to Congress'.[21] Fourth, an active and open US support for dollarization might be politically counter-produc-tive and spur nationalist, anti-dollarization, movements. Official statements warning countries to consider carefully before giving up their currency should be seen in this light. The US prefers to leave this task to the IMF. For example, as soon as the Ecuadorian government's intention to dollarize became public, the IMF sent a team of experts (on 12 January 2000) to 'advise' the government.[22] On 26 February 2000 an IMF delegation arrived in Ecuador as its Congress was debating the dollarization bill to illustrate its objections to that bill. The session was suspended and the weekend used for last-minute negotiations.[23]

Finally, it is (fractions of) the local bourgeoisies of the dominated countries (especially of Latin America) which push for dollarization. The US need not push. The job is being done for them. Dollarization is favoured by large sections of the local bourgeoisie for a number of reasons. First, the high inflation/high devaluation Latin American model of the 1970s and 1980s has become unfeasible. Those policies resulted in the destruction of the national currencies' purchasing power on the one hand and in the 'social instability' associated with increasing levels of exploitation and poverty on the other. Resistance to increasing misery had brought a wave of anti-capitalist movements and of military regimes which, in order to maintain capital's rule and keep the masses at bay, did not hesitate to engage in cruelties and crimes comparable to some committed by Nazi Germany. One of the main justifications for these regimes was that only they could prevent their countries from sliding into communism. With the fall of the Soviet Union, these regimes saw a basic aspect of their legitimation vanish; almost everywhere popular resistance was crushed, both militarily and ideologically. The situation was ripe for a return to 'normality'. However, the return of 'democracy' had to be combined with the maintenance of those traditionally high rates of exploitation. Within the changed political-ideological climate, dollarization represents one, but only one, such opportunity. It has the further advantage that it legitimizes neoliberal policies.[24]

Dollarization has been supported also by other sectors of the population, basically because it is perceived as a drastic remedy against the high rates of inflation which erode both salaries and pensions. While this is of course a legitimate concern, dollarization will not deliver the promised increase in the level of living (as Panama, dollarized since 1904, shows). First, if the country in question cannot compete through devaluation, it will have to rely on lower labour costs. Wages might fall in nominal terms. They will certainly fall in real terms, given that wages and pensions are fixed by government institutions and employer associations while there are no agencies for imposing controls on the level of prices.[25] However, given that too high a rate of inflation is detrimental to international competitiveness, governments will intervene to hold inflation down for non-tradables because of its impact on the prices of internationally traded goods. The former are the goods that are consumed by the working class (food, transportation, etc.). Second, inasmuch as the disappearance of the lender of last resort makes more difficult the rescue of ailing businesses, labour will be hit by higher unemployment rates. Third, if the dollarized country needs to borrow dollars for the conversion of the local currency, the repayment of that loan will lead to budget cuts with concomitant lower real wages. Furthermore, the justification for this will be found in an impersonal development — dollarization — itself an aspect of a supposedly inevitable process — globalization.

We can now return to dollarization as a strategy to hold back EU imperialism. From its inception, the EU (then the EEC) had the imperialist virus inscribed in its genes. Initially, due to its limited economic size, it was incapable of challenging the US and, in the Cold War climate, it had to remain under the aegis of the US and hence also of NATO. In the course of the years, the EU has emerged as an economic power comparable to the US, at least in terms of indicators such as GNP and world trade. The imperialist countries within the EU participate (through international as well as strictly European institutions) in the appropriation of international surplus value. However, until recently, neither they nor the EU as a whole was close to challenging US hegemony. The creation of the EMU and the introduction of the Euro has marked a qualitative change. Through the introduction of the Euro which has the potential to challenge the dollar's seigniorage, the EU is now a potential competitor for the systematic appropriation of value along this dimension. Whether the Euro will become a real competitor to the dollar, only time will tell. But if this will be the case, the non-imperialist countries within the EU will benefit to some extent from seigniorage along with the imperialist European countries. *This* is the real meaning of seigniorage sharing.

This notion has nothing to do with the orthodox one of seigniorage sharing criticized above, which refers to the refunding by the US of (part of) the interest lost by the dollarizing countries due to the conversion of the US Treasuries held in their vaults into dollar bills. Notice also that the correct notion of seigniorage sharing applies to the Euro but not to the dollar. Assuming that the Euro will indeed become a rival of the dollar, when the European Central Bank, a supra-national body, will print more Euros, all EMU countries will receive a share of them, thus sharing in Euro seigniorage. By contrast, if the Fed, a national institution, prints more dollars, it is only the US that appropriates value. To see this, consider the country to have fully dollarized recently, Ecuador. It could be held that every time Ecuadorians import commodities, they pay with dollars. If those dollars did not re-enter Ecuador as a consequence of other countries' unofficial dollarization, Ecuador would share with the US in the appropriation of value from other countries. However, Ecuador must earn somehow the dollars it uses for its imports. For example, it must have exported. Or, if it borrows in order to import, it has to repay that debt. For the Ecuadorian central bank neither prints dollars nor shares in the dollars newly printed. There is thus no seigniorage sharing for the countries that dollarize. This is the difference with the EMU countries and this will be a further advantage for the US even if the Euro will become a truly international currency.

It has been said that the outcome of the contest between the dollar and the Euro is far from certain. Let us mention a few factors that are likely to undermine the Euro project. To begin with, the commitment to a strong Euro will be more trying for weaker than for stronger member states, which intensifies the tendency towards inflation and devaluation. Enlargements might aggravate this difficulty. But, more importantly, the EU is not yet able to impose the non-economic conditions for its hegemony, due to a twin disadvantage: political fragmentation (basically, the lack of a supranational, possibly federalist, European state) and military weakness. The former drawback is not likely to disappear for the time being. Nevertheless, the EMU member states have already relinquished part of their sovereignty. This sets an important precedent. Military weakness too is a brake for EU imperialist ambitions. The fall of the USSR could have provided an opportunity to break out of this straitjacket. However, it was the US and NATO that have grown in importance. This has been due to a number of factors, like the impenetrability of 'the European security architecture'.[26] But the most important reasons are the lack of preparation on the part of the WEU, the military arm of the EU, to pick up a greater role, and UK reluctance to sever its 'special relationship' with the US.

Official economic literature resorts to concepts like 'inertia in international currency use' in order to explain the persistent importance of the dollar: 'international traders and investors face the lowest transaction costs in those currencies which are already the most used, reinforcing their incentives to continue using them and causing inertia. Hence, once a dominant international currency is established, it will usually not lose its role quickly even if the issuing country has lost its leading status'.[27] This is true. But that persistence itself needs to be explained with reference to the above mentioned reasons; it is only marginally reinforced by 'inertia'.

But this situation might change. First, the EU is aware that it will have to become militarily more powerful if it is to further its economic interests. Military power should be understood not so much as a precondition for gunboat diplomacy (even though this will be an aspect in the future as well as in the past, as the recent war on Yugoslavia shows). The threat of intervention can be just as effective as intervention itself. Rather, a strong military arm is needed to ensure both the economic and the non-economic conditions for hegemony. Second, UK reservations are mainly based on its fear that an integrated military power independent of the US would give a strong impulse to a move towards further European political integration. But once the UK will have joined the EMU, a further obstacle towards greater political unity and thus towards a European army will have been removed.[28] Third, the member states' military industries are also pushing for greater military integration in order to create firms capable of competing with US giants and of manufacturing standardized weapon systems.[29] And fourth, the US will have to share power with the EU because it is becoming too onerous for them to police the world by themselves.

The recent agreement to form a 60,000 strong European rapid intervention force is no indication that a truly European army is in the making, since it is composed of segments of national armies employing NATO infrastructures. However, the fact that the WEU will cease to exist and that this rapid intervention force will be part of the EU (rather than remaining an organization independent of it, as it would have been under the WEU) is an important new development. The US will allow, or even spur, the EU to create its own army but under conditions such that it will remain an extension of the NATO. These, however, are exactly the conditions the EU wants to break out of.

The terrain on which the struggle for world hegemony is fought is ultimately that of technological leadership. This requires constantly higher levels of productivity in the leading economic sectors. It is uncertain whether the EU will manage to achieve this leadership. But the signs and tendencies are there, most visible in the economic areas (capital penetration and levels of productivity) and in the monetary field (the EMU) but already discernable also in the political and military fields. It would be a mistake to ignore them and consider US hegemony as absolute just as it would be a mistake to consider the EU as a fully hegemonic power, side by side the US. A more balanced view should stress both US hegemony and the real challenges to that hegemony. The Euro is one such challenge.

4. IMPERIALISM AND TRANSNATIONAL CLASSES

The above has important ramifications for the class structure emerging from present-day imperialism. Just as the previous sections have focused on some aspects of supranational imperialism (rather than of national imperialisms), this section focuses on just a few aspects of the two basic classes in their supranational manifestations.[30] Let us begin with the bourgeoisie.

Firstly, there exists, side by side with the national bourgeoisies, a world bourgeoisie, inasmuch as elements of the national bourgeoisies (1) share common interests relative to other classes (2) are conscious of these common interests, and (3) dispose of instruments (legal, institutional or otherwise) for pursuing, and limiting the contradictory nature of, those interests. These bourgeoisies relate to each other in a hierarchical way, i.e. the bourgeoisies of the imperialist countries (with the US bourgeoisie playing the dominant role) are dominant vis-à-vis those of the other countries. It is the former's interests that are basically catered for by institutions such as the UN, NATO, the IMF, the World Bank, and the WTO. These institutions both mediate between the interests of different national bourgeoisies (primarily those of the imperialist powers) in order to allow the emergence of common supranational interests and more or less overtly impose those common interests upon other classes or countries.

The terms 'national bourgeoisies' should be properly understood. As opposed to the notion that bourgeoisies are national because they are external to, and separate from, each other, Poulantzas stressed forcefully that they are the result of the mutual interpenetration of nationally based capitals.[31] The point is well taken. However, Poulantzas' emphasis was on US capital's penetration of other national capitals and thus on its reproduction within those national realities. This was a partial rendition that was perhaps consonant with the reality of the early 1970s when US penetration in Europe could be seen as the 'new' structure of European dependency. But nowadays the opposite is also the case. Capitals of other imperialist countries penetrate US capitals as well. This holds not only for productive capital (Poulantzas' focus) but even more for financial and speculative capital. The dominant role of US capital (bourgeoisie) thus does not rest on a one-way reproduction of US capital within other socio-economic formations (with the concomitant ideological and political effects). Rather, it rests on the reasons mentioned in the previous section, on the appropriation by US capitals of surplus value from other imperialist countries and on the imposition upon these countries of the economic and non-economic conditions for the continuation of this appropriation. Moreover, Poulantzas writes off too hastily those capitals that continue being based only or principally on a national process of accumulation. It follows that a national bourgeoisie is composed of *both* those agents who represent nationally based capitals *and* those agents who represent the result of national capitals' mutual interpenetration. It is the interests of these two fractions of the national bourgeoisies (in their interrelation) that are moulded by international institutions into the world bourgeoisie's common interests relative to other classes (countries) and under the hegemony of US bourgeoisie.

Second, it is usually held that financial capital is dominant *vis-à-vis* industrial (and more generally productive) capital. This should be properly understood. Since financial capital lives off the surplus value produced by productive capital, it is the latter which is the condition of existence (the determinant) of the former. Financial capital, in its turn, is the condition of reproduction of (determined by) industrial capital. This can, and does, imply that financial capital sets its own rules, including the destruction of units of industrial capitals, in order to ensure the reproduction of the latter and thus of the system as a whole. The conspicuous way in which financial capital does this is wrongly perceived as dominance vis-à-vis industrial capital. The size of financial and speculative capitals moving around daily on the world market lends further credence to this illusion. Nevertheless, the dominant fraction within the world bourgeoisie is the productive (including the industrial) one, even if under specific circumstances it might delegate the task of its own (and of the system's) reproduction to other fractions.

Third, we have seen that national states ensure the reproduction (possibly on an enlarged scale) of nation-based oligopolies by pursuing economic and other support policies ultimately in the interests of the oligopolistic sector. This holds whether an oligopoly is based in one nation (the rule) or in more than one (the exception). Thus, the dominant fraction within the world bourgeoisie is the oligopolistic one, with the national bourgeoisies, including the national political elites, making its reproduction possible. Consonant with the main argument of this essay, within the world bourgeoisie it is still the US bourgeoisie that is dominant. To sum up, the dominant fraction within the world bourgeoisie is that of the US productive oligopolistic capitalists.

But we are witnessing the emergence of a European bourgeoisie as well. It is composed of the various national European bourgeoisies inasmuch as they have common interests, are conscious of these interests and have at their disposal common instruments to further them. Paramount in expressing these interests are the European Summits, the Councils of Ministers, the Commission, the Parliament, and the European Central Bank. These institutions are the instruments through which the European bourgeoisie manifests itself. They are at the same time the arena in which both purely national, i.e. opposite, interests and supra-national, i.e. common, interests are furthered. Sometimes the distinction is purely analytical but at other times the differences are clear. By focusing only on the mediation between national interests, the European dimension of the bourgeoisie is denied. The specificity of these institutions, relative to those at the disposal of the world bourgeoisie, is that they formulate policies in a relatively autonomous manner since some areas of decision making have been transferred to them from national states. The European bourgeoisie thus is a more unified class formation than the world bourgeoisie, due to the institutions which make it possible for the former to carry out its own class based policies, but a less unified class formation than the national bourgeoisies. The emergence of (supranational) classes is a gradual process. Within the European bourgeoisie, the German industrial oligopolies followed by the French and English ones, are the dominant fractions, and thus the fractions that have privileged access to the centres of European decision making.

The situation is far less favourable for the European working class, not to mention the world proletariat. While common objective interests clearly exist,[32] European workers lack awareness of them. Usually, inasmuch as the national proletariats defend their interests on an international level, they do so only as national classes and thus in opposition to each other. The reasons for this weakness are many, both conjunctural and not. Here only three can be briefly addressed.

First, a class emerges as an active agent of class struggle inasmuch as it aggregates through and around its own institutional and otherwise means of domination of other classes.[33] The European bourgeoisie's means of domination (including EU institutions) are at the same time the means through which the emergence of the European working class as an agent is held back (or its disaggregation is fostered) through blackmail, individual co-optation, ideological barrage, and the creation of divisions among its different sectors. For example, the influence of European oligopolies, e.g. through their pressure groups such as the European Roundtable of Industrialists, on European institutions is far greater than that of other classes.[34] But the question is not only one of how those institutions are used. It is their nature itself that is inherently anti-labour. As Accattatis remarks, they have been fashioned after the French Bonapartist, institutional model which is characterized by the concentration of power in the executive, by a passive democracy and by active paternalism, all aimed at fostering entrepreneurial interests.[35] The European working class lacks not only its own European institutions that would allow it to unite and emerge as an active player. It is also denied significant influence within the existing institutions.

Second, new technologies cause a tendency towards the proletarianization and de-qualification (and a counter-tendency in the opposite direction) of class positions. Those positions that combine both the function of labour (transformation of use values) and the function of capital (control and surveillance) are proletarianized if the function of capital disappears either because it is incorporated in the means of production or internalized by labourers.[36] A position is de-qualified if the value of the labour power of those who fill it is reduced. New technologies cause proletarianization and de-qualification of positions either by simplifying them or by eliminating some of the tasks constituting them. They also can (and mostly are designed in order to) introduce new forms of control by the ultimate controllers upon both the controlled and the other controllers.[37]

While in the 1970s, due to a strong labour movement, a re-composition of tasks into new positions usually indicated its re-qualification, this is not the case anymore. Nowadays, capital, especially in the technologically dynamic sectors, needs both 'flexible' workers, who can shift from one de-qualified position to another, and a reassembling of de-qualified tasks, which does not result in new re-qualified positions but in new de-qualified ones. Moreover, these new positions can contain, again, elements of the function of capital. In the present ideological conjuncture, and partly because of the reintroduction of the function of capital into many positions, 'flexibility' and de-qualification can be smuggled into the labourers' consciousness as re-qualification, greater responsibility, independence, opportunity for personal growth and ultimately 'escape' from the proletarian condition. An important role here is played by the use of the computer and related technologies for tasks which, even though de-qualified, are regarded, just because of this use, as qualified. The greater this mystification, the weaker the collective labourer's class consciousness.

Imperialism reinforces this false perception in at least two respects. First, very broadly speaking, inasmuch as material labour processes are exported to the dependent countries and mental labour processes remain in the technologically advanced, imperialist, countries,[38] the perception is created that the working class-condition is exported to those countries. This is false both because mental labour processes can, and do, imply de-qualified mental labour and because the identification of classes depends on criteria other than mental or material labour (often misunderstood as intellectual and manual labour), whether qualified or not.[39] Second, this mystification rests on the redistribution of part of the surplus value from the dependent countries to the labourers of the imperialist ones. The higher standard of living gives rise to a false feeling (skilfully cultivated by capital) that workers are not workers any more but 'middle class'. This, together with the political weakness of the Left (which was reflected in the disintegration of the USSR and the shift to the right in social democracy), goes a long way in explaining the fall in the European workers' class consciousness in the 1990s.

The third factor accounting for this weakness is the blackmail to which the European working class is subjected: the great mobility of capital and thus of the threat of relocation should workers' demands be 'excessive'. At the same time, the influx of 'foreign' labour into the imperialist countries of the EU is used to decrease wages and to threaten job security. While it is true that the European collective labourer 'profits' from the crumbs of imperialism (the above mentioned redistribution of value), it is also true that many sectors are increasingly subjected to pauperization (relative to the socially determined level of living in the EU). Job and wage insecurity are, again, powerful allies of capital. Moreover, false conflicts of interest are created. Capital's ideologists play an important role here. If, as neoclassical economists hold, lower wages were the way out of crises, it would make sense to expel foreign workers in order to reduce the 'social' wage (old age pensions, medical care, education, etc). If, as Keynesians hold, higher wages were the way out of crises, it would make sense to increase wages by forcing foreign labourers' repatriation. But both views are anti-labour and both are wrong.

Crises and unemployment are caused neither by too high nor by too low wages. Lower wages do increase profits but on the other hand they increase real-ization difficulties as well. Higher wages do reduce realization difficulties but at the same time they reduce profits as well. The level of wages can only modify the shape of the cycle, not eliminate it.[40] But if wages impact only on the shape of the cycle, a policy of closed doors can only have a marginal and temporary effect on one of the *main* reasons behind anti-foreign labour policies, the fear of unem-ployment. There are no inherently contradictory economic interests between the two sectors of the European collective labourer. This contradiction appears to emerge only if labour is seen as a cost rather than as the source of all value and wealth.

But this is Capital's view, not Labour's view. And this reflects a real weakness of the European working class that this essay has tried to address, i.e., the tendency of its leaders and intellectuals to embrace the view of Labour's class enemy especially as it is manifested today in the ideology of globalization and the bourgeois economic thinking that underpins it. As always, the Right wins not because it is strong but because the Left is weak.

NOTES

1   G. Carchedi, *For Another Europe. A Class Analysis of European Economic Integration*, London: Verso, 2001, ch. 2.

2   For the possibility of a truly radically alternative type of society see G. Carchedi, 'Democracy, the Market, and Egalitarianism', in J. Milios, L. Katseli, and T. Pelagidis, *Rethinking Democracy and the Welfare State*, Athens: Ellinika Grammata, 1999.

3   G. Carchedi, *On the Economic Identification of Social Classes*, London: Routledge and Kegan Paul, 1977, and *Frontiers of Political Economy*, London: Verso, 1991.

4   More precisely, the proletariat is given by all those who sell their labour power to the owners of the means of production either directly or indirectly (such as through the state and its institutions). It encompasses both produc-tive and unproductive labourers, both mental and material labourers, both the employed and the unemployed, both those who hold full-time jobs and those who must be content with part-time, short-term and subsistence jobs, no matter in what branches of the economy (i.e., not only in the industrial but also in the agricultural, commercial, etc. sectors). It excludes those who,

while selling their labour power to capital, either directly or indirectly, perform what Marx calls the work of control and surveillance (since they are an extension of capital) but it encompasses those who perform the work of coordination and unity of the labour process. It also excludes those who belong to the middle classes, either old or new (see G. Carchedi, *Frontiers of Political Economy*, London: Verso, 1991). The proletariat needs to be conceived as a world entity (the collective labourer on an international scale) rather than only a collage of national proletariats because of the international dimension of what Marx calls the socialization of the labour process. Although the conditions under which the world proletariat can develop consciousness of itself cannot be dealt with here, it would be wrong to deny the existence of a proletariat simply because of this lack of consciousness.

5   '[S]tates, and above all the world's most powerful state, have played an active and often crucial role in making globalization happen. Increasingly, they are now encumbered with the responsibility of sustaining it' (L. Panitch, 'The New Imperial State', *New Left Review*, 2, March–April, 2000, p. 5).

6   Japan and Asia are generally disregarded here. Contrary to the EU, Japan cannot be seen as a real, not even as a potential, rival of the US. Its international weight is not comparable to that of the EU. Right before the introduction of the Euro, the EU had a GDP roughly comparable to that of the US, while Japan's was only half. The US dollar was used in almost half of all international transactions, while the currencies of the EU countries were used in about 30 percent and the yen in only 5 percent of those transactions (C. Sabhasri, 'Euro and Asia: Hope and Fear', *Euro*, 46, 1999, p. 58). As for its relations to the other Asian countries, Japan has nothing even remotely similar to the pre-EMU European institutions.

7   Panitch, 'The New Imperial State', p. 15. Reporting information may be thought unimportant. But this is not so. The BIS requires that the ratio between a bank's capital and its risk assets (primarily loans) be no less than 8% (the 'capital adequacy ratio'). Take Japan. Since Japan's lending is denominated in dollars but its capital is denominated in yen, to make the numerator and the denominator of the capital adequacy ratio compatible, yen-denominated capital is converted into dollars. Now, in case the yen depreciates, this ratio is reduced and with it Japanese banks' ability to lend. If depreciation is needed to revitalize the economy (through exports), credit must be reduced just at a time when it should be increased. This constraint could be avoided if the ratio would be expressed in yen (i.e. if the risk assets would be denominated in yen). Since the BIS requires that the ratio be expressed in dollars, not only Japan but all other countries are at a disadvantage, except the US. See C.H. Kwan, 'A Yen Bloc in Asia?', *Euro*, 46, 1999, p. 64.

8   Like, for example, (American) English as the world language of business and science, US universities and research institutes as centres of excellence to be imitated, and the 'American way of life' as something to be aspired to. In his

farewell speech on 18 January 2000, President Clinton spoke of the desirability that 'the world shares our cherished values'. The US, of course, can accept cultural traits from other countries but these are not realized conditions for the economic predominance of these countries upon the US.

9   Generally speaking, efficiency differentials lead to prices reflecting an average efficiency that penalizes the technological laggards and rewards the technological leaders. If a producer increases its efficiency, there is an increase in the appropriation of value (or a reduction in the loss of value) at the cost of all other producers in proportion to their level of efficiency. A new structure of prices arises reflecting this changed situation. Exchange on the basis of these prices hides that appropriation of value and is called unequal exchange. Unequal exchange presupposes that all similar commodities are sold at the same price, a price that tendentially gives the average productivity producers the average rate of profit. However, this constant advantage (value appropriation) makes it possible for the technological leaders to undersell their competitors. This price competition reinforces value appropriation but is not unequal exchange.

10   The discussion of dollarization that follows is a shorter version of Carchedi, *For Another Europe*, ch. 5. See also G. Carchedi, 'La Dolarización, el Señoraje, y el Euro', *Cuadernos del Sur*, 16, (30), 2000.

11   K. Schuler, *Basics of Dollarization*, Staff Report, Joint Economic Committee (Office of the Chairman, U.S. Congress, 1999, available at http://www.senate.gov/~jec/106list.htm, section 4.

12   US Federal Reserve, Federal Reserve Statistical Releases, H3 Historical Data, *Aggregate reserves of depository institutions not adjusted for changes in reserve requirements and not seasonally adjusted*, Washington DC, 27 January 2000. All data refer to December.

13   US Federal Reserve, Board of Governors of the Federal Reserve System, *The Federal Reserve System: Purposes and Functions*, Washington DC, 1994, p. 17.

14   Schuler, *Basics of Dollarization*.

15   As Stein remarks, '[m]uch of Latin America is already *unofficially* dollarized' (R. Stein, *Issues Regarding Dollarization*, Subcommittee on Economic Policy, US Senate Banking, Housing and Urban Affairs Committee, 1999, p. 2). By 2001 half-a-dozen countries were semi-officially dollarized including, most recently, El Salvador and Guatemala. So far two countries have dollarized completely: Panama (in 1904) and Ecuador, in 2000.

16   Of course, paper money has a value, its purchasing power. However, to understand seigniorage, it is its lack of intrinsic value that should be focused upon.

17   Stein, *Issues Regarding Dollarization*, p. 7.

18   Prepared Testimony of Senator Chuk Hagel, Hearing on Official Dollarization in Emerging-Market Countries, 22 April 1999, available at http://www.senate.gov/~banking/99_04hrg/042299/hagel.htm. See also

Schuler, *Basics of Dollarization*, section 4; and Speech by Deputy Treasury Secretary Lawrence H. Summers at the Senate Banking Committee Subcommittee on Economic Policy and Subcommittee on International Trade and Finance, *Treasury News,* US Treasury, Office of Public Affairs, 22 April 1999.

19 C.F. Bergsten, 'Dollarization in Emerging-Market Economies and its Policy Implications for the United States', statement before the Joint Hearing of the Subcommittee on Economic Policy and the Subcommittee on International Trade and Finance, Committee on Banking, Housing and Urban Affairs of the US Senate, Institute For International Economics, 22 April 1999.

20 A. Acosta and J. Schuldt, *Dolarización vacuna para la Hiperinflación?* Unpublished paper, 2000.

21 J.A. Frankel, Transcript of a Speech on 'Dollarization: Fad or Future for Latin America?' *IMF Economic Forum,* 24 June 1999. The conventional notion of 'seigniorage sharing' derives from that of international seigniorage as a flow of interests, which has been rejected above. In that view, if the dollarized country changes its US treasuries into dollars in order to buy back its own currency, it loses interests on those treasuries. That country's compensation by the US for a part of that loss is called seigniorage sharing. While this loss sharing is not appealing to the US, its absence is not appealing to the countries considering full dollarization. Contrary to Schuler (*Basics of Dollarization*, section 4) the prospect of losing 'seigniorage' is only a minor factor explaining why official dollarization is rare today 'despite potential benefits'. See below, however, for an alternative notion of seigniorage sharing.

22 *El Comercio*, 13 January 2000.

23 Ibid., 27 February 2000.

24 Not all sectors of the bourgeoisie favour full dollarization. For example, a managed devaluation might benefit export-oriented capital by cheapening exports, and speculative capital by creating the possibility of selling local currencies at a relatively high rate and re-buying them at a lower rate.

25 According to *El Comercio* of 16 January 2000, wages in Ecuador will be 'fixed by the Government' but prices could not be fixed in a free market economy. As if wages were not the price of labour power in such an economy!

26 J. Oberg, *The Imminent Militarisation of the European Union*, paper available at http://www.transnational.org/pressinf/2001/pf110_EU_imperial.html.

27 P. Hartmann, 1999, 'Trimetrics, the Euro in the New Order of International Currencies, *Euro*, 46, 1999, pp. 71.

28 This suggests the existence of conflicts within the EU, a topic which cannot be dealt with here. See Carchedi, *For Another Europe*.

29 S. Cararo, 'Globalizzazione o competizione globale? Quattro considerazioni sull'imperialismo nel XXI° Secolo', *Contropiano*, Rome, June 2000.

30 I disregard thus the middle classes, both old and new, the peasantry, etc.

31 N. Poulantzas, *Les Classes Sociales dans le Capitalisme Aujourd'hui*, Paris:

Éditions du Seuil, 1974, ch. 1, part II.

32 See Carchedi, *For Another Europe*, ch. 8.

33 From this angle, the distinction between class in itself and class for itself is insufficient.

34 Ibid., ch. 1. The European Roundtable of Industrialists was founded in 1983 by Umberto Agnelli of Fiat, Wisse Dekker of Philips and Pehr Gyllenhammer of Volvo

35 V. Accattatis, *Quale Europa?*, Milan: Edizioni Punto Rosso, 2000.

36 Carchedi, *On the Economic Identification of Social Classes*, ch. 1, especially section VI, and ch. 4.

37 Ibid.

38 This is an extreme generalization, useful only to localize a broad trend.

39 For a theory of material and mental labour see Carchedi, *Frontiers of Political Economy*.

40 Carchedi, *For Another Europe*, ch. 8.

THE NEW INTERNATIONAL FINANCIAL ARCHITECTURE: IMPOSED LEADERSHIP AND 'EMERGING MARKETS'

SUSANNE SOEDERBERG

The Asian bust of 1997 caught the international financial community by surprise. It also opened the floodgates to a torrent of criticism about the ability of financial liberalization to create sustained prosperity. The United States government launched an impassioned defence of capital mobility by blaming the 'emerging markets'. In the larger framework of the G7 (Group of Seven) the US sought to strengthen the existing rules of the game through the creation of the so-called New International Financial Architecture (NIFA) at the Cologne summit in 1999. The chief significance of the NIFA lies in its attempt to incorporate what are called 'systematically important' emerging market economies into a carefully-structured international policy-making environment, so as to ensure that they adopt the rules and standards of the West, by integrating these countries more closely with the International Monetary Fund (IMF) and the World Bank.

Yet securing their compliance is not entirely easy, given the waning level of public support for the neoliberal project in the wake of ever-widening income inequality and increased poverty rates.[1] The political and social effects of the vicious cycle of crisis and bailout over the past two decades have made the principle of free capital mobility more difficult to sustain and caused a crisis of legitimation among those who pay the costs whenever short-term debt falls due and asset price bubbles implode. The production by the IMF and World Bank of numerous 'second generation' policies aimed at addressing issues of social justice and anti-poverty may be viewed as an attempt to address the waning legitimacy of the existing neoliberal agenda, and more fundamentally, of American interference in other countries' politics and economies. Indeed, governments of emerging market economies have begun to make explicit their discontent with the ideas that underpin the Washington consensus. Some have gone so far as to call for a new development agenda and increased policy autonomy to assist them in overcoming what the Executive Secretary of the UN Economic Commission for Latin America and the Caribbean (ECLAC), José Antonio Ocampo, refers to as a 'crisis of the state'.[2]

Alongside this general dissatisfaction with the existing international financial system in 'emerging markets', doubts about the logic of the Washington consensus are also evident in the United States. While to a certain extent due to political squabbles, the refusal of the US Congress to co-operate with the Clinton Administration in a $20 billion bailout for Mexico in 1994 — not to mention its baulking at a request to contribute $18 billion to the IMF for the Asian crisis in 1998 — signalled the growing unwillingness of the American public to clean up the mess made by corrupt governments and greedy investors in emerging markets. Crucially, this agitation equally threatens what Peter Gowan aptly calls the 'Dollar-Wall Street Regime' (DWSR), as it makes it more difficult for the United States to reap the economic benefits of the Structural Adjustment Policies (SAPs) imposed on 'emergent markets', and to respond rapidly to bail out American investors.[3]

In view of the NIFA's potential for generalizing and enforcing the rules governing the international financial system, and especially to redefine what constitutes a *successful* 'emerging market', it is important to investigate this project critically. Why was new architecture required? Whose building is it? What shape is it taking? This essay argues that the NIFA constitutes a transnational class-based strategy to reproduce the power of financial capital in the world economy and, in effect, the structural power of the United States. More specifically, the NIFA may be seen as a novel attempt to refurbish the political and ideological elements of the existing international financial architecture — the so-called Washington consensus — by way of what I call 'imposed leadership'.

The main elements of the NIFA are outlined below, in section five. First, however, it is necessary to outline the key structural contradiction upon which imposed leadership rests. As the scope of the DWSR expands, the conditions for continued accumulation in the global South weaken, and this in turn threatens the viability of the DWSR. More specifically, since the expansion of the DWSR depends on global financial liberalization, there has been a continual disarticulation between esoteric financial instruments and the real economy. This leads both to greater volatility in the international financial system and a more and more interconnected and interdependent world economy. The latter condition implies, amongst other things, the ability of crises to spread more rapidly. Yet for the DWSR to continue to grow there must be enough stability in the system to guarantee the continuation of free capital mobility across national borders. On the other hand, as the emerging market countries are forced to pry open their capital accounts as well as their current accounts, distribution tensions grow. The need to address the resulting 'crisis of the state' has produced the demand for increased policy autonomy in the South, which could easily lead to departures from the rules and policies needed to guarantee the continued expansion of the DWSR and the power of global finance.

1. CONTESTING THE CONSENSUS

The Asian crisis shook the foundations upon which neoclassical hegemony rested. Despite the fact that these economies were revered as 'growth tigers', won high praise from the International Financial Institutions (IFIs) up to the year of the devaluation of the Thai baht in 1997 and possessed sound fundamentals, investors were badly burnt. Those associated with the Washington consensus were quick to blame 'crony capitalism' for the debacle, as opposed to the reckless and excessively herd-like behaviour of electronic speculators, and the IMF 'made reforms of corporate governance and related institutions a condition for its bail-outs in the region'.[4]

There is far from a consensus on this issue, however. High-profile US policy-makers and economic pundits, such as the former Federal Reserve Chairman, Paul Volcker, and the former Chief Economist of the World Bank, Joseph Stiglitz, have begun to question not only the wealth-creating power of free capital mobility but also whether the structure of the global financial system is sufficiently coherent for continued capital accumulation. In the words of the celebrated financier, George Soros,

> [w]hat makes this crisis so politically unsettling and so dangerous for the global capitalist system is that the system itself is its main cause ... the origin of this crisis is to be found in the mechanism that defines the essence of a globalized capitalist system: the free, competitive capital markets that keep private capital moving unceasingly around the globe in a search for the highest profits and, supposedly, the most efficient allocation of the world's investment and savings.[5]

Events in the so-called IMF-3 (South Korea, Indonesia and Thailand) made it painfully clear that the underlying tenets of the Washington consensus were more than faulty. For instance, liberalized financial markets will *not* 'consistently price capital assets correctly in line with future supply and demand trends', and it is not true that 'the correct asset pricing of liberated capital markets will, in turn, provide a continually reliable guide to saving and investment decisions ... and to the efficient allocation of their economic resources'.[6] Alexandre Lamfalussy, the former General Manager of the Bank for International Settlements (BIS), shares this view, writing that the exuberant behaviour of lenders and investors from the industrialized world played a major role in spurring on the past several crises in the emerging markets.[7] Other 'organic intellectuals' of capital tend to agree. The MIT economist, Paul Krugman, for example, has argued that 'most economists today believe foreign exchange markets behave more like the unstable and irrational asset markets described by Keynes than the efficient markets described by modern finance theory'.[8] Jagdish Bhagwati, an eminent defender of free trade, nonetheless accepts that the dominance of short-term, speculative capital flows is not productive, but is characterized by panics and manias which will continue to be 'a source of considerable economic difficulty'.[9]

The significance of these debates is that they have generated a renewed interest in capital controls as a necessary mechanism to reduce market volatility by seeking to curb 'hot money'. One popular way of achieving this is by imposing a tax on short-term inflows, such as the Tobin tax. The tax, ranging anywhere from 0.1 to 0.5 percent, would be applied to short-term capital flows. It is estimated that it would enhance the efficacy of macroeconomic policy whilst encouraging longer-term investment and raising some tax as a by-product.[10] But to be effective it would need to be implemented both uniformly and universally, and in conjunction with other reforms to deter speculation, such as domestic financial transaction taxes, and, more fundamentally, within a new international system of stable relationships between major currencies, or what some have called a new Bretton Woods. This solution would thus drive a stake through the heart of Washington consensus, for a new Bretton Woods would necessitate an interstate system based on major political and economic compromises, such as re-pegging the value of the dollar as well as limiting the amount of hot money that was allowed to flow out of the United States.

Those opposed to the implementation of any general controls have argued that the Tobin tax is unfeasible due to technical and administrative barriers. Yet as Tobin himself has pointed out,

> while the implementation of the tax may appear complex, it is not any more complicated, probably much less so, than the detailed provisions of many existing taxes ... Indeed if the standards of what is feasible employed [by opponents of the tax] had been used before imposing income tax or VAT they would never have been introduced! The dominant feature in the introduction of new taxation has always been the political will rather than administrative feasibility.[11]

As Benjamin J. Cohen notes, of all the possible reasons why governments may hesitate to implement capital controls, the political opposition of the United States appears to be the most decisive.[12] Despite the fact that the burden of proof has shifted from those advocating capital controls to those in favour of continued capital mobility, this debate has not received much attention. But it has not been ignored. The transnational bourgeoisie and the caretakers of the global economy have become painfully aware of the concerns raised by capital's own organic intellectuals, as well as of the declining support for global capitalism in the South.

2. THE ANATOMY OF AMERICAN LEADERSHIP

In contrast to the era of the Bretton Woods system (1944-71), the current period is marked by a free floating exchange rate system in which states use their power over monetary policy formation to engage in beggar-thy-neighbour tactics and currency devaluations, so as to attract financial inflows. Also unlike the Bretton Woods system, the present one is characterized by a de-linking of the overriding concern for continued economic stability at the international level from national prerogatives. How do we make sense of the role of the United States in this context? More specifically, how does the DWSR reproduce itself in a multilateral interstate system that promotes, and, in turn, feeds off growing competition between other nation states? Giovanni Arrighi's notion of 'forced leadership' is useful in beginning to conceptualize the changing nature of US leadership:

> A dominant state exercises a hegemonic function if it leads the system of states in a desired direction and, in doing so, is perceived as pursuing a general interest. It is this kind of leadership that makes the dominant state hegemonic. But a dominant state may lead also in the sense that it draws other states onto its own path of development. Borrowing an expression from Joseph Schumpeter (1963: 89), this second kind of leadership can be designated as 'leadership against one's own will' because, over time, it enhances competition for power rather than the power of the hegemon.[13]

While Arrighi's notion is helpful in drawing a distinction between hegemonic and non-hegemonic leadership, the term 'forced leadership' presents two problems for the analysis at hand. First, the argument being pursued here is not about the United States seeking to establish leadership in terms of regional or coalitional hegemony; but about a highly contradictory and complex form of world dominance by capital. Second, whereas Arrighi's notion of 'forced leadership' seems to imply that American headship is itself forced, the focus here is on the followers who are forced. Put differently, the crisis of American hegemony involves forcing other states to follow suit. As such, *imposed leadership* seems more aptly to capture the nature of the DWSR as a moment of American leadership. The DWSR is largely reproduced and regulated through coercion rather than consensual arrangements. Yet this coercion does not involve brute force, but operates through less visible and highly complex networks within the transnational bourgeoisie and political elites.[14] In the management of both the global economy and national economies, for example, the coercion we are talking about has taken the form of a shift of the *locus* of decision-making to forums that are independent of public opinion and democratic accountability.

In what follows I will consider two dimensions of this kind of coercion: (1) *core-alliance coercion*, and (2) *core-periphery coercion*. Both interpretations draw on Antonio Gramsci's understanding of hegemony. *Core-alliance coercion* involves capitalists in the core — especially the US — building an alliance with other fractions of the dominant class; in particular, it refers to the US state constructing institutions that incorporate other powerful industrialized countries (the G7, the OECD) and global finance. *Core-peripheral coercion* entails the relationship between the US state and those of the 'emerging market economies' (in what follows, this relationship will be examined through the evolution of the 'Washington consensus').

Core-alliance coercion is at work in the networks of transnational capital and political elites who have been the key players in defining the international financial regulation (or lack thereof) developed under the DWSR. Since the fall of Bretton Woods various international financial regulatory institutions have been established: the G10 Central Bank Governors, with their Basel Committee on Banking Regulations and Supervisory Practices, formed in 1975; the globally oriented International Organization of Securities Commissions, formed in 1984; and the International Association of Insurance Supervisors (IAIS), formed in 1994. Alongside these regulatory bodies, the Bank for International Settlements and the G10's Eurocurrency Standing Committee produce information on and analysis of global financial markets. Both these forms of transnational political authority emerged as a response to the need of financial capital for a regulatory regime in an interstate system characterized by increasing forms of competition for, and dependency on, private, short-term financial inflows. Correspondingly, both kinds of institution are closed policy communities 'wherein an elite group works out the management of its own vital interests without wider public involvement'.[15] As we shall see, it is precisely the power of these highly clandestine global management webs and linkages that the NIFA is attempting to strengthen through tighter communicative lines and increased co-operation.

Core-periphery coercion is embodied in the so-called 'Washington consensus'.[16] This was an important feature of the DWSR, not only because it expanded markets, but also because it assisted in defining and universalizing the norms and values of global financial capital, which in turn strengthened the position of the United States in the global economy. The consensus orthodoxy is based on the hypotheses of efficient markets and rational expectations; it assumes that progress will be brought about via free trade, free capital mobility and non-interventionist states. It sees globalization as an inevitable and natural progression and holds that governments and societies must embrace it if they wish to share in increased prosperity. These help to reproduce the DWSR by legitimating free capital mobility and free trade as conditions necessary to the market, while drawing attention away from the active role states are playing in ensuring that these conditions are met and reproduced.[17]

This orthodoxy was primarily transmitted through the IMF's Structural Adjustment Programs (SAPs), which were tenaciously pursued by the IMF and the World Bank in the global South after the debt crisis of 1982. SAPs locked Latin American, Asian and African economies into an open world market economy, guaranteeing freedom of entry and exit for mobile capital across the globe. Countries that were willing to play the game by Washington's rules were rewarded with generous financial assistance and other forms of support.[18]

The consensus should not be conceived in deterministic terms, however; it was not just a blunt policy and ideological package that the United States forced onto the governments of the global South. Although the consensus clearly supported the DWSR, it also, albeit unevenly, benefited the political elites and bourgeoisies in emerging market economies, who were restructuring their relations of production in order to overcome declining profit levels; 'it was not the Washington consensus idea that taught people to transform social relations; it was the material transformations of social relations which produced the power of the Washington consensus idea'.[19] For this reason, contradictions in the DWSR fundamentally affect changes in the Washington consensus, which, in turn, help us understand the nature of the NIFA.

3. THE CONTRADICTIONS OF IMPOSED LEADERSHIP

How should we understand the internal relations of the DWSR? I suggest that the relationship between the United States government and global finance is symbiotic yet constraining. It is symbiotic because as international financial markets grow in size and power, so, too, does the US economy. Because of its low level of domestic savings, the US is dependent on a constant inflow of funds from abroad, and the market in US government bonds is the biggest financial market in the world.[20] The mutually reinforcing elements of global finance's insatiable greed and Washington's obsession with neoliberal practices to maintain its structural power in the world economy resulted in a constant thrust toward financial liberalization. Indeed, prior to the Asian crash, the Interim Committee of the IMF was attempting to revise the Fund's charter so as to impose a legal obligation on its members to open their capital accounts.[21] As Benjamin J. Cohen rightly observes, this was the high-water mark of the attempt to consecrate 'free market mobility as a universal norm'.[22]

It is important to note that the DWSR thrives not only in periods of systemic stability, but also during times of instability. As Gowan notes, it feeds off crises in the following way. First, funds flee towards the safe haven of Wall Street. Second, SAPs encourage the export-oriented industrialization so that countries can pay off their debt; exports into the dollar zone further strengthen the dollar's centrality. Third, the risks faced by US financial operators are widely covered by the IMF, enabling them to return to international activity more aggressively than ever. Fourth, the weakening of states in the South strengthens the bargaining power of the Wall Street credit institutions in determining the form of future financing. Creditors are enabled to turn to forms that are safer, such as securitized debt and short-term rather than long-term loans.[23]

This has had two important consequences for the DWSR. First, it has increased the dependency of emerging market economies on short-term flows as their primary source of credit. Back in 1981, for example, bank loans made up 77 per cent of the foreign investment in such emerging markets as Mexico, Brazil, Chile, Argentina and Sri Lanka. By 1993, 74 per cent of private foreign investment in these same countries came from mutual funds, hedge funds, and pension funds.[24]

Second, this move has led to the concentration of power in the hands of a smaller and smaller number of institutional investors, so that decisions relating to capital allocation have in effect become more and more centralized.

This apparently win-win situation for the DWSR is not without its problems, however. A major limitation worth examining here concerns the global South.

Given the growing interconnectedness brought about by the DWSR, its viability has become increasingly dependent on the health and stability of financial markets regardless of their location. As the former Secretary of the Treasury department, Robert Rubin, stated in reaction to Indonesia's economic woes in 1997, '[f]inancial stability around the world is critical to the national security and economic interest of the United States'.[25] With each debacle in the 'emerging markets', the neoclassical premises upon which the Washington consensus rests — especially the equation between free capital mobility and sustained prosperity — become harder to legitimate. Susan Strange noted this contradiction almost fifteen years ago when she remarked that

> the sorry state of the financial system is undoubtedly aggravating the difficulties in the path of economic development for poor countries while conversely the difficulties of the deeply indebted developing countries, so long as they persist, will aggravate the instability of the banking system.[26]

As Ilene Grabel points out, the predominant type of inflows to the South — i.e. short-term and speculative in nature — have two negative and mutually reinforcing effects on governments in the South. First, they impose constraints on policy autonomy. Eager to ensure a steady inflow of credit, states in the South have been keen to pursue the policies laid down by the IMF, whose seal of approval is the ultimate sign of creditworthiness for the financial markets. Second, these inflows lead to increased vulnerability to financial volatility and crisis.[27] To earn hard currency via exports, these countries need to keep their own currencies low, but they also require capital inflows to finance state expenditures, which push the value of their currencies upwards. Take for example the strength of the Mexican peso, which recently hit its highest levels since mid-1998, thereby weakening its export industry. Unsurprisingly, in view of the new interconnectedness of the global economy, one of the main reasons for the peso's revaluation is that Mexico has been a haven for short-term capital fleeing problems in Argentina and Brazil.[28]

Given their high dependence on exports, a currency revaluation can be, and has proven, fatal for an emerging market economy. In addition, high interest rates choke their heavily indebted private sectors and aggravate their already high levels of poverty. These policy constraints pose a threat both to the emerging market economies and the DWSR. Viewed together, these constraints appear as political expressions of the underlying contradictions of the capital relation in these countries. They place an extremely heavy burden on their governments, which have to maintain the political and social conditions for continued capital accumulation by trying to meet the constantly increasing demands of both the private sector and society at large. What is more, 'imposed leadership' demands that they overcome these policy constraints in such a way as to continue to support free capital mobility. To protect themselves from this 'trilemma' the governments of emerging markets call for increased policy autonomy in the management of their capital accounts and in the determination of their exchange rates.[29] Both responses clearly run contrary to the interests of the DWSR. How has Washington responded? The next section focuses on how the NIFA attempts to contribute to the management of these contradictions.

4. THE NIFA: A PROCRUSTEAN BED FOR THE EMERGING MARKETS?

In response to various issues relating to the financial crisis of the emerging markets in the late 1990s the United States, acting through the esoteric community of the G7, unilaterally pushed through an agenda that would officially link 'systematically important' emerging markets with the IMF and the World Bank. The objectives of this project were clearly mapped out by the primary directive of the G7 Summit meeting in Cologne: to integrate emerging market economies more fully and flexibly into the global financial system by getting the IMF and its member states to increase their 'transparency' by publishing economic data, especially on short-term indebtedness and the state of their foreign exchange reserves. The G7 also 'urged the IMF to co-ordinate surveillance of the degree to which countries comply with international standards and codes of conduct. In addition, the G7 demands greater disclosure of the degree to which private sector financial institutions are exposed to hedge funds and other highly leveraged institutions.'[30] After hearing provisional reports from various ad hoc committees — whose membership was selected under the watchful eye of the US — the G7 leaders created the G20, or Group of 20, in Washington, D.C. on September 25, 1999. Unsurprisingly, the G20's membership structure reveals an important tendency in regard to the two types of coercion involved in imposed leadership.

The G20 includes the G7/G8, representatives from the European Union, the IMF, the Fund's new International Monetary and Financial Committee (IMFC) and the World Bank, as well as the Bank's Development Committee, and the following 'systematically important' emerging market countries: Argentina, Australia, Brazil, China, India, Indonesia, Mexico, Saudi Arabia, South Africa, South Korea, and Turkey. Taken together the constitution of the G20 represents a new attempt at *core-periphery coercion* by inviting these countries into the highly exclusive G7/G8, or more bluntly, coopting them into the rules and standards of the *core alliance* by involving them in official, and thus more tightly integrated, relations with the IMF and World Bank. This has never been attempted before. The mission of this esoteric community of IFIs, emerging markets and core states is to fulfil the primary objectives listed at the Cologne Summit.[31]

Through its annual meetings, the G20 seeks to promote consistency and coherence in the various efforts aimed at reforming and strengthening the international financial system as defined by the IMF and World Bank.[32]

As with the G7, however, and in the interests of a similar wish for low visibility, the G20 does not have a permanent secretariat but is 'based' in the country of its chairperson, who in mid-2001 was the Canadian Minister of Finance, Paul Martin.

Again following the imposed leadership of the United States, the G7 finance ministers also created the Financial Stability Forum (FSF, or Forum). The Forum is a political body that reports to and is supervised jointly by the G7 leaders. Unlike the G20, however, the FSF is a type of *core-alliance coercion*. Its membership is confined to a total of forty members from G7 countries. The FSF, which was first convened in April 1999, was established to promote international financial stability through information exchange and international cooperation in financial supervision and surveillance. In its own words, '[t]he *Forum* brings together on a regular basis national authorities responsible for financial stability in significant international financial centres, international financial institutions, sector-specific international groupings of regulators and supervisors, and committees of central bank experts.'[33]

The FSF seeks to co-ordinate the efforts of these various bodies in order to promote international financial stability, improve the functioning of markets, and reduce systemic risk. Crucially, the initial Chairman of the FSF was drawn not from a 'strategically important' emerging market economy but was the General Manager of the BIS. Moreover, the Forum is also housed in the BIS in Basel, Switzerland.

As stated on its website, the key objectives of the FSF are: (1) to evaluate the vulnerabilities in the international financial system; (2) to identify and oversee action needed to address these vulnerabilities; and (3) to improve co-ordination and information exchange among the various authorities responsible for financial stability. The FSF meets twice a year, or as many times as needed to carry out its objectives. Some important developments that have emerged from these meetings have been the establishment of three working groups to extensively assess and recommend policy actions regarding: (a) highly-leveraged institutions; (b) capital flows; and, (c) offshore financial centres. Together with the International Association of Insurance Supervisors (IAIS), one of the FSF's recent accomplishments was to put together and disseminate a 'Compendium of Standards'. The Compendium establishes a common reference for the various standards and codes of good practice that are internationally accepted as relevant to sound, stable, and well-functioning financial systems. Furthermore, the FSF has approved a Financial Supervision Training Directory, which was created jointly by the managers of global capitalism, namely the IMF, the World Bank, and the BIS.

The above sketch of the G20 and the FSF sheds some light on whose building the NIFA actually is. The key role played by the United States in initiating the NIFA, and the fact that it is aimed at strengthening, as opposed to transforming, the existing power structures in the world economy, makes it clear that the edifice is an annex of the US state. This becomes particularly evident in light of the importance attached to linking the 'systematically important' emerging markets more closely to the IMF and World Bank. It is common knowledge that the US is disproportionately represented in the IMF and World Bank; with about 18 per cent of the Fund's quotas, the United States is able to veto any decision by this institution. Nevertheless, it should be emphasized that the interests served are also those of the *core-alliance* and the transnational bourgeoisie as a whole, all of whom benefit from this strategy to address the key structural contradiction inherent in the DWSR.

The NIFA's ideological impact is as significant as its practical structures. It reinforces the commitment of governments in emerging market economies to continue to adhere to the tenets of free trade and capital mobility, in three overlapping ways. First, it reinforces the view that increased volatility in the international financial system is due to home-grown policy-errors in emerging markets — not so much those of profligate governments, which have been largely 'corrected' by SAPs, but those resulting from bad structures of corporate governance (relatedly, this presupposes that the regulatory structures of the advanced industrialized countries, especially those of the United States, do not need reform). Second, it shifts the blame for the crises onto the emerging markets and absolves the international financial markets, which thus need not be subject to reform. Third, it induces the governments of emerging market countries to endorse the status quo by means of inclusionary politics. As the G7 made clear during the Cologne summit, the key objective of this interstate initiative was to integrate emerging market economies more fully and flexibly into the DWSR.[34]

This move is not an attempt to shift the balance of power between the *core* and *periphery* but to strengthen the existing system through collective surveillance. The existing hierarchy of power will also be reflected in the structure of the G20 and the FSF. Yet as Geoffrey Underhill notes, these closed and highly technical transnational communities only provide *ad hoc* and patchy forms of regulation and supervision of financial markets. This lackadaisical governance plays a major role in facilitating the growth of both capital mobility, and, in turn, volatility associated with highly leveraged institutions such as hedge funds.

Drawing other states into the path of the consensus: imposed leadership

The NIFA is an attempt to strike a balance between financial deregulation and stability by encouraging governments of emerging markets to adopt only 'prudent' policies to restrain the inflow of speculative capital and to encourage more productive, long-term capital formation. Top officials from the IFIs have argued that certain limited capital controls (as opposed to universal controls, such as the Tobin tax) in emerging markets are acceptable as temporary, second-best options — that is, next to the first-best option of complete liberalization, which allows the magical self-corrective forces of the market to do their trick through open capital accounts.[35] It must be stressed, however, that their position is not a big departure from the orthodoxy of the Washington consensus. As John Williamson notes, convention has always held that to ensure stability during the reform process, policymakers should concentrate on liberalizing other parts of the economy first, before opening the capital account.[36] In this spirit limited capital controls are also acceptable as temporary policy instruments to achieve a breathing space for corrective action — which, of course, involves the implementation of neoliberal reforms. Stanley Fischer, the IMF's deputy director, summarized this view when he said that the Fund 'is prodding countries toward the importance of pursuing sound macro-economic policies ... and phasing capital account liberalisation appropriately — which means retaining some capital controls in the transition is virtually axiomatic now.'[37] Thus emerging markets should employ 'certain' types of controls so that they may undertake the necessary reforms — the adoption of First World financial and banking structures — to achieve the end goal of full financial liberalization.

Not all limited capital controls are acceptable, however. Fourteen emerging market economies have employed a variety of capital controls over the past decade, but Washington has only endorsed the Chilean capital controls of 1991–98 (the unremunerated reserve requirement or URR). The URR attempted to limit the free outflow of portfolio investment by requiring all non-equity foreign capital inflows to buy a one-year, non-interest-bearing deposit, in effect charging a fee to anyone taking funds out of the country less than a year after moving them in.[38] When viewed in light of the Washington consensus, however, the reasons underlying this endorsement are not far to seek: Chile's fastidious adherence to the principles of neoliberalism, since General Pinochet so inhumanely introduced this policy and ideology in 1973, and especially the fact that apart from these controls the Chilean government had fully liberalized capital outflows. Apart from this, spokespeople for the international financial markets (including George Soros) as well as the US government have condemned states that curtail free capital mobility. In stark contrast to the Chilean endorsement, the IMF passed a hostile judgement on the much shorter-lived but more far-reaching Malaysian controls on outflows (1998-99) as clearly abandoning the liberalization of capital accounts.[39] Although the jury is still out regarding the effectiveness of both types of controls, the US remains vehemently opposed to the Malaysian controls.[40] Despite the fact that Malaysia modelled its controls on China's, it was not only exposed to disciplinary action by both the IMF and capital markets (capital flight and investment strikes) but was also denied entry into the 'elite' club of the G20, on the ostensible grounds that 'some among the G7 felt that Thailand, on the size of its economy and the absence of currency controls, [was] better suited.' Significantly enough, given China's geopolitical importance in the global political economy, it was admitted to membership of the G20 in spite of its use of the controls for which Malaysia was excluded.

There are at least three overlapping reasons — all of which can be traced to the interests of the DWSR — for the US rejection of the Malaysian currency controls. First, controls on capital outflows restrict the liquidity needed to nourish Wall Street and Main Street. This is particularly compelling in light of the fact that the Asian region has the highest saving rates in the world.[41] Second, the general opposition of the United States to restricting short-term capital flows, and its corresponding vilification of the 'Asian model' as 'crony capitalism', arise logically enough from the fact that these controls do pose an ideological threat to the logic of financial liberalization. Neoliberals cannot deny that countries such as China and Taiwan, and later Hong Kong, which closed their economies to these volatile flows, escaped the direct impact of the Asian crisis in large part because their currencies were non-convertible, preventing both inflows and outflows of hot money yet *not* preventing foreign direct investment.[42] The Malaysian currency controls were opposed by the United States because they reflected a larger historical tradition in the region to rely on a form of state intervention that runs directly against the neoclassical spirit of the Washington consensus, namely the 'developmental state'. John Zysman defines developmental states as non-Anglo-Saxon state regulations, strong-state technocratic dirigisme, and corporatist structures, like Japan's.[43] This conception of development does not see state economic intervention as an unproductive and at best necessary evil. More importantly, the developmental state is closely associated with specific practices that run contrary to the NIFA project of implementing 'good corporate governance' (i.e., a separation between management and ownership) and transparency (i.e., public availability of information) — policies aimed at destroying the exclusive family-based capitalist business networks common in the region, the so-called 'bamboo networks' and 'pyramids' which are effectively closed to foreign penetration.[44] Because this type of state intervention and accumulation regime has been highly successful in the past, its renewed attractiveness to these governments as a viable alternative to the Washington consensus — particularly in light of the present economic downturn in the region — poses a powerful threat to Washington's bid to consecrate global capital mobility.

5. CONCLUSION:
THE CONTRADICTION OF IMPOSED LEADERSHIP

The NIFA, a project of the caretakers of the global economy to refurbish and fortify the political and ideological scaffolding of the DWSR, reveals an overriding concern to address some of the more salient contradictions involved in free capital mobility. Nonetheless, far from smoothing over these contradictions, imposed leadership has led to new ones. Although the power of the DWSR and global finance has been reproduced in the process of guaranteeing the continuation of global capital accumulation, the process has served not only to intensify the competition for power (as opposed to the establishment of a new era of capital accumulation — a new Golden Age of growth) but also to aggravate uneven development, manifested in increasing inequality between the core and periphery, and between rich and poor in the global South. Moreover additional obstacles have been placed in the path of governments of the emerging markets seeking both to regulate their economies in ways compatible with the expansion and reproduction of the DWSR and to compete for FDI. As a result, imposed leadership will more than likely beget yet more coercion.

There is also the problem that 'peripheral' political elites woo foreign capital by making significant concessions to global players. Governments have to address and subdue the escalating social conflicts to which these concessions give rise in ways that will not lead to capital flight or investment strikes — but, under the NIFA/DWSR rules, with one hand tied behind their backs. Yet governments must also depoliticize these struggles in order to maintain their own legitimacy. Take for example the policy contradiction in which the Mexican government was caught in 2001. The Fox administration was being pressured by Standard and Poor, a major credit-rating agency and spokesperson for global finance capital, to undertake a tax reform that would lower borrowing costs for companies and governments alike. The payback for this concession would be an award of investment–grade status.[45]

It was also, however, under pressure to make concessions to the growing numbers of Mexicans who found themselves below the poverty line, as well as from the general discontent of voters with the neoliberal policies of the past two decades. To deal with these pressures Vicente Fox needed the revenue from planned tax *increases* to pay for, *inter alia*, anti-poverty programmes, social programmes, and education.

To put it more generally, far from capital mobility disciplining the governments of 'emerging markets' to adhere to the rules of the West, its inherent contradictions have touched off a general 'crisis of the state' for many governments of the global South, especially those involved in the G20. This crisis has enormous consequences for the ability of these states to adhere to the dictates of imposed leadership. To gain more elbow-room for policy formation these governments have predictably turned to populist politics. More fundamentally still, their attempts to deal with the key structural contradiction between the DWSR and the global South appear to be moving them in the direction of a new 'double movement', particularly in the two regions most vulnerable to a downturn in demand in the US, namely Latin America and East Asia. This is the larger significance of the exclusion of Malaysia from the G20; it was not merely intended to discipline an 'anti-Washington consensus' rogue state, but rather to serve as a general deterrent to a regional movement toward what Karl Polanyi referred to as a Phase II type of economic and social development — a decisive shift toward explicit state intervention, not only to stabilize and regulate the markets, but also to create conditions for wealth creation and efficient resource allocation.[46] A significant development that has the potential to be part of such a shift is the establishment by the Association of Southeast Asian Nations (ASEAN) +3 (i.e., the ASEAN countries plus Japan, South Korea, and China) of a 'network of currency swap/repurchase arrangements, designed to protect member countries against the sudden withdrawal of hot money investment by Western speculators'.[47] China's dual role in the G20 and ASEAN+3 will prove quite interesting vis-à-vis imposed leadership. The question that arises here is the effectiveness of the ASEAN currency swap, given that China remains tied to the DWSR. In Latin America, too, there is a nascent and patchy move towards what is loosely referred to as the 'Buenos Aires consensus', which is essentially an alternative to the orthodoxy of the Washington consensus in that it is aimed at 'sharp tax reforms, productivist integration of national economies, social safety nets and democratized state and political systems.[48] The potential threat posed to the DWSR by these regional 'double movements' is that they could result in the re-introduction of the developmental state, which by its very definition implies protectionist policies that could be more than merely rhetorical. In short, the peril these alternative political forms of capitalism pose to the United States is their ability to delegitimize the principle of free capital mobility throughout the global political economy.

A domestic variant of the 'double movement' is an attempt to cope with the crisis of the state by defying the orthodox development strategy prescribed by the Washington Consensus and re-embedding the market economy in society — but without ceding material concessions and political empowerment to the masses. José Ocampo, the Executive Secretary of ECLAC, points out that Latin America implemented the most extensive reforms based on the Washington consensus yet 'growth in the 1990s was on 3.2% a year, far below the 5.5% record set during the three decades of State-led development from the 1950s to the 1970s.'[49] Noting that other major players and pundits agree that liberalized capital accounts do not create economic prosperity, Ocampo argues that emerging market states can only hope to strengthen the international financial system if the international community grants them freedom to increase their policy autonomy — especially over capital account liberalization and exchange rate regimes — so that they can devise policies to shield their countries from the devastating socio-economic effects brought about by speculators. This would allow governments more breathing space in which to find a new balance between the market and the public interests, aligning public policy with the objectives of civil society.

It is very clear that neither of these two kinds of 'double movement' is reformist, let alone revolutionary. Indeed, they are attempts by political elites and bourgeoisies to secure export competitiveness whilst repressing domestic class struggle. Yet these strategies, aimed at salvaging political legitimacy whilst over-coming the obstacles to capital accumulation, do have the potential to throw a spanner in the works of imposed American leadership and could lead to discipli-nary reactions from the World Bank, the IMF and the credit-rating agencies. Nevertheless the structural contradictions of imposed leadership could continue to weaken the political strategy of DWSR and global finance, which in turn could open up fresh space for political protest and the struggle to radically trans-form class relations in the emerging market countries and beyond.

NOTES

I would like to thank Benjamin J. Cohen, Colin Leys, Leo Panitch, Christopher Roberts, and Marcus Taylor for commenting on earlier drafts of this essay. The usual disclaimers apply.

1   World Bank, *World Development Report 2000/2001: Attacking Poverty*, Oxford: Oxford University Press, 2000, p. 3.

2   José Antonio Ocampo, 'Rethinking the Development Agenda', Santiago, Chile: ECLAC, http://www.eclac.org/noticias/articulos/4/5784/rethinking3.pdf.

3   Peter Gowan, *The Global Gamble: Washington's Faustian Bid for World Dominance,* London: Verso, 1999.

4   'A Survey of Asian Business: In praise of rules', *The Economist*, 7 April 2001, p. 3. The 'crony-factor' as an explanatory variable has been criticized by many authors across the political spectrum: see, for example, Jeffrey Sachs,

'The IMF and the Asian Flu', *The American Prospect*, No. 37, March–April 1998, http://epn.org/prospect/37/37sachf.html; and Walden Bello, 'East Asia: on the eve of the great transformation?', *Review of International Political Economy*, 5(3) 1998.

5   George Soros, 'Capitalism's Last Chance?' *Foreign Policy*, 113 (Winter 1998–99), p. 55.

6   David Felix, 'The Economic Case Against Free Capital Mobility', in Leslie Armijo Elliot, ed., *Debating the Global Financial Architecture*, New York: SUNY Press, forthcoming, p. 172.

7   Alexandre Lamfalussy, *Financial Crises in Emerging Markets*, New Haven: Yale University Press, 2000, pp. 47–66.

8   Philip Arestis and Malcolm Sawyer 'What role for the Tobin tax in world economic governance?', in J. Michie and J. G. Smith, eds., *Global Instability: The Political Economy of World Economic Governance*, London: Routledge, 1999, p. 153.

9   Jagdish Bhagwati, 'The Capital Myth: The Differences between Trade in Widgets and Dollars', *Foreign Affairs*, (May/June) 1998, p. 10.

10   James Tobin, 'A proposal for international monetary reform', *Eastern Economic Journal*, 4 (3-4), 1978.

11   Arestis and Sawyer, 'What role for the Tobin tax', p. 163.

12   Benjamin J. Cohen, 'Capital Controls: The Neglected Option', in Geoffrey R.D. Underhill, ed., *What is to be Done? Global Economic Disorder and Policies for a New International Financial Architecture*, forthcoming, 2001.

13   Giovanni Arrighi, *The Long Twentieth Century: Money, Power, and the Origins of Our Times*, London: Verso, 1994, p. 29.

14   Following Antonio Gramsci hegemony entails both coercion and consensus, which are intimately intertwined in a dialectical relation — albeit consensus is more predominant than coercion in a hegemonic situation. The inverse is true during non-hegemonic periods.

15   Geoffrey R.D. Underhill, 'Private Markets and Public Responsibility in a Global System: Conflict and Co-operation in Transnational Banking and Securities Regulation', in Geoffrey R.D. Underhill, ed., *The New World Order in International Finance*, London: Macmillan Press, 1997, p. 31.

16   For more policy-oriented discussion of the Washington Consensus, see John Williamson, 'Democracy and the Washington Consensus', *World Development* 21(8), 1993; John Williamson, *Latin American Adjustment: How much has happened?*, Washington, DC: Institute for International Economics, 1990.

17   On the importance of the role of the state in globalization, see, for example, Leo Panitch, 'The New Imperial State', *New Left Review*, (March–April) 2000, pp. 5–20.

18   Cohen, 'Capital Controls'.

19   Gowan, *The Global Gamble*, p. 58.

20   Doug Henwood, *Wall Street: How it Works and For Whom*, London: Verso,

1998, p. 24: '[a]t the centre of the market are 38 major investment and commercial banks who are certified as primary dealers by the Federal Reserve Bank of New York — the choice inner circle with which the Fed conducts its official monetary business'.

21   IMF, 'IMF Builds on Initiatives to Meet Challenges of Globalisation', *IMF Survey*, Washington, D.C.: IMF, September 1997, p. 8.

22   Cohen, 'Capital Controls', p. 4.

23   Gowan, *The Global Gamble*, pp. 35ff.

24   John Dillon, *Turning the Tide: Confronting the Money Traders*, Ottawa: Canadian Centre for Policy Alternatives, 1997, p. 70.

25   *New York Times*, 1 November 1997.

26   Susan Strange, *Casino Capitalism*, Oxford: Oxford University Press, 1986, pp. 92-5.

27   Ilene Grabel, 'Marketing the Third World: The Contradictions of Portfolio Investment in the Global Economy', *World Development*, 24 (11), 1996, p. 1763.

28   'Mexico: Slowing economy, quickening politics', *The Economist*, 19 May 2001, p. 33.

29   José Antonio Ocampo, 'A Broad Agenda For International Financial Reform, in J. A. Ocampo *et al.*, eds., *Financial Globalization and the Emerging Markets*, Santiago, Chile: UN Economic Commission for Latin American and the Caribbean, 2000.

30   'The New Financial Architecture', *Financial Times*, 24 September 1999.

31   For more information, see the G20 website at www.g20.org.

32   The first meeting of the G20 was convened in Berlin in 1999. The second was held in Montreal in 2000. The 2001 meeting is to be announced.

33   http://www.fsforum.org

34   'The New Financial Architecture', *Financial Times*.

35   Recently, the former chief economist of the World Bank, Joseph Stiglitz, as well as officials of the IMF, such as Deputy Managing Director Stanley Fischer, have championed the use of limited, or country-specific, capital controls in select emerging market economies. See, for example, J. Stiglitz, 'The Role of International Financial Institutions in the Current Global Economy', Washington, DC: World Bank, 27 February 1998.

36   John Williamson, 'Orthodoxy is Right: Liberalize the Capital Account Last', in C. P. Ries and R. J. Sweeney, eds., *Capital Controls in Emerging Economies*, Boulder, CO: Westview Press, 1997, pp. 13-16.

37   IMF, 'Report of the Acting Managing Director', p. 12; Barry Eichengreen, *Toward a New International Financial Architecture*. Washington, DC: Institute for International Economics, 1999; IMF, 'Capital Account Liberalization and the Role of the IMF', *IMF Survey*, Washington, DC: IMF, 20 October 1997.

38   See, for example, D. J. Mathieson and G. J. Schinasi, *International Capital Markets: Developments, prospects, and Key Policy Issues*, Washington, DC: IMF,

September 2000, sections 1-7.

39   On 1 September 1998, Mahathir Mohamad, the Malaysian Prime Minister, announced a system of currency controls on short-term capital, which was explicitly based on the Chinese capital controls. In effect, this prevented purchasing of foreign exchange for speculative purposes by both residents and foreigners.

40   See, for example, IMF, *Recovery from the Asian Crisis and the Role of the IMF*, Washington, DC: IMF Staff Essays, 2000; IMF, *Capital Controls: Country Experiences with their Use and Liberalization*, Occasional Essay 190, Washington, DC: IMF, 17 May 2000 parts 1-3.

41   Asian countries have always had a high rate of savings vis-à-vis the rest of the world. However, in the post-Asian environment, these rates have risen considerably. Malaysia and Singapore, for example, had rates hovering around 45 per cent of their respective GDP levels, while savings levels in Hong Kong registered at about 30 per cent of GDP and Japan at 27 per cent. *Taipei Times*, 9 July 2000.

42   Robert Wade and Frank Veneroso, 'The Asian Crisis: The High Debt Model Versus the Wall Street-Treasury-IMF Complex', *New Left Review*, 228 (March/April) 1998, p. 22.

43   John Zysman, *Governments, Markets, and Growth: Financial Systems and the Politics of Industrial Change*, Ithaca: Cornell University Press, 1983.

44   Cf. 'In Praise of Rules', *The Economist*, 7 April 2001.

45   See, for example, Jorge Casteñada, 'Mexico: Permuting Power', *New Left Review*, 7 (January-February), 2001; 'Slowing economy, quickening politics', *The Economist*, 19 May 2001.

46   Karl Polanyi, *The Great Transformation*, Boston: Beacon Press, 1968.

47   Tim Armstrong, 'Asia is going it alone', *Globe and Mail*, Monday, 12 February 2001.

48   J. Casteñada, 'Mexico: Permuting Power', p. 16. Cf. S. Soederberg, 'From Neoliberalism to Social liberalism: Situating the National Solidarity Program within Mexico's Passive Revolutions', in *Latin American Perspectives*, 28 (3), May 2001.

49   Ocampo, 'A broad agenda', p. 56ff.

MAKING POVERTY WORK

Paul Cammack

Those that get their living by their daily labour ... have nothing to stir them up to be serviceable but their wants which it is prudence to relieve, but folly to cure. ... From what has been said, it is manifest, that, in a free nation, where slaves are not allowed of, the surest wealth consists in a multitude of laborious poor (Bernard de Mandeville, *The Fable of the Bees*, 5th edition, London, 1728, p. 328, cited in K. Marx, *Capital*, Vol. 1, London, 1976, Ch. 25, p. 765).

The international development community, led by the World Bank, has recently committed itself to the abolition of poverty; and the World Bank has set out, in its most recent World Development Report, *Attacking Poverty*, the means by which the target of reducing the proportion of people living in absolute poverty by half by 2015 is to be achieved.[1] Indeed, the website of the World Bank Group now proclaims: 'Our Dream Is A World Free of Poverty'. Rather than dismiss this as a flight of fancy, we should ask why the claim is made, and why it is the World Bank that makes it. The answer touches on two key contradictions in global capitalism — its need to represent the interests of a single class as those of society as a whole, reflected today in the systematic effort to present as benevolent a neoliberal revolution intended to deliver people everywhere into the clutches of capital; and its need to operate as a single system across a fragmented world of competing states with no overarching political authority, reflected today in the search for international regimes and organizations through which the global system might be managed. The World Bank's affected concern for poverty, I argue, is a response to the combined effects of these two contradictions.

Over two centuries ago, it was possible for the Reverend Townsend to celebrate hunger, comparing it favourably to compulsion by force on the grounds that it 'is not only a peaceable, silent, unremitting pressure, but as the most natural motive to industry and labour, it calls forth the most powerful exertions'.[2] It is no longer prudent to sing the praises of starvation in quite these blunt terms, so capitalism must be sold as a *solution* to poverty. In broader terms, global capitalism must be represented as a universal good, rather than as what it is, a system which benefits a minority to the detriment of the majority. Secondly, in so far as capitalism operates on a world scale, its contradictions operate and must be addressed on a world scale. This creates a problem which elsewhere in this volume Ellen Meiksins Wood identifies as a key contradiction of globalization:

> The economic imperatives of capitalism do indeed permit the reach of capital to extend far beyond the scope of direct political and military domination. Yet at the same time, capital can never dispense with the enforcement of market imperatives, and the system of property relations in which they are rooted, by legal and political means. If anything, capitalism more than any other system needs a stable and predictable political and legal order. That kind of order is, for all practical purposes, impossible on a global scale, and capital has hitherto found no better instrument of social order than the nation state, nor is it likely to find one in the foreseeable future.[3]

This argument is taken a step further here. In the long run capitalism may be doomed by its fundamental contradictions, but the agencies dedicated to staving off the contradictions which beset it are neither powerless nor stupid, and the World Bank is currently positioning itself as the leading agency overseeing the coordination and global marketing of strategies intended to cement the core disciplines of capitalism in place. It is putting in place new mechanisms — principally, its Comprehensive Development Framework and its newly devised Poverty Reduction Strategy Papers — to oblige the poorest countries to adopt its chosen policies, and seeking ways to extend their discipline to the 'middle-income' countries which make up the majority in the global economy. It is also building some key global alliances, the most significant of which is with the British New Labour government and its Treasury-led 'development' arm, DFID. Behind its proclaimed wish to see an end to poverty lies a diametrically opposite intention: to impose universally the conditions through which poverty is created and maintained. Far from wanting to abolish poverty, the World Bank wants poverty to work for capitalism.

MARX ON POVERTY: THE ABSOLUTE GENERAL LAW OF CAPITALIST ACCUMULATION

The logic of the Bank's proposal to 'abolish' poverty is perfectly disclosed in Marx's discussion of the reserve army of labour in *Capital*, to which it is useful to return in this context. Marx's view of the relationship between capitalism and poverty can be expressed in six related propositions: an ever-expanding proletariat is part and parcel of capitalist accumulation; supposedly 'free' workers themselves produce and reinforce the mechanisms by which capitalism exerts discipline over them; this process reaches maturity when rising labour productivity becomes the driving force behind accumulation; mature capitalism requires and generates a 'relative surplus population' without which its discipline cannot work; the presence of an 'industrial reserve army' within this surplus population keeps wages low, and tending towards subsistence level; and a proportion of the surplus population is always in absolute poverty. In short, to abolish poverty would be to abolish capitalism itself.

Noting at the beginning of *Capital*, Volume 1, Chapter 25, that wages may temporarily rise when demand from capitalists for labour outstrips supply, Marx goes on:

> [t]he more or less favourable circumstances in which the wage-labourers support and multiply themselves in no way alter the fundamental character of capitalist production. As simple reproduction constantly reproduces the capital-relation itself, i.e. the presence of capitalists on the one side, and wage-labourers on the other side, so reproduction on an expanded scale, i.e. accumulation, reproduces the capital-relation on an expanded scale, with more capitalists, or bigger capitalists, at one pole, and more wage-labourers at the other pole. The reproduction of labour power which must incessantly be re-incorporated into capital as its means of valorization, which cannot get free of capital, and whose enslavement to capital is only concealed by the variety of individual capitalists to whom it sells itself, forms, in fact, a factor in the reproduction of capital itself. Accumulation of capital is therefore multiplication of the proletariat.[4]

The system is thus driven forward not by the needs of the majority of the population, but by the opportunities for capitalists to make profits. These features are the *differentia specifica* of capitalist production:

> [l]abour-power is not purchased under this system for the purpose of satisfying the personal needs of the buyer, either by its service or through its product. The aim of the buyer is the valorization of his capital, the production of commodities which contain more labour than he paid for, and therefore contain a portion of value which costs him nothing, and is nevertheless realized through the sale of those commodities. The production of surplus-value, or the making of profits, is the absolute law of this mode of production.[5]

Capitalism as a system comes into its own when increasing amounts of capital are applied to the labour process, increasing the productivity of labour and cheapening the price at which commodities can be produced. Competition between capitalists, attended by the failure of some, the 'centralization' or amalgamation of others and the emergence of new ones, drives the process forward in a dynamic but uneven fashion, generating cycles of activity punctuated by regular crises in an overall pattern of expansion. In the process, the 'organic composition of capital' — the ratio between the 'constant' part represented by means of production, and the 'variable' part reflected by the labour-power needed to set them in motion — steadily rises. Although the enormous expansion in the means of production allows an expansion in the absolute size of the proletariat, 'the additional capital formed in the course of further accumulation attracts fewer and fewer workers in proportion to its magnitude. On the other hand, the old capital periodically reproduced with a new composition repels more and more workers formerly employed by it'.[6]

It follows that 'it is capitalist accumulation itself that constantly produces, and produces indeed in direct relation with its own energy and extent, a relatively redundant working population, i.e. a population which is superfluous to capital's average requirements for its own valorization and is therefore a surplus population'.[7] This is the 'law of population peculiar to the capitalist mode of production': '[t]he working population ... produces both the accumulation of capital and the means by which it is itself made relatively superfluous; and it does this to an extent which is always increasing'. This process creates a 'disposable industrial reserve army', a 'mass of human material always ready for exploitation by capital', which makes possible rapid expansion when new opportunities for profit-making appear.[8] Capitalism requires this relative surplus population at all times, if its self-expansion is to continue. Its production is therefore 'a necessary condition for modern industry'.[9]

The existence of a 'relative surplus population', then, is an essential element of an efficient capitalist system. Marx identifies three forms it may take — floating (members of the modern industrial proletariat who move in and out of work in accordance with the fluctuations of the market), latent (the surplus population in the countryside, 'freed' by capitalist investment in agriculture, and drawn to the towns when demand for labour rises), and stagnant (the 'inexhaustible reservoir of disposable labour-power' which provides a broad foundation for special branches of capitalist exploitation precisely because 'its conditions sink below the average normal level of the working class').[10] The lowest sediment of the relative surplus population — those able to work but last to be employed, orphans and pauper children, 'the demoralized, the ragged, and those unable to work', and the 'actual lumpenproletariat' of vagabonds, criminals and prostitutes' — 'dwell in the sphere of pauperism'.[11] Marx argues, in sum, that capitalism requires, and produces, a relative surplus population, and that this in turn requires pauperism: 'its production is included in that of the relative surplus population, its necessity is implied by their necessity; along with the surplus population, pauperism forms a condition of capitalist production, and of the capitalist development of wealth'.[12] From this set of circumstances there arises what Marx terms 'the absolute general law of capitalist accumulation':

> [t]he greater the social wealth, the functioning capital, the extent and the energy of its growth, and therefore also the greater the absolute mass of the proletariat and the productivity of its labour, the greater is the industrial reserve army. The same causes which develop the expansive power of capital, also develop the labour-power at its disposal. The relative mass of the industrial reserve army thus increases with the potential energy of wealth. But the greater this reserve army in proportion to the active

labour-army, the greater is the mass of a consolidated surplus population, whose misery is in inverse ratio to the amount of torture it has to undergo in the form of labour. The more extensive, finally, the pauperized sections of the working class and the industrial reserve army, the greater is official pauperism. *This is the absolute general law of capitalist accumulation.*[13]

This is not a natural law, but a central aspect of the 'antagonistic character of capitalist accumulation', and part and parcel of a set of characteristic features of capitalism — proletarianization, alienation, the subjection of the worker to the dictates of capital, and the systematic mystification of these processes in bourgeois ideology. Within this context,

> the law which always holds the relative surplus population or industrial reserve army in equilibrium with the extent and energy of accumulation rivets the worker to capital more firmly than the wedges of Hephaestus held Prometheus to the rock. It makes an accumulation of misery a necessary condition, corresponding to the accumulation of wealth. Accumulation of wealth at one pole is therefore, at the same time accumulation of misery, the torment of labour, slavery, ignorance, brutalization and moral degradation at the opposite pole, i.e. on the side of the class that produces its own product as capital.[14]

The self-expansion of capital is a dynamic but uneven process, which needs to carry workers-in-waiting along with it. This 'reserve army of labour' is held effectively in place and available where all social institutions are oriented towards the enforcement of market dependence. Capitalism also requires potential new workers to be prepared for it, in areas where its disciplines are not yet fully in place. This process, described by Marx as original or primitive accumulation, consists in the main of *proletarianization* — forcibly depriving free producers of access to the means of subsistence, in order to convert them into an available proletariat. Capitalism requires that the great majority of the population should have no other means of survival than to offer themselves for work at the market wage; where competition between capitalists is allowed to operate untrammelled on as wide as possible a scale, the market wage tends towards subsistence; in an efficiently operating capitalist system there is always a fluctuating proportion of the proletariat out of work; and there is always a further layer of the utterly impoverished ('absolutely poor') at the edge of or beyond the reserve army of labour itself.

In the particular global circumstances of the late twentieth and early twenty-first centuries, the World Bank has assumed responsibility for outlining and enforcing the policies that are necessary for these conditions to obtain, and for securing their general acceptance by the majority whom they oppress. What the Bank envisages, in its grand plan for reducing absolute poverty by half by 2015, is an efficient global labour market in which the existing proletariat will 'float' easily in and out of work, and the 'latent' proletariat, whether small peasant producers or young women as yet insufficiently accessible to capital's reach, will be 'freed' and fully proletarianized.

And despite its headline claims to the contrary, it recognizes that a third layer of the absolutely poor will continue to exist beyond these two, as a reservoir for further workers, and valuable source of discipline for the rest.

PROMOTING PROLETARIANIZATION, FACILITATING EXPLOITATION, ENHANCING MARKET DEPENDENCE

The World Bank has taken a new mission upon itself over the last decade. Spelled out discreetly but explicitly in successive World Development Reports since 1990, it is to complete the process of primitive accumulation on a global scale, and to promote reforms which enforce market dependence throughout the resulting global capitalist economy.[15] In adopting this dual mission, it implicitly endorses the truth of capitalism as a social system — that 'the surest wealth consists in a multitude of laborious poor'. As we shall see, the substance of World Bank policy recognizes this with unerring accuracy, while its rhetoric declares the opposite. Nor is this surprising — to advertise its goal as 'Exploitation or Misery!' would capture the truth but weaken its appeal. The Bank claims, in its latest World Development Report, *Attacking Poverty*, to be 'promoting opportunity', 'facilitating empowerment', and 'enhancing security'.[16] These phrases, on investigation, prove to conceal a fundamental contradiction of capitalism — that it 'frees' individuals by making them entirely dependent upon capital. The resources of the Bank are overwhelmingly devoted to defining policies which will promote proletarianization, facilitate exploitation, and enhance market dependence, guiding national governments in their adoption and implementation, structuring knowledge to minimize the availability and appeal of alternatives, and propagandizing the virtues of global capitalism. These are presented as offering freedom, but prove at every turn to replace constraints on the operations of the market with inescapable dependence upon the market.

The clues are there for anyone to read. The Bank places at the head of the second chapter of attacking poverty a graphic which helpfully translates the policy of global labour market expansion pursued for over a decade into the new language of liberation:

> *From World Development Report 1990 ...*
> *   Labor-intensive growth
> *   Broad provision of social services
> *... to World Development Report 2000/2001*
> *   Opportunity
> *   Empowerment
> *   Security

And if this were not clear enough, it quotes directly from its previous 1990 Report, Poverty, the paragraph which spelled out its commitment to a policy of global proletarianization:

[c]ountries that have been most successful in attacking poverty have encouraged a pattern of growth that makes efficient use of labor and have invested in the human capital of the poor. Both elements are essential. The first provides the poor with opportunities to use their most abundant asset — labour. The second improves their immediate wellbeing and increases their capacity to take advantage of the newly created possibilities. Together, they can improve the lives of most of the world's poor.[17]

It was clear, in 1990, that proletarianization was to be sold as an 'opportunity' that would allow the poor to 'take advantage' of their lack of other assets by selling their labour on the open market. But the truth behind it could be clearly discerned: when the World Bank spoke of providing the poor with 'opportunities to use their most abundant asset' — labour — it intended denying the poor any option *but* to use it. They were to be obliged to sell their labour power, while the Bank would support its efficient extraction by promoting targeted investment in health and education. Ten years on, the logic is the same, but the attempt to disguise it is more elaborate. Labour-intensive growth in which the poor are kept poor and obliged to sell their only asset is to be presented as offering the triple benefits of opportunity, empowerment and security. However, the process of mystification still shows through.

'Promoting opportunity' turns out to mean securing market dependence. It is initially translated as 'expanding economic opportunity for poor people by stimulating overall growth and by building up their assets and increasing the returns on these assets, through a combination of market and nonmarket actions'.[18] The specific content is then spelled out. First, 'a business environment conducive to private investment and technological innovation is necessary, as is political and social stability to underpin public and private investment'. Second, 'markets are central to the lives of poor people'.[19] The majority of the poor are to be proletarians. A minority are to be highly competitive small producers, particularly where patterns of land ownership and agriculture are currently inefficient. Basic social services and infrastructure — subsidies to capital — are presented as 'assets of the poor'; and for good measure the poor are offered the 'opportunity' of providing local services for themselves, for the further benefit of capital: 'local service delivery, engaging poor people and communities, can have a powerful impact on effectiveness'.[20]

'Facilitating empowerment' turns out to mean attacking two obstacles to the free action of capital — 'rent-seeking' and other forms of corruption by representatives of the state, and political, legal and social barriers that limit access to sections of the potential working class. The World Bank advocates 'building administrative and regulatory capacity and reducing corruption', and challenging 'customary practices and discrimination on the basis of gender, ethnicity, race, religion, or social status' that hinder growth and development. As usual in the World Development Reports, no direct reference is made to the underlying theory — as usual, standard public-choice concerns regarding rent-seeking behaviour by holders of state power:

> [e]mpowerment means enhancing the capacity of poor people to influence
> the state institutions that affect their lives, by strengthening their partici-
> pation in political processes and local decisionmaking. And it means
> removing the barriers — political, legal, and social — that work against
> particular groups and building the assets of poor people to enable them to
> engage effectively in markets. Expanding economic opportunities for poor
> people indeed contributes to their empowerment. But efforts are needed
> to make state and social institutions work in the interests of poor people
> — to make them pro-poor.[21]

Again, the logic is transparent. The targets are cultural practices on the one
hand, and the actions of the state on the other. The goal is to enable the poor
'to engage effectively in markets'; the result is to deliver the poor into greater
dependence upon markets. In other words, what is presented as a 'pro-poor'
strategy is in fact a pro-capital strategy. The Bank is effusive about its 'progressive' potential, but silent about the envisaged outcome, in which the poor
themselves act as vigilantes to enforce the disciplines which perfect and maintain their subordination to capital.

This is confirmed when the Bank turns to 'enhancing security'. It first
announces that enhancing security for poor people 'means reducing their vulnerability to such risks as ill health, economic shocks, and natural disasters and
helping them cope with adverse shocks when they do occur'. But it is immediately made clear that the purpose is not really to reduce 'vulnerability to risk' but
to transform its character:

> [p]overty reduction strategies can lessen the vulnerability of poor house-
> holds through a range of approaches that can reduce volatility, provide the
> means for poor people to manage risk themselves, and strengthen market
> or public institutions for risk management. The tasks include preventing
> or managing shocks at the national and regional level — such as economic
> downturns and natural disasters — and minimizing the impact on poor
> people when they do occur. Supporting the range of assets of poor people
> — human, natural, physical, financial, and social — can help them manage
> the risks they face. And supporting the institutions that help poor people
> manage risk can enable them to pursue the higher-risk, higher-return
> activities that can lift them out of poverty.[22]

The purpose behind 'risk management institutions' — health insurance, old age
assistance and pensions, unemployment insurance, workfare programs, social funds,
microfinance programs, and cash transfers — is to lock the poor into a permanent
exposure to the risk of market dependence, by so calibrating those institutions that
they propel the poor smartly back into the risk environment when they happen
to fall out. What is going on? Simply, as the World Bank itself signals at the outset,
that it has re-presented its 1990 message that the poor must work for a living in
the captivating language of opportunity, empowerment and security — opportunity meaning the ultimate denial of opportunity, the removal of any alternative but

submission to the disciplines of capitalism; empowerment meaning the ultimate form of disempowerment — delivery entirely into the hands of capital; and security meaning the ultimate, most comprehensive abolition of security — eternal dependence upon the market. In other words, the mission of the Bank is not to abolish poverty, but to make it work to promote accumulation.

MAKING POVERTY WORK

The stated goal of the World Bank is to reduce the proportion of the world's population living in extreme poverty (defined as having an income of less than $1 per day) by half over the period from 1990 to 2015. On the estimates published in the 2000/2001 Report, this would mean a decline from 1.2 billion to 0.8 billion over the period. First, then, this is not a policy to abolish extreme poverty, but to reduce it slowly over time — the Bank may dream of a world free from poverty, but it is not going to bring it about. Second, however, the target appears to be unrealistically high. According to the Report itself, between 1987 and 1998 the share of the population of developing and transitional countries living on less than $1 a day fell from 28 per cent to 24 per cent, but as a consequence of population growth 'the number of people in poverty hardly changed'.[23]

To put it another way, a reduction in the number of extremely poor of 2.7 per cent per year is needed to reach the target, and the current level recorded by the Bank is 1.7 per cent per year[24] — just about enough to keep the number of extremely poor constant if it were to continue. Third, the dismal record of poverty reduction over the last decade or so has been accompanied by spiralling inequality, on a global scale. Again, the Bank reports that per capita GDP in the richest twenty countries is thirty-seven times higher than in the poorest, and that the gap has doubled over the last forty years. It accepts, too, that income inequality between individuals, on a clearly upward trend for two centuries, has increased sharply over the same forty year period, and especially sharply in the very recent past.[25]

And when the Bank turns to an alternative, variable measure of 'relative poverty' (less than one third of a country's average consumption level), nearly a third (32.1 per cent) of the world's population are classified as poor in 1998 — and over 50 per cent in both Latin America and Sub-Saharan Africa.[26]

Keeping the 'nonpoor' working for capital

Having selected an income level of one dollar a day to define poverty, the World Bank coins the term 'nonpoor' to describe individuals above this level of austerity. This arbitrary and indefensible dividing line between the poor and the 'nonpoor' then plays a crucial strategic role in its analysis and policy prescriptions, making it clear that its principal intention is not to reduce poverty at all, but to subject the majority of the poor as commonly understood to dependence upon the market. The Report accepts the need to build coalitions between the poor and the 'nonpoor' in order to secure public acceptance of targeted poverty reduction programmes, and recognizes that whatever the system of targeting employed some benefits regrettably 'leak to the nonpoor'.[27] At the same time, it is alive to the consequences, and vigilant to guard against them:

> [c]hanges in the incentive system embedded in targeted programs could also facilitate cuts for nonpoor beneficiaries during periods of austerity. The argument is this: it is often said that for political economy reasons some of the benefits of targeted programs have to go to the nonpoor — through 'leakage' — to ensure continuing support for programs. The same forces will presumably act to limit the welfare losses to the nonpoor from cuts. One way to avoid this political economy constraint is to design programs with low marginal benefits or high marginal costs for the nonpoor.[28]

The explicit logic of the programmes it proposes, then, is to make labour markets work efficiently by keeping income levels for those supported by public provision below market rates, and support programmes sufficiently unattractive to deter all but the most desperate. In the topsy-turvy world of the Bank, this approach goes under the benevolent heading of 'Helping Poor People Manage Risk', overlooking the fact that this risk is what the Bank is seeking to create in the first place. Accepting that even sound macro-economic policies and efficient labour markets will not fully eliminate the risk of unemployment or underemployment, the Bank calls for unemployment benefits to 'protect workers from large income losses and poverty'. It rules out unemployment insurance on the grounds that contributory systems do not work well in economies with large informal sectors and weak administrative structures: 'Better options for assisting the unemployed are means-tested social assistance and public work programs (workfare)'.[29]

The logic of workfare programmes is two-fold. First, they are structured to attract only those who cannot find work at the bottom end of the labour market. Second, they incorporate initiatives intended to maximize the likelihood that those who are employed will remain available to re-enter the labour market in the future. In principle, therefore, they both preserve a reserve army of labour in times of recurrent crisis, and keep the total labour force at its maximum size over time. According to the Bank, their principal virtue is that by paying wages below market rates, such schemes can be self-targeting — in other words, in a manner impeccably consistent with the strategy of silent compulsion which eliminates the need for costly bureaucratic regulation, only the very neediest will contemplate entry to them. Beyond this, they can keep workers from falling permanently out of the labour market by being forced to sell assets and reduce food intake, and they can provide training to enhance skills. The Bank usefully provides a summary of the principles of successful workfare programmes, prefaced by the statement that '[i]n many programs for the poor a large share of benefits go to the nonpoor. This problem has stimulated interest in self-targeting schemes, such as public work programs (workfare), which have been especially effective':

[w]orkfare programs can improve their effectiveness by adhering to several principles.

• The wage rate should be determined by the local market wage for unskilled labor, not by the program's budget. If resources are insufficient to meet demand, the program should target areas with a high concentration of poor people. Using additional eligibility criteria should be avoided.

• Wage schedules should be gender neutral. Women can be encouraged to participate through suitable project selection, decentralized work sites, and the provision of child care.

• Labor intensity should be higher than the local norm for similar projects.

• Communities should be involved in project selection to maximize the capture by the poor of indirect benefits of the infrastructure created.

• To get the most risk mitigation, the program should be available at all times, expanding automatically during crises as demand increases.[30]

In every point, these maxims reflect a strategy of creating and maintaining a reserve army of labour without competing with (and thereby driving up wages in) the local labour market. They confirm that the logic of World Bank proposals to 'free the world of poverty' corresponds exactly and in detail to a strategy of extending the breadth and depth of proletarianization on a global scale, and imposing the disciplines of capitalist competition upon the global proletariat.

BUILDING A GLOBAL ARCHITECTURE OF GOVERNANCE

The World Bank, in cooperation with the IMF and the WTO, is seeking to perfect a strategic division of labour and to delegate key tasks to nation states, under the closest supervision. This strategic coordination, seen as the appropriate response to the contradiction between the limited scope for agency by nation states, and the global reach of the imperatives of capitalism, is exemplified by the 'World Bank Group Strategic Framework' published on 24 January 2001. This outlines the mechanisms through which its 'Comprehensive Development Framework' is to be imposed upon societies throughout the world, and celebrates a strategic alliance with the IMF, with 'the Bank leading the dialogue on social/structural issues, and the Fund leading on macroeconomic and related issues'.[31] It confirms the intention of the World Bank — originally conceived as an agency for channelling scarce capital to 'underdeveloped' countries — to reinvent itself as a vehicle for shaping institutions and policies from top to bottom in supposedly independent sovereign states.

At the same time it betrays an acute awareness that this project of aggressive global intervention creates a level of 'governance' far less legitimate and far more precarious than that operated by national governments. Hence its insistence that a central element of the strategy is to engineer 'ownership' of its policies by the target governments themselves. It is essential to the realization of its ambitions that its policy framework should be adopted and internalized by governments throughout the world. The Comprehensive Development Framework seeks to shape social and structural policies so that they reinforce and extend macroeconomic discipline, principally by 'freeing' labour for capital. In order to enforce it, the World Bank has introduced the 'Matrix', a comprehensive tracking system, to be 'kept up-to-date using modern communication and information technology, possibly with open designated websites', to enable it to monitor national programmes in real time, down to provincial, state, city and municipal levels.In sum, says World Bank President James D. Wolfensohn, '[t]he Matrix will allow us to see quickly what is going on in a country from the point of view of structural and social development, and will also show us what is not going on'.[32]

The operational tool through which the CDF and the Matrix is to be implemented is the Poverty Reduction Strategy Paper (PRSP), first proposed in 1999 and subsequently imposed as a contract between heavily indebted countries on the one hand, and the IMF and the World Bank on the other. The PRSP is to be monitored and updated annually, and reworked completely at three-year intervals. Through it, governments are to sign up to policies agreed on the basis of 'guidance that does not breach the principle of ownership in the context of joint missions to discuss strategy formulation with governments', backed by a comprehensive 'PRSP Sourcebook' and a programme of 'outreach and learning events'. *In extremis*, the Bank will kindly offer 'extra guidance on the expected core content of PRSPs and the participatory processes to be used in preparing them'.[33] Considerable progress has already been made in building the proposed system of global surveillance. By 2000 there were twelve pilot CDFs in place, and in ten of the twelve cases a Matrix was being developed or about to be adopted.[34] Six months later four full PRSPs and thirty-two Interim PRSPs had been agreed,[35] and the Bank was moving (with a target date of 1 July 2002) to a point where all Country Assistance Strategies (CAS) presented by the International Development Association to the Boards of the IMF and the World Bank would be underpinned by sector-by-sector SSPs (Sector Strategy Papers) and by an agreed PRSP, with the intention that 'all Bank lending and nonlending activities in IDA countries will be organized under a CAS business plan responding to the PRSP'.[36]

Finally, the CAS-CDF-PRSP framework was being extended, beyond the small group of low-income countries covered by the Heavily Indebted Poor Countries initiative within which the system was initially developed, to the much larger group of World Bank-classified 'Middle-Income Countries', with the intention of generalizing the disciplinary framework developed in the CDF and the PRSP to all countries eligible for IBRD lending. Middle-income countries were to be invited to present a 'vision of development' in the form of a 'Letter of Development Strategy', incorporating a systematic and comprehensive diagnosis of their priorities. The matching Country Assistance Strategy would identify a programme of Economic and Sector Work (ESW), so that all the Bank's 'lending products' could be aligned to support medium-term reform programmes. Thus the CDF–PRSP framework, with its supporting matrix, has been trialled with the most heavily indebted countries, prior to being extended to the remaining clients of the Bank and the Fund as a generalized means of intervention in economic and social policy and political governance.

NEW LABOUR SIGNS UP:
DFID AND THE WORLD BANK

No government has been more active in adopting and promoting the World Bank agenda of global proletarianization than New Labour in Britain. Successive White Papers in 1997 and 2000 issued by the Department for International Development (DFID) have endorsed every element of the programme, while behind the scenes the British government has emerged as the World Bank's strongest supporter. While NGOs queued up, in response to a World Bank 'consultation' on its proposed Poverty Reduction Strategy Papers, to counsel against the tying of debt relief for the poorest countries to the adoption of poverty reduction strategies defined by the Bank, the British government came in right on cue with the most supportive of advice. The British Government's views on the Heavily Indebted Poor Countries (HIPC) Initiative were summarized by the World Bank's Development Committee as follows:

> British government regards closer link between debt relief and reducing poverty as the very rationale of a revived HIPC. Relief should only be available to countries seriously committed to poverty reduction — should reward progress, outcomes. For this reason, wary of adding new short-term conditions. Instead, debt relief should be integrated with strategies aimed at encouraging long-term poverty reduction. i) The Comprehensive Development Framework provides mechanism for national leadership and integration of donor support. ii) Medium-Term Expenditure Frameworks, as developed in Special Program for Africa (SPA) and in consultation with IMF. iii) Code of Social Principles being discussed by World Bank and UN, building on Copenhagen Social Summit resolutions. Framework for ESAF conditionality and new Enhanced Poverty Framework called for by G-7 need to be brought together, and analysis is needed on how closely HIPC relief should be linked to ESAF.[37]

In fact New Labour's commitment to neoliberal principles, and its desire to promote itself as a leading ally of the international organizations seeking to develop a framework for global governance, have shaped the activity of DFID since its creation.[38] The first White Paper endorsed the theme of 'eliminating world poverty', while the second adopted lock, stock and barrel the policies of global proletarianization backed by universal surveillance advocated by the Bank.[39] Following World Bank prescriptions to the letter, the British government urged that the poor should be 'freed' by being obliged to become workers or competing small producers within a thoroughly competitive global capitalist economy, while contributing further unpaid labour to community organization and the provision of essential infrastructure.[40] The 1997 White Paper echoed the World Bank line on the need to submit the poor to the logic of capitalist markets: 'Individuals, households, enterprises and communities need the capacity to take advantage of opportunities to initiate and participate in new economic activity, to be provided with the appropriate incentives to stimulate their efforts to pursue and sustain income-generating activities, and to be encouraged through targeted instruments that promote economic activity'.[41] It then set this micro-level discipline, applied to households, enterprises and communities, firmly in the macro-disciplinary framework provided by the World Bank, the IMF and the WTO: '[w]e will support a closely integrated approach in which the IMF contributes to the establishment of sound macro-economic and financial policies to encourage pro-poor growth, while the Bank complements these efforts by promoting policy, institutional reforms and projects that focus on the elimination of poverty'.[42]

To support the effort, the British government volunteered to use its influence to persuade international actors that all aid and support should be conditional on signing up to the policies promoted by the World Bank and its allies, and offered partnership only to low-income countries 'committed to the elimination of poverty and pursuing sensible policies to bring that about'.[43] Potential partners in the developing world would have to adopt policies and budgetary allocation processes to the liking of the IMF, the World Bank, and the WTO, accept banking supervision and IMF surveillance of their financial systems, allow extensive evaluation and monitoring of their performance, and agree mechanisms for civil society oversight of government performance: '[t]here will thus be a range of relationships reflecting the circumstances of each country. What will remain consistent is the principle that the level of resources, length of commitment and flexibility in the use of resources provided to governments will be related not only to their needs but also to the confidence that we have in their policies not actions.'[44]

Against this background, the 2000 White Paper proposes that international organizations should 'work with countries and international institutions to design 'road maps' for the opening up of capital accounts',[45] and calls for the IMF and the World Bank to play closely coordinated central roles, with developing countries obliged to adopt IMF-approved Poverty Reduction Strategies to gain access to funds.[46] The IMF's powers of surveillance are to be strengthened, for developed and developing countries alike, and extended to cover all aspects of the operation of financial markets: '[f]irst, we need improved surveillance — better monitoring of the performance of developed and developing country economies, and greater transparency in this process … We believe that an enhanced IMF surveillance process … provides the best framework'.[47] At the same time, domestic social policy must 'provide a better foundation for coping with shocks and help build the political consensus required to undertake adjustment and restore private sector confidence'.[48] The White Paper reflects pride in the fact that debt relief under the Heavily Indebted Poor Countries Initiative has been tied 'at

UK prompting' to the adoption of World Bank and IMF approved poverty reduction strategies, and proposes that this policy should be extended to cover *all* concessional resource flows:

> [a]t the meetings of the World Bank and the IMF in 1999, it was agreed, at UK prompting, that the support provided by the World Bank and the IMF to developing countries should be focused around debt reduction strategies. These would be drawn up by the developing country government in consultation with its civil society. This new approach will be applied not only to the Heavily Indebted Poor Countries, but is intended also to become the basis for all concessional resource flows from the World Bank and the IMF and other development agencies. Implementation has so far focused on low income countries in Africa. We believe that the principle of a country-led poverty reduction strategy should apply to middle income countries and to other developing country regions too.[49]

In support of this goal, the British government promises to develop 'country strategy papers' that will 'address the full range of policy reforms needed to enable countries to adapt successfully to the challenges of globalisation'. And the White Paper concludes with an ambitious programme for the creation of an international system in which the UN, the IMF, the WTO, the World Bank and the multilateral development banks, the G8, the OECD and the Commonwealth would all work together, guided by the World Bank's 'Comprehensive Development Framework' and the 'International Development Targets', to ensure that all countries in the global economy face a unified international framework from which there can be no escape.[50]

CONCLUSION

The distinctive feature of World Bank policy and the British proposals which so closely echo it is that they have shifted decisively from promoting US (or British) capital abroad to promoting the development of *capitalism* on a global scale. The strategy is to make the extremely poor exploitable, by their own 'local' capitalists as much as by foreign capital, as a means of creating a vast army of workers on subsistence-level wages across the world. In other words, World Bank proposals for 'poverty reduction' reflect — for a *global* capitalist system — precisely the logic set out by Marx in *Capital*. First, policy is geared towards ensuring that the 'floating' proletariat does indeed float easily between employment and unemployment. Labour markets are to be deregulated, and every care is to be taken to avoid the introduction of unemployment support which competes with those markets. Second, a battery of measures is proposed, some operating over the short term and some over the long term, to draw the 'latent' proletariat into the proletariat proper. Third, the Bank proposes safety nets and other forms of support at a minimal level for a 'stagnant' surplus population of over a billion living below a 'poverty line' of $1 a day. The policy, recognizing precisely the categories of 'relative surplus population' identified by Marx, is to create and maintain a reserve army of labour, to throw the bulk of the cost onto the poor themselves, and to turn the poor systematically, by institutional and ideological means, into the agents of their own subordination to the disciplines of global capitalism.

In all of this, the definition of a poverty line at an income level of one dollar a day plays a crucial strategic role. The 'nonpoor' above it are to be a genuinely global proletariat, fully exposed to market dependence. The level itself denotes the border, policed on the one side to prevent the 'nonpoor' from sticking their greedy fingers into the resources targeted on the poor, and arrayed on the other side with mechanisms to suck new waves of workers into the global proletariat. And out on the margins a mass of the absolutely poor providentially acts as the ultimate guarantee that the disciplines of market dependence will operate with the maximum effect. Nothing could better illustrate practical commitment to the truth that the surest wealth consists in a multitude of laborious poor — a view to which the Bank clearly subscribes.

At this point, then, we may return to the two contradictions in global capitalism identified at the outset — its need to operate as a single system across a fragmented world of competing states with no overarching political authority, and its need to represent the interests of a single class as those of society as a whole. The World Bank is seeking to address the first by proposing itself as the source of strategic guidance on policy frameworks within which the conditions for capitalist accumulation can be secured and reproduced. This is the key to its role in the contemporary global economy. The manner in which it promotes its policies, passing off strategies of subjection to market dependence as promises to bring direct benefits to the poor, reflects but cannot overcome the second, more fundamental contradiction — that capitalism must subject the majority to poverty, but cannot admit it.

NOTES

1. IMF, OECD, UN, World Bank, *A Better World For All: Towards the International Development Goals*, Communications Development, Washington, 2000; 'United Nations Millennium Declaration', 55th General Assembly, Resolution 55/2, 18 September 2000; World Bank, *World Development Report 2000/2001: Attacking Poverty*, New York: Oxford University Press, 2001.
2. Cited in Karl Marx, *Capital*, Vol. 1, London: Penguin/New Left Review, 1976, Ch. 25, p. 800.
3. See Ellen Meiksins Wood, *infra.*
4. Marx, *Capital*, pp. 763-4.
5. Ibid., p. 769.
6. Ibid., pp. 780-1.
7. Ibid., p. 782.
8. Ibid., pp. 783-5.

9. Ibid., p. 786.
10. Ibid., p. 796.
11. Ibid, p. 797.
12. Ibid.
13. Ibid., p. 798.
14. Ibid., p. 799.
15. See Paul Cammack, 'Attacking the Poor', forthcoming, *New Left Review*, 2001.
16. World Bank, *Attacking Poverty*, p. 33.
17. World Bank, *World Development Report 1990: Poverty*, New York: OUP, 1990, p. 51.
18. Ibid.
19. Ibid., p. 38.
20. Ibid., pp. 38–9.
21. Ibid., p. 39. See also pp. 88–96.
22. Ibid., pp. 39–40.
23. Ibid., p. 21.
24. Ibid., p. 6.
25. Ibid., Box 3.3, p. 51.
26. Ibid., p. 24.
27. Ibid., p. 168.
28. Ibid., p. 169.
29. Ibid., pp. 154–5.
30. Ibid., Box 8.9, p. 156.
31. World Bank, 'World Bank Group Strategic Framework', Washington DC, 24 January 2001, p.8. For a fuller analysis, see Paul Cammack, 'The Mother of All Governments: the World Bank's Matrix for Global Governance', forthcoming in R. Wilkinson and J. Hughes, eds., *Engaging Global Governance: towards a new agenda?*, London: Routledge.
32. James D. Wolfensohn, 'A Proposal for a Comprehensive Development Framework', memo to Board, Management and Staff of World Bank Group, 21 January 1999, pp. 24, 28.
33. 'A Joint Memorandum from the Managing Director of the IMF and the President of the World Bank', 7 September 2000, in Development Committee, 'Heavily Indebted Poor Countries (HIPC) Initiative and Poverty Reduction Strategy Papers (PRSP): A Joint Memorandum from the Managing Director of the IMF and the President of the World Bank and Reports on Progress in Implementation', DC/2000-18, 8 September 2000, p. 6.
34. Development Committee, 'Comprehensive Development Framework: Progress Report', DC/2000-17, 7 September 2000. The twelve pilots were in Bolivia, Côte d'Ivoire, Dominican Republic, Eritrea, Ethiopia, Ghana, Kyrgyz Republic, Morocco, Romania, Uganda, Vietnam, and the West Bank/Gaza.

35. IBRD/IDA, 'Strategic Directions for FY02-FY04: Implementing the World Bank's Strategic Framework', 28 March 2001, p. 2.
36. International Monetary Fund and International Development Association, 'Poverty Reduction Strategy Papers — Progress in Implementation', para 45, p. 21, in Development Committee, 'HIPC Initiative and PRSP', op. cit.
37. Development Committee, 'Heavily Indebted Poor Countries (HIPC) Initiative: Strengthening the Link Between Debt Relief and Poverty Reduction', DC/99-24, 17 September 1999, Annex 1: Respondent's Views on HIPC Initiative, p. 39.
38. For the background, see Rorden Wilkinson, 'New Labour and the Global Economy', and Ralph Young, 'New Labour and International Development', in David Coates and Peter Lawler, eds., *New Labour in Power*, Manchester University Press, 2000, pp. 136-48 and 254-67.
39. HMSO Cm 3789, *Eliminating World Poverty: A Challenge for the 21st Century* (Stationery Office, 1997); Cm 5006, *Eliminating World Poverty: Making Globalisation Work for the Poor* (Stationery Office, 2000).
40. For a detailed analysis see Paul Cammack, 'Making the Poor Work for Globalisation', *New Political Economy*, forthcoming November 2001.
41. *A Challenge for the 21st Century*, Panel 10, p. 29.
42. Ibid., para. 2.10, p. 34; see also para. 3.15. p. 58: 'The Government supports an open, fair and sustainable multilateral trading system — from which all countries can benefit. The World Trade Organization (WTO) provides the rule-based framework which underpins the system. We will encourage and assist developing countries to become more fully integrated into the multilateral system and to participate in the WTO. We want to support their efforts to reduce their trade barriers, taking account of the time needed for their economies to adjust'; and para. 3.47, p. 67.
43. Ibid., para. 2.21, p. 38.
44. Ibid., para. 2.25, p. 40. See also paras 2.13, 2.19, 2.22, and 3.56.
45. *Making Globalisation Work for the Poor*, paras 161-3, pp. 51-2.
46. Ibid., paras 165-71, pp. 52-3.
47. Ibid., paras 173-5, p. 53.
48. Ibid., para. 179, p. 54.
49. Ibid., paras 306-7, p. 91.
50. Ibid., paras 314-50, pp. 92-101.

CAPITALISM AND DISABILITY

Marta Russell and Ravi Malhotra

Having a disability is conventionally regarded as a personal tragedy which the individual must overcome, or as a medical problem to which the individual must become adjusted. In 1976, however, the Union of the Physically Impaired Against Segregation in Britain made a significant advance when it pointed out that 'disability is something imposed on top of our impairments by the way we are unnecessarily isolated and excluded from full participation in society'.[1] Among those concerned with disability it soon became common ground that 'it is society which disables persons with impairments'.

This social model of disability[2] necessitates a rethinking of prevalent definitions. Leaving aside biological or physical-anthropological definitions of disability which make it appear that impaired persons are 'naturally' and, therefore, justifiably, excluded from the 'labour force', even mainstream definitions have serious shortcomings. The World Health Organization, for instance, defines impairment (the condition of being deaf or blind, or having impaired mobility or being otherwise impaired) as the physiological 'problem'; disability as restricted functions or activities resulting from an impairment; and handicap as the 'disadvantage resulting from the impairment or disability, that limits or prevents the fulfillment of a role'.[3] This terminology has been criticized by social model theorists of disability because it relies primarily on medical definitions and uses a bio-physiological definition of normality. Further, 'the environment' within which this 'disadvantage' is located, 'is represented as "neutral", and any negative consequences of this approach for the person with an impairment are regarded as inevitable or acceptable rather than as disabling barriers'.[4]

Reconceptualizing disability as an outcome of the political economy, however, also requires acknowledging the limitations of the 'minority' model of disability, which views it as the product of a disabling social and architectural environment. In this view the fundamental source of the problems encountered by disabled persons is prejudicial or discriminatory attitudes, implying that by erasing mistaken attitudes society will accept 'difference' and equality will flourish.[5] This approach diverts attention from the mode of production and the concrete social relations that produce the disabling barriers, exclusion and inequalities facing disabled persons.

In contrast, we take the view that disability is a socially-created category derived from labour relations, a product of the exploitative economic structure of capitalist society: one which creates (and then oppresses) the so-called 'disabled' body as one of the conditions that allow the capitalist class to accumulate wealth. Seen in this light, disability is an aspect of the central contradiction of capitalism, and disability politics that do not accept this are, at best, fundamentally flawed strategies of reform or, worse, forms of bourgeois ideology that prevent this from being seen.

CAPITALIST BEGINNINGS AND THE COMMODIFICATION OF THE IMPAIRED BODY

The primary oppression of disabled persons (i.e. of people who could work, in a workplace that was accommodated to their needs) is their exclusion from exploitation as wage labourers.[6] Studies show that disabled persons experience lower labour-force participation rates, higher unemployment rates and higher part-time employment rates than non-disabled persons.[7] In the US, 79% of working-age disabled adults say they would prefer to work,[8] yet in 2000 only 30.5% of those with a work disability between ages sixteen and sixty-four were in the labour force and only 27.6% were employed; while 82.1% of non-disabled persons in this age group were either employed (78.6%) or actively seeking work for pay.[9] Though having a job does not always translate into an above-poverty-level existence, disabled persons' historical exclusion from the labour force has undoubtedly contributed to their poverty. Disabled persons are nearly three times as likely to live below the current poverty line — 29% live in poverty, compared to 10% of non-disabled people.[10] In the USA fully one third of disabled adults live in a household with an annual income of less than $15,000,[11] while the 300 to 400 million living in developing countries have even less chance of employment and exist in abject poverty, usually with no social safety nets at all.[12]

Historical materialism provides a theoretical base from which to explain these conditions and outcomes. Under feudalism, economic exploitation was direct and political, made possible by the feudal concentration of land ownership. While a few owners reaped the surplus, many living on their estates worked for subsistence and disabled people were able to participate in this economy to varying degrees.[13] Notwithstanding religious superstition about disabled people during the Middle Ages, and significant persecution of them, the rural production process that predominated prior to the Industrial Revolution permitted many disabled people to make a genuine contribution to daily economic life.[14]

With the advent of capitalism, people were no longer tied to the land, but they were forced to find work that would pay a wage — or starve; and as production became industrialized people's bodies were increasingly valued for their ability to function like machines. Bosses could push non-disabled workers to produce at ever increasing rates of speed. Factory discipline, time-keeping and production norms broke with the slower, more self-determined and flexible work pattern into which many disabled people had been integrated.[15] As work became more rationalized, requiring precise mechanical movements of the body, repeated in quicker succession, impaired persons — the deaf or blind, and those with mobility difficulties — were seen as — and, without job accommodations to meet their impairments, were — less 'fit' to do the tasks required of factory workers, and were increasingly excluded from paid employment.[16] And so 'the operation of the labour market in the nineteenth century effectively depressed handicapped people of all kinds to the bottom of the market'.[17]

Industrial capitalism thus created not only a class of proletarians but also a new class of 'disabled' who did not conform to the standard worker's body and whose labour-power was effectively erased, excluded from paid work.[18] As a result, disabled persons came to be regarded as a social problem and a justification emerged for segregating them out of mainstream life and into a variety of institutions, including workhouses, asylums, prisons, colonies and special schools.[19] Exclusion was further rationalized by Social Darwinists, who used biology to argue that heredity — race and genes — prevailed over the class and economic issues raised by Marx and others. Just as the 'inferior' weren't meant to survive in nature, they were not meant to survive in a competitive society. Legislation, influenced by Social Darwinism and eugenics theory, was enacted in a number of jurisdictions for the involuntary sterilization of disabled people.[20] Advocates of eugenics such as Galton, Dugdale and Goddard propagated the myth that there was an inevitable genetic link between physical and mental impairments and crime and unemployment.[21] This was also linked to influential theories of racial superiority, according to which the birth of disabled children should be regarded as a threat to racial purity.[22] In the notorious Buck v. Bell decision of 1927, the US Supreme Court upheld the legality of the forced sterilization of disabled people. At the extreme, Nazi Germany determined that disabled individuals were an economic burden and exterminated tens of thousands of them.[23] But even in 'democratic' America bean-counting logic prevailed: by 1938, thirty-three American states had sterilization laws and between 1921 and 1964 over 63,000 disabled people were involuntarily sterilized in a pseudo-scientific effort to prevent the births of disabled offspring and save on social costs.[24] Whether or not codified into law, the sterilization of disabled people was common in a number of countries in the first half of the twentieth century, including Britain, Denmark, Switzerland, Sweden, and Canada.[25]

After World War II the expansion of the welfare state in most industrialized countries gave rise to two contradictory trends for disabled people. On the one hand, there was increased state provision of social services. On the other hand there was also a greater attempt to regulate the lives of the recipients of these services. This was particularly the case in Britain and other European countries. The Beveridge Report in Britain symbolized this project and it clearly envisaged an 'ableist' and patriarchal system in which white male able-bodied workers were the primary breadwinners, married women worked in the home, and disabled people were defined as a medical problem and relegated to the expertise of specialists.[26] However, even in the USA, which adopted a relatively modest welfare state, one saw increased provision of social programs such as segregated sheltered workshops which exploited disabled workers in part by paying below minimum wages. This was a component of the 'dictatorship over needs' inherent in the bureaucratism of the welfare state which transformed people into objects of state policy called 'clients'.[27]

The 'medicalization' of disablement and the tools of classification clearly played an important role in establishing divisions between the 'disabled' and the 'able-bodied'. Disability became an important 'boundary' category whereby people were allocated to either a work-based or a needs-based system of distribution. In the US, disability came to be defined explicitly in relation to the labour market. For instance, in some workers' compensation statutes, a labourer's body is rated by the degree of its impairment suffered by each of its functioning parts.[28] In Social Security law, 'disabled' means medically unable to engage in substantial work activity.[29] The disability category was essential to the development of an exploitable workforce in early capitalism and remains indispensable as an instrument of the state in controlling the labour supply today.[30] By focusing on curing so-called abnormalities, and segregating those who could not be cured into the administrative category of 'disabled', medicine cooperated in shoving less exploitable workers out of the mainstream workforce.[31]

So, just as capitalism forces workers into the wage relationship, it equally forcefully coerces disabled workers out of it.[32] Disabled workers face inherent economic discrimination within the capitalist system, stemming from employers' expectations of encountering additional production costs when hiring or retaining a non-standard (disabled) worker as opposed to a standard (non-disabled) worker who has no need for job accommodations, interpreters, readers, environmental modifications, liability insurance, maximum health care coverage (inclusive of attendant services) or even health care coverage at all.[33] 'Disability' is a social creation which defines who is offered a job and who is not, and what it means varies with the level of economic activity.

This is because the root cause of the work-place discrimination experienced by disabled people is to be found in an accountant's calculation of the present cost of production versus the potential contribution the employment of a given worker will make to future profits. If 'disabilities' among the direct producers add to the cost of production without increasing the rate of profit, owners and managers will necessarily discriminate against them. Expenses to accommodate the 'disabled' in the workplace will be resisted as an addition to the fixed capital portion of constant capital. Hence the opposition of small and medium businesses, especially the US Chamber of Commerce, to the 'Americans with Disabilities

Act'. Managers and owners will only tolerate the use of 'disabled' workers when they can save on the variable portion of cost of production, e.g. by paying low wages to disabled workers,[34] or through tax breaks and other subsidies. So an employee who is too costly (i.e., significantly disabled) to add to net profits at the current level of output will not likely become (or remain) an employee at all.[35] US Census data consistently show that, as compared with the four-fifths of working-age persons with no disability who have jobs, only just over one-quarter of people with a significant disability do so.[36]

Employers and investors rely on the preservation of the status quo labour system which does not require them to absorb the non-standard costs of employing disabled workers under the current mode of production, let alone the 800 million people who are totally or partially unemployed worldwide. Consequently, disabled individuals who are currently not in the mainstream workforce, who are collecting disability benefits and who could work if their impairments were accommodated, are not tallied into employers' costs of doing business.[37] The disability benefit system thus serves as a socially legitimized means by which the capitalist class can avoid hiring or retaining non-standard workers and can 'morally' shift the cost of supporting them onto poverty-based government programs — thereby perpetuating their poverty.

Being categorized as 'disabled', however, and the subsequent impoverishment that so many face when struggling to survive on disability benefits,[38] serves another class function: it generates a very realistic fear among workers of becoming disabled. At base, the inadequate safety net is a product of the owning class's fear of losing full control of what they do with the means of production;[39] the American work ethic is a mechanism of social control that ensures capitalists a reliable work force for making profits. If workers were provided with a social safety net that adequately protected them through unemployment, sickness, disability, and old age, labour would gain a stronger position from which to negotiate their conditions of employment. American business retains its power over the working-class through a fear of destitution that would be weakened if the safety net were to actually become safe.

Disabled persons who do not offer a body which will enhance profit-making as labourers are used to shore up US capitalism by other means. Entrepreneurs and rehabilitation specialists have made impaired bodies of use to the economic order by shaping disablement into big business[40] and turning the disabled body into a commodity around which social policies get created or rejected according to their market value.[41] The corporate solution to disablement — institutionalization in a nursing home, for instance — evolved from the realization that disabled people could be made to serve profit because public financing guaranteed the revenue (in the USA, Medicaid funds 60% of the cost, Medicare 15%, private insurance 25%). Disabled people are worth more to the Gross Domestic Product when occupying a 'bed' than a home. When a single impaired body can generate $30,000 — $82,000 in annual revenues Wall Street counts it as an asset that contributes to companies' net worth. Despite the efforts of the disability rights movement to de-institutionalize disabled populations and shift policy towards the provision of in-home services, the logic of capital reasserts itself via the recommodification of the disabled body in the home (insofar as public funding permits — with the advent of 'managed care', trying to limit costs, there is an increased financial motive to underserve). Corporations have taken an interest in the money-making potential of the in-home services field, and indeed promote the in-home services model as they build their new 'home-care' empires. As Jim Charlton puts it, 'the transformation of people into commodities hides their dehumanization and exploitation by other human beings: it becomes simply an economic fact of life'.[42]

It is also evident that the definition of disability is not static but fundamentally linked to the needs of capital accumulation. Hence, when the welfare state entered into 'crisis', governments attempted to narrow the definition of disablement and to cut entitlement levels. There have also been widespread closures of the institutions that warehoused disabled people, but without an allocation of adequate resources and services to enable them to live independently. Yet this withdrawal of the state from certain types of benefits does not entail any rupture in the intervention of the state in the lives of disabled people. The state's interventionist role remains but is refocused on the ruthless cutting of social expenditures, including services and income support programmes to disabled people, in the name of neoliberal efficiency.[43]

The rise of capitalism has thus seen dramatic changes in the ideological classification and treatment of disabled people. Yet while socialists have considered the relationship between the rise of capitalism and, for instance, the enactment of the English Poor Laws,[44] the classification, marginalization and oppression of disabled people have been largely ignored. Speaking generally, the rise of capitalism clearly had contradictory outcomes for disabled people. On the one hand, there were positive effects in terms of better medical technology that lengthened the life span and increased the quality of life for those who could afford it. On the other hand there were some very negative effects, including classification into rigid and arbitrary diagnostic categories and incarceration in oppressive institutions. Exclusion from exploitation in the wage-labour system, as the 'deserving poor', lies at the core of disabled peoples' oppression in every aspect of modern life.

DISABILITY RIGHTS MOVEMENTS: PROSPECTS AND LIMITATIONS

While new social movements fighting against racism, patriarchy and homophobia were gaining prominence in many Western countries in the 1960s,[45] movements of disabled people, with more or less coherent programmes and ideologies, also slowly emerged. Unlike other social movements, the various disability rights movements[46] to date have received relatively little attention from socialists, union activists or academics, even in the USA, which arguably has one of the strongest and oldest disability rights movements.[47] Yet an examination of their various trajectories suggests useful insights that those seeking to challenge capitalism in other struggles can learn from and incorporate in them. To the extent that widespread accommodation to the needs of disabled workers would necessarily transform the workplace and challenge expectations of ever increasing productivity rates, the disability rights movement can be seen as radically democratic and counter-hegemonic in potential and scope.

An important analytical distinction must be made between charitable organizations established for disabled people, sometimes by parents of disabled children, and organizations directly controlled by disabled people. In the former category, the organizations, usually based on a diagnostic category linked to impairment, do not necessarily reflect the views and experiences of disabled people themselves, notwithstanding that they may do occasional work that is beneficial. In fact, the implicit ideological agenda of these paternalistic organizations is that disabled people are unable to advocate on their own behalf.[48] Moreover, the fact that their mandate rests on usually arbitrary diagnostic categories places unwarranted emphasis on medical issues and not enough on the barriers imposed by the physical environment and the class system. The resulting fragmentation — splintering disabled people into literally hundreds of different categories — also works to make cross-disability solidarity that much more difficult. Just as importantly, these organizations, like NGOs in other sectors, are often directly tied to the state through funding arrangements. Consequently, they are extremely limited in their ability to criticize government policy, even if they were so inclined, for fear of losing funding and access to decision-makers. In fact, organizations run *for* disabled people dramatically outnumber those controlled *by* disabled people, and receive far more generous funding.[49] The severe limitations of their politics should come as no surprise, given the questionable and co-opted record of NGOs in all contexts.

In sharp contrast, organizations run by disabled people have at least the potential for more radical politics. In the late 1960s, the Independent Living (IL) movement emerged in Berkeley, California, spearheaded by a disabled students' group known as The Rolling Quads. It sought to promote the empowerment of disabled people and focused attention on the structural barriers imposed by the built environment, not on the impairments of individuals. The first Independent Living Centre (ILC), based on the social-political model of disablement, was founded in Berkeley and sought to broaden struggles for empowerment to include students and non-students alike. Within a few years, a network of hundreds of ILCs had sprouted across the United States, as well as a number of other countries including Britain, Canada and Brazil.[50]

The emergence of the IL movement was unquestionably a step forward for the disability rights movement. The shared sense of consciousness fostered by collective action is an important first step in the building of any social movement. By redefining as political issues requiring redress by society at large what had been previously regarded by most people as private troubles (just as the women's movement had done), the IL movement provided a basis for a vital social movement;[51] and the vitality of the women's movement, the Black civil rights movement, the gay and lesbian movement, the Chicano movement and other new social justice movements created an opening in which the case for eradicating disability oppression could also get a hearing.

Nevertheless, there were and are serious contradictions in the IL philosophy. On the one hand, it seeks to promote autonomy and self-determination for disabled people. On the other, it implicitly accepts the foundations of free market ideology by framing the debate in terms of the right of disabled people as consumers to receive equal treatment from the marketplace. The ability to access the marketplace is cold comfort to the huge proportion of disabled people living in poverty or near-poverty conditions. In a capitalist society, after all, access to the marketplace is predicated on having the purchasing power to buy the services in question. A strategy of disability liberation politics entirely dependent on that purchasing power is so impoverished as to be of assistance to only a tiny fraction of the most privileged disabled people. It also tends to marginalize the concerns of women and minorities. By accepting free market principles as a given the IL movement undermined its radical potential to truly empower disabled people. In the worst cases, some IL centres, afraid of rocking the boat and losing state funding, have become little more than venues for peer counselling and organizing picnics. Only by questioning the very basis of the rules of the market can there be liberation for disabled people.

Yet there have always been some strands of the disability rights movement that have resisted the dangers of state co-optation and engaged in militant, in-your-face tactics that demonstrate the possibility for resistance and broader social change. For example, decades before the emergence of the IL movement, the League for the Physically Handicapped, a group of some three hundred disabled pensioners in New York, engaged in civil disobedience during the Great Depression to protest their discriminatory rejection from the employment offered by the Works Progress Administration.[52] Much later, in 1970, an organization called Disabled in Action (DIA) was founded and adopted the tactic of direct political protest. During the 1972 Presidential Election DIA militants joined with disabled and often highly politicized Vietnam veterans, clearly an influential base of support, to demand an on-camera debate with President Nixon. They also organized a demonstration at the Lincoln Memorial after President Nixon vetoed a spending bill to fund disability programs.[53]

Perhaps the most memorable moment in recent disability rights history in the USA came during the struggle in 1977 to have the regulations pursuant to section 504 of the Rehabilitation Act of 1973 issued. The regulations were to outline how it was illegal for federal agencies, contractors, or public universities to discriminate on the basis of disability. They had been delayed by previous Administrations but there was an expectation that the new Carter Administration would fulfill its promise to issue the regulations. When it became obvious that policy-makers were stalling and wanted to substantially modify the regulations, so as to permit continued segregation in education and other areas of public life, disability rights activists mobilized in a number of cities across the USA. While most demonstrations ended fairly quickly, in Berkeley the movement took on a truly extraordinary trajectory. There, disability rights activists occupied the Department of Health, Education and Welfare (HEW) federal building for some twenty-five days, culminating in total victory: the issuing of the regulations without any amendments.[54]

In the process, the participants in the occupation found themselves transformed by the experience. They discovered their ability to change the world through political action. Whereas divisions along arbitrary diagnostic categories based on a flawed medical-model approach to disablement have often created serious tensions in building social movements, in this instance people with different impairments were able to unite around a common strategy and build solidarity in what was clearly a key turning-point. Links were also forged with other social movements. For instance, unions and civil rights organizations donated food for the demonstrators and it was prepared by the local branch of the militant Black Panthers Party. It is clear, however, that the HEW protests built on the legacy left by the pioneering work of the IL movement, notwithstanding its structural and ideological limitations.

In both the USA and Britain a small cadre of militant disability rights activists have continued a tradition of struggle from below. In 1983 a new organization, the American Disabled for Accessible Public Transit (ADAPT), was established by disability rights activists in several important cities in the USA to highlight the inaccessibility of public transport for people with mobility impairments. It quickly became known for its confrontational and often successful tactics. For instance, it repeatedly disrupted the conventions of the American Public Transit Association, leading to mass arrests, in protest against their unwillingness to implement modifications to make public transport more accessible. They also demonstrated a dramatic flair when they engaged in symbolic forms of protest, like crawling up the numerous stairs at the entrances of public buildings to highlight their inaccessibility.[55] It is hardly surprising that more moderate disability organizations have largely shunned or even attacked ADAPT; a coalition of IL centres in Michigan went so far as to condemn its actions in a letter to the state's governor.[56] More recently ADAPT has switched its priorities to securing better funding for a national attendant services program that would permit disabled people to live in the community as opposed to being institutionalized.

Yet, ultimately, even the most grassroots disability organizations in both the USA and Britain appear theoretically ambiguous in their ideological formulations. They have yet to adopt an anti-capitalist agenda that sees disablement as a product of the class system. Moreover, in both the USA and Britain the passage of disability rights legislation, which is individualistic at base, removes an element of coherence from the political praxis of even the most militant disability rights organizations. A failure to see their common links with other marginalized members of society, including the reserve army of the unemployed, welfare recipients, the increasingly large segment of society working in part-time jobs or in jobs that do not pay a living wage, and others, may result in the squandering

of the promise of the various disability rights movements on the shoals of identity politics — or, worse, on postmodern discourse whose theorists refuse to name
capitalism as a cause for their oppression. A turn to class politics and historical
materialism, fully cognizant of its risks and limitations, is what the disability rights
movements need most.

THE CIVIL RIGHTS IMPASSE

Though it might seem contradictory that a US Republican President (representing the GOP which is, after all, the reactionary voice of capital) signed the
Americans with Disabilities Act of 1990 (ADA) into law,[57] the goals of the ADA
are completely in line with neoliberal and Third Way politics which emphasize
ending dependency and increasing productivity. There has been a convergence
of neoliberal and Third Way discourses, resulting in the mantra that 'rights entail
responsibilities'. Both discourses adopt the supply-side theory that the economy
is burdened by rigid labour markets and overly-generous welfare provisions. In
this spirit former President Clinton declared that the 'era of big government is
over' and called for 'more empowerment, less entitlement'. There is keen
government interest in policies that will shift the long-term unemployed and
disadvantaged into employment.

These politics are underscored in the ADA legislation itself. Congress specified three major goals when it enacted the ADA: eliminating arbitrary barriers
faced by disabled persons, ending inequality of opportunity, and reducing unnecessary dependency and unrealized productivity. The ADA promotes the inclusion
of disabled persons in the majority workforce through the establishment of consti-
tutional law and regulations which are geared to creating 'equal opportunity' in
the labour market for disabled job applicants by 'leveling the playing field' and
requiring employers to accommodate impairments on the job, unless to do so
would cause an 'undue hardship' for the business[58] — which makes the 'entitlement' to accommodation no entitlement at all. In other words, disabled people's
quasi-civil rights would be tolerated by the anti-government and anti-regulatory
GOP as long as the ADA cost the federal government next to nothing, was
largely voluntary for business (no quotas, no affirmative action), and promised to
get people off state-funded entitlements.[59]

Though disability civil rights are relatively new in Britain, Prime Minister
Tony Blair has gone even further. 'New policies to offer unemployed people jobs
and training are a social democratic priority — but we also expect everyone to
take up the opportunity offered', says Blair. These remarks were soon followed
by a notice from officials telling disabled persons to seek work or lose benefits.
The Independent reported that '[s]ick and disabled people who refuse to look for
work will face the withdrawal of their state benefits under a tough new government drive to slash "welfare dependency."'[60] The disability unemployment issue
is increasingly defined in both the USA and in Britain as one of dependency
which the faulty individual on welfare must overcome, not as the structural
outcome of an exclusionary market.

It is no surprise that the neoliberal plan has not worked in the USA. In 2000, ten years after passage of the ADA, despite a growing US economy and a low aggregate national official unemployment rate of 4.2%, the unemployment rate for working-age disabled population has barely budged from its chronic level of 65-71%.[61] According to a recent study, while many Americans reaped higher incomes from an economy that created a record number of new jobs during seven years of continuous economic growth (1992-98), the employment rates of disabled men and women continued to fall so that by 1998 they were still below the 1992 level.[62] Civil rights laws have not produced the gains in employment levels, wage rates, or employment opportunities for disabled people that their advocates expected.[63] Census data confirm that there has been no improvement in the economic well-being of disabled persons since the passage of the ADA. In 1989, 28.9% of working-age adults with disabilities lived in poverty; in 1994, the figure had climbed very slightly to 30.0%.[64] Some scholars suggest that the law is 'a compromise that is failing'[65] and is 'least likely to help those workers with disabilities who are most disadvantaged in the labor market'.[66]

Other studies echo these findings. In a 1998 report on the performance of the Equal Employment Opportunity Commission (which enforces employment discrimination laws) the US Civil Rights Commission concluded that enforcement of the ADA has fallen short. Businesses have resisted hiring and retaining workers with disabilities by vigorously fighting ADA discrimination cases in the courts. A 1998 study by the American Bar Association's Commission on Mental and Physical Disability Law shows that disabled workers bringing discrimination suits are unlikely to succeed in court. Of the more than 1,200 cases filed under Title I of the ADA from 1992-98, employers prevailed 92% of the time. By 2000, employers were prevailing more than 95% of the time.[67] Ohio State Law Professor Ruth Colker concludes that 'only prisoner rights cases fare as poorly'.[68]

In 2001, during his first hundred days, President-Select George W. Bush (whose father-president had signed the ADA) declared that 'too many Americans with disabilities remain trapped in bureaucracies of dependence'.[69] This exemplifies the key contradiction that disablement now represents: the ruling class would like to cut state spending on keeping disabled people out of work, but redistributionist laws like the ADA are necessarily in tension with business class interests, which resist such cost-shifting. Representatives of small and medium businesses (GOP supporters), such as the US Chamber of Commerce, the National Association of Manufacturers, the American Banking Association, and the National Federation of Independent Business, were all opposed to the ADA. Supply-side economist Paul Craig Roberts warned on the day the Act was signed that it would 'add enormous costs to businesses that will cut into their profits'.[70] A leading economist in the Law and Economics movement, Richard Epstein, states that the employment provisions of the ADA are a 'disguised subsidy' and that 'successful enforcement under the guise of "reasonable accommodation" necessarily impedes the operation and efficiency of firms'.[71]

Writing for the 7th Circuit in 1995, Judge Richard Posner, a self-appointed protector of the interests of business, applied cost/benefit analysis to the ADA:

> If the nation's employers have potentially unlimited financial obligations to 43 million disabled persons, the Americans with Disabilities Act will have imposed an indirect tax potentially greater than the national debt. We do not find an intention to bring about such a radical result in either the language of the Act or its history. The preamble actually 'markets' the Act as a cost saver, pointing to 'billions of dollars in unnecessary expenses resulting from dependency and nonproductivity'. The savings will be illusory if employers are required to expend many more billions in accommodation than will be saved by enabling disabled people to work.[72]

The cost-benefit view (whether real or perceived) of the business class at large runs up against their political representatives' expectations in sponsoring the ADA. Those who believe that liberal civil rights are the solution to the unemployment predicament of disabled people confront the problem that within capitalism equal treatment is in contradiction with macro-economic realities. Unemployment is a permanent feature of any capitalist economy. Civil rights, though still necessary to counter individual acts of prejudice and discrimination, have only the power (if enforced) to randomly distribute the maladies of unemployment, income and wage inequality throughout the population,[73] not to meet everyone's material needs. Is there social justice in promoting bourgeois liberal remedies that may liberate some but not all disabled persons from oppression? Liberal anti-discrimination laws cannot end systemic unemployment and individual rights cannot override the economic structure. Neither the market nor civil rights laws can end the exclusion of disabled people from the labour force. Business has obtained both the legal and political legitimacy necessary to discriminate and exclude millions from the workforce in the name of work-place and market efficiency.[74] Transforming this reality, not the (unachievable) accommodation of disabilities under a liberal 'rights' model, must clearly be a goal of any socialist praxis worthy of its name.

AFTERWORD: BEYOND WORK

So how, then, can disability politics help to end capitalist exploitation? While to address this question fully is beyond the scope of this paper we will offer some food for thought. Oliver, for instance, suggests 'if the game is possessive individualism in a competitive and inegalitarian society, impaired people will inevitably be disadvantaged, no matter how the rules are changed'.[75] Finkelstein recognizes that a society may be willing to absorb a portion of its impaired population into the workforce, yet this can have the effect of maintaining and perhaps intensifying the exclusion of the remainder.[76] Indeed, former US President Clinton suggested that bringing disabled persons into the workforce could be a tool to fight inflation in a tight labour market.[77] Abberley suggests that we abandon the notion that production be at the centre of any new conceptualization of Utopia: 'even in a society which did make profound and genuine attempts to integrate impaired people into the world of work, some would still be excluded by their impairment'.[78]

But need the ability to labour in some socially recognized sense be a requirement for full membership in society? In a work-based society, productivism is the 'normal' activity. A radical disability perspective could offer great liberatory potential by proposing to abolish this notion and to offer counter-values to those of productivism. Is work the defining quality of our worth? Employability, aptitude for earning money and even work chosen during one's free time are not, a priori, the measure of what it means to live, to be part of the human race. Moreover, a counter-hegemonic praxis of disability politics, challenging productivism, opens the door to alliances with many other groups who are also marginalized by the imprisoning dictates of a market economy. These include single mothers, welfare recipients, part-time workers, parts of the incarcerated population, and all those unable for various reasons to earn a living wage. Indeed, the fostering of grassroots solidarity amongst those oppressed by productionism can only serve to enrich the disability rights movements themselves and enhance the chances of achieving reformist goals of physical and structural access while pursuing a longer term agenda of economic transformation. After all, what is the alternative? Eugenics, sterilization, euthanasia and the institutionalization of the impaired and others have all been productivist societies' answers to what to do with the 'unproductive'. If the goal of social justice is to ensure the dignity of each and every person, then buying into the largely capitalist-induced belief that work equates with self esteem or is a condition for membership of the human race — that people are labourers first and human beings second — only serves to oppress us all.

NOTES

1   UPIAS, *Fundamental Principles of Disability*, London: Union of the Physically Impaired Against Segregation, 1976, p.3.
2   Michael Oliver coined the phrase. See his *Politics of Disablement*, New York: St. Martin's Press 1990.
3   *International Classification of Impairments, Disabilities and Handicaps: A Manual of Classification Relating to the Consequences of Disease*, Geneva: World Health Organization, 1980, p.29.
4   Colin Barnes, Geof Mercer & Tom Shakespeare, *Exploring Disability: A Sociological Introduction*, Cambridge: Polity Press, 1999, p.25.
5   Harlan Hahn, 'An Agenda for citizens with disabilities: pursuing identity and empowerment', *Journal of Vocational Rehabilitation*, 9, 1997 (explaining the minority model), p.34; Nirmala Erevelles, 'Disability and the Dialectics of Difference', *Disability & Society*, Vol. 11, No. 4, 1996, p.522 (explaining limitations of liberal concept).
6   Marta Russell, 'Disablement, Oppression and Political Economy', *Journal of*

Disability Policy Studies, 2001 (forthcoming).

7 Edward Yelin and Patricia Katz, 'Making Work More Central to Work Disability Policy', *Milbank Quarterly*, 72, 1994; R.L Bennefield and John M. McNeil, 'Labor Force Status and Other Characteristics of Persons with a Work Disability: 1981 to 1988', *Current Population Reports*, Series P-23, No. 160, Washington, DC: U.S. Bureau of the Census, 1989.

8 Louis Harris & Associates/National Organization on Disability, 'Americans with Disabilities Still Face Sharp Gaps in Securing Jobs, Education, Transportation, and in Many Areas of Daily Life', 1998. On-line available at http://www.nod.org/presssurvey.html (visited Feb. 12, 2001).

9 United States Current Population Survey, U.S. Census Bureau, Current Population Survey (March 1998). <http://www.census.gov/hhes/www/disable/disabcps.html> (visited April 27, 2001).

10 Louis Harris, *The 2000 National Organization on Disabilities/Harris Survey of Americans with Disabilities*, New York: Louis Harris and Associates, 2000.

11 Ibid.

12 James I. Charlton, *Nothing About Us Without Us: Disability Oppression and Empowerment*, University of California Press, 1998, p.45.

13 Victor Finkelstein, *Attitudes and Disabled People*, New York: World Rehabilitation Fund, 1980, p.8.

14 The focus here is necessarily on European feudal societies. A discussion of precapitalist Asian societies and the politics of disablement is beyond the scope of this article.

15 Joanna Ryan and Frank Thomas, *The Politics of Mental Handicap*, London: Penguin, 1980, p.101.

16 Finkelstein, *Attitudes*, p.8.

17 Pauline Morris, *Put Away*, London: Routledge & Kegan Paul. 1969, p.9.

18 Russell, 'Disablement, Oppression and Political Economy'.

19 Finkelstein, *Attitudes*, p.10; Oliver, *Politics*, p.28.

20 David Pfeiffer, 'Overview of the Disability Movement: History, Legislative Record, and Political Implications', *Policy Studies Journal*, Vol. 21(4), 1993, p.726; Joseph Shapiro, *No Pity: People with Disabilities Forging a New Civil Rights Movement*, New York: Random House, 1993, pp. 158-60.

21 Colin Barnes, *Disabled People in Britain and Discrimination*, Hurst & Co., 1991, p.19.

22 Ibid.

23 See Robert J. Lifton, *The Nazi Doctors, Medical Killing and the Psychology of Genocide*, New York, Harper Collins, 1986, pp.45-133; Robert Proctor, *Racial Hygiene: Medicine Under the Nazis*, Cambridge: Harvard University Press, 1988, pp.185-94; Hugh Gallagher, *By Trust Betrayed: Patients, Physicians and the License to Kill in the Third Reich*, New York: Henry Holt, 1990; and Henry Friedlander, *The Origins of Nazi Genocide: From Euthanasia to the Final Solution*, Chapel Hill: University of North Carolina Press, pp.39-165.

24 Pfeiffer, 'Overview', p.726; Marta Russell, *Beyond Ramps: Disability at the End of the Social Contract*, Maine: Common Courage Press, 1998, pp.46-47, 61.

25 Gunnar Broberg and Nils Roll-Hansen, eds., *Eugenics and the Welfare State: Sterilization Policy in Denmark, Sweden, Norway, and Finland*, Michigan State University Press 1996; Mathew Thomson, *The Problem of Mental Deficiency: Eugenics, Democracy, and Social Policy in Britain c. 1870-1959*, Oxford: Clarendon Press, 1998; and Sandra A. Goundry, *Final Recommendations to the Royal Commission on New Reproductive Technologies*, Winnipeg: Canadian Disability Rights Council, 1992, p.15.

26 J. Harris, B. Sapey, and J. Stewart, 'Blairface: Third-Way Disability and Dependency in Britain', *Disability Studies Quarterly*, Vol. 19(4), 1999, p.365; Oliver, *Politics*, pp.104-5.

27 Andre Gorz, *Reclaiming Work: Beyond the Wage-Based Society*, Cambridge, UK: Polity Press, 1999, p.4.

28 Edward Berkowitz, *Disabled Policy, America's Programs for the Handicapped*, Cambridge University Press, 1987, p. 49.

29 H.S Erlanger, and W. Roth, 'Disability Policy: the Parts and the Whole', *American Behavioral Scientist*, 28 (3), 1985, pp.319-45.

30 Deborah Stone, *The Disabled State*, Philadelphia: Temple University Press, 1984, p.179.

31 Marta Russell, 'The Political Economy of Disablement', in Marc Breslow, Ellen Frank, Cynthia Peters, and the Dollars & Sense Collective, eds., *Real World Micro*, 9th edition, Cambridge, MA: Economic Affairs Bureau, Inc., 2000, pp. 94-7.

32 Russell, 'Disablement, Oppression and Political Economy'.

33 Marta Russell, 'Backlash, the Political Economy, and Structural Exclusion', *Berkeley Journal of Employment & Labor Law*, February 2000, p. 349.

34 Goodwill and other not-for-profit employers are known to pay well below-minimum wages but data from John McNeil of the Census Bureau show a negative association between earnings and disability in employment generally. In 1995, workers with disabilities holding part-time jobs (disabled persons are more likely to work part-time) earned on average only 72.4% of the amount non-disabled workers earned annually. H. Stephen Kaye, 'Is the Status of People with Disabilities Improving, *Disability Statistics Abstract*, (Disability Statistics Center, San Francisco, Cal), May 1998, p. 2.

35 Russell, 'Structural Exclusion', p. 349.

36 John McNeil, *Americans with Disabilities: 1994-95*, Washington, DC: Bureau of the Census, 1997. <http://www.blue.census.gov/hhes/www/disable/sipp/disab9495/oldasc.htm>.

37 Russell, 'Disablement, Oppression and Political Economy'.

38 The US Federal poverty guideline for one is $8,350 (FY2000). Since $759 is the average per month benefit that a disabled worker receives from SSDI, and $373 is the average federal income for the needs-based Supplemental

Security Income (SSI), the annual income of over 10 million disabled persons on these programs is between $4,000 and $10,000. The extremely low SSI benefit was set up for those with no work history or not enough quarter-years of work to qualify for SSDI: the least valued disabled members of society.

39   Russell, *Beyond Ramps*, pp.81-3.
40   Gary Albrecht, *The Disability Business*, London: Sage, 1992.
41   Russell, *Beyond Ramps*, pp.96-108.
42   Charlton, *Oppression*, p.46.
43   H. Radice, 'Taking Globalisation Seriously', *Socialist Register 1999*, pp.1-28.
44   Karl Polanyi, *The Great Transformation. The Political and Economic Origins of Our Time*, Boston: Beacon Press, 1944, pp. 70-1.
45   B. Epstein, 'The Marginality of the American Left: The Legacy of the 1960s', *Socialist Register 1997*, pp.146-53.
46   There are various and distinct social movements struggling around disablement politics including the physical disability rights movement, the psychiatric rights movement, the blind people's movement and others.
47   T. Fagan and P. Lee, '"New' Social Movements and Social Policy: A Case Study of the Disability Movement', in M. Lavalette and A. Pratt, eds., *Social Policy: A Conceptual and Theoretical Introduction*, Sage Publications, 1997, pp.140-60; H. Meekosha and A. Jakubowicz, 'Disability, Political Activism, and Identity Making: A Critical Feminist Perspective on the Rise of Disability Movements in Australia, the USA and the UK', *Disability Studies Quarterly*, vol. 19(4), 1999, pp.393.
48   Oliver, *Politics*, pp. 114-5.
49   Tom Shakespeare, 'Disabled People's Self-Organisation: a New Social Movement?', *Disability, Handicap and Society*, vol. 8(3), 1993, p.260.
50   Charlton, *Oppression*, p.138.
51   Fagan and Lee, *Social Movements*.
52   Shapiro, *No Pity*, pp.63-4; Paul Longmore and David Goldberger, 'Political Movements of People with Disabilities: The League of the Physically Handicapped, 1935-1938', *Disability Studies Quarterly*, Vol. 17, No. 2, 1997, pp.94-8.
53   Shapiro, *No Pity*, p.58.
54   Ibid., pp.64-70.
55   Ibid., pp.127-39.
56   Charlton, *Oppression*, p.122.
57   The ADA prohibits employers from discriminating on the basis of disability. See 42 U.S.C. Sec. 12112(b)(5) (1994). To prevent discrimination, employers must provide reasonable accommodations for qualified employees or applicants with disabilities.
58   See 29 C.F.R. Sec. 1630.2(o)(1) (1999).
59   Russell, *Beyond Ramps*, pp. 112-4.
60   Paul Waugh and Sarah Schaefer, 'Disabled Told To Seek Work Or Lose

Benefits', *The Independent*, 27 November 2000.

61 During the pre–ADA research phase, Congress found that 'two thirds of all disabled Americans between thee age of 16 and 64 [were] not working at all'. Hearing on H. R. 2273, The Americans with Disabilities Act of 1989: Joint Hearing before the Subcommittee on Select Education and Employment Opportunities of the House Committee on Education and Labor, 101st Cong.,1st Sess. (July 18 & Sept. 13, 1989) (two hearings). S. Rep. No. 101–16, at 9.

62 Peter Budetti, Richard Burkhauser, Janice Gregory, & H. Allan Hunt, *Ensuring Health and Security for an Aging Workforce*, W.E. UpJohn Institute for Employment Research, 2001.

63 Walter Y. Oi, *Employment and Benefits for People with Diverse Disabilities. Disability, Work and Cash Benefits*, Michigan: W.E. Upjohn Institute for Employment Research, 1996, p.103.; S.A. Moss and D.A. Malin, Note, 'Public Funding for Disability Accommodations: A Rational Solution to Rational Discrimination and the Disabilities of the ADA', *Harvard Civil Rights-Civil Liberties Law Review*, vol. 33, 1998, pp.197-8.

64 Stephen H. Kaye, 'Is the Status of People with Disabilities Improving?', *Disability Statistics Abstract*, San Francisco: Disability Statistics Center, May 1998, p.2.

65 Sue A. Krenek, Note, 'Beyond Reasonable Accommodation', *Texas Law Review*, Vol. 72, 1994, p.1969.

66 Marjorie Baldwin, 'Can the ADA achieve its employment goals?', *Annals American Academy of Political & Social Science*, 549, January 1997, p.52.

67 'Study Finds Employers Win Most ADA Title I Judicial and Administrative Complaints', *Mental and Physical Disability Law Reporter*, Vol. 22, May-June 1998, pp.403, 404 and May-June 2000.

68 Ruth Colker, 'The Americans with Disabilities Act: A Windfall for Defendants', *Harvard Civil Rights-Civil Liberties Law Review*, 34, 1999, p.100.

69 George W. Bush, New Freedom Initiative at http://washingtonpost.com/wpsrv/onpolitics/elections/bushtext020101.htm

70 Robert Shogun, 'Halt Bush's Tilt to Left, Conservatives Tell GOP', *Los Angeles Times*, 17 July 1990, p.A26.

71 Richard Epstein, *Forbidden Grounds: The Case Against Employment Discrimination Law*, Cambridge, MA: Harvard University Press, 1992, p. 485.

72 Vande Zande v. State of Wisconsin Department of Administration (ruling for employer-defendant).

73 Russell, 'Structural Exclusion', p.364.

74 Russell, 'Structural Exclusion', p.366.

75 Michael Oliver, 'A Sociology of Disability or a Disablist Sociology?' in Len Barton, ed., *Disability & Society: Emerging Issues and Insights*, New York: Longman, 1996, p. 35.

76 Victor Finkelstein quoted by Paul Abberley, 'Work, Utopia and

Impairment', in Barton, ed., *Disability & Society*, p. 71.

77   Marta Russell, 'The New Reserve Army of Labor?' *Review of Radical Political Economics*, Vol. 33, No. 2, p. 226.

78   Abberley, 'Work, Utopia and Impairment'. p. 71.

THE INJURED SELF

Michael Kidron

Two hundred years ago the personal columns of newspapers read by the literate middle class stressed the most general social and personal characteristics of the advertiser and of the prospective respondent. From *The Times* (London), Tuesday, 15 December, 1801: 'Gentleman (a Bachelor), about 26 … man of good property, agreeable person, and in an old-established profitable Business … Any Lady (Widow or Spinster) not exceeding 30 years of age'; or, from *The Times* Wednesday, 28 December, 1803: 'A Tradesman, in a pleasant part of London wishes to meet with a Partner for Life … an agreeable, prudent Person; a Widow would not be objected to if her age did not much exceed his own which is under 30. Some fortune is expected'.

Today the typical advertiser concentrates on his or her singular characteristics, idiosyncratic proclivities, desires, interests, passions, hates and so on, and those of the target reader. Thus, from a recent issue of *The New York Review*: 'loving good music, cats, nature', 'great listener/ great lover', 'seeking non-smoking, dynamic, sensitive, Jewish male 40-55', 'gay', 'deep feelings for nature and expressionistic art', 'socially/environmentally responsible, enjoys long walks, the arts, travel, mountains, skiing', 'loves to travel, go for walks, and have good conversations', 'attracted to Moroccan pillows'.

In two hundred years personal advertisers made the passage from representing themselves in terms of a wider social identity (a lineage or family, an occupation), through presenting themselves as individual personalities, increasingly free of a social dimension, to, finally, presenting themselves as a collection of attributes or characteristics without a unifying principle. The transition marked a momentous change in the socio-psychological landscape of market society as it lurched into its industrial-urban phase.

CAUSES

Curious things happened in the course of the eighteenth century in Europe, England in particular. The impersonal, single-shot, single-purpose transaction between strangers which constitutes the essence of a market broke free from age-old constraints, and took over economic life. God began to be approached on His day, not on any other day; the person one married was no longer a person one lived near; the space between people became more real than the people themselves; an 'enough' society gave way to a 'more', or 'never quite enough' one.

The transition was catastrophic for most of those who experienced it. Their family and social networks were torn apart. They were detached from fixed locations and clear identities. Their material life deteriorated. Their moral world, their understandings, their sense of self were damaged, often beyond repair. For a few the changes amounted to an anastrophe ('a coming together of disparate elements to form a coherent, connected whole'). For them a new, living creation emerged — the modern capitalist market system. Driven by the interactions between people, rather than by individual natures, this society became free to pursue its logic to the limits of human capacity, and beyond. It created ever-rising standards of performance, physical and mental — standards that few achieve, that some approach, that many aspire to but fail to attain.

True, the vast mass of Market Being that resulted — average Market Beings — are better fed, better protected against disease, more knowledgeable, able to accomplish more than is conceivable in any other society, past or present. The exceptional individual in our midst would appear little short of superhuman anywhere else. But that is not the whole story. Even the most remarkable of individuals could not accomplish one iota of the achievements routinely expected of ordinary Market Being — in terms of strength, speed, agility, consistency, concentration — without help.

These miracles are possible because human capabilities are augmented by machines — by desktop computers that compute at three million times the speed of a numerically competent human, tirelessly and with (mostly) perfect reliability; cars that typically carry their occupants 20-30 times faster than they can walk — without tiring; airplanes that multiply that multiple by a factor of 8 or 10. At best a human can lift 50 kilos one metre, compared to an earthmoving machine's 2,700 kilos and seven metres in the same time; a fighter can kill a handful where a nuclear weapon can wipe out millions.

But these machines really confirm people in their deficiencies, encouraging them to settle for what they can do without effort, and result in the kind of dependence that reduced the American GI in Vietnam to impotence: can't move without the chopper, can't see without the glasses, can't smell without the sniffer, can't hear without the booster, can't sense without apparatus, adjuncts, aids. In short, can't live without a vast supply train — the pills, the pre-cooked food, the ice cream. For the mass of people machines widen the gap between the possible and the probable. What people can accomplish themselves loses importance.

People lose coherence, find it easy to dissociate persona from person or even to replace a vestigial person with many personas.

Consider the entertainment business, where self-estrangement and self-thingi-fication reach an apogee. Hear Arnold Schwarzenegger — who redesigned his body, punishingly, over many years — speaking about himself (if 'self' can be said to come into it):

> I know one thing. I have been very fortunate that every year the public's interest in me and in my films has gone up, whatever is on the market. If it is magazine covers, they sell better this year than last year, and last year they sold better than the year before, so there is increase all the time. When you look at the last five years there has been a steady increase. We hope it will continue like that … I really only had a plan to creating and publicizing myself… I went to a lot of acting classes, voice classes, accent removal classes and on and on and on. I mean I covered myself really well.

The effort clearly paid off. By the mid-to-late nineties the fees demanded by his agents started approaching the GDP of a small country.

Or look at Michael Jackson, constantly recreated at vast expense, constantly remodelled, constantly mutating. Supported by a retinue of plastic surgeons, dermatologists, hair specialists, and other personscape artists, he produced a supremely marketable product, neither black nor white, neither man nor woman; ageless, with narrowed nose, straightened hair, sculpted eyebrows, bleached skin — an embodiment of fantasy, and a far cry from the rather appealing little boy launched into superstardom in the early seventies. Schwarzenegger and Jackson are, however, only highly visible exponents of a culture in which we permit ourselves to be treated like commodities in the hope that we may, one day, be treated like valuable commodities, a culture which encourages extreme professionalization, a slide from participation to spectacle, and the use of drugs to enhance (and recover from) performance.

It is a culture that supports an army of counsellors and therapists devoted to creating 'new expectations' and to persuading people to 'rethink their self-images'; that has spread psychometric testing, adapted from educational, military and clinical uses, to selecting applicants for almost any job; that rewards behavioural consultants with six-figure salaries for helping managers handle workplace relationships by projecting an acceptable image; that brings fashion consultants and sartorial psychologists to match dress to station (rather than to self); which divorces behaviour from feeling (as in Tokyo's smile classes); which supports a multi-billion dollar market for cosmetic surgery, cosmetic products, beauty salons, health farms, fitness centres, body shapers, exercise instructors, cosmetic prostheses and so on, each with its magazines, manuals, treatises and experts; and which brings a third of all adults in Britain (41 percent of women) to try slimming at any one time. Altogether the personal packaging business, the business of presenting a self-other-than-self, of separating persona from person, of constructing a presence distinct from the essence, accounts for perhaps $200 billion in sales worldwide. And this is apart from the huge sums spent on clothing, housing and generally providing this persona with its accoutrements.

It is a culture which demands of the body, particularly the female body, heroic feats of adaptation. The ideal figure, the one composed by fashion designers on their drawing boards, is one that is impossible in nature. Magazine art departments elongate necks, enhance breasts, narrow waists. And where depiction is not enough, the plastic surgeon is invoked: $3 billion a year was spent on some 2 million cosmetic procedures in the US alone in the early nineties, keeping as many as 15,000 cosmetic surgeons in relative luxury. In the early 1960s there were 108 plastic surgery clinics in Tokyo, serving 200,000 women a year. Today South Africa is bolstering its currency with 'scalpel safaris', in which women from Europe fly in, have eyes and other parts lifted, get a tan while watching a wild beast or two in a national park, and return home — all for one third of the cost of the procedure (minus tan and tour) at home. A recent development in the field is the adjustable breast implant, into which silicone can be added or siphoned out, according to the dictates of fashion or the tastes of the current partner in a woman's life.

The sense of self rests, ultimately, on three bases, or pillars, which the death of subjectivity undermines.

First, it depends on a broad, balanced understanding of the social and physical world, and of one's place in it — an understanding which can withstand the test of performance, which can therefore be self-reinforcing and cumulative. This has been seriously weakened by the narrowing of cognitive modes in market society. Of the four major modes of understanding on which our sense of self is based — the scientific, the religious, the intuitive, and the sensuous — only the scientific has triumphed and been dignified. Exhausted it may be, too weak to carry the full weight of traffic between society and its environment, or between the individuals who make up society, it is nevertheless active, powerful, and the more imposing because of its rivals' even greater decline.

The second pillar of the self is the sense, based on accomplishment, of being an autonomous agent in the world,. That sense is not encouraged by current arrangements. Natural events — puberty, ageing, change, death and bereavement — have become the province of specialists, consultants, counsellors. Every organ, every biological event, every infection has its experts; health comes to depend on drugs and specialist care. Life is medicalized; health, illness, pregnancy, birth, sexuality, death, eating and drinking, are standardized. We lose our capacity to take charge of our own physical state and to face the events and trials of our own existence. We don't recover; we are cured. We don't die in the natural course of life, but are carried off by a disease in hospital, and then often only with the doctor's permission. Death ceases to be for amateurs: it's a professional business. You don't control even the passages of your life: surgery takes over the function of the fallopian tubes and womb-management increases in scope.

This passivity is reinforced by the disconnection of most work from a direct relationship with nature and by its migration from the household. For most people work takes place in a dedicated workplace, separate from social and cultural life (which also becomes the business of specialists), separate from the household and the wider community which it sustains, separate from everything but personal survival. Dependency supplants agency. Loss of control over work, its culture and hygiene, leads to a desire to avoid or escape from it and, by a natural progression, to the development, by specialists, of 'objective', 'scientific' criteria, for 'justified' idleness and unjustified 'malingering'.

Medicine aligns itself with school, army, and prisons, in producing individuals adjusted, by chemical means if need be, to the social roles assigned them: company doctors steer workers back to jobs they cannot abide; prison and army psychiatrists try to make prisoners and troops adjust to inhuman conditions. The loss of agency leads to the treatment of symptoms rather than underlying causes, and converts medical care into, ultimately, a licensed purveyor of normative Market Being.

The third pillar of self — the third condition for self to exist — is that it be recognized by others. It cannot exist without relatedness, in two senses. To be aware of one's self is to see something distinct from its physical or cultural surroundings, capable of a changing relationship; something in motion, with an orientation which might be changing at a different pace or in a different direction from that of its surroundings. That orientation forms the substance of all our feelings of meaningfulness — the deepest substratum of ethics. A condition of self — as every physician, counsellor or priest knows — is having 'something to live for.' Second, the self cannot exist in a void — it is formed by bonding to others from birth (gradually enlarging the 'I' into a 'we' which includes the 'I', but is distinct from it). It requires a secure base, derived in large measure from the relative permanence of our bonds-folk and our surroundings.

One source of the strain on the pillars of self is the pervasive uncertainty about where one stands, a relativism which, at best, turns moral life into an optional extra, and at worst, into a void, empty of purpose, experienced as a lack of reference to what is good, significant, or meaningful. In our world, activities may have purpose, but life no longer has. Individual lives do not assimilate different conducts, or make sense as part of a larger entity; they are no longer a focus of meaning. Nor is there a single entity they might represent. You might be a paid up member of a family, a loyal colleague at work, a dedicated fan or hobbyist, a good neighbour — a multitude of things each of which is enmeshed in a larger entity. But there is no compelling reason for all these connexions to coalesce.

Another pressure undermining the sense of self comes from the transformation of intention into behaviour, of purpose into law, whereby the individual is relieved of responsibility for outcomes so long as he or she conforms.

The self has also suffered from increasingly rapid changes in social and physical circumstances, which turn attachment into contact — a superficial, evanescent thing; from the narrowing of family relationships to the conjugal or sub-conjugal family; from urbanization and the loss of direct links with nature,

which have dulled our sense of the uniqueness and variety of individual consti-
tutions, and replaced our easy acceptance of variety with seeing it as something
discordant, unnerving (and which have also promoted a slide from strong associations through mutual stimulation, to the weak associations of agglomeration
and contiguity).

The weakening of self feeds back to the social detachment and disconnected-
ness which are its chief cause. It occurs most easily when the individual is denied
the repeated relationships and exchanges of community life, and is propelled into
a series of mobile, changing, revocable associations designed for highly specific
ends — a series of partial relationships..

In these circumstances, other people's motives cannot be inferred with convic-
tion; what happens, while apparently being the intended action of a human agent,
is often unintelligible and non-negotiable. We do not know what to make of it,
how to respond to it, how to distinguish between human responsibility and the
nature of things. It is a world of bafflement and disassociation. It is also a world
of rage, of watchfulness, of dulled enthusiasms, suspicion, pessimism, defensive-
ness and quickness to take offence. In precapitalist times people knew what other
people thought or believed or saw or heard — they shared common values and
assumptions, common experiences and purposes. Nowadays you don't know
without asking. Consumer surveys, opinion polls, elections, referenda have taken
the place of shared awareness. The basis for relatedness has moved from the
unmediated and spontaneous to the external and formally-structured.

One of the ways personal detachment expresses itself is in criminal behaviour.
People with little or no stake in society do not feel bound by its rules, and may
even have little idea of what they are. A more general expression is the way
people typically behave in an urban setting. Even in a small suburb, like Nassau
County in New York, one can meet 11,000 people on the street within a ten-
minute radius; in mid-town Manhattan the figure climbs to 220,000. In these
conditions personal contacts become narrow and superficial, reduced to formulae,
measured in terms of their cost in psychic energy, protected by inhibitory screens.
Norms of non-involvement evolve to cope with the threatened sensory overload
(norms which also permit greater tolerance of the unusual than is likely to be
found in a small community). At the extreme this moral atonality allows indifference to homicide, or homicidal indifference, to flourish, as when neighbours
hear or even watch murder or rape without doing anything about it.

Ironically, the cultivation of non-involvement leads to understimulation and
attempts to create artificially, and within a controlled sphere, the stimuli which
it denied in the first place. So urban dwellers manufacture unnecessary problems
which they then have to, and can, solve, in games such as Scruples; they over-
react to normal stimuli by compulsive intimacy or confessionalism.

Another expression of personal detachment is the conversion of normal activities into specialist 'recreational' pursuits — compulsive gratification unattenuated
by contextual restraints.

Sex, stripped of an emotional and social setting, becomes a mechanical pastime, repeated to the limits of physical capacity, drained of content as a means of communication or propagation. Eating becomes detached from energy require-ments and, at the extreme, from social intercourse, and turns into ingestion or 'grazing'. Travel ceases to be a purposeful activity, used 'to regulate imagination by reality' (as enjoined by Dr Johnson), and becomes an accumulation of expe-riences divorced from everyday life — time taken out of real time: most cruises no longer have much to do with going anywhere in particular. Each activity becomes a uniform, monotonic pursuit, unrelated to others, a single thread, attracting measurement rather than appreciation, not part of a web.

A common companion of personal detachment, or loneliness, is gregarious-ness — being amongst, but not with, others, relating to an outside agent in common, not to each other. It is encouraged by, and sustains, the gigantism of modern urban facilities — enormous astrodomes and arenas, huge rallies orga-nized for pop concerts or politics or sport. Often it is only when these gigantic facilities break down that social intercourse takes place. Gregariousness substitutes a spurious identity — nation, class, occupation, belief— for personal identity. For too many people 'I am I' is replaced by 'I am as you wish me to be'.

The impairment of spontaneous, unforced relatedness has not gone without response. Large hotel chains have automated check-in kiosks and room service in order to eliminate contacts between guests and staff. Banks are beginning to charge account holders for communicating with a human being rather than an automated telephone system or an ATM. A Japanese theatrical agency runs a stable of amateur actors who play the parts of friends, colleagues, bosses, univer-sity professors and teachers — even siblings and parents — at weddings: fake colleagues with no speeches to give other than deflecting inquisitive questions begin at around 30,000 yen (£190) plus travel expenses. 'Old friends of the family', who might have to propose toasts or deliver long, sentimental reminis-cences, might cost ten or twenty times more. In China, 'apology companies' are sprouting in the spaces emerging between the ever-present bureaucratic cells. Charities and voluntary organizations everywhere attach themselves to the lonely and frightened with help-lines ('Contemplating suicide? Contact the Samaritans — 1-800 784 2433 — or a local crisis centre'), soup kitchens, Christmas treats and so on. The clergy trundle through hospitals which also deploy their own social workers. Mandatory altruism in the form of community service is proposed for high schools in Texas as a condition of graduation. The Japanese Ministry of Labour publishes advice on how to avoid becoming lonely.

The most extreme form of dissociation is estrangement from self, or self-alien-ation. People who suffer from it experience themselves as they experience things, with the senses, but without a sense of self. They do not feel they are the subject of their experiences, their thoughts, their feelings, their decisions, their judg-ments, their actions. They do not feel they are the centre of their world, creators of their own acts. They do not have a sense of wholeness and proven agency that is their own, not others'. They are as out of touch with themselves as they are with others. Alienation at work is a core element of this inside-out experience.

As mechanical power took over from human power and standardized machine production replaced craft production the deep-seated need to see oneself and one's abilities reflected in the things one produced was progressively denied, and with it the affirmation of identity. One became an anonymous part of an external production system, a disposable, interchangeable, appendage.

Alienation is not a natural condition. At the extreme, it is pathological, denying the social nature of the human species and its cultural development, threatening the very existence of those affected. It is at least suggestive, not only of changes in perception and fashion amongst psychotherapists, but of the underlying change in the predicament of their clients, that the dominant patterns of psychopathology changed markedly over the last century, from hysteria, phobias and fixations, to 'ego loss' — a sense of emptiness, flatness, futility, lack of purpose or loss of self-esteem, a pathological disorientation in which people do not know what to think of, or where they stand on, issues of cardinal importance to them.

Its signs are all around. There is the enforced isolation, the institutionalized suspicion — living constantly with Big Brother, or rather a lot of little brothers chattering and exchanging information over computer networks, professionally suspicious of you and, by their very presence, stirring up your doubts about others. Public streets and private malls, stores and halls, churches and parks are open to the unblinking eyes of their TV cameras. Many campuses have police officers on patrol three shifts a day, seven days a week. They are beaded with intensified lighting and strewn with emergency telephones that can call up a policeman within ninety seconds. Every large commercial building has its security guards and checks; many have entry passes. Nothing is considered safe, and no one does not have the finger pointing at him or her. Avoid contact; avoid being listed; dig a moat around yourself.

But can you? On a typical day, you might be tracked to work by an intelligent traffic system, your employer might listen, legally, to your telephone conversations, or tap into your computer, e-mail and voice-mail. You may be tracked by the ever-present closed circuit camera when shopping, and have your image stored. There are peepholes in the fitting rooms of clothes stores, and hidden microphones. The supermarket will log information about your purchases if you belong to its buyers' or loyalty club. Your credit card company keeps tabs on where and what you buy, and sells the information to eager marketers. Toll-free numbers identify a caller's number even if it is unlisted, and may sell it on. Should you change your job, your new employer may legally obtain your medical history from your insurance company, and your credit history from a credit bureau, ask you to submit to a drug test, a lie-detector test, or a personality test, ask you to disclose the prescription drugs you take and whether you have smoked in the preceding twelve months. If you're a nanny your new employers might track you with a concealed camera.

To see alienation's private face, walk down main street anywhere in the world. As likely as not you will encounter a run of Walkman-wearing, eye-shaded individuals, secluded, avoiding contact in the most crowded circumstances. Get on a commuter train, tube or bus, to find the passengers pressed against each other, reading, avoiding eye contact. Shuttered faces. Stop for a moment, observe gait, posture, personal furniture: many, particularly if young, saunter rather than walk; act cool and laid back rather than purposefully; carry cans of coke, lager, even bottles of Evian, and crisps ('I eat and I drink whenever I want to, wherever I want to; it's no business of yours'); telephoning on the trot, isolated in crowds, and crowded in their isolation. They look defiant rather than compliant; distant. See the clothes inspired by every style in the world and by none at all. All of which is saying, 'make of it what you will, but don't try to rule it. I'll do as I please. I'm as good as you'.

Dissociation goes farther than the weakening and dissolution of social links. It colours our view of our place in nature. If we are all there is, the final arbiters — encompassing, not coexisting with, all reality; if we inflict such damage on the world as to make it unpredictable; if we threaten to become the largest untamed living beings; if we consider there to be no limits to our powers to define and 'create' nature through genetic and other engineering, and our individual fate is only loosely connected with that nature; then the world becomes a lonely place, a vortex of meaninglessness, a source of anguish and of personal dislocation, in which the mind, in weariness or leisure, recurs constantly to its obsessions.

CONSEQUENCES

The void in subjectivity and self, and the widening gap between ever-more demanding standards of achievement and improving but increasingly inadequate accomplishments, between 'achievers' and others, is teeming with illness and unhappiness. Stress is undoubtedly more pervasive and acute for today's Market Beings than it was for people in precapitalist times. The kinds of stress that we share with them — due to natural disasters, poverty, bereavement — are much less easily dissipated through ritual, religious or other forms of public expression, and the individual is also less protected by community, family, kinship or neigh-bourhood group. In other words, the stressful life-events might be similar — and even attenuated — but the individual is more exposed to them

A standard objective measure of stress is the presence of coronary heart disease (CHD). A sudden heart seizure in an apparently healthy person was first reported in the US only in the 1920s. Heart attacks were not even mentioned in most medical textbooks until after World War II. Now cardiovascular diseases cause 30 percent of all deaths worldwide. Although some of the increase might reflect changes in reporting procedures and conventions (which bias diagnosis towards a talked-about disease), the real increase has nonetheless been dramatic, despite new drugs, closer monitoring, and attempts at prevention through changes in lifestyle. Accompanying the increase has been a drop in the social level of patients.

Another objective indicator of stress is obesity, which is spreading in epidemic proportions. In Britain in 1998 21 percent of women and 17 percent of men were classed as sufficiently overweight to seriously endanger their health — (compared with 8 percent and 6 percent respectively in 1980), and the proportion of overweight people rose by more than one-sixth to 54 percent of men and 45 percent of women.[1] In the US, more than half of adults are overweight and over three-tenths clinically obese — only arthritis, high blood pressure and diabetes affect more people, and only cigarette smoking causes more deaths.

The most obvious and dramatic of the objective indicators of stress are mental illness and madness. Difficult as it is to plot their epidemiological history (for reasons of definition, diagnosis, official policy and coverage, and for reasons to do with the late emergence of psychiatry as a distinct profession with lobbying power), they are attaining a progressively greater prominence: mental disorders were not included in the World Health Organization's International Classification of Disease until its 6th Revision in 1948, when they accounted for 10 pages out of 187 (5 percent). The 7th Revision (1957) also had 10 pages devoted to mental disorders (slightly less as a share of the total); the 8th (1967) had 14 pages (3 percent), the 9th (1977) 38 pages (7.4 percent) and the 10th (1992) 76 pages (6.2 percent). By then, the WHO thought it necessary to publish a separate 362-page volume on *Mental and Behavioral Disorders*, one third as long as the main book. The WHO predicts that clinical depression will be the leading cause of disability and the second leading contributor to the global burden of disease, accounting for 15 percent of the total, by 2020.[2] And British insurers have announced that stress, anxiety and depression have overtaken back problems as the main causes of long-term absenteeism from work.

Beyond mental illness lies madness — a profound, prolonged inability (including refusal) to know and deal in a rational and autonomous way with oneself and one's social and physical environment. It is unreason, disorder, a condition which the ruling culture of the time finds difficult, for whatever reason, to engage with positively. Modern market society is particularly conducive to madness, or so it seems. In its first phase a large population of misfits found themselves hauled into the Gulag-cum-madhouse of the time. One-tenth of all arrests made in Paris from the mid-seventeenth century to the end of the eighteenth concerned 'the insane'. As time progressed, those who could not, or would not, adapt to the new system and its work ethic were separated out semi-permanently so that they became, by the nineteenth century, a confined population. Madness became distilled, concentrated, not part of everyday life. It was segregated physically behind bars, morally and emotionally beyond the realm of meaning and control, a demon to be avoided except as an object of fascinated horror.

In time the frontier of madness drew back, but never again to its pre-market society lines, most dramatically from the middle of the last century. Until then the number of involuntary inmates in mental hospitals in the US rose steadily from 183 per hundred thousand population in 1904 to peak at 409 in 1945, putting severe strains on medical budgets. The trend changed direction in the second half of the century when funding was centralized and psychotropic drugs, primarily chlorpromazine (Thorozine), that tamed the recipients (or made them tractable), became available. Far cheaper than bricks and mortar, and cheaper to administer, they paved the way for a privatization and individualization of control. Numbers in institutions fell steeply — to 380 per hundred thousand in 1956 and 194 in 1970. All but the criminally insane were let loose into 'the community' — an effective de-institutionalization rate of 91.3 percent from 1955 to 1994.[3] In England and Wales, prescriptions of anti-depressants rose from 27 per thousand men patients in 1994 to 33.3 in 1996 (19.2 to 71.3 for women patients).

Madness is defined with ever-greater fastidiousness: there is mental retardation (physiological impairment); personality disorders (the disposition to behave in abnormal ways present continuously from early adult life); mental disorders (abnormalities of behaviour with a recognizable onset); adjustment disorders (in response to stressful, changed circumstances); and 'other' disorders (significantly, abnormalities of sexual preference, drug dependence). The perimeters of madness are under constant review and adjustment, fought over with bitterness and tenacity — it was only after a postal ballot held in 1975 that homosexuality was removed from the American Psychiatric Association's list of mental illnesses.

At the same time madness is becoming more ambiguous. A realm of *conditional sanity* is opening up, pacified by the psychotropic bombs that subdue, cow and curtail. There are two issues here. One is of definition: whether to consider the neurotic and, especially, the chemically-constrained, mad or sane. In terms of the culture's ability to make them function in some sort of concert with the majority, they are sane, if only conditionally. In this sense, psychotropic drugs are a shining example of modern medical culture, enabling people with a culturally-defined deficit to live and function adequately without becoming ill. They also illustrate the supreme vulnerability of a society where normalcy is dependent on the existence of an intricate logistical system to supply and administer the means of maintaining it to a large, and growing, clientele scattered amongst the general, not quite so mad, population.

The other issue is of scope: in the heartlands of the modern world the number of the potentially-mad, as defined by the culture, is growing, but being held down. In the world at large, it is exploding: mental disorders accounted for 10 percent of the world's disease burden in 1999 (as measured by years of healthy life lost), and are expected by the World Health Organization to account for 15 percent by 2020.[4] In rich countries the cost per unit of madness, the cost of 'treatment' or prevention or control per 'mental patient', has come down. But world spending on madness, the madness market as it were, has not dipped at all.

Monitoring is sketchy. The social infrastructure is poor. The distinctions between personal and institutional intractability, and between political and subcultural, intractability, are blurred. When, on 14 February 1989, Ayatollah Khomeini, then spiritual leader of Iran, issued a *fatwa* calling on all Muslims to kill Salman Rushdie and his publishers for *The Satanic Verses*, who was criminally insane? Iran's ruling circles *knew* it was Rushdie. Many others thought differently…

Another view of stress is subjective: people who feel their ability to cope with normal life sufficiently impaired for them to disrupt its daily routine.

They include those who seek medical advice and consume medication, a larger number who believe themselves to be ill without having recourse to a physician. The number of times people sought professional care for illness more than doubled in the USA last century, from an average of under once a year in the 1920s to more than twice a year in the late 1980s. In Britain the number of consultations with a National Health Service general practitioner rose by half between 1975 and 1996, from 196 million to 294 million.[5] Even more significant is the growing recourse to complementary and alternative medicine (CAM), which is more purely voluntary since it is not tied to the requirements of employers, insurance companies, state agencies, police authorities and so on. In 1997 42.1 percent of Americans resorted to CAM, compared with 33.8 percent in 1990 (an increase of a quarter in just seven years).[6]

Beyond the host of people who seek help publicly and formally there are those, almost certainly greater in number, who do so hidden from view, as part of their normal round, and the even larger number who cope under strain. The ultimate effect of strain is, of course, death. And nowhere is *karoshi* (death as a result of overwork) more closely monitored than in Japan where, on some lawyers' estimates, it claims between 10,000 and 30,000 victims a year. In Russia a sharp rise in the number of deaths following the collapse of the Soviet regime is attributed not, as might be expected, to simple poverty or the increasingly parlous state of the post-Soviet health service, but to a 'psycho-social crisis' due to greatly rising insecurity. Life expectancy for men at birth was 15 years *less* in 1995 than in 1983, before the transition, as 20-65 year olds succumbed to a complex cocktail of homicide, suicide, accidents, falls, burns, drownings and other symptoms of psychological stress and alcoholic bingeing.[7]

There is a huge and growing market for psychotherapy, ranging from psychoanalysis (an intricate, demanding craft), to its simplified, routinized, modular, gadget-ridden but more-easily-marketed derivations — an industry dedicated to reassembling or constructing the self. A lot of it provides little more than comfort. Some of it addresses the underlying condition, and sometimes succeeds in self-realization or (re)assembly. The growth of psychotherapy from the day in 1896, when Freud first hung out his shingle in Vienna, has been remarkable, and one which shows no signs of abating. One survey dating from 1959 listed thirty-six different kinds. Less than twenty years later, in 1977, no fewer than 200 conceptually distinct psychotherapies were noted. The growth in professional activity has been far greater than the growth in the activity as such. Psychological and emotional cures and comforting have always been available, part of normal social intercourse. That is still the case, within functioning families and friendship networks. But it has been extended and partially supplanted by external, professional, marketed versions.

Embracing both the subjective and objective indicators of stress are the epidemics of hysteria that sweep ever more frequently through the market system's heartlands — from belief in alien abduction to satanic ritual abuse — a 'cultural symptom of anxiety and stress' in the words Elaine Showalter, the phenomenon's theorist and historian.[8]

'I'm sick and can't work' often stands in for 'I can't work and so I'm sick'. Absenteeism from work is a mass phenomenon: in Western Europe alone it embraces around 14 percent (one in seven) of the total number of people not at work for whatever reason. In some countries declared illness accounts for astonishingly high proportions: 60 percent of time lost in the US, 43 percent in Belgium, 35 percent in Germany, 34 percent in Ireland and Portugal, 31 percent in Italy and Holland, 28 percent in France, 25 percent in Canada, 20 percent in the UK and Spain. In the early nineties days lost to sickness in Western Europe averaged 80-90 times the number lost in labour disputes. These figures do not constitute cast-iron evidence: different states define absenteeism and its causes differently and different social security laws and regulations induce different behaviour on the part of workers. The figures also do not fully account for fake or phantom illnesses, logged in order to take up unused entitlements to paid sick leave, to join a public rally, to pursue romance or revenge, to care for children or others, or to slop about and enjoy simply being. There are many, many reasons to avoid work, even in a society that ultimately punishes non-work. On the other hand the figures do not allow either for those who turn up to work feeling ill, but bound by duty, fear, solidarity, circumspection or pressing material need.

If early retirement is considered a form of absenteeism, as surely it must be, when not imposed by mass firing — a meta-absenteeism if you like — the evidence is striking. Labour-force participation of men aged 60-64 has declined from over 80 percent in most rich countries in 1960 to 50 percent in America and below 35 percent in Germany, Italy and France. In Britain eight out of ten employees retire before reaching the normal pension age as defined by their pension-scheme rules, two-thirds before the age of sixty. By contrast, late retirement — after normal pension age — is negligible, even in countries with no compulsory retirement age.[9]

Then there is drug taking. It combines a number of functions, some of them mutually contradictory. On one view it is a promoter of connectedness — a social activity, a pipe of peace, a shared joint, which lowers barriers, removes or reduces inhibition, lubricates a common experience. On another view it is precisely the opposite — an escape from connectedness, a substitute for sociability, a 'solitary vice', an avoidance of taking responsibility for one's own life. On both views it relieves stress. Drug-taking of all sorts is rising. Of course drugs do not enter mouths or veins unassisted. They are pushed in many ways — through advertising (legal drugs) and through personal inducement and example (illegals). There are large numbers of people with a stake in extending the market for each and every one. But that goes for all of them. The important point is that the drugs most indicative of social detachment — which, incidentally, are the most restricted in the marketing methods available to them — are the ones that are spreading fastest.

The supreme subjective indicator of stress is suicide. It lies at one extreme of a range of actions that start with unconscious self-harming behaviour like incautious cutting of vegetables, jay-walking or swimming out of depth, and progress through 'indirect self-poisoning' through over-eating or wrong-eating to deliberate self-harm such as impulsive overdosing without the preparation (of dosage, secrecy) that would ensure 'success', to, finally, the successful denouement. It is mostly committed by men, sometimes suffering from a psychiatric disorder, often under great strain from incompatible roles or duties or expectations. Not all suicides are a cry of despair or for help — they can be a response to unbearable physical pain, a fulfilment of a sense of public duty, a quest for martyrdom, or whatever. Significantly, urban suicide is higher in areas with relatively high boarding-house populations, immigrants and divorcees, and in the spring and early summer, when more people are flaunting their attractions and thereby underlining the suicide's isolation.

It is not easy to gauge the prevalence of *real* suicide — that is, 'completed', successful suicide. It is usually planned carefully, with precautions taken against discovery, and often camouflaged so that the death appears to be accidental (traffic accidents, falls, drownings). Recording is haphazard; coroners' courts in England and their equivalents elsewhere operate under different regimes of stringency for evidence; doctors and officials often connive with families to shift the cause of death to morally safer (and insurance-covered) ground. Changes in reporting practice compound the difficulties. In many countries the true figure, as attested by psychiatrists is way above the official figure. Suspect as the figures are, the number of recorded suicides is rising steadily, increasing by 122 percent between the early-to-mid 1950s and the mid-to-late 1990s in the twenty-nine countries, comprising a seventh of the world's population, for which comparisons could be made.[10]

Confused, with a damaged sense of self and ragged connectedness with others, it is not surprising that Market Being is ill, uncertain, stressed, inadequate and in need of comfort. At any one time a quarter of the world's population exhibit signs of physical morbidity and mental distress. And the proportion is growing.

COSTS

Although not all of it can be attributed directly to market society, the coincidence of its spread and deepening, and the increasing prevalence of illness and distress, is remarkable. Recorded spending on health care is on the up-and-up: from an (unweighted) average 3.8 percent of GDP in 1960 to 8.5 percent for the same eighteen rich countries in 1998; and from 115 international (PPP) dollars a head to 1974 dollars in the same years. It rose from 5.1 to 13.6 percent of GDP in the US, from 3.0 to 7.6 in Japan, 6.3 (1970) to 10.6 in Germany, 4.2 to 9.6 in France, 3.6 to 8.4 in Italy, and 3.9 to 6.7 in the UK. Spending per head rose eighty-seven times in Spain in the same years, seventy times in Japan, fifty-three times in Norway, thirty-six times in Italy, thirty-one times in Switzerland, twenty-nine times in the US and France, and twenty times in Britain.

Saturation medication is becoming general: more than half of all adults and nearly one-third of children in Britain take some form of medication every day. In Britain and the US there are as many renewal prescriptions for psychotropic drugs as there are inhabitants. In England the number of medical prescriptions rose from 6.7 per head in 1982 to 9.7 in 1995.

Yet people are not noticeably healthier. In the mid-1970s, the life expectancy of a person over 60 in France was just two years higher than in 1900. For men it remained constant. While life expectancy in the US and Britain has been rising, the proportion of healthy people (alive and not diseased or disabled) has declined — from 81.8 percent to 79.2 percent for men in the US between 1970 and 1980 (from 81 percent to 77.8 percent for women); and from 83.1 to 81.8 percent for men, 81.1 to 79.2 percent for women, 1976 to 1985, in the UK.

In France the mortality rate for fifteen-to-twenty-year-olds is rising at 2 percent per year. In all rich countries, for men aged forty to fifty it rose from the mid-1960s to the mid-1970s. For British workers over fifty it is higher than during the 1930s. In some countries (and not only the 'usual suspects' of the former Soviet Union and AIDS-afflicted sub-Saharan Africa) life expectancy at birth has stopped increasing or even entered a decline.

There are several ways to understand the apparent diminishing returns to medical intervention which these statistics suggest. One is that the underlying morbidity of the population is rising faster than medicalization in all its forms (drugs, treatment, hospitalization), because of a deterioration in social circumstances or a decline in human quality, or both. It might be difficult for readers in rich countries to grasp the fact that most people are getting poorer as their environment deteriorates. Since the agents of health and disease are largely social (between 80 and 90 percent of the differences in life expectancy across the world can be explained by the presence of clean drinking water and of literacy), it is understandable that health suffers. In addition, countless studies show that city life is debilitating psychologically, and that migration contributes greatly to psychopathology.

A deterioration also seems to be occurring in the human stock. Modern genetics has highlighted the ubiquity of inborn disease. In Britain about one child in thirty is born with a genetic defect of some kind. Over a third of registered blind people are blind for genetic reasons and more than a half of all cases of severe mental handicap have an inherited cause. If diseases that have an inherited component, such as cancer or heart disease, are included, two thirds of the population will suffer from, and possibly die of, a genetic disease. Advances in medical and public health techniques have permitted debilitating mutations to accumulate through the generations, without being cleansed by natural selection through death in infancy and childhood.

Another way of interpreting the apparent diminishing returns to medical intervention, particularly in the rich countries, is to say that the refinement of medical treatment — its fragmentation into ever-narrower specialisms, its reductionism, its resistance to participation by the patient, the support it lends to the loss of self and to medical dependency — has made it less effective in securing well-being. And it is a fact that a fifth of the patients in a typical research hospital in the US acquire a doctor-induced illness in the course of their treatment. But at a certain point these distinctions divert attention from a more fundamental and obvious truth: it is in the nature of market society to blight a large proportion of its people with *mens insana in corpore insano*.

NOTES

This essay is drawn largely from my book, *The Presence of the Future: the costs of capitalism and the transition to ecological society,* forthcoming 2002.

1   Report from UK National Audit Office, reviewed in *The Financial Times,* 15 February 2001.
2   See http://www.who.int/whosis.
3   E. Fuller Torrey, *Out of the Shadows, Confronting America's Mental Illness Crisis,* New York, etc: John Wiley & Sons, 1977, pp. 206-7.
4   See http://www.who.int/whosis.
5   UK Department of Health, *General Medical Services Statistics, England and Wales, 1994, National FSA,* Table 4.20.
6   House of Lords, Select Committee on Science and Technology, *Complementary and Alternative Medicine,* London: The Stationery Office, 2000, Table 2, p. 14.
7   Helen Epstein, 'Time of Indifference', *The New York Review,* 12 April 2001, pp. 36-7.
8   Elaine Showalter, *Hystories: Hysterical Epidemics and Modern Culture,* London: Picador, 1997.
9   World Resources Institute, UN Environment Program, UN Development Program, World Bank, *1998-99 World Resources, a Guide to the Global Environment,* New York and Oxford: Oxford University Press, 1998, data table &.2, pp. 246-7.
10 *UN Demographic Yearbook, 1955* (Table 29B), *1966* (Table 20) and *1998* (Table 21).

MEDIA POWER AND CLASS POWER: OVERPLAYING IDEOLOGY

DAVID MILLER

The media have a contradictory role in relation to class power. They do predominantly carry corporate and state friendly messages, but not exclusively. They do have a role in legitimating capitalist social relations, but the role of ideology in maintaining social order has been overplayed by some theorists. A variety of other mechanisms employed by the powerful to pursue their interests are arguably as important as the mass media in the maintenance of 'ruling ideas'. In attempting to rethink the relationship between media power and class power, this essay uses the work of Stuart Hall as the starting point for a critique of cultural and media studies. It argues that Critical Theorists such as Hall overemphasized the importance of ideology and the 'function' of the media in capitalist social order.

The primary interest of this kind of argument was in the alleged 'ideological effect' of the media on the public and how this might help to secure hegemony. A key assumption was that definitional power was 'always already' power in society. The argument advanced here is that definitional power is just power over definitions and has no necessary link with either popular ideology or societal power. The media do play a role in 'keeping America [and the rest of us] uninformed', as Donna Demac put it.[1] They also mislead key sections of western populations about their own interests, and persuade some that happiness lies in the pursuit of goods. But this is not the only role of the media in relation to class power. The media play a direct role in the system of governance in which the public have very little say, or are really heard only *in extremis* (e.g. following successful campaigns or demonstrations — i.e. when opposition is effective). The public are in many circumstances mere spectators at what James Connolly in a different context described as the 'carnival of reaction'.

Furthermore, huge swathes of decision making and power-broking occur not just beyond the reach and influence of the public but also outside the purview of public and media debate. For example, the existence of the multimillion dollar/pound lobbying industry is a standing rebuke to those who argue that the media are overwhelmingly important. Ironically, then, a 'Marxist' analysis of the media assumes, along with liberal analyses, that the public have a fundamental legitimating role in liberal democracies, when in fact public consent is only needed to legitimize decision-making in certain circumstances. And even strong, consistent and popular protest can be ignored by the powerful under many circumstances. We need an alternative model of the relationship between media power and class power, on the lines outlined towards the end of this essay.

MEDIA POWER AND CLASS POWER

I have adapted the title of this essay from an essay written by Stuart Hall in the mid-1980s. It was a short and simplified piece for a book which attempted to make an intervention in media debates in the UK at the time. In it the media are said to be:

> *the machinery of representation* in modern societies. What they exercise is the power to represent the world in certain definite ways. And because there are many different and conflicting ways in which meaning about the world can be constructed, it matters profoundly what and who gets represented, *what* and *who* regularly and routinely gets left out; and *how* things, people, events, relationships are represented. What we know of society depends on how things are represented to us and that knowledge in turn informs what we do and what policies we are prepared to accept.[2]

There are four points to be made here. First, what we know of society depends only in part on how things are represented to us, since we also experience the world directly. Second, the world is not only represented to us by the mass media. There is an elision here between representation in general and the mass media in particular. Third, this is a model which assumes fairly powerful media effects. Fourth, note the assumption that the argument stops at the level of the public. But what we are constantly being 'prepared to accept' is often not the same as what the public actually consents to.

Hall acknowledges the importance of ownership and control and of direct and indirect censorship and policing of the media in curtailing diversity. But he argues that these are not by themselves adequate explanations:

> [t]here is also the way in which the hierarchy of *power* in the society is reproduced, in the media, as a structure of *access*. Or how the respect for, orientation towards and reproduction of power in the media surfaces as a set of limits and constrictions on knowledge. That is how, without a single Ministerial or MI5 intervention, 'topics' come to be defined, agendas set and frameworks deployed which ultimately define the 'sayable and 'unsayable' in society. The area of what is considered as 'reasonable talk'

about anything, as the appropriate and inappropriate registers, as the intangible boundaries which rule the inclusion or exclusion of certain things, certain points of view, is one of the most powerful of the ways the media's regimes of truth come to be established.[3]

This seems like a mysterious process. How is the structure of access determined? How exactly is it that topics come to be defined? What set of processes establish the boundaries of the sayable? Hall does acknowledge that 'we know far too little' of such processes. He asks: '[h]ow can we pinpoint, in the endless, diverse, flow of "talk" in the media, the precise ways in which the state stands as the "definer of the limits of political reality" for the media'.[4]

THE IDEOLOGICAL EFFECT?

Perhaps the mysteriousness of this process arises as a result of the simplified content of this particular article. But when we turn to Hall's earlier formulations, the process becomes if anything more mysterious. Here the media are the preeminent ideological institutions. They furthermore operate effectively to ensure the reproduction of capital:

> [t]he 'definitions of reality', favourable to the dominant class fractions, and institutionalised in the spheres of civil life and the state, come to constitute the primary 'lived reality' as such for the subordinate classes. In this way ideology provides the 'cement' in a social formation.[5]

This assumes on the basis of theory (rather than evidence) that bourgeois ideology actually does indoctrinate the masses. But how does this happen? To understand this we need to look at the theoretical heritage on which Hall's work is based.

In particular we need to note the way in which two bodies of literature were drawn together in an attempt to renovate Marx. First there was contemporary work on language and semiotics. These approaches relied heavily on speculation about the meanings of texts. Drawing on semiotics, structural linguistics and anthropology via Levi-Strauss and Saussure, Hall attempted to posit a homology between Levi Strauss' proposition, that a speaker can use a language without any consciousness of its generative code, and Marx's famous statement that people make history but not in circumstances of their own choosing. The point of this was to show that language and discourse have their own determinate rules and can be seen to operate autonomously from the economic and political levels of society. On this basis Hall could argue for the 'relative autonomy' of the ideological and for an apparently autonomous 'class struggle in language', or for the 'specificity of the cultural'.[6]

Second and perhaps most importantly was the influence of Althusser. Althusser's work on ideology was an attempt to avoid the economism of certain strands of Marxism. Althusser conceived of society as being a complex totality of different 'levels' or 'instances'.[7] Of particular note was the instance of ideology, which had a 'relative autonomy' from the political and the economic. The economic level of society determined the ideological 'in the last instance'. [8] But if the last instance guarantees ideology for capital, relative autonomy is really not very autonomous at all and only narrowly, if at all, escapes the charge of economism. It certainly does not escape the charge of functionalism, as Hall notes, but his take on Althussser is also vulnerable to the same problem of assuming a function for the media even if it is only a 'systemic tendency'. [9]

Hall's model blurs together, under the heading of ideology, the distinct moments of the propagation and promotion of particular ideologies by the dominant class, the work done on them to transform them into media products, the understanding and response to them of audiences and the impact of this in societal outcomes. [10] It does this by conceiving of language and ideology as nearly indistinguishable and assuming that understanding language is tantamount to 'being spoken' by ideology. [11] Ideology, in other words, is an unconscious process. Hall discusses 'effective communication' [12] as the site of ideology. It is as if it were not possible to step outside of ideology; language itself is ideological regardless of the intentions or views of the speaker.

> To put it in its extreme form, a statement like, 'the strike of the Leyland tool-makers today further weakened Britain's economic position' was premised on a whole set of taken for granted propositions about how the economy worked ... for it to win credibility, the whole logic of capitalist production had to be assumed to be true.

So far so good, but the key to this passage is the way that Hall goes on to assume that the statement wins credibility simply by virtue of having been understood:

> Much the same could be said about any item in a conventional news bulletin, that, without a whole range of unstated premises or pieces of taken-for-granted knowledge about the world, each descriptive statement would be literally unintelligible. But this 'deep structure' of presuppositions, which made the statement ideologically 'grammatical' [was] rarely made explicit and [was] largely unconscious ... to those who were required to make sense of it. [13]

To win credibility for the proposition that strikes are a 'problem' for the nation (or whatever is the latest piece of capitalist ideology or state propaganda) certainly requires that it is repeated and elaborated on the 'unbiased' TV news as if it were simply a statement of fact; but it also requires that people believe it, which is not guaranteed simply by virtue of it being an intelligible statement. We may understand the message but not accept that it is true, valid or fair. This has been found extensively in critical audience research in recent years. [14] In formulations like Hall's the problem of the reproduction of capital is solved not by direct investigation of the relationship between the media, popular ideology and societal outcomes, but by theoretical fiat. [15]

In later formulations (in the early 1980s) Hall moved towards the Foucauldian notion of discursive practice, where ideology is said to speak through people without their knowledge:

> [w]hen in phrasing a question, in the era of monetarism, a broadcasting interviewer simply takes it for granted that rising wage demands are the sole cause of inflation, he is both 'freely formulating a question' on behalf of the public and establishing a logic which is compatible with the dominant interests in society. And this would be the case regardless of whether or not the particular broadcaster was a lifelong supporter of some left-wing trot-skyist sect … In the critical paradigm, ideology is a function of discourse and of the logic of social process, rather than an intention of the agent … The ideology has 'worked' in such a case because the discourse has spoken itself through him/her.[16]

It strains credulity to suggest that left journalists would not and do not notice their contributions to dominant ideologies. The MI5 vetting office in the BBC certainly does not take that view, nor did the management of Fox TV when they sacked two journalists in Tampa, Florida for their reporting of Monsanto.[17] But for Hall, what is important is the mysterious functioning of ideology, which we have imbibed so thoroughly that we no longer notice.

Hall, following Althusser, goes on to discuss ideology as an unconscious process:

> [i]mportant modifications to our way of conceiving dominance had to be effected before the idea was rescuable. That notion of dominance which meant the direct imposition of one framework, by overt force or ideolog-ical compulsion, on a subordinate class, was not sophisticated enough to match the real complexities of the case. One had also to see that dominance was accomplished at the unconscious as well as the conscious level: to see it as a property of the system of relations involved, rather than the overt and intentional biases of individuals; and to recognise its play in the very activity of regulation and exclusion which functioned through language discourse, before an adequate conception of dominance could be theoret-ically secured.[18]

If anything, however, the idea of the unconscious as the last guarantor of bour-geois ideology is less sophisticated than the model it seeks to replace, in the sense that it explains everything by a hidden principle. It does not match the complex-ities of actual societies in which people do continuously and consciously struggle for a better tomorrow. Elegant and sophisticated the theory and the delivery might be, but it does not conform to the available evidence on public belief and popular ideology. As McDonnell and Robins put it:

> [i]deology [is] … not a factor of the unconscious as Althusser maintains. This latter position would … make class consciousness impossible … Ideology does not permeate people's minds: the working class does not find it impossible to unmask the ideological mystifications of capitalist society.

> For ideology is far from watertight; it requires an incessant struggle by the capitalist class to maintain its precarious validity. A validity that is constantly called into question, not in a separate sphere of ideological struggle, but throughout the daily struggles in the workplace, the community etc.[19]

This is a much more adequate position and lets us theorize the role of state and corporate information management, censorship and secrecy in the reproduction of inequality. It lets us see the importance not of the 'system of relations' but of concrete actions by concrete institutions and individuals in concrete historical circumstances not of their choosing. What else is the whole machinery of state and corporate public relations (together with confidentiality, intimidation, the use of the law etc) but a massive daily attempt to 'nobble' the media and 'indoctrinate' the people? The capitalist class is perfectly aware of the need to brief, spin, dissemble and lie.

GRAMSCI TO THE RESCUE?

Hall's greatest achievement, so far as many commentators are concerned, was his use of the concept of hegemony to avoid the disabling reductionism and functionalism of Althusserianism. Hegemony meant that consent was important and that the class struggle in language was or could be a two-sided affair. Hall noted that a problem with Althusser's work was that it was difficult to see how anything but the dominant ideology could ever be reproduced.[20] Volosinov and particularly Gramsci were deployed to show that there can be a class struggle in language. This appeared to mean that intelligibility was not guaranteed and could be ruptured by oppositional codes or subordinate meaning systems. There was not always 'an achieved system of equivalence between language and reality'.[21] This gave the possibility of a struggle for hegemony in language. This struggle was conceived as emanating from within the technical aspects of signs and language: there were 'mechanisms within signs and language which made the "struggle" possible'.[22] These mechanisms included the multi-accentuality of a discourse, or the fact that some words can mean more than one thing or can be interpreted differently. Against this we can say that the struggle over language is made possible not by the alleged technical features of language, but by the material facts of conflicting power and interests. Instead of seeing challenges to hegemony as emerging from separate discourses, we need to see them as emanating from experience, material and ideal interests, and struggles in which ideology and language play a role that we can only sensibly grasp in terms of totality. The example Hall gives is the conflict over the term 'Black' as a term of abuse, or as a positive sign of beauty and empowerment. But it is the fact of racist discrimination and violence, on the one hand, and the struggle for self determination and self respect, on the other, which make this conflict possible, not the technical features of language. These conditions form the material circumstances in which people 'become conscious of conflict and fight it out', as Marx put it.

Hall discusses the level of the discursive as if it were a separate domain.

Gramsci's notion of the war of position is transposed from political and class strug-gles to the 'field of discourse'. As a result Hall holds that 'now we have to talk about texts that are never closed, about discursive systems that are not unified but the product of articulation and always contradictory; about the possibilities of transcoding and decoding the dominant definitions in play'.[23] But we only have to talk in this way if we swallow all of this elegant theoretical edifice. Included in the bargain is the separation and elevation of discourse, as opposed to the importance of the reproduction of the means of survival. A materialist view holds rather that language is a product of human culture and is a part of the social rela-tions of production of a 'whole way of life'. It is a tool used by humans to communicate and negotiate, even if we do not understand the rules which generate it. To see the level of the discursive as a separate level is to privilege language over experience, consciousness, and material and biological reality. The problem is that this is not how 'discourse' functions. Discourses, or ideologies (as Hall seems increasingly unwilling to call them) arise out of the material and ideal interests of real people. There is no abstract struggle over language, only a struggle over power and resources of which ideological battles form part. There is no 'class struggle in language' which is separate and distinct from the class struggle over resources and the organization of society. Changing the word is not changing the world, as Sivanandan memorably put it.[24]

The notion that it was ideology that pre-eminently explained the reproduc-tion of capital foundered on the rock of all sorts of evidence that people were able to understand the world (and the word). On the part of some formerly radical theorists, this led to some confusion about the possibilities of using concepts such as ideology and to a renewed pluralist emphasis on the indeterminacy of power.[25] The narrow focus on the media, or on the moment of decoding or interpreta-tion, meant that the wider picture of the assault on social democracy seemed simply to vanish from the academic agenda of media studies.[26]

BACK TO MARX

As a potential way out of some of these problems I want to try and advance an alternative approach by going back to Marx and briefly re-examining his classic formulations about the relations between economics, power and ideas. There are three main points I want to make here. The first relates to the misunderstanding of the notion of the social relations of production, the second to the base-super-structure metaphor, which has often been interpreted as indicating that the ownership of the means of production endows the capitalist class with fantastic powers of persuasion, and the third relates to the notion of ruling ideas.

1. In one of the most famous passages on the question of ideology Marx argued that:

> [i]n the social production of their existence, men inevitably enter into defi-nite relations, which are independent of their will, namely relations of production appropriate to a given stage in the development of their mate-rial forces of production. The totality of these relations of production

constitutes the economic structure of society, the real foundation, on which arises a legal and political superstructure and to which correspond definite forms of social consciousness. The mode of production of material life conditions the general process of social, political and intellectual life. It is not the consciousness of men which determines their existence, but their social existence that determines their consciousness.[27]

It is fairly clear from this passage that the 'social relations of production' are not simply a set of mechanistic 'economic' processes. They are a set of social processes which are determined by the need to reproduce the material basis of life and the forces of production. Such social processes act on the 'forces of production' and shape them in determinate, if historically contingent, ways. Social relations are profoundly ideological and are the real foundation on which capitalist self-interest — and opposition to it — are built. In other words, ideology is constitutive of the social relations of production. Further, ideology, and how people become conscious of their world, affects how those struggles are fought out and the resulting changes in both the forces of production and the social relations surrounding them. Ideology is not simply a reflection of the level of the economic, it is part of the means by which interests are welded to action and by which certain actions or states of affairs are justified and legitimated.

We should not reduce ideology to the system or structure of relations, but rather see the conscious (if ideological) actions of human beings as constitutive of the social totality and as causative agents in historical processes. This approach necessitates first and foremost empirical research to ascertain how human activities constitute history. It also means that we see the determinate actions of real human beings as being consequential for the reproduction of capital. Rather than seek power in some mysterious unobservable process of ideological interpellation or articulation, or simply in understanding language, we must seek it in the actions of real people in the (would-be) secret (but sometimes discoverable) low conspiracies which are a continuous and inevitable part of capitalist rule; in censorship, spin, lobbying, public relations, marketing and advertising;[28] in the institutions of 'disinformation and distraction' as Raymond Williams put it.[29] These, in the context of economic power and resources, are some of the key means by which capitalism is reproduced, and we treat them as mere epiphenomena of the real, hidden nature of ideology at our peril.

2. The base/superstructure metaphor is rather unpopular these days. Critics have suggested that it reduces ideas and ideologies to the economic, whether in the first or last instance. And to be sure, in some hands it does. But following Terry Eagleton,[30] I would like to enter a few words for the defence.

Speaking crudely there were two interpretations of the base-superstructure metaphor. One was the vulgar Marxist interpretation which saw the media simply as an agency of class control and the population as brainwashed (or subject to 'ideological effects' in Hall's more sophisticated versions). The second was that associated with Raymond Williams, who suggested that we see the economic (the ownership of the means of mental production) as setting limits on what could appear in the media.[31] This does seem to provide a reasonable description of much media behaviour. We could query it on the grounds that the imperative to make money sometimes pulls against the supposed imperative to support the system. Or we might query it on the issue of popular ideology, since it is arguably not that case that economic power determines popular ideology, at least not in a simple sense. But this again betrays a misunderstanding about the sources of power and experience in society. The position advanced here is that ideas come from and indeed are inseparable from interests. Accounts of the world and evaluations of it emerge from material experience as well as from the media and other symbolic systems. So there is every reason to suppose that there will always be sources of opposition to capitalism.

And who could deny that material factors have a determining role in moving culture in particular directions? To pick an example from California, which comes to hand as I write, it is apparent that the development of new forces of production in Silicon Valley has involved a set of changing social relations of production. Capital has been poured into the development of dot.com companies in the latter half of the 1990s (prior to the transformation from dot.com to dot.gone as the NASDAQ index plummeted). This made a small number of relatively young people very rich very fast. One consequence of this has been an alleged deleterious effect on social solidarity in some neighbourhoods in the Bay area. The *San Francisco Chronicle* reports:

> [i]t was the new millionaires, made rich by cashing in their abundant stock options, that changed the playing field here. They thought nothing of bidding up houses several hundreds of thousands of dollars over the asking price or paying cash for $60,000 Mercedes-Benzes ... For many, the irrationality of it all came at a price: skyrocketing housing costs, maddening traffic jams, shortages of skilled labor and perhaps most frustrating, a diminished sense of community. The nouveau riche were moving into old neighbourhoods, tearing down vintage homes, building bigger ones and erecting giant fences.[32]

Now we might say that the 'culture' of the new rich and how they behave is not 'determined' in a mechanistic sense by the social relations of production. It was of course possible for the new rich to have given all their money away to anti-globalization protesters or for them to rip off the firms in which they work to fund the activities of revolutionary writers. The latter course was taken by Friedrich Engels at his family firm as a means of supporting Karl Marx.[33] But this has not happened — as far as we know — widely in the Bay area. Instead they put up fences and further dehumanized 'community'. Why must we say that this was simply a cultural matter with no deterministic link to the social relations of production? To say that the fences were built as part of a new cultural formation simply begs the question of what caused the culture to change. It seems more adequate to say that this was a 'determinate' outcome of the change in the social relations of production. Without wanting to reduce everything to such clear cut causation, it is clearly imperative to understand the social and material genesis of ideas and values and how these then ripple through the social fabric, provoking approval, desire, opprobrium or opposition. We cannot explain phenomena such as this without a model in which the social relations of production 'condition', 'determine' or 'influence' how people live in the world and relate to each other.

3. But the extent to which particular ideologies or ideas require to be believed (and by how many people) for the system to function is not a straightforward affair. The key question was how far does the ownership of capital allow the capitalist class to dominate the thinking of subordinated classes? According to Marx and Engels:

> [t]he ideas of the ruling class are in every epoch the ruling ideas, i.e. the class which is the ruling *material* force of society, is at the same time its ruling *intellectual* force. The class which has the means of material production at its disposal, has control at the same time over the means of mental production, so that thereby, generally speaking, the ideas of those who lack the means of mental production are subject to it ... The individuals composing the ruling class possess among other things consciousness, and therefore think. Insofar, therefore, as they rule as a class and determine the extent and compass of an epoch, it is self evident that they do this in its whole range, hence among other things rule also as thinkers, as producers of ideas, and regulate the production and distribution of the ideas of their age: thus their ideas are the ruling ideas of the epoch.[34]

The widespread interpretation of this is that those who own the means of production dominate the production of ideas, with the result that their ideas are adopted by the masses, thus assuring capitalist rule. This is the clear assumption in the work of Stuart Hall, quoted at the beginning of this essay.[35] But there is not much in the passage from Marx and Engels to encourage this interpretation. One way to pose this is to ask what a ruling intellectual force might be? Is it a set of ideas with which everyone agrees, or at least with which the mass of the (working class) population agrees? Or is it a set of ideas that rule because they are the most powerful in the society, or because they are the operating assumptions of the power structure, without necessarily commanding widespread consent?

If we assume that it is the first of these it is not very difficult to slip into a rather condescending view of the proletariat as being 'subject' to ideology. But suppose we take the second definition. It does not assume that a majority of the population agrees with or accepts every piece of bourgeois ideology. But then the question arises, if such ideas are not accepted how do they rule? To assume that capitalist societies are so transparently responsive to popular belief and opinion is to assume a rather pluralist version of the theory of democracy. (In fact Hall is explicit about this, observing that the advantage of pluralism is that it has a firm grasp of the place of consent in the social order.[36]) But liberal capitalist democracies are founded on consent of an extremely limited and provisional sort.

DEMOCRACY

What does liberal democracy entail? Does it entail the government of the people, for the people and by the people? Or does it entail simply voting once every four or five years? Assuming for a moment that the will of the people in terms of votes cast is respected in Western countries,[37] we can probably agree that the practice of democracy is somewhere between these two poles. There are occasions, albeit rare, when popular pressure forces concessions — from the defeat of the Poll Tax in the UK to the anti-WTO protest in Seattle. But overall the exercise of power in society does not seem to bow easily to public opinion or the popular will — let alone to principles of justice and equality. While the media have a central role to play here, it also seems to be the case that much of the decision-making in society occurs elsewhere, out of sight of the population and sometimes of the media too. It is a task of social activism to illuminate such processes and bring them to wider attention and sometimes that task is successfully accomplished. But we should be aware that class and corporate power occur 'behind our backs' in the sense that we do not know about them, rather than in the sense that we unconsciously consent to them via the mysterious mechanism of ideology. One neat way to sum this up is with Alex Carey's aphorism: '[t]he twentieth century has been characterised by three developments of great political importance: the growth of democracy, the growth of corporate power, and the growth of corporate propaganda as a means of protecting corporate power against democracy.'[38]

Empirically this means widening the focus of media and cultural studies to examine the interaction of the symbolic and the material throughout society and to examine the communicative processes which accompany and make possible the operation of power. This means more than studying the media as texts or as institutions. It means studying their whole range of interactions with the rest of the society. I would highlight two areas where this is especially important. The first of these is the role of corporations, states and activists in pursuing strategies for power and influence and the role that the media do (or do not) play in these. This means examining the intentions of actors and the planning and execution of strategies. Much of this will involve public relations and lobbying consultancies and these need to be a serious object of attention in media and cultural studies (and not just in terms of cultural industries). A second area is the question of the 'success' or failure of strategies. This is a much more complex area, which we might group under the heading of 'reproduction'. It involves questions about the role of the media in informing/influencing public opinion and the variety of questions associated with the notion of the 'active audience'. However, this notion has severe limitations, not least because it has not led on to questions intrinsic to the notion of reproduction, such as the question of outcomes. What happens as a consequence of popular belief or disbelief, or of 'negotiated' or 'oppositional' 'readings' of texts (to use the inadequate language derived via Hall from the pluralist Frank Parkin)? And what difference does this make to class power? We need to discuss these points under the specific heading of power in society, rather than in terms of media power alone.

CORPORATE POWER AND THE MEDIA

It is clear enough that corporations regularly get a good deal from the mainstream media in the UK (and even more so in the US). But, there are occasions on which essentially anti-corporate themes become major running news stories. In the UK, food safety issues such as Salmonella and BSE,[39] and the campaign against 'fat cats' in the mid-1990s, are good examples.[40]

It is not that the coverage has always been progressive, although it sometimes has been, but that the stories' news values entail a concern for the 'public' as victims of state or corporate power, greed and arrogance. (It also helps that the corporations in question are not media corporations.) In such circumstances radical and liberal pressure groups can help to make the story run and can get some of their message across. Some recent writers describe this observation as a 'pluralist point', to which I would say the following: definitional power is not identical to political and economic power. It is important that we look beyond the front pages of the tabloids and the nightly news headlines to the issue of what happens as a result. In the examples of food safety, there can be little doubt, given the evidence of slump in the market for eggs, cheese and beef, that the radical view was widely shared by the public. Further evidence comes in the form of opinion poll and focus group research carried out by government and academic researchers,[41] but the key question then is what happens as a result of this.

For a long time at the level of government, nothing beyond cosmetic changes occurred. Indeed after the 1988 salmonella scare in the UK public health interests were marginalized in policy-making, thus contributing to the appalling treatment of the issue of BSE.[42]

Then under the Conservatives came an admission that BSE-infected meat was the 'most likely' cause of human deaths from CJD. Under New Labour this was followed by the BSE inquiry, and a Food Standards Agency — one of the key demands of the food activists from the late 1980s — was established. Both of these developments were 'nobbled' — the BSE inquiry by official spin, the Food Safety Agency by its limited powers and the fact that its head was a natural scientist unsympathetic to the critique of science and its increasingly close relationship with corporate power and money. There were no moves to reverse the deregulation which was at the root of the problems and very little 'political demand' (i.e. demand in policy circles as opposed to amongst the public) for change. So in terms of outcomes, even if we regard the media as having been on the side of the angels in this case — which would be a massive distortion — this does not lead us in a pluralist direction. The media may sometimes be the only ally that democrats and socialists have, given the foreshortened avenues for democratic change in current conditions, but they are not necessarily a powerful ally.

In what has been described as the information age, it is obvious that capitalism as a system, and corporations as institutions, require large amounts of information to function. Indeed the development of information technology has been an essential requirement for capital to increase its own mobility in the past couple of decades.[43] Corporations need market data, data on their customers and potential customers, information on political movements and regulatory regimes. Some of this information comes from the media. But they also need to communicate to function. They need to debate internally and amongst their competitors in the same or differing industries. And they need to discuss issues with politicians and decision-makers. Much of this information and communication is private, confidential or secret. Some is public in a very limited sense and some is public and on view in the mainstream media, although it is often tucked away on the margins of the business pages. In the following section I outline four ways in which corporate and class power operate beyond the reach of the popular will.

CORPORATE AND CLASS POWER BEYOND THE MEDIA

1. Lobbying

In recent years the power of the legislature has declined while lobbying and other covert means of influencing policy have massively expanded — from the hard money/soft money debate in the US to the 'cash for questions' and other lobbying scandals in the UK.[44] Although there is some measure of transparency in terms of the regulation of lobbying in the US, lobbying itself is an almost completely covert business. It trades influence for cash and generally does not attempt to influence public opinion. In its day-to-day activities it is beyond the reach of public debate. It is an organized conspiracy against democracy in the sense that private interests try to influence legislation and decision-making directly, rather than democratically or by means of debate. The role of the media here is negligible, with one exception. That is when lobbying misdeeds are exposed in the media. This does not happen nearly regularly enough, but the role of the media is sometimes to undermine this or that piece of corporate self-interest. Except in such cases, much decision-making in both the US and UK goes on in secret away from the prying eyes of the media and with precious little popular involvement. This is not an insignificant point given the very large sums of money and resources that the rich have managed to expropriate from the poor (especially in the US and UK) in the last couple of decades, through redistributive tax, cutting social spending and privatizing public assets.

Two examples might be worthwhile. The corporate campaign to open up China to global capital required that the US Congress pass the China Trade Bill. According to Public Citizen's Global Trade Watch at least $113.1 million was spent lobbying on this bill alone.[45]

Yet this is not part of the agenda of mainstream news or of widespread public debate. In this example power is exercised away from the media rather than by the media. Secondly, let us take the example of the negotiations over the Free Trade Area of the Americas (FTAA), a major and audacious attempt to abolish the minimal democratic controls that still exist over the abuses of big money throughout North and South America. There is very little discussion of this in the mainstream media and the public are kept in almost total ignorance.[46]

To be sure, a lot more people may have heard of it after the protests against it in Quebec in April 2001, but one indication of where power resides is that the text of the agreement was kept secret by the state and corporate personnel nego-tiating it. 'Consumers' are almost completely ignorant of all such debates. This does not suggest that they are dupes of the system or that they have been ideo-logically spoken — it is just that they don't know.

As the system of global 'governance' emerges the global public becomes more and more disenfranchised and powerless, denied basic information with which to make up its mind. The trend toward global 'governance' has been boosted by the progressive dilution of democratic controls on capital as corporations have increasingly sought to buy their way into the political process. There has been a flurry of books across the Anglophone world with very similar titles on this 'corporate takeover' and on the 'sleaze' and 'scandals' which go with it.[47] These developments suggest a weakening of democratic controls. Do they also suggest that the role of the media as some form of check or balance within the system is becoming less important? On the contrary, media agendas are increasingly being set by corporate priorities to maximize profits.[48]

2. Private debates in public

There is also a sense in which much of what appears in even mainstream news-papers is not really for the bulk of the audience who consume the news. Private debates among the powerful can surface in the media as part of a struggle within the state apparatus or corporations, such as the struggle between the Special Branch of the Metropolitan police and the intelligence agency MI5 over anti-terrorist operations in Britain,[49] or the 'dirty tricks' battle between British Airways and Virgin Atlantic,[50] or a thousand other pieces of intrigue and power struggle. We can sometimes listen in if we are able to read between the lines, but there are few ways in which we can be part of the conversation.

3. Withstanding hostile coverage

The question is not 'is there definitional advantage?', but 'what difference does definitional disadvantage make?' When does it matter if the media are hostile? The issue of 'sleaze' in the UK did mean the end of ministerial careers and to some extent the unpopularity of the Tories and there was a field day on 'fat cats', as the bosses of the privatized utilities were dubbed. But this did not necessarily cause much angst in the business world — or at least it did not significantly mate-rially alter board room pay rates which continued to rise, nor (beyond some populist rhetoric) did it result in any significant move by the Labour Government against boardroom pay rises or corporate power. Media coverage hostile to corporate interests often has little impact.

4. Ignoring public opinion, opposition and protest

There is a further stage beyond hostile coverage, which is the question of public opinion and action. Corporate and state decision-makers are able to ignore popular opinion and protest even when there is widespread support for or against a particular decision. Popular protest too can be resisted. In the UK the protests against the Poll Tax were ignored for a long time and it was only when the tax threatened to split the Conservative Party that it was removed. Throughout the counterinsurgency campaign in Northern Ireland virtually every opinion poll showed that the public was in favour of British military disengagement, yet no mainstream party ever attempted to carry through the will of the people on this issue.[51] In the UK and the US large sections of the population oppose corporate pollution and approve of public funding for everything from power and transport to health and education, yet governments in both states move further towards the market in their social and economic policy. The protests in Seattle 'shut down' the WTO talks, but they didn't stop the organization functioning and there is little sign of it fundamentally changing its course.

CONCLUSION

All this is only to say that change is hard to achieve. It has to be struggled for in language and in action. Changing the word is not changing the world. But this essay has also tried to draw attention to the fact that capitalism reproduces itself by means not just of ideology, but by a myriad of social processes in which ideology is ever-present, but only as part of a wider struggle for power and resources.

So what is the role of the media in the reproduction of class power? The media do have a role in promoting dominant ideologies and in spreading them variably amongst sections of the population. The media can on occasion help to convince elements of the public of states of affairs and evaluations of them which are thoroughly ideological, even where this is not in their own interests. But the media also have a direct role which is arguably as important for the reproduction of inequality as ideological power over the masses. Furthermore, there is a variety of mechanisms and practices in society, by which power is exercised and resources distributed, in which the media have a minimal role. Lobbying is an obvious example. Of course ideology and communication are ever attendant on such processes.

Consent is not simply an ideological process, but interacts with material and ideal interests, even though ideology can affect the perception of interests. Consent, as in post-1945 Britain for instance, was gained not only by ideology but by real compromises such as the nationalization of key industries and the creation of the welfare state. Dependence on ideology as a privileged explanatory principle severs the connection between interests and ideas and neglects the importance of material interests in conditioning and creating ideas.

Secrecy, censorship and information management are all daily conspiracies against democracy. The way in which questions are ruled in and out are not mysterious processes but eminently researchable. Such research must not only examine media ownership, institutions and ideology, as much valuable work has, but also the real activities and strategies of corporations and states which are incessantly being planned and deployed. I am speaking of course of the promotional and information management activities of governments and corporations and of their secretive and covert lobbying and espionage activities. These are not distracting epiphenomena the state and capital could do without, but some of the key ways in which our system works.

Some people under some circumstances believe some things that are against their own interests and in the interests of the powerful. But the working classes do not believe every bit of bourgeois propaganda. Nor is it necessary for them to do so for capitalism to survive — or more accurately, if we take the current historical epoch, to go from strength to strength. There is no straightforward and automatic relationship between ideology and public consciousness. Ideology has been overplayed as an explanation of the reproduction of class and other divisions. 'Ruling ideas' rule by a variety of mechanisms. These include media propaganda and the systematic distortions of ideology which do successfully fool some of the people some of the time, but not all of us all of the time.

NOTES

Thanks to Barbara Epstein and Steve Marriott.

1   Donna Demac, *Keeping America Uninformed: Government Secrecy in the 1980s*, New York: W. W. Norton, 1984.
2   Stuart Hall, 'Media power and class power', in J. Curran *et al.*, eds., *Bending Reality: The State of the Media*, London: Pluto, 1986, p. 9. Note the Foucauldian language which Hall had adopted by the mid-1980s.
3   Hall, 'Media Power', p.12
4   Ibid.
5   Stuart Hall, 'Culture, the media and the ideological effect', in J. Curran, M. Gurevitch and J. Woollacott, eds., *Mass Communication and Society*, London: Edward Arnold, 1977, p. 333.
6   Note how this severely tests the 'last instance' part of the formulation and threatens to let the cultural float free of all determination. For a critique of this position see Dan Schiller, *Theorizing Communication: A History*, New York: Oxford University Press, 1996.
7   See Louis Althusser, *For Marx*, London: Allen Lane, 1969, and *Lenin and Philosophy and other essays*, London: New Left Books, 1971.
8   Although the phrase was apparently first coined by Engels. See Leszek Kolakowski, 'Althusser's Marx', in R. Miliband, and J. Saville, eds., *The Socialist Register 1971*, London: The Merlin Press, 1971.
9   Hall, 'Culture, the media and the ideological effect', p. 346.
10   See David Miller, 'Dominant Ideologies and Media Power: The Case of Northern Ireland', in M. Kelly and B. O'Connor, eds., *Media Audiences in Ireland*, Dublin: University College Dublin Press,1997.
11   In a caveat Hall notes that language and ideology are not the same thing: '[a]n analytic distinction needed to be maintained'. But it is hard to see much of a gap between the concepts since he goes on to note the close relationship between understanding language and being spoken by ideology:

'one cannot learn a language without learning something of its current ideo-logical inflections' (Stuart Hall, 'The rediscovery of "ideology": return of the repressed in media studies', in M. Gurevitch *et al.*, eds., *Culture, Society and the Media*, London: Methuen, 1983, p. 80). Once again this blurs together learning something, about which we might suspend judgement, with being 'spoken' by ideology.

12   Hall, 'Culture, the media and the ideological effect', p. 344; see also Stuart Hall, 'The "Structured Communication" of Events', Paper for Obstacles to Communication Symposium, UNESCO, *University of Birmingham Centre for Contemporary Cultural Studies Stencilled Occasional Papers*, Birmingham: CCCS, 1973.; Stuart Hall, 'Encoding/decoding', in S. Hall, D. Hobson, A. Lowe and P. Willis, eds., *Culture, Media, Language*, London: Hutchinson, 1980.

13   Hall, 'Rediscovery', p. 74.

14   See for example John Corner, 'Meaning, genre and context: the problem-atics of public knowledge in the new audience studies', in J. Curran and M. Gurevitch, eds., *Mass Media and Society*, London: Edward Arnold, 1991; J. Kitzinger, 'A Sociology of Media Power: key issues in audience research', in G. Philo, ed., *Message Received*, London: Longman, 1999; David Miller, *Don't Mention the War: Northern Ireland, Propaganda and the Media*, London: Pluto, 1994.

15   See Kevin McDonnell and Kevin Robins, 'Marxist Cultural Theory: the Althusserian Smokescreen', in S. Clarke *et al.*, *One-Dimensional Marxism: Althusser and the Politics of Culture*, London: Allison and Busby, 1980, pp. 160-1.

16   Hall 'Rediscovery', p. 88.

17   See http://www.foxgbhsuit.com.

18   Hall, 'Rediscovery', p. 88. This sits nicely with the appropriation of Lacanian psychoanalysis by Althusserians in the 1970s around the journal *Screen*, and later by Hall himself. The Lacanians saw the entry into consciousness as being the entry into ideology, via the mirror phase or the Oedipus complex. As late as 1996 Hall was hailing the importance of the 'suturing of the psychic and the discursive' (Stuart Hall, 'Introduction: Who Needs "Identity"', in S. Hall, and P. du Gay, eds., *Questions of Cultural Identity*, London: Sage, p. 16. For a critique of this position see Greg Philo and David Miller, *Market Killing*, London: Longman, 2001).

19   McDonnell and Robins, 'Marxist Cultural Theory', pp. 167-8.

20   In response to Thompson's *The Poverty of Theory*, Hall went furthest along the road of disavowing certain Althusserian positions, but this seems only to have had a limited effect on the extent to which the Althusserian 'prob-lematic' continued to inform his thinking on ideology and media power. See Stuart Hall, 'In defence of theory', in Raphael Samuel, ed., *People's History and Socialist Theory*, London: Routledge and Kegan Paul, 1980.

21   Hall, 'Rediscovery', p. 78.

22   Ibid.

23   Stuart Hall, 'Ideology and Communication Theory', in B. Dervin, L. Grossberg, B. O'Keefe, and E. Wartella, eds., *Rethinking Communication: Vol I Paradigm Issues*, Thousand Oaks, CA: Sage 1989, p. 51.

24   Ambalavaner Sivanandan, *Communities of Resistance: Writings on Black Struggles for Socialism*, London: Verso, 1990, p. 49.

25   For critiques, see Terry Eagleton, *The Illusions of postmodernism*, Oxford: Blackwell, 1996; and Greg Philo and David Miller *Market Killing*, London: Longman, 2001.

26   Although it should be acknowledged that Hall and his colleagues had produced a pioneering account of such questions in *Policing the Crisis* (London: Macmillan, 1978). In addition Hall did produce a wide range of political writings on Thatcherism, collected in his books, edited with Martin Jacques, *The Politics of Thatcherism* (London: Lawrence and Wishart in association with *Marxism Today,* 1983) and *New Times*, (London: Lawrence and Wishart, 1989). Unlike *Policing the Crisis*, however, these writings were not based on original empirical research, and much of the political analysis derived from the theoretical agenda being described here. This work encouraged the left to abandon much of its radical platform and embrace a kind of left mirror image of Thatcherism in order to build a new counter-hegemony. For critiques see David Harris, *From Class Struggle to the Politics of Pleasure*, London: Routledge, 1992; M. Rustin, 'The Politics of Post-Fordism and the Trouble with "New Times"', *New Left Review*, 175, 1989. This trajectory also fitted well with those tendencies which resulted in the virtual disappearance of the concept of class across academia. See Graham Murdock, 'Reconstructing the ruined tower: Contemporary Communications and Questions of Class', in M. Gurevitch and J. Curran, eds., *Mass Media and Society*, 3rd Ed. London: Edward Arnold, 2000.

27   Karl Marx, 'A Contribution to the Critique of Political Economy', in *Early Writings*, Harmondsworth: Pelican, 1975, p. 425.

28   D. Miller and W. Dinan, 'The rise of the PR industry in Britain 1979-1998', *European Journal of Communication*, 15(1), January 2000; J. Stauber and S. Rampton, *Toxic Sludge is Good for You: Lies, Damn Lies and the Public Relations Industry*, Monroe, Maine: Common Courage, 1995.

29   Raymond Williams, *Towards 2000*, London: Penguin, 1985, p. 268.

30   Terry Eagleton, *Ideology: An Introduction*, London: Verso, 1991, p. 82.

31   Raymond Williams, *Problems in Materialism and Culture*, London: Verso, 1980.

32   D. Walsh and S. Finz, 'Bay Area gloaters see upside in dot-com downturn', *San Francisco Chronicle*, Sunday 13 May 2001, pp. A1+A17.

33   Francis Wheen, *Karl Marx: a life*, London and New York: W. W. Norton, 2000.

34   Karl Marx, and Friedrich Engels, *The German Ideology*, New York: International Publishers, 1947, p. 39. The example that Marx gives of the

doctrine of the separation of powers as the dominant idea which is expressed as an 'eternal law' is also compatible with this interpretation. This is what is expressed in the 'dominant' ideology, but in order to rule it may not be necessary for it to be shared by the vast bulk of the population. This is particularly the case if we hold a weak model of hegemony where dominance need only be secured by the absence of effective opposition. See Ralph Miliband, 'Counter-hegemonic struggles', in *The Socialist Register 1990*, London: The Merlin Press.

35 To be fair it is not only 'Marxists' influenced by Althusser who have endorsed this interpretation.

36 Hall, 'Rediscovery', p.85

37 Which is somewhat adrift from practice, as the US election of George W. Bush in 2000 showed.

38 Alex Carey, *Taking the Risk out of Democracy: Corporate Propaganda versus Freedom and Liberty*, Sydney: University of New South Wales Press, 1995, p. 18.

39 David Miller, 'Risk, Science and Policy: BSE, definitional struggles, information management and the media', *Social Science and Medicine* special edition 'Science speaks to policy', Vol. 49, 1999; David Miller and Jacquie Reilly, 'Making an Issue of Food Safety: The media, pressure groups and the public sphere', in Donna Maurer and Jeffrey Sobal, eds., *Eating Agendas: Food, Eating and Nutrition as Social Problems*, New York: Aldine De Gruyter, 1995.

40 Lewis Bastion, *Sleaze: the State of Britain*, London: Channel Four Books, 2000; Ed Vulliamy and David Leigh, *Sleaze*, London: Fourth Estate, 1997.

41 Sally Macintyre, Jacquie Reilly, David Miller and John Eldridge, 'Food Choice, Food Scares and Health: The Role of the Media', in Murcott A., ed., *The Nation's Diet*, London: Addison Wesley Longman, 1998.

42 See Miller, 'Risk'.

43 See the various contributions in R. Babe, ed., *Information and Communication in Economics*, Boston, Dordrecht, London: Kluwer Academic Publishers, 1994.

44 Elizabeth Drew, *The Corruption of American Politics: What went wrong and why*, Woodstock, NY: Overlook Press, 2000; Mark Hollingsworth, *MPs for Hire: The secret world of political lobbying*, London: Bloomsbury, 1991; Charles Lewis and the Center for Public Integrity, *The Buying of Congress: How special interests have stolen your right to life, liberty and the pursuit of happiness*, New York: Avon Books, 1998.

45 P. Woodall, L. Wallach, J. Roach, and K. Burnham, *Purchasing Power: The Corporate-White House alliance to pass the China Trade Bill over the will of the American people*, Washington, DC: Public Citizen's Global Trade Watch.

46 See http://www.ifg.org.

47 C. Derber, *Corporation Nation: How corporations are taking over our lives and what we can do about it*, New York: St Martins Press, 1998; James Lull, and

Stephen Hinerman, eds., *Media Scandals*, London: Polity, 1997; George Monbiot, *Captive State: The Corporate Takeover of Britain*, London: Macmillan, 2000; Rod Tiffen, *Scandals: Media, Politics and Corruption in Contemporary Australia*, Sydney: University of New South Wales Press, 1999; John B. Thompson, *Political Scandals*, Cambridge: Polity, 2000.

48   Robert McChesney, *Rich Media, Poor Democracy*, rev. ed., New York: The New Press, 2000; D. Underwood, *When MBA's rule the newsroom*, New York: Columbia University Press, 1995.

49   See Miller, 'Primary Definition'.

50   Martin Gregory, *Dirty Tricks: British Airways' secret war against Virgin Atlantic*, rev. ed. London: Warner Books, 1996.

51   See Miller, *Don't Mention the War*.

NEGOTIATED CONTRADICTIONS

Pablo González Casanova

One of the great achievements of Marxist thinking lies in identifying the class struggle as the principal contradiction of the capitalist system, which the dominant forces who benefit from it are the first to want to hide. It was not the mere existence of class struggle, which was hardly new to capitalism, but rather the nature of the class struggle within capitalism, its potential to not only be its 'grave digger', but the midwife of a classless social order, that Marx insisted was significant.[1] But the significance of class struggle for Marx was not, in fact, limited to its transformative potential alone. Indeed, when Marx identified as contradictions the imbalances, incoherencies and inconsistencies between means and mediations in the capitalist system, he identified them in terms of their being expressed in and through class struggles — including struggles that took place within, as well as between, classes. Contradictions seem more humane when they are considered as struggles, since when they are only seen as imbalances, incoherencies or inconsistencies, they almost always evoke natural or technical determinations. Protagonists, and social actors generally, stand out more clearly in the perspective of struggles, whereas to speak of contradictions without this is to suggest reified forces, whether expressed as currents and flows, or as factors and variables. But it is also very important to be able to distinguish between those struggles/contradictions that are system transforming and those that are not. Especially given the proven capacity of capitalism, from Marx's time to ours, to reproduce itself with a greater degree of viability than is recognized by any voluntarist or determinist theory of change, we need to retain the notion of contradiction to understand, not only the crises, but also the dynamics of capitalist reproduction and extension (including through crises), and the way these are expressed in class struggles that do not necessarily entail the end of the system, much less its desirable transition into a classless society, as a probable or imminent event.[2]

Among the flaws that traditionally beset a good deal of Marxist thinking was an idealization of the workers without taking into consideration that historically, politically and ethically, the workers are a class not only in permanent conflict but also in permanent negotiation with those who pay them wages, and that within that permanent conflict and negotiation, their awareness, their organization, their morality and their politics are often such as to be unable to take them beyond the system. Within this system, the most powerful negotiators, who are the entrepreneurs, are going to do everything they can to weaken the negotiating power of the workers. They are also going to seek or construct social spaces, organizations and technologies in which the owners are stronger and the workers are weaker. This means that in the capitalist system the workers are negotiators, and that the dominant forces in the system make them negotiate from a position of weakness, or remove them from the market and only let them in if they accept the conditions set by them for the negotiation. This reaches the extreme, during times of crisis, of excluding many workers who want to be employed even under the worst of conditions. In order to increase their negotiating and accumulative powers, the employers use migrant workers and home-workers as well as calling on the national and global 'reserve army' of those previously excluded from the labour market.[3]

Within much 'critical thought' in general, the idealization of the workers, or at least the people, as a liberating category, takes them out of their condition as negotiators. The idealistic preconception of workers sees them only as liberating victims, and does not consider, much less say, that within capitalism they are also negotiators; they are also the merchants of their own labour power. This idealization seriously affects our ability to know what needs to be done in terms of constructing a world that is less unjust, because it does not see that exploitation and liberation necessarily involve negotiation. One of the main problems regarding the contradictions of capitalism lies in understanding that the exploited and oppressed, even in their rebelliousness, may still be negotiating their status as the merchants of their labour power. This is a restricted form of *negotiated contradiction* quite different from that of daring to say no to the current terms of negotiation and trying to impose new terms of negotiations in which workers can secure sufficient autonomy to realize their potential to usher in a new classless society.

The history of capitalism, and the history of the struggle for socialism, involves, in other words, not just a history of class conflict and repression, but a history of *negotiated contradictions*. The strength from which classes negotiate, and the terms of what is negotiable and what is not negotiable (over which there is also necessarily a struggle between class factions amongst themselves), determines the variation of outcomes. Both the negotiated contradictions between class enemies and those arising within each class alter the history of class structuring and the nature of conflict and accommodation within and between classes. The structures, or internal and external relationships, of classical capitalism are not the same as those of today's neoliberal globalization. But while this fact is obvious, what is less obvious is that the ability to predict and explain the changes in question continues to be very poor when the 'workers' are treated as mere victims or idealized as inherently revolutionary, rather than as negotiators who have been embroiled in the class contradictions that generate change within capitalism.

Within the capitalist system, negotiation tends to encompass everything and everyone. Although negotiations were already present in the precapitalist world, they did not enjoy the prestige they do now: 'I am a gentleman, I do not negotiate', said a Mexican entrepreneur of late feudalism in a semi-colonial country that was yet to undertake its national bourgeois revolution. Neither was negotiation valued in those societies that saw repression alone as the surest way to preserve slavery and servitude. But, since the onset of classical capitalism, the masters and entrepreneurs, as the merchants who purchase a labour force, have been studying how to improve their own strength through negotiation. They seek the best prices here and now, or go to other parts of the country or the world, or build politico-military-cultural-technological systems that favour them in the areas in which they live or the places they haunt.

Since the emergence of capitalism, the purchaser of labour has found that he can negotiate the price of labour with the worker who is selling it. Day in and day out, he experiences in his factory the same thing other proprietors experience in theirs. From the generalization and common usage they make from this, he and his kind deduce policies of domination that strengthen them in the face of those peddling their labour. They promote an increase of their own strengths and the weakening of the workers'. They apply the old policy of 'divide and conquer' to those selling labour. Between violence and negotiation, they make repeated concessions to some workers or groups of workers of various types.

Since the middle of the nineteenth century, concessions have created new social blocs within the working class. These were given new impetus by Bismarck in Germany — the first 'state socialism' led by the bourgeoisie — and became generalized in Europe by the end of the nineteenth century. This redefined the working class and the socialist forces. Bernstein, and reformism generally, expressly manifested this change, virtually confirming that the working classes' primary mode of action is negotiation. The problem immediately revealed was that working class negotiations contained intrinsic contradictions, and these could be seen even at those moments when the class appeared combative, defiant and even fearless, as well as when it was willing to make sacrifices. Even so, it was already also clear that socialist and revolutionary expressions of the working class would not necessarily be predominant in history, as opposed to the reformist and even opportunist ones Rosa Luxemburg confronted in the Second International.

But the really great negotiations between workers and proprietors in the twentieth century began with the Bresk Litovsk Treaty, and lasted until the end of the Cold War. Negotiated concessions reached their highest expression with the Keynesian welfare state as a response to the possible spread of communism amidst the crisis of the thirties and the war, and the threat to the dominant classes this constituted. They were forced to diminish the danger through collective negotiations and concessions that many workers accepted. At the same time, the outcomes of these negotiations increasingly opened up new contradictions within the working class itself, including restructuring the internal contradictions within the 'labour aristocracy' and establishing a sizeable group of organized workers with standards of living more or less equal to those of the middle class, and much above those of unorganized or marginalized workers.

On an international level, the policy of differentiation through negotiation was also used in the development of colonialism and technological development. The meaning of *uneven development*, for the underdeveloped regions and their workers, salaried or not, was manifested in the colonialism that partly began with the movement of dominated ethnic groups within the European nations themselves, and then implicated the peoples of Africa, Asia, Latin America and the Caribbean. Colonialism showed the clearest facets of violence as terror, but also of negotiation as corruption. (It would, however, be difficult to affirm that terror as repression, and negotiation as corruption, had any less dramatic features within North America and Europe, as evidenced by the genocide of the native nations, by the locus of fascism and Nazism, and even by the more contemporary organized gangsterism in the United States and Russia.) In any case, the main point is that in both the internal and international history of colonialism we find phenomena of negotiation, and not only repression. Negotiation with the colonies took on the nature of a new worldwide policy with the independence movements of the new states in the Americas during the eighteenth and nineteenth centuries, and the buying-selling and concessionary aspects became even more pronounced with the decolonization policy of the postwar period in the twentieth century. It was in this context, in which the 'developmental' model arose, that capitalism was sometimes forced to negotiate with, and even show some respect for the policies of, revolutionary nationalism, as part and parcel of the cooption of the forces that advanced it. The differentiation and disarticulation of the workers' forces through negotiation as well as repression thus includes the history of workers in the colonialist countries (and their social democratic movements) *and* those of the workers of the colonized nations (and their revolutionary nationalist and 'socialist oriented' movements).

Negotiated contradictions also are involved in the differentiation among workers brought about by technological development. The appearance of white collar or office workers, and the no less important growing distinction between qualified and unqualified workers, and between those achieving specialized knowledge and highly valued 'symbolic' labour as compared to those with medium or low levels of specialization — all this aggravated the old differentiation between organized and unorganized, metropolitan and peripheral workers. Multiform differentiations altered and restructured the terms of class struggle in its aspects of repression and negotiation. Stratification in terms of direct and indirect income and horizontal and vertical social mobility both functioned as escape valves for the system and as the basis for new forms of mediation and influence, distribution and participation, marginalization and exclusion. The redefinitions of the exploiter and exploited classes did not only come about through confrontation, but also through negotiation. The logic of confrontation is insufficient to explain the contradictions of modern capitalism and of the complex, adaptive and self-regulated system to which it has today given rise in the form of neoliberal globalization; nor can it explain the way in which the military-industrial complex of the Group of Seven under the shared hegemony of the United States, which dominates the world, thinks and acts.

Negotiated contradictions are also the basis for understanding the foundation of the capitalist mega-organizations of our time and the role they have played in the construction of contexts that contributed to transforming 'closed' systems into 'open' systems,[4] which thereby try to prolong their existence by drawing on the strength and energy of global capital. This reduces or nullifies the entropic tendencies of the capitalist system, at least for a future period that is difficult to estimate, and which can be understood not so much by means of projections or extrapolations, as by means of uncertainty theory, open to the possible construction of ever new adaptive organizations and complexes.[5]

The new systems theory, which accepts the challenge of being a paradigm or scientific theory based on dominant power, has among its antecedents Hobbes' rich concept of the contradictions of paradise lost, as well as William James' notion of pragmatic adaptability to achieve goals, which Piaget took to a higher level as one of the main precursors of constructivism. The new theory comes from the so-called 'new sciences' or 'techno-sciences', in which a great scientific revolution was brought about based on cybernetics and mathematical modeling, communications sciences and the science of organization, bringing an end to the paradigm dominant since Newton, Bacon and Descartes.[6] The new sciences developed after World War II included within their revolution the dynamic systems of a historical cosmology,[7] but the irreversible changes in physics this brought about was nothing in comparison to the techno-scientific advances in the construction of adaptive and complex self-regulated systems. These are able to achieve their goals under conditions of uncertainty and able to stop the natural tendency of systems to age, weaken and become extinct, as they would if they remained closed systems, thanks to entropy.[8]

Science and technology have been systematically combined in order to develop a negentropic[9] mega-policy for the capitalist system, allowing it to create subsystems in which the conditions of domination and negotiation are improved. Biological struggles may be taken as metaphors. AIDS, a parasite in the cells defending the organisms it wishes to attack and dominate and at whose expense it lives and develops, mimics the mechanisms for the natural protection of the invaded organisms and undermines the categories available to science for making it possible to identify it. In the same way we may say that through techno-science the dominant forces renew their skill in remaining undetected by terms such as 'imperialism' or 'capitalism', thereby forcing those who used such terms to abandon their icons, symbols and moralities, their organizations and their policies — and even making them recant their philosophies and their pedagogical or scientific ideals, such as occurs today with Marxism–Leninism, revolutionary nationalism, and radical democracy, all amid direct and subliminal pressures stimulating the use of 'politically correct' language.

Just as biology discovers that there are aerobic animals that, under adverse conditions, become anaerobic, the new science of business discovers how to transform managers into politicians who are looking for 'partners', soldiers into terrorists who perform charitable acts, and bankers into apostles who 'seek to re-establish the kingdom of God on earth' (in the words of Camdessus before his Holiness the Pope). Just as the new physics replaces the old determinism of mechanical systems, or the probabilistic determinism of quantum physics, with an analysis of multiple possible paths, so the new forms of capitalist repression-negotiation use these metaphors to design alternative scenarios. They try to follow those most functional for their ends, and to establish policies for dialogue and negotiation, as well as repression and stimuli, in which the workers appear to freely decide what the bosses want them to decide. This is a system of 'human' performance that is studied in depth by the philosophy of 'rational choice', where what is rational is to think and do what the dominant forces want one to choose, think and do. 'Technical progress', wrote Marcuse, 'occurs as political progress in domination; thus it is progress in the suppression of the alternatives'.[10]

The implication of thinking about negotiated contradictions in this context is that it helps us appreciate that the old determinist concepts prevalent in many pages of Marxism are useless for understanding the neoliberal globalization of capitalism, its origins and meaning. Today's negotiated class struggle, breaking with previous negotiations and pacts, involves the construction of subsystems for a worldwide negotiation in which the positions of the dominant corporate capital and the military industrial complexes that lead it are enhanced, and in which those of workers, nations, peoples and most citizens are further weakened. These and other features of neoliberal globalization are not only incomprehensible, but also unpredictable and invulnerable if one is unaware of how they have been restructured and have, in turn, restructured the world thanks to their strengthening through the techno-sciences. Not only the ideological, but the technological nature of the 'new sciences' ensures the maximization of utilities, the accumulation of property and the increase in the power of corporate capital and its 'partners', be they large or small.

After the defeat of social democracy, of revolutionary nationalism and communism, the new neoliberal expansion of capitalism came about under conditions which were far from given. In such circumstances, one cannot think in a linear fashion of the development of the empire, nor of the crisis of the empire, much less of the progressive development of democracy, of the struggle against poverty and extreme poverty, or the struggle for peace. Corporate capital gave up the idea of changing the world. It retains nothing Faustian, humanitarian, or religious, nothing about creating a society in which mankind is the measure of all things. Its civilizing project and its conception of progress are replaced by an ideology of negotiating those 'differences' that will maintain the inequalities and contribute to its increasing domination. It renounces universalizing 'Western values' in favour of respecting differences — as long as they also increase inequities. 'Human rights' are reduced to subsystems in which they are systematically violated, and in which they are defended casuistically.[11]

This predatory and mercantile philosophy invades politics, ethics, society, culture, as much as it can. It demands the privatization of conscience and rationalizes negotiation with moral values. It implements a culture and a policy of *negotiated plunder* of public, social and national property. It organizes the complicity of its 'partners' in the negotiated global pillage. With them, it carries out an exchange of matter and energy in which financial flows and foreign debt are the 'cement of a global power'. Associated armies and police and individuals belonging to the dominant military-industrial complex watch over the proper functioning of the process and use at will violence, bombings and invasions which are justified on 'humanitarian' grounds (and accompanied by the use of radioactive material that include calculated 'miscalculations'). The 'elites' of each country engage in a mockery of democracy with the *democracy of minorities*, which they and their abysmally cynical publicists present as admirable, amid the ailing conformism of citizen abstention, which they welcome. The dominant system controls its politicians by corrupting them, or denounces them if they disobey its orders or when they are no longer useful as mediators and controllers of the people. It implements state terrorism, corruption and drug trafficking, on a scale that goes beyond even the ability of a Chomsky to document fully. It spreads cooption through stimuli mixed with repression, and it combines this with the exclusion of scientists who are humanists, and moralists who would be revolutionaries, as well as delinquents and the poor.[12]

Everything this capitalism touches becomes merchandise, but it constantly generates new contradictions because it increasingly marginalizes more and more of humanity.[13] Those who are marginalized not only include the four-fifths who only receive one-fifth of the income, but also a growing number of people who are dissatisfied and leaning toward the attractions of an alternative of democracy tempered with socialism. But the contradictions converge in unpredictable fashion, non-linearly. If we lived in a closed historical system, the end of capitalism would be nigh, and the alternative 'socialism or barbarism', or at least 'reform or revolution', would remain valid. But we do not live in such a system. The only alternative in the general interest, and that of the survival of humanity, appears to lie in the development of democratic forces capable of uniting while respecting a pluralism of ideas, and able to gain strength through organizations structured for struggle. This struggle will still involve negotiation, but of a kind in which militants would lose the fear of conflict, learn how to bring about and articulate unity without erasing diversity, and develop negotiating strategies that will cumulatively strengthen the position of the working classes. This will involve, above all, making market values secondary to the values of citizens and peoples. In this sense, even those still employing a historical materialist theory, must recall, dialectically, that the highest expression of the material lies in ethical ideas, and that the incorporation of these into organizations of the exploited and oppressed is the necessary and historical creative link between ideal and material impulses.

The history of the class struggle is the history of both class repressions and negotiations. In capitalism, even struggle is negotiated, and, if the workers, the citizens and the peoples think like merchants who buy labour power, they *will morally or materially lose a struggle in which the casualties are not only physical*. It is not a matter of individual ethics, nor even of the ethics of a group, but of classes, citizens and peoples rebelling, negotiating and making a new politics in which negotiated conflict forces new concessions. In this struggle, revolutionaries will have to be more than 'good generals and bad economists'. They cannot be good generals if they are bad negotiators; and they cannot be good economists for the workers, citizens and peoples if they negotiate for their own — or their own specific groups' — profit and against the general interest (which unfortunately remains merely a 'catchphrase' even among progressive forces today). 'Man is the only little animal that will die for a symbol', said a great Caribbean leader, but that symbol must more than ever today truly represent the prediction-construction of a democratic, socialist and liberating future.

The road to the future forks into three main paths. One leads to the exhaustion of options, an entropy delayed only by techno-scientific 'fixes'. Another leads to the Mode of Production of Androids, or the World Animal Farm. But there is a third one which leads, through a negotiated liberation, to 'islands of growing negentropy'.[14] It takes us in the direction of universal democracy, constituted in terms of a true pluralism of power, a truly representative and participatory democracy. This would be the only kind of democracy capable of achieving the predominance of a socialist mode of production in which budgets for the use of the surplus will be decided by democratic discussion and determination by the workers, the citizens and the peoples.[15]

Awareness of the importance of negotiations among contradictions, and of the contradictions in the negotiations, is a necessary starting point for the prediction-construction of another form of negotiation in a future social order that is classless, democratic and socialist. This is the challenge which critical techno-scientific thought and critical postmodern thought, as well as Marxism, must face today.

NOTES

1   Karl Marx, 'Letter to J. Wedermeyer', (March 5, 1952) in Marx and Engels, *Selected Works*, Volume One, Moscow: Progress Publishers, 1969, p. 528.

2   István Mészáros, *L'alternativa alla societa del capitale. Dal 'secolo americano' al bivio socialismo o barbarie*, Milano: Punto Rosso, 2000.

3   Samir Amin and Pablo González Casanova, eds., *Mondialisation et Accumulation*, Paris: L'Harmattan, 1993. See also Pablo González Casanova and John Saxe Fernández, eds., *The World Today*, in *Social Justice*, Vol. 23 (Spring/Summer), 1996.

4   Norbert Wiener, *The Human Use of Human Beings. Cybernetics and Society*, Cambridge, Mass.: Houghton, 1950.

5   Uri Merry, *Coping with Uncertainty. Insights from the New Sciences of Chaos, Self-Organization, and Complexity*, Westport: Praeger, 1995.

6   Jean Piaget, ed., *Logique de la connaissance scientifique. Encyclopédie de la Pléiade*, Vol. XXII, Paris: Gallimard, 1967; Immanuel Wallerstein, *Unthinking Social Science: The Limits of XIXth Century Paradigms*, New York: The New Press, 1991; Pablo González Casanova, 'Restructuring the Social Sciences: Toward a New Paradigm', in Roberto Briseño and Heinz R. Sonntag, eds., *Social Knowledge: Heritage, Challenges, Perspectives*, Sociology in Latin America, 1998, chapter 11. See also Göran Therborn ed., *Globalizations and Modernities. Experiences and Perspectives of Europe and Latin America*, Uppsala: Suecia, 1999, pp. 52-72.

7   Illya Prigogine and Isabelle Stengers, *La Nouvelle Alliance. Métamorphose de la Science*, Paris: Gallimard, 1986; Illya Prigogine, G. Nicolis and A. Babloyantz, 'Thermodynamics of Evolutions', *Physics Today*, 25 (11), 25 (12), 1972; Illya Prigogine, *Etude Thermodynamique des phénomenes irréversibles*, Liege: Desoer, 1947.

8   Raymond A. Eve *et al.*, eds., *Chaos, Complexity and Sociology. Myths, Models and Theories*, Thousand Oaks: Sage, 1997.

9   Negentropic processes are associated with greater organization, information and complexity. They reduce a positive measure of disorder called 'entropy' through 'self regulated systems'. Vid, Wiener, *The Human Use of Human Beings*, See also: Daniel F. Brooks and E. O. Wiley, *Evolution as Entropy Toward a Unified Theory of Biology*, Chicago: the University of Chicago Press, 1988.

10   Herbert Marcuse, 'Socialist Humanism' in Erich Fromm, ed., *Socialist Humanism*, New York: Garden City, 1965.

11   Ralph Miliband, *Socialism for a Sceptical Age*, Cambridge: Polity Press, 1994.

12   Noam Chomsky, *Deterring Democracy*, New York: Hill and Wang, 1992. See also Noam Chomsky, *Year 501: The Conquest Continues*, Boston: South End Press, 1993.

13   Michel Chossudovsky, *The Globalization of Poverty*, Penang: Third World Network, 1997; Pablo González Casanova, 'La Explotación Global', in M. Monereo and Pedro Chávez, eds., *Diversidad y Desigualdad*, Madrid: El Viejo Topo, 2000.

14   Cf. Wiener, *The Human Use of Human Beings*, p. 25.

15   Pablo González Casanova. 'The Third World and the Socialist Project Today' in William K. Tabb, ed., *The Future of Socialism. Perspectives From the Left*, New York: Monthly Review, 1990. See also Pablo González Casanova, 'Theory of the Rain Forest Against Neoliberalism and for Humanity', *Thesis Eleven*, 53, May 1998.

CONTRADICTION: ONLY IN CAPITALISM?

ELLEN MEIKSINS WOOD

For many years, one of my most prized possessions was a Chinese pamphlet (in English translation, of course) called *Serving the People with Dialectics*, which I acquired in London's Chinatown some time in the 1970s. Its purpose was to give practical advice, based on the maxims of Mao, to ordinary people, from farmers to mailmen, about problems they might encounter in their daily work. I have to confess that I never treated this historic document with the seriousness it deserved. My favourite bit was a chapter with the sublime title, 'Solving the Principal Contradiction of Onions'.

Still, this pamphlet was at least intended to mobilize the concept of contradiction to useful ends, and, if nothing else, it had the virtue of being intelligible. At about the same time, that concept was undergoing more tortuous elaborations at the hands of some prominent Western Marxist intellectuals. In their brand of scholasticism, distinctions such as that between 'principal' or 'dominant' and 'fundamental' contradictions could be the subject of positively Jesuitical disputation.

Against that background, it was not surprising, for instance, that a distinguished Marxist historian, G.E.M. de Ste. Croix, in his magisterial study of class struggle in the ancient Greek world, felt obliged to explain and defend his conception of 'class struggle' by emphatically dissociating it from 'contradiction'. 'The very existence of classes', he wrote,

> in the sense in which (following Marx, as I believe) I have defined that term, inevitably involves tension and conflict between the classes. Marxists often speak of 'contradictions' in this context. As far as I can see, although Marx himself could speak of 'contradictions' between (for example) the relations of production and the forces of production, between the social character of production and private appropriation of its products by a few,

and between private landownership and rational agriculture, it is not at all characteristic of him to describe a situation of what I am calling class struggle as a 'contradiction': this terminology is more often found in Engels and especially in Lenin and Mao Tse-tung. I realise that Mao in particular has made some important contributions to this subject; but I am not myself satisfied with any discussion I have seen in English of the concept of 'contradiction' in a Marxist context, and I feel reluctant to employ the term in a peculiar sense which has not yet established itself in the English language and become accepted into normal usage, as it doubtless has in French, for instance. I therefore prefer to speak of class 'struggles', 'conflicts', 'antagonisms', 'oppositions' or 'tensions', arising as (in a sense) the *result* of 'contradictions'.[1]

I have to admit to a certain sympathy with Ste. Croix's approach to contradiction. In fact, it is tempting to go even further. The use of the concept by Marxists (with some notable exceptions, of course) has tended to oscillate between the absurd and the trivial, between pretentious and empty theoretical verbiage and ritual cliché, vague enough to cover almost anything we Marxists happen not to like. That would be reason enough to be nervous about using it, not only in relation to class struggle but altogether, and I have more than once been accused of ignoring 'contradiction' or at least of avoiding the word when clearly alluding to something that other Marxists would call a contradiction. Still, I have used the word, probably far too often, and my usage has been as vacuous as anyone else's. So, when asked to provide this theoretical overview, I agreed with some hesitation.

And yet, there is something in Ste. Croix's observations that demands closer scrutiny, which may help to salvage the concept of contradiction by identifying a specific meaning with a real explanatory value, capable of shedding light on our contemporary realities. The concept, as a key to social explanation, may in fact have more meaning today that at any other time in history.

MARX ON CONTRADICTION

Consider, first, Ste. Croix's three examples of Marx's own usage: the contradiction between relations and forces of production, between the social character of production and private appropriation, and between private landownership and rational agriculture.

The contradiction between relations and forces of production as a mechanism of major social transformations has been a staple of Marxist theory ever since Marx himself, in a shorthand passage in his 1859 preface to *The Critique of Political Economy*, sketched out a historical (or transhistorical) process in which the development of productive forces, coming up against the barrier of the prevailing production relations, breaks through their restrictive integument and transforms them to allow further development.

In that passage, the formula is presented as a general law of history. But Marx himself never pursued this line of argument in any of his own more systematic historical investigations, in particular, his account of the transition to capitalism.[2] His life's work, in fact, argues against the kind of technological determinism implied by this simple formula. Marx's critique of political economy, and the analysis of capitalism that lies at its heart, are intended precisely to repudiate the generalization of specifically capitalist laws of motion and their attribution to history in general. Yet the 'contradiction' between forces and relations of production as Marx elaborated it represents precisely an internal dynamic specific to capitalism, and *not* a general law of history.

Only capitalism is driven by the need constantly to revolutionize the forces of production, while capitalism's own relations of production, although they impel the development of productive forces, at the same time constitute a barrier to the fulfilment of that constant need:

> The *real barrier* of capitalist production is *capital itself*. It is that capital and its self-expansion appear as the starting and the closing point, the motive and the purpose of production; that production is only production for *capital* and not vice versa, the means of production are not mere means for a constant expansion of the living process of the *society* of producers.... The means — unconditional development of the productive forces of society — comes continually into conflict with the limited purpose — the self-expansion of the existing capital.[3]

That contradiction, to be sure, propels a historically unique process of self-sustaining development, but at the same time, it repeatedly creates obstacles and tensions within capitalist society. Ultimately, that irreducible contradiction lays a foundation for the transition to socialism. It is in this sense, and only in this sense, that Marx himself ever elaborated in any detail the contradiction between forces and relations of production.

Ste. Croix's second contradiction is just another aspect of the contradiction between capital's need to develop the productive forces and the obstacles its own self-expansion puts in the way of that development. Capitalism creates the conditions for the transformation of the labour-process into a social process. The imperatives of self-expansion and the development of productive forces to meet the requirements of competition and profit-maximization have transformed 'the conditions of production into general, common, social conditions'.[4] Capitalist production tends to be a collective, cooperative process with a highly refined and interdependent division of labour, creating the most socialized system of production the world has ever known.

Paradoxically, the *disunity* of capitalism, its fragmentation into competing capitals obliged to act independently of one another, itself acts as a socializing force: capitalist enterprises, in an integrated competitive market, are compelled to transform the labour process because they have to adapt to certain common social conditions, in particular the social average of labour productivity or the 'socially necessary labour time', that set the conditions of survival and profitability. Yet the independence and disunity of these competing capitals is itself in constant tension with the socialization of production; and capitalism remains a system of private appropriation in which the needs of individual capitals for relentless self-expansion are constantly thwarted by other capitals, as well as by their own exploitation of labour (about which more in moment). So '[t]he contradiction between the general social power into which capital develops, on the one hand, and the private power of the individual capitalist over these social conditions of production, on the other, becomes ever more irreconcilable...'.[5] Again, the only final resolution of this contradiction would be socialism.

These examples have two essential things in common. The first is that they apply specifically to capitalism, identifying certain relations and processes that distinguish it from other social forms. The second is that these relations and processes are internal to the system and that both sides of the contradiction are equally essential to it. They represent a contradiction in the sense that the very forces that produce an irreducible systemic need at the same time constitute a barrier to the fulfilment of that need. The imperative to overcome that self-imposed barrier drives capital relentlessly forward, only to throw up another obstacle in its place. Capital is driven to break down all barriers to its own self-expansion, to the development of productive forces and to the universalization of the capitalist system, its extension across all geographic boundaries and its penetration into every human practice and the natural environment. Yet the same imperatives that drive it forward constantly recreate the barriers that stand in their way. These contradictions 'are constantly suspended in the system of production resting on capital, but also constantly created again'.[6] Contradiction, in this sense, is capitalism's basic operating principle, in a way that is true of no other social form. It is the source, at one and the same time, of both the capitalist system's unique dynamism and its constant self-subversion.

Ste. Croix's third contradiction, between private landownership and 'rational' agriculture, is more complicated. This one seems to apply not only to capitalism but to any system of production based on private landed property, 'the general contradiction between private land-ownership and a rational agriculture, the normal social utilisation of the soil'.[7] The passage appears in Marx's discussion of the genesis of capitalist ground rent, where he identifies the various ways in which different forms of private landed property erect barriers to 'rational' cultivation.

On the one hand, according to Marx, small landed property, specifically peasant property in which 'not social, but isolated labour predominates', 'excludes the development of social productive forces of labour, social forms of labour', and thereby rules out 'wealth and development of reproduction, both of its material and spiritual prerequisites'.[8] On the other hand, large — and specifically capitalist — landed property thwarts development in a completely different way:

> ...large landed property reduces the agricultural population to a constantly falling minimum, and confronts it with a constantly growing industrial population crowded together in large cities. It thereby creates conditions which cause an irreparable break in the coherence of social interchange

prescribed by the natural laws of life. As a result, the vitality of the soil is squandered, and this prodigality is carried by commerce far beyond the borders of a particular state....[9]

So, concludes, Marx,

While small landed property creates a class of barbarians standing halfway outside of society, a class combining all the crudeness of primitive forms of society with the anguish and misery of civilised countries, large landed property undermines labour-power in the last region, where its prime energy seeks refuge and stores up its strength as a reserve fund for the regeneration of the vital force of nations — on the land itself. Large-scale industry and large-scale mechanised agriculture work together. If originally distinguished by the fact that the former lays waste and destroys principally labour-power, hence the natural force of human beings, whereas the latter more directly exhausts the natural vitality of the soil, they join hands in the further course of development in that the industrial system in the country-side also enervates the labourers, and industry and commerce on their part supply agriculture with the means for exhausting the soil.[10]

At first glance, then, in the 'contradiction' between private property and rational agriculture, we seem to have a contradiction different from the others, which applies to other historical forms and not just to capitalism, even if it works in various ways. Yet on closer inspection, it appears that the 'contradiction' of small or non-capitalist landed property may not be a contradiction at all, at least not in any sense specific enough to give the concept real explanatory weight. Peasant property, argues Marx, thwarts 'rational' agriculture and human development only in the simple sense that it provides no adequate foundation for the development of productive forces. There is no *contradiction* here. There is a simple linear relation between cause and effect: insufficiency breeds insufficiency.

The case of large, or more precisely, capitalist landed property is very different. Here, according to Marx, the conditions are present for a more than adequate development of social productive forces, sufficient to provide the 'material and spiritual prerequisites' not only of rational agriculture but of human emancipation in general. Yet those very same conditions, the imperatives of capital accumulation that drive the advance of productive forces, at the same time destroy the foundations of rational production and human development, indeed the ecological conditions of life itself.

Marx's argument here is vitiated by his tendency to conflate the size of landholdings with the social property relations that constitute particular forms of landholding irrespective of size (not to mention his prejudices about 'rural idiocy' and peasants as 'undifferentiated potatoes'). There is, of course, no reason to accept, and much reason to reject, the notion that smallholding, just by virtue of its size, can never be productive, or that 'rational' agriculture requires some kind of (albeit non-capitalist) large-scale enterprise. But let us not be deflected from his principal point: that the way in which capitalism militates against 'rational' agriculture is very different from the limits imposed on it by insufficient resources or inadequate productive capacities. Capitalist agriculture is 'contradictory' not because of its scale but because of the logic of its property relations, which create a dynamic inimical to 'rational' agriculture despite, or precisely because of, the specific imperatives that enable, indeed compel, it to develop the productive forces.

In this case, then, we do have something more like, and inextricably bound up with, the other contradictions, those internal and self-generated barriers that constitute a systemic contradiction, which both propels development and at the same time undermines it; and here too this contradiction is specific to capitalism. In capitalism, argues Marx in the *Grundrisse*, 'For the first time, nature becomes purely an object for humankind, purely a matter of utility.'[11] Capital is destructive toward nature as to all other obstacles that stand in its way, 'tearing down all barriers which hem in the development of the forces of production, the expansion of needs, the all-sided development of production, and the exploitation and exchange of natural and mental forces'. Capital, in the process of its self-expansion, devours its own human and natural substance.

IS CLASS A CONTRADICTION?

If we now revisit Ste. Croix's objection to the usage that applies the term 'contradiction' to class relations, we may begin to see it in a different light. We may be inclined to ask whether there is here too a difference between capitalism and every other system, and whether capitalist class relations uniquely represent a 'contradiction'.

Let me state the case baldly: although I have myself in careless moments described class relations as a 'fundamental contradiction' in any class society, I would, on reflection, insist that class is not, in itself, a 'contradiction' in any but the most vague and general sense, which could just as easily, and for the most part with greater precision, be denoted by 'opposition', 'antagonism', 'conflict' and 'struggle'.

These terms need not be understood as synonymous and may be taken to refer to different aspects of the class relation. Two classes, which stand in opposition to each other as exploiters and exploited, may have antagonistic interests — such that what benefits the one is to the detriment of the other — without any open conflict between them, at least for a time, and without active struggle. Class oppositions and antagonisms, with or without conflict and struggle, manifest themselves in any form of class society, and certainly class struggle can lead to major social transformations. But none of these relations, or even all of them together, necessarily entail a contradiction.

All precapitalist class societies, as varied as they were, had in common the appropriation of surplus labour by 'extra-economic' means, the use of direct coercive force to extract surplus labour from direct producers. This was true in a wide range of different forms: the master-slave relation, the relation between landlord and peasant (in all its varied forms), or the relation between appropriating states and subject producers. As complex as all these relations are, and as fraught with oppression, suffering, conflict, and struggle, their logic is fairly straightforward: the exploited producer produces, and the exploiting appropriator takes part of the product, whether in kind, labour services, or monetary rent. There is a direct, as it were linear, relation between appropriator and producer, and the relation is fairly transparent — requiring quite elaborate ideological mystifications to disguise. The gain of one class is indeed the other's loss, but that kind of relation is, so to speak, more complementary than contradictory. There is nothing in this world so simple and straightforward as a zero-sum game.

To be sure, these precapitalist forms of exploitation are generally not conducive to the development of productive forces. The lord may even squeeze his peasants to the limit of their physical capacity, and if he goes too far, he will, of course, undermine his own source of wealth and self-reproduction (unless there are, as there have so often been, land-hungry peasants waiting in the wings). But there is nothing inherent in that class relation that requires the lord constantly to go to a self-undermining extreme. Needless to say, these systems can come to an end when resistance by the producers to exploitation by the appropriators forces a change in their relations. But it is hard to see what the concept of contradiction adds to our understanding of such processes that is not adequately covered by other nouns denoting the oppositional relations between the two classes.

Consider now the class relation between capital and labour. Here is what Marx himself says about it:

> To each capitalist, the total mass of all workers, with the exception of his own workers, appear not as workers, but as consumers, possessors of exchange values (wages), money, which they exchange for his commodity.... The greater their number — the number of the industrial population — and the mass of money at their disposal, the greater the sphere of exchange for capital....Every capitalist knows this about his worker, that he does not relate to him as producer to consumer, and [he therefore] wishes to restrict his consumption, i.e. his ability to exchange, his wage, as much as possible. Of course he would like the workers of *other* capitalists to be the greatest consumers possible of *his own* commodity. But the relation of *every* capitalist to *his own* workers is the *relation as such* of *capital and labour*, the essential relation.... Capital itself then regards *demand by the worker* — i.e. the payment of the wages on which this demand rests — not as a gain but as a loss.... *Here again it is the competition among capitals*, their indifference to and independence of one another, which brings it about that the individual capital relates to the workers of the entire remaining capital *not as to workers*: hence is driven beyond the right proportion.[12] [Original emphasis.]

So here we do have a situation not adequately covered by words that are meant to describe the social relations between exploiting and exploited classes, words like 'opposition', 'antagonism', 'conflict', or 'struggle'. Here, we can indeed apply the concept of 'contradiction' with some degree of specificity, in a way that fits no other system of class relations. In capitalism, as in any other form of class society, there are antagonisms, conflicts, and struggles between the two opposing classes, which have to do with exploitation by one class and resistance by the other. But there is something else too: a self-negating process in the inter-action between classes, which is governed by mutually subverting but equally essential principles.

Consider, first, the situation described by Marx in the passage just quoted. The capitalist relates to his own workers — in the 'essential relation' between capital and labour — as exploiter to exploited: the more surplus he can extract from them, the better for him. In that respect, this class relation is much like any other. At the same time, in order to realize the benefit of the workers' labour, the capi-talist has to be able to sell the products of that labour, and workers constitute a large part of the market. Yet every other capitalist relates to his own workers in the same way, not as consumers but as producers, and the producers' gain — which constitutes their power as consumers — is the capitalist's loss. So capital is driven at one and the same time by two contradictory needs, and the relation among independent and competing capitals inevitably creates a tendency to over-shoot in production what can be realized in consumption. It should probably be added here that these contradictions may apply even where appropriator and direct producer are the same person, subjected to 'self-exploitation' by general-ized conditions of capitalist competition.

But there is, of course, a more fundamental contradiction here. In every rela-tion of class exploitation, there is a distinction between necessary and surplus labour: the direct producers must, in one way or another, labour for their own subsistence, and transfer surplus to the exploiter. In capitalism, the relation between necessary and surplus labour is more complicated. Capital can realize itself only by pushing the worker beyond necessary labour, the labour needed to reproduce the direct producer. At the same time, capitalism is a system in which direct producers have no access to the means of labour at all except by selling their labour-power to capital, and their labour must be set in motion by capital. But capital has no interest in necessary labour, unless it produces surplus labour and can be realized in the market as surplus value. In contrast to other systems, where the direct producers must, in effect, produce for their own necessary consump-tion before their surplus is appropriated by an exploiting class, in capitalism no labour is performed at all unless the capitalist anticipates the production of a surplus that he can realize in the market.

The problem is that, in the conditions of capitalist competition, no capitalist can know in advance whether realization will succeed. He cannot determine the price at which his commodity will sell, nor can he be sure what conditions of production are required for realization. To put it another way, using a distinc-tion that figures centrally in Marx's account of capitalist contradictions, the market is indifferent to the amount of actual or 'concrete' labour that goes into any given commodity, and the possibility of profitable sale is, instead, determined by a certain quantity of 'abstract' labour, a social average of productivity or 'socially necessary labour time', which is not within any individual capitalist's control. This uncertainty compels capitalists to pursue 'maximizing' strategies, which will achieve an optimal price/cost ratio and increase surplus value by increasing labour productivity. So capital both requires and restricts labour and the creation of value:

> By its nature, therefore, it posits a barrier to labour and value-creation, in contradiction to its tendency to expand them boundlessly. And in as much as it both posits a barrier specific to itself, and on the other side equally drives over and beyond every barrier, it is the living contradiction.[13]

THE CONTRADICTIONS OF MARKET DEPENDENCE

The class relation between capital and labour, then, is a contradiction in the same sense and for the same reasons as the other contradictions that constitute capitalism. But more needs to be said about what those reasons are and about the underlying common source of all these contradictions. We can, again, begin with Marx, and the comment that introduces his remarks on the contradictory relation between capitalists and workers:

> But in production based on capital, consumption is mediated at all points by exchange, and labour never has a direct use value for those who are working. Its entire basis is labour as exchange value and as the creation of exchange value.[14]

The capitalist class relation is mediated by exchange, and that is what makes it a 'contradiction' in a distinctive way. This mediation is, among other things, what makes class relations in capitalism less transparent than the direct opposition of precapitalist exploitation. While the exploitative relation between lord and peasant may require elaborate ideological constructs to disguise it, the relation between capital and labour presents a contrary challenge: capital certainly needs ideological mystifications and supports, but it may be harder to *reveal* than to conceal the exploitative nature of the capitalist relation, or to conceptualize and capture it in theory.

At any rate, the mediation that makes this class relation contradictory applies to every capitalist relation and process, in production, appropriation, and distribution. There are no use values in capitalism that are not first and above all exchange values, and there is no relation or process that is not determined by that fact. This is the bottom line: that the whole capitalist system of social reproduction is mediated by the market, and this mediation is what makes contradiction the operating principle of capitalism as it is in no other social form.

The contradiction between use value and exchange value in a system where social reproduction is 'mediated at all points by exchange', with all the dynamic contradictions that proceed from this most basic one, is hardly news to anyone persuaded by the Marxist analysis of capitalism. But the implications of this proposition are not consistently pursued. To say, for instance, as Marxists typically do, that the market is merely 'the sphere of circulation', a surface appearance beneath which lie more fundamental social property relations, is to miss the point that, in capitalism as in no other system, the market is something more than that. The fundamental property relations of capitalism are themselves mediated, indeed defined, by the compulsions of the market. The specifically capitalist contradictions of class are what they are because — indeed, they are *contradictions* only because — they are rooted in the contradictions of market dependence and the imperatives that follow from it. Market dependence is not something that just happens in the sphere of circulation. It has to do with the conditions of access to the means of survival and self-reproduction. Market dependence in capitalism constitutes a *fundamental* contradiction because, as in no other social form, it is a fundamental condition of survival and social reproduction, on which it imposes its imperatives of competition and profit-maximization.

What, then, follows from perceiving the capitalist market as a social property relation? The point I am making here could, I suppose, be put provocatively by saying that class is not the 'fundamental contradiction' of capitalism. It would be possible to say that this distinction belongs to the contradictions of market dependence, of which class contradictions are only one manifestation. Yet this observation by itself would tell us nothing about the ways the class relation between capital and labour affects and intensifies the contradictions of market dependence, nor would it tell us anything about the importance of class struggle in the operations of capitalism, and even less about its role in the transition to socialism (though it might tell us a great deal about the *possibilities* of class struggle, and the terrain on which it can be fruitfully pursued). It would simply mean, again, that capitalist class relations are what they are because both classes are market-dependent — dependent on the market for the most basic conditions of their self-reproduction — in a way that is true of no other class relations.

This means not only that every transaction between capital and labour is 'mediated at every point by exchange' but also that the relation of each to the means of production and appropriation is mediated by the market from the start. The moment access to the means of production and appropriation becomes market-dependent — and even before market dependence takes the form of the general commodification of labour power — the 'fundamental contradiction' of capitalism is already at work, and the market's imperatives of competition and profit-maximization come into play.

It is certainly true, as a historical proposition, that once these imperatives were set in motion, the complete commodification of labour power and the mature class relation between capital and labour were inevitable consequences of market dependence. It is also certainly true that the contradictions of market dependence were transformed and intensified (even if they were not, in the first instance, caused) by that class relation. But it is equally important to acknowledge that even in a fully developed capitalism, with all its contradictory relations between capital and labour, there are still irreducible contradictions among competing capitals, which remain intractable irrespective of the class regime and however much the working class restrains its struggles in the interests of 'competitiveness'. That is why, for instance, it is an illusion to believe that working-class restraint, or social-democratic policies of 'progressive competitiveness', whatever else they may achieve, will eliminate the instabilities of capitalism or its tendency to crisis and more prolonged downturns.[15]

Let us then look more closely at exactly what it means to talk about market-dependent access to the means of production and appropriation. Here again the point can be made by contrast with non-capitalist societies, especially those where producers and appropriators have direct, unmediated access to the means of production and/or appropriation. In precapitalist societies direct producers (above all, peasants) have typically been in direct possession of the means of production, in particular land. Producers deprived of non-market access to the means of subsistence, and especially those who are obliged to enter the market not only to obtain the most basic means of subsistence but even access to the means of production, have been a historical rarity. Where producers have direct, non-market access to the means of production, exploiting appropriators — whether landlords or states — must possess the means of direct coercion, in the form of military, political, and legal power, which allow them to extract surplus labour from producers, in the form of labour services, rent, tribute, or tax. These 'extra-economic' powers of appropriation are not mediated by the market.

It should be emphasized, too, that the existence of markets and even a highly developed system of trade does not by itself entail market-dependent appropriation, nor does wealth derived from commercial activity necessarily imply market-dependent access to the means of appropriation.[16] For instance, urban patriciates or merchant elites in commercial centres in medieval and early modern Europe often extracted great wealth from commercial activities, but they relied in large part on the privileges and powers associated with their status in the city. The success of these commercial centres was dependent less on competitive production than on 'extra-economic' factors such as military superiority, command of trade routes, monopoly privileges, superior shipping, together with sophisticated commercial methods and instruments, elaborate trading networks, and far-flung trading posts. Ruling elites in these centres depended on their civic status not only for privileged access to such commercial advantages but typically also, as officeholders, for exploitation of domestic producers by means of direct extra-economic surplus extraction in the form of dues and taxes of one kind or another. It is not for nothing that these commercial cities have been described as collective lordships. Great wealth, in other words, still depended here on what has been called 'politically constituted property'; and this form of appropriation shaped the particular and self-limiting course of economic development in these non-capitalist commercial centres.

In early modern England, by contrast, there emerged a dominant appropriating class — a landlord class — which, generally lacking extra-economic powers of appropriation, increasingly depended on purely *economic* relations with tenants, and on their tenants' success in competitive production, instead of on surplus extraction by direct extra-economic coercion. The tenant paying economic rents, in a system of competitive leases, was effectively dependent on the market for access to land, and that access presupposed the producer's success in competitive production. By the same token, the landlord's access to wealth and the means of self-reproduction was mediated by the market and depended on the producer's competitive success, rather than on politically constituted property, on extra-economic privilege or direct political, legal, or military coercion. The landlord's rents entailed the tenant's profit, derived from competitive, cost-effective production.

These social property relations set in motion a historically unique process of self-sustaining economic development, but it also brought the system's contradictions to the fore. The end result of the market imperatives entailed by these property relations — in which competitive failure meant complete loss of access to the means of production and self-reproduction — was the complete commodification of labour power, the mature relation between capital and labour, and a system of appropriation 'mediated at every point by exchange'.

From its inception, the system of market-dependent appropriation had another significant consequence. In precapitalist societies, extra-economic powers of appropriation entailed the performance of certain public functions — judicial, political, or military. In capitalism, private appropriation is completely detached from the performance of such public functions. Capitalism certainly needs enforcement by the state to maintain the system of social property relations, but, just as the capitalist can exploit workers without directly wielding extra-economic power himself, his exploitative power does not entail public responsibilities. To be sure, a system of private appropriation by public means entails problems of its own, which could even be called 'contradictions', contradictions that the complete privatization of appropriation in capitalism appears to have resolved.[17] But the capitalist dissociation of private appropriation from any public responsibility represents a contradiction in an even deeper sense.

There is certainly no system of appropriation more private than the capitalist one. Yet there is no system that implicates the whole of society in the way that private appropriation in capitalism does. The mediations of the market make the realization of capitalist profit a uniquely social business. At the same time, while public institutions exist uniquely apart from private appropriation, they must all be mobilized to sustain this system of private property which carries no public responsibilities. Since use values in capitalism must first be exchange values, and since the condition of necessary labour is surplus labour, or the creation and realization of surplus value, even the most basic needs of society, insofar as their provision is organized under the auspices of capital, cannot be met without satisfying the conditions of capitalist profit and the self-expansion of capital. This means that social reproduction in general is here always subject to the requirements of private appropriation. Yet at the same time, the process of private appropriation is at every point subject to social processes — not, of course, to the needs of society at large but to the social conditions that determine the imperatives of competition and the possibilities of realization. It is difficult to think of a system more riddled with contradictions than this.

CAPITALIST CONTRADICTIONS TODAY

I: *Ecological Degradation*

There is bound to be a temptation to dismiss 'contradiction' as a theoretical abstraction with no tangible manifestations 'on the ground'. But even a brief overview of capitalism as it is today will illustrate its very concrete meaning. Take just two of the most salient characteristics of our current capitalist moment: ecological degradation and globalization.

In his remarks on the incompatibility between capitalist property and rational agriculture, Marx already identified the contradiction that inevitably leads capitalism to ecological destruction. It is surely self-evident that the relentless drive for unlimited accumulation is inimical to sustainable development. Human practices have always impinged on the environment, and even the most basic exploitation of the soil has often had some damaging effects. But, even setting aside the unprecedented technological capabilities of industrial capitalism to destroy no less than to produce (capabilities that, for better or worse, have themselves been a product of capitalist imperatives), no other system has been required constantly to drive production beyond the limits of human consumption.

Aristotle long ago pointed out the difference between production for use and production for exchange. Above all, he stressed the absence of *limits* in production which has profit as its object. There is, in principle, no end to it. But in no other system before capitalism was this limitless production a presupposition of necessary labour, a necessary condition of basic survival and social reproduction. More particularly, no system has ever so completely detached the requirements of profit from the benefits of use. Of course, realization requires consumption. But use value in capitalism is never a guarantee of exchange value, while production for exchange value can produce both inadequate provision of the most basic use values (for instance, affordable housing) and wasteful excess at the same time (such as new and obsolescent models of cars or mobile phones every year) — to say nothing of all the other ways in which considerations of quality, or even safety, are subordinated to the requirements of profit.

Even while capitalism has brought with it unprecedented productive capacities which have for the first time in history made possible a fairly consistent freedom from scarcity and have provided the material means of looking beyond tomorrow, the system is nonetheless driven by short-term imperatives that override the possibility of planning in advance. The short-term needs of profit consistently subvert the long-term strategies required to ensure ecological sustainability — the kind of planning, for instance, required for safe and energy-efficient public transportation. Yet the needs of profit at the same time come in conflict with themselves, as capital consumes its own substance; and the more it erects barriers to its own realization, the more it destroys its own human and natural foundations.

In earlier systems, preservation of the means of production, and conservation of their material foundations, were basic survival strategies and conditions of social reproduction, especially for direct producers. Needless to say, strategies of preservation were often impossible, and they surely often failed. But those failures were indeed failures — as, indeed, was ecological destruction in the old Communist regimes. And, to be sure, precapitalist modes of predatory exploitation often had destructive effects. But only in capitalism are constant waste and destruction requirements of systemic reproduction and emblems of success.

It should be emphasized here that capitalism poses a unique ecological threat not simply because it has created technologies with an unprecedented capacity to strain the earth's resources. No doubt the same technological advances that have made capitalism uniquely capable of waste and destruction are also capable of *conserving* resources by means of enhanced productivity and more efficient use. Nor is it impossible for capital itself to benefit from using energy-efficient technologies and even from producing and marketing them. The point is rather that the relentless imperatives of capitalist self-expansion are dissociated from the production and consumption of use values. This means that the logic of capitalism, just as it inevitably drives production beyond the limits of use, also requires destruction long before the possibilities of use are exhausted. Whatever capitalism may do to enable the efficient use of resources, its own imperatives will always drive it further. Without constantly breaching the limits of conservation, without constantly moving forward the boundaries of waste and destruction, there can be no capital accumulation.

II: *Globalization*

Our historical moment is marked by the *universality* of such contradictions, with the universal and complete subordination of use value to exchange value in the commodification of all human life and the natural environment. The contradictory imperatives of market dependence have penetrated to the depths of social life in advanced capitalist societies, into every human practice and social relation. At the same time, these imperatives have expanded spatially, around the globe, as the drive for accumulation seeks to break down (as Marx said it would) every spatial barrier as well as every natural, material, and human one, every obstacle presented to capitalist self-expansion by the physical and social limitations of human labour and the natural environment. It is in this sense — as the universalization of market dependence — that we should understand the process of 'globalization'.

To say this is not to deny that globalization, whatever else it may be, is a specific set of conscious policies undertaken by advanced capitalist powers, and by one in particular, to impose their will on the world. But this new imperialism is different from the old, and it is different largely because it operates in a different context. That context is defined above all by the universalization of capitalism and its contradictory imperatives, which, on the one hand, gives capital new capabilities and, on the other, new weaknesses and vulnerabilities.

One way of defining the difference is to say that the new imperialism, especially in the form of globalization, is not a simple matter of military conquest or direct political domination but a new form of hegemony by economic means.[18] In this respect, we can draw an analogy between globalization and class domination in capitalist society. Unlike class domination in precapitalist societies, which depended on direct 'extra-economic' coercion, capital dominates labour by 'economic' means, by means of the economic imperatives that come with market dependence. Workers must forfeit their surplus labour in advance (indeed their necessary labour too, in exchange for a wage) just to gain access to the means of labour itself.

This is, among other things, what it means to talk about the specific separation of the 'economic' and the 'political' in capitalism. That separation, as well as the detachment of private appropriation from public responsibility, gives capital a unique capacity to dominate without exercising direct extra-economic power. Needless to say, capitalism's economic imperatives still have to be sustained by state coercion, but capitalists themselves have no need for direct political rule or a monopoly on political rights. Where workers have lost complete non-market access to the means of their self-reproduction, and even to the means of their own labour, capitalist classes have been able to exercise power over them even where political rights have become universal.

Much the same can be said about capitalist imperialism. The separation of the 'economic' and the 'political', the detachment of economic power from political coercion, and private appropriation from public responsibility, gives capital a unique capacity not only to dominate without direct coercive power but also to extend its spatial reach. Market imperatives can far exceed the scope of direct political or military rule. The major capitalist powers can exercise their imperial hegemony by subjecting subordinate peoples to market imperatives, even while permitting them — in fact, often compelling them — to develop as more or less sovereign states. It is, in fact, only under capitalism that the nation state has become the universal political form. Capitalist imperialism is uniquely capable of extending its hegemony over those states without direct coercive extra-economic power, by imposing and manipulating market imperatives; and globalization (with the help, for example, of 'structural adjustment') represents the universalization of this distinctively capitalist form of imperial rule.

But here we come again to contradictions. We have seen how the mediations in the relation between capital and labour introduce a historically specific element of contradiction into age-old class oppositions, antagonisms, conflicts, and struggles. The same is true of capitalist imperialism in general, and globalization in particular. This form of mediated imperial domination carries with it all the contradictions of market dependence, for exploiters no less than exploited. It introduces into the relations between them all the familiar instabilities of capitalism, and all the constant self-subversion of capitalist accumulation, not least the crises of overcapacity that come with capitalist competition, now infinitely expanded and intensified as they are raised onto a global plane.

The increasing polarization between rich and poor which is by now a familiar mark of globalization — a tendency that far outstrips whatever capacity the rising capitalist tide may have to lift all boats — is no longer a simple matter of the rich robbing the poor. That effect is now produced by subjecting subordinate economies to market imperatives, while the dominant powers manipulate those forces to their own advantage. This kind of exploitation can be achieved without surplus appropriation by direct, coercive means. All that is needed is to make the subordinate economy dependent on the market and subject to its 'laws' — in much the same way that direct producers in the early days of capitalist develop-ment, expropriated by market imperatives, were subjected to exploitation by purely 'economic' means.

In some cases, this kind of imperial exploitation can have the effect of pushing subordinate economies to the very margins of poverty — as, for instance, when the agencies of capital have compelled developing economies to replace subsis-tence farming with cash-crop production for the export market, or forced them to specialize in one or another form of resource extraction. Inevitably, as the global market for their commodities declines, and as rich capitalist economies subsidize their own agricultural producers, such economies are completely marginalized in the world economy, while having lost the means to sustain them-selves at home. In other cases, where developing economies have been more or less successfully integrated into the global economy, the condition of relative success has typically been the exploitation — both by foreign and domestic capital — of low-cost production in the interests of 'competitiveness'. To put it simply, capital profits from uneven development, the differentiation of social conditions among national economies, the preservation of low-cost labour regimes, and hence the reproduction of relative poverty.

Yet, as in every process mediated by the capitalist market, this is also a deeply contradictory process not wholly different in its logic from the capitalist class rela-tions described by Marx, in which capital's exploitation of producers undermines its own need for realization in consumption. One difference is that here, on the global plane, it is much harder to operate the corrective measures that have evolved in advanced capitalist societies to compensate, to some degree, for the tendency of capitalism to undermine its own human and material foundations, the economic policies designed to stabilize the contradictions of the market and social policies intended to pick up the pieces when, inevitably, that balancing act fails.

At the same time, when subordinate economies do succeed in generating capi-talist 'growth', they simply deepen the contradictions of overcapacity; while a universal equality of capitalist development, if it were even remotely conceivable in the contradictory conditions of uneven development, would spell ecological doom. Capitalism produces this ultimate contradiction not because the earth cannot in principle sustain an equitable distribution of material comfort and even prosperity but because the logic of the system has nothing to do with the distri-bution of use values and everything to do with the wastefully unlimited and destructive imperatives of capital accumulation.

There is one contradiction specific to the globalization of market dependence, which does not manifest itself in the same way in local class relations. The economic imperatives of capitalism do indeed permit the reach of capital to extend far beyond the scope of direct political and military domination. Yet at the same time, capital can never dispense with the enforcement of market imperatives, and the system of property relations in which they are rooted, by legal and political means. If anything, capitalism more than any other system needs a stable and predictable political and legal order. That kind of order is, for all practical purposes, impossible on a global scale, and capital has hitherto found no better instrument of social order than the nation state, nor is it likely to find one in the foreseeable future. If US military power is the closest thing the world has ever seen to a global power of coercion, it is completely unsuited to provide the daily regulation and stability required by capital accumulation. That is why, in an era that is supposed to be marked by the decline of the nation state, the eclipse of the state by 'global' capital and its transnational agencies, the nation state is more than ever before the world's universal political form and the indispensable medium of global capital.

The result is, yet again, a contradiction. The very detachment of economic domination from political rule that makes it possible for capital to extend its reach beyond the capacity of any other imperial power in history is also the source of a fundamental weakness. On the one hand, global capital relies not only on the state in its own domestic base, particularly in the US, but also on local states elsewhere to enforce its imperatives. It has not only promoted the nation state as the universal political form but has sought to reconstruct all states to serve the interests of foreign capital as well as domestic. On the other hand, in so doing, it has opened up new spaces for resistance. As long as relations of exploitation remain relatively localized, political powers of coercion can more or less keep up with economic domination. But the economic reach of capital is increasingly extending beyond its extra-economic grasp, and the distance between them is growing — with everything this implies for oppositional struggles. In that sense, the separation of the 'economic' and the 'political', which is one of capital's great strengths, may also prove to be a growing weakness.

This is one of the deepest contradiction in today's global capitalism: that the nation state is more than ever the point of concentration of capitalist power, the indispensable medium without which capital cannot navigate, let alone dominate, the global economy. National states implement and enforce the global economy, and they remain the most effective means of intervening in it. This means that the state is also the point at which global capital is most vulnerable, both as a target of opposition in the dominant economies and as a lever of resistance elsewhere. It also means that now more than ever, much depends on the particular class forces embodied in the state, and that now more than ever, there is scope, as well as need, for class struggle.

That, then, is the lesson to be drawn from the contradictions of capitalism: while they give it an unprecedented strength and dynamism, they are also the source of vulnerabilities. The system's strengths are at the same time its weaknesses, creating the terrain on which opposition and class struggle can take place.

NOTES

I would like to thank David McNally for his comments and suggestions.

1   G.E.M. de Ste. Croix, *The Class Struggle in the Ancient Greek World*, Ithaca: Cornell University Press, 1981, pp. 49-50.
2   This point is developed at greater length in my *Democracy Against Capitalism: Renewing Historical Materialism*, Cambridge: Cambridge University Press, 1995, chap. 4.
3   Karl Marx, *Capital* III, Moscow: Progress Books, 1974, p. 250. Emphasis in this quotation, as in all others in Marx, is in the original.
4   *Ibid.*, p. 264.
5   *Ibid.*
6   Marx, *Grundrisse*, Harmondsworth: Penguin, 1973, p. 406.
7   *Capital* III, p. 812.
8   *Ibid.* p. 813.
9   *Ibid.*
10   *Ibid.*
11   *Grundrisse*, p. 410.
12   *Ibid.*, pp. 419-20.
13   *Ibid.*, p. 421.
14   *Ibid.*, p. 419.
15   For this reason, I was very puzzled by Sam Gindin's account of my argument, as well as his critique of Robert Brenner, in last year's *Register*, and even more puzzled when we engaged in an email debate after I had seen the article just before it went to press. I was mystified, among other things, by a question Sam asked me, about whether I had ever before the debate on Brenner's economic analysis treated competition as a 'fundamental contradiction', suggesting that this was a dangerous new departure in my work (I wonder, by the way, whether he would react in the same way to Marx's observation in the *Grundrisse* that '*competition* is nothing other than the inner *nature* of capital, its essential character' [p. 414]). In fact, it was this exchange that obliged me to consider more carefully the failure of Marxists to think through the implications of the contradictions rooted in market dependence. Although this is not the place to reproduce our lengthy exchange, I will say, regretfully, that it made no difference to the final product and that, in the published version, Sam still attributes to me positions I decidedly do not hold — such as, for instance, that 'the nature of capitalism in its earliest stage remains the same *after* a full-fledged working class has entered history'. (346) Or that competition is 'pre-eminent' over class (n. 11). Or that workers can happily engage in militant adventurism without fear of consequences (though he does concede that this seems 'uncharacteristic' of me). And so on. In one of my letters to Sam, I spelled out my argument about the contradictions of market dependence, more or less as it is laid out here. My

purpose, in the specific context of that discussion, was simply to emphasize that 'there's a difference between saying, as you seem to think I am, that only competition, and not class struggle, has anything to do with economic trends, and saying that there is a fundamental source of crisis in the relations of competition that's there whatever the specific configuration of class power, and in a wide variety of class regimes'.

I wanted to emphasize that, while class struggle can certainly affect profitability, and while capital certainly seeks to counteract that effect by squeezing labour harder, there is a fundamental contradiction in the relation among capitals (which, according to Brenner, lay at the heart of the long downturn after the postwar boom) that is not caused by class struggle and cannot be corrected by the absence of class struggle — and that this has political consequences. What puzzled me about Sam's response more than anything else is that the politics that seems to me to follow inevitably from a failure to recognize this fundamental contradiction is the politics that Sam himself has most powerfully repudiated.

16 This argument is based on my 'The Question of Market Dependence', forthcoming in the *Journal of Agrarian Change*.

17 I owe this suggestion about the contradictions of precapitalist societies to George Comninel.

18 Some of the arguments that follow here are developed at greater length in my 'Global Capital, National States', in eds. Mark Rupert and Hazel Smith, *Now More than Ever: Historical Materialism and Globalization* (London: Routledge, forthcoming).